THE ROGUE'S MARCH

Potomac's
THE WARRIORS
Series

Acclaimed books about combatants throughout history who rose to the challenges of war. Other titles in the series:

God's Samurai: Lead Pilot at Pearl Harbor
Gordon Prange, with Donald N. Goldstein and
Katherine V. Dillon

*Jungle Ace: Col. Gerald R. Johnson, the USAAF's Top Fighter Leader
of the Pacific War*
John R. Bruning

*Spitfires, Thunderbolts, and Warm Beer: An American Fighter Pilot
Over Europe*
Philip D. Caine

Strike Eagle: Flying the F-15E in the Gulf War
William L. Smallwood

The Pattons: A Personal History of an American Family
Robert H. Patton

*Victory at Any Cost: The Genius of Viet Nam's
Gen. Vo Nguyen Giap*
Cecil B. Currey

Warthog: Flying the A-10 in the Gulf War
William L. Smallwood

Women Warriors: A History
David E. Jones

THE ROGUE'S MARCH

JOHN RILEY AND THE
ST. PATRICK'S BATTALION

Peter F. Stevens

Potomac Books, Inc.

WASHINGTON, D.C.

First Warriors edition published in 2005

Copyright © 1999 by Potomac Books, Inc.

Maps by Larry Hoffman, courtesy of COMMAND *Magazine.*

Library of Congress Cataloging-in-Publication Data

Stevens, Peter F.
The rogue's march : John Riley and the St. Patrick's Battalion,
1846–48 / by Peter F. Stevens. — 1st ed.
p.   cm.
Includes bibliographical references and index.
ISBN 1-57488-145-0
1. Mexico. Ejército. Batallón de San Patricio—History.
2. Mexican War, 1846–1848—Regimental histories—Mexico.
3. Mexican War, 1846–1848— Desertions.   4. Mexican War,
1846–1848—Participation, Irish American.   5. Riley, John, b. 1817.
6. Defectors—United States—History—19th century.
7. Defectors—Mexico—History—19th century.   I. Title.
E409.8.S74   1998

973.6'2—DC21   98–6552
ISBN 1-57488-738-6 (paperback)
CIP

Potomac Books, Inc.
22841 Quicksilver Drive
Dulles, VA 20166

Designed by Pen & Palette Unlimited

10   9   8   7   6   5   4   3   2   1

Printed in Canada

War-battered dogs are we,
Fighters in every clime;
Fillers of trench and of grave,
Mockers bemocked by time.
War-dogs hungry and grey,
Gnawing a naked bone,
Fighters in every clime—
Every cause but our own.

—Emily Lawless,
"With the Wild Geese"

Contents

List of Maps

Preface and Acknowledgments

M Y INTRODUCTION TO THE STORY of John Riley and the St. Patrick's Battalion was a plaque in the Plaza San Jacinto, in San Angel, Mexico, 12 years ago. The memorial contained the names of 71 soldiers and the following inscription: "In Memory of the Heroic Battalion of St. Patrick, Martyrs Who Gave Their Lives for the Mexican Cause During the Unjust North American Invasion of 1847." I noticed that 48 of the names were Irish, 13 German.

Intrigued by the tablet, I began to research the battalion for an article for *American History Illustrated*. I quickly discovered that the subject was one that few novelists could have dreamed up: during the Mexican-American War of 1846-1848, deserters from the U.S. Army had formed a unit in the Mexican Army and had fought against their old tent-mates in the conflict's fiercest battles and had "settled scores" against their former American officers "with the malignity of private revenge." In the words of the St. Patrick's Battalion's leader, John Riley, the unit was predominantly made up of Irish immigrants who had "gone over the hill to Mexico." Riley, a tough, charismatic Galwayman and a veteran of the British army, had been one of the first to desert and was captured outside Mexico City in the war's bloodiest battle. His command's ammunition had run out. He was taken only after a savage hand-to-hand fray and only after the Americans had suffered, at the hands of the St.

Patrick's Battalion, their severest casualties of the war. Courts-martial, whipping and branding, and mass hangings in front of the city during the war's climactic battle awaited Riley and his men. So, too, did lies, myths, controversy, and cover-up in the ensuing decades.

I felt that no one had presented the sheer drama of the story or the full military history of the unit's key role in the war. As I dug into the story of the St. Patrick's Battalion during the past 12 years, I started with a question: How could this episode have happened? Gradually, as I studied the "rising tide" of Irish and German immigration to America in the 1840s, the woes that sent the Irish to the United States, and the corresponding rise of Nativism—the anti-Catholic, antiforeigner movement infecting American society of the era—an explosive mix of history, culture, religion, and nationality emerged. These factors collided with harsh economic conditions driving desperate Irishmen and Germans into the U.S. Army for a private's seven dollars a month, a pittance. The bulk of the immigrant recruits were not even citizens. They could die for their new land but could not vote there. In the ranks of a Protestant nation that loathed them, disaffected Irish and German immigrants went off "to soldier" in the name of Manifest Destiny against Catholic Mexico. The worst desertion problem in America's foreign wars soon erupted, fueled by the abuse of Nativist officers.

For me, the chief question about the St. Patrick's Battalion changed. I asked: How could this tragedy *not* have happened? In the words of an immigrant in Winfield Scott's army, "harsh and unjust treatment by their [immigrants'] officers operated ... to produce these deplorable results [desertions]." He added: "The various degrading modes of punishment often inflicted by young, headstrong officers ... were exceedingly galling to ... the sons of the Green Isle. And I have not the slightest doubt that those barbarous modes of punishment ... were the principal causes in the majority of these cases of desertion that were so lamentably frequent."

"As they [Irish deserters] were Roman Catholic, they imagined they were fighting against their religion by fighting the Mexicans," he wrote. "There was truth in that statement."

The Rogue's March addresses the controversies that have long surrounded the story of John Riley and the men who deserted the U.S.

Army and were willing to die in the Mexican ranks beneath a green banner emblazoned with a glittering image of Ireland's patron saint. The book also focuses upon the Irish who stayed in the American ranks despite brutal, biased treatment from their officers. Throughout this work, immigrant Mick Maloney, one of the U.S. Army's most decorated soldiers of the war, stands juxtaposed against the most famed deserter, John Riley.

In researching and writing the book, I am indebted to many. The National Archives, in Washington DC, provided the courts-martial transcripts of the St. Patrick's Battalion; the muster rolls of the U.S. Army during the Mexican War; general orders from the field; correspondence from the theater of operations to the War Department; congressional records; letters and communiqués from American Generals Zachary Taylor and Winfield Scott; and the "John Riley" file, which included a key letter from Riley to his ex-employer in Michigan. From the Archives, I was also able to draw upon the letters of American soldiers. My special thanks go out to David H. Wallace, of the Archives I Reference Division. Also in Washington, the Library of Congress was a tremendous resource throughout my research.

Early on in this project, John J. Slonaker, Chief of the Historical Reference Branch, U.S. Military History Institute, furnished me with a wealth of material and pointed me in the direction of other helpful collections. At Harvard University, I was granted access to the Houghton Library's collections relating to the Mexican War and the St. Patrick's Battalion. Professor Harmon Murtagh, of the Military History Society of Ireland, shared insights about the "Wild Geese" and Irish soldiers who served in the British army in the first half of the nineteenth century.

I am grateful to Marie Mannion and the Galway (West) Family History Society and to the National Archives, in Dublin. From the office of the Registrar General and the National Library of Ireland, both in Dublin, I found gracious assistance. So, too, at the Public Records Office of Great Britain.

In Mexico, the *Archivo Nacional de Mexico* and the *Museo de las Intervenciones,* at Churubusco, contain key documents and periodicals relating to the St. Patrick's Battalion. The memoirs of Mexican officer Manuel Balbontin and *The Other Side,* the work of Ramon Alcarez, are indispensable sources.

Closer to home, I want to thank my friend and colleague Bill Forry, the editor of *The Boston Irish Reporter,* for his interest in and unflagging support for this story. I also want to express my appreciation to Mary Clark and Linda Beeler of the Thomas Crane Public Library in Quincy, Massachusetts. They patiently tracked down seemingly countless 19th-century volumes necessary to this book.

Professor Robert Ryall Miller's academic study *Shamrock and Sword* contains the first actual analysis of the desertion rates of the Mexican War in comparison to America's other foreign wars. He also unearthed six letters written by John Riley; and Professor Miller's deep knowledge of Mexico, the Southwest, and military life of the 1840s is second to none. Several recent articles about the St. Patrick's Battalion have made no mention of their debt to him.

For anyone interested in the Mexican War, Justin Smith's two-volume *The War with Mexico,* published in 1919, remains a landmark work. Ray Allen Billington's *The Protestant Crusade* is a seminal work on the Nativism of the 1840s, and Professor Kerby Miller's *Emigrants and Exiles* brilliantly details what the Irish faced in Ireland of the early 1840s and of the Great Famine and what they found in America.

In the documentary *The San Patricios* (Day Productions, 1996), on which I appeared as an on-screen commentator and analyst, both Robert Ryall Miller and Kerby Miller also lent their voices—literally—and their knowledge to the controversial story.

To my editor at Brassey's, Don McKeon, I offer my boundless thanks for his patience, his firm and fair editorial hand, and his insight. Historian and author Curt Johnson, who poured over the manuscript, shared his vast expertise in military history, and I am vastly grateful to him.

I must offer my special thanks to Mark Day, a terrific print and film journalist who wrote, directed, and produced the documentary *The San Patricios.* Mark and I first met in early 1993, when he was just beginning the film. He is a man unafraid to take a stand—and all the flak that comes with it. I am proud to have been a part of his documentary and even prouder to call him my friend. *The San Patricios* is a must for anyone interested in the Irish-American experience and the Mexican War.

This book would not have been possible without the support and skill of my literary agent, Frank Weimann. Special thanks go out to Debra Greinke, Linda Smith, and researcher Alexander Bacon.

Finally, I offer my deep thanks to Peg Stevens and Patricia Marsh, fiercely proud of their Irish roots and "O'Connells to the core." They prodded me to stick with John Riley and company over the past 12 years. Paula, Greg, and, last here but certainly not least, Karen Stevens and David Pearlman did likewise. I'm glad I listened.

Introduction

IN THE GRAYNESS JUST BEFORE DAWN OF SEPTEMBER 13, 1847, 15 mule-drawn wagons creaked across the cobbled plaza of Mixcoac, Mexico. They lurched up a small, steep hill and halted in front of a long wooden crossbeam that was supported by four sturdy posts. Dangling from the beam were 30 nooses.

Each of the wagons, flanked by neat rows of American soldiers clad in visored campaign caps and sky-blue jackets and trousers and shouldering muskets, held three men, a muleteer and two soldiers, who wore darker blue uniforms and whose hands and feet were bound with ropes.

At 5:30 in the morning, as the first fiery streaks of sunlight seeped across the Valley of Mexico, the muleteers nudged their wagons beneath the nooses. Guards' bayonets prodded the prisoners to their feet. Two hours later, several hundred yards to the northwest of the gallows, some 7,000 American troops formed up and surged toward a hilltop bastion. Batteries of American artillery opened up in front of the scaffold, and their roundshot streaked eastward and tore chunks of masonry from the gleaming white walls of the distant fortress. The climactic battle of the Mexican-American War had begun. An equally dramatic and tragic episode was unfolding on that little hill where the nooses hung slack.

The ropes awaited 30 men of the Saint Patrick's Battalion, prisoners who had "fought like Devils" against the American armies of occupation

1

of General Zachary Taylor and Winfield Scott in every major battle of the Mexican War and who had nearly beat Taylor at the Battle of Buena Vista, in February 1847. On August 20, 1847, at Churubusco, a convento and bridgehead just south of Mexico City, the Saint Patrick's Battalion had torn apart several American regiments and had "settled old scores by seeking and killing dozens of West Point officers with the malignity of private revenge."[1]

The American hatred for the "San Patricios" blazed on the morning of September 13, 1847, for the doomed men were not ordinary prisoners of war. "The Legion of St. Patrick" had been "organized from the Irish deserters from our [the U.S.] army and numbered over 700 men who fought with a rope around their necks."[2] Although men had switched sides during the American Revolution, the U.S. Army had never encountered its own deserters forming a unit in a foe's army to fight against their ex-comrades—until the appearance of the St. Patrick's Battalion.

Many of the men wearing American blue later dwelled upon motives that had compelled the Irishmen, as well as many Germans and other immigrants, to desert the American army, to form a battalion in the Mexican army, and to march into the war's major battles beneath a green silk banner emblazoned with gold-threaded images of St. Patrick, the harp of Erin, and a shamrock. In the heat, haze, and dust of that Mexican morning of September 13, 1847, however, only revenge against the deserters who had claimed such a fearsome toll from their old regiments mattered to most of the Americans. They blamed the tragedy on "the evil influence and example" of the deserters' leader, a man named John Riley.[3]

Of the Irishmen, Mexican commander Santa Anna would write: "Give me a few hundred more men like Riley's, and I would have won the victory."[4]

No U.S. Army has ever encountered the problems of desertion that plagued Generals Zachary Taylor and Winfield Scott during the Mexican-American War, 1846–48. Of the nearly 40,000 regulars who saw duty during the conflict, a stunning 5,331—nearly 13 percent of the ranks—deserted. Of that figure, nearly 1,000 were Irishmen, 445 Germans, and 457 other Europeans. Approximately 5,000 Irish enlisted in the regular army, and nearly 20 percent went over the hill. Many were apprehended; many more simply disappeared. Many others fought in the St. Patrick's Battalion alongside John Riley.

The combined desertion rates of regulars and volunteers, 3,876 among the latter, were nearly 10 percent—double that of any of America's foreign wars. Center stage in the unprecedented controversy stood John Riley and an antiforeigner, anti-Catholic movement called Nativism that infected America and its army and made recently arrived Irish and, to a lesser degree, German immigrants willing not only to desert the U.S. Army, but also to fight for Mexico against their former officers and old messmates. These deserters did so in the ranks of the St. Patrick's Battalion, one of the war's hardest-fighting and most effective units. For nearly 150 years, the story of that controversial battalion was covered up and distorted.

Part One

"To Attain My Former Rank or Die"

1

"To the Golden Door"

IN THE SPRING OF 1843, a stranger arrived at Mackinac Island. Tall, blue-eyed, dense black hair curling to the bottom of his neck, he stepped down a skiff's gangplank and onto the main dock of the Michigan trading outpost and strode down the quay with the "straight as a ramrod" grace of the born soldier.[1] Crowds of fur trappers in buckskins and beaver caps and of prosperous merchants sporting stylish claw-hammer frock coats and brimmed planter hats milled about the waterfront. Women in calico skirts and oblong bonnets, children in tow, always filled the trading post's rutted main road in the spring to shop at the island's three general stores. To pursue this activity they had to dodge ox carts piled high with pelts, lumber, and fish slated for barges and Great Lakes steamships moored in the little harbor.

In the newcomer's ears, teams of men loading and unloading the ships and sweating in homespun linen shirts and woolen pants fastened with a bit of rope shouted syllables with familiar inflections of "the ould [*sic*] sod," including the stranger's own county, Galway. Those dock workers had stepped onto the town quay with the same destination in mind as the Galway native: a two-story, red-oak blockhouse emblazoned with a green- and gold-lettered sign—*Charles O'Malley*. Nestled among other trading posts; a cluster of Huron Indians' lakeside wigwams; and a few hundred sturdy frame houses built in a long clearing below stands of beeches, white spruces, and oaks covering limestone cliffs, O'Malley's blockhouse offered a proverbial mecca for "footloose" or desperate Irishmen who happened upon it from points Canadian or American and begged for work.

The Galway man entered O'Malley's and was granted an interview by the man locals had dubbed "the Big Lord," "Big Boss," and "the Irish Dragon." In his mid-thirties, O'Malley possessed fierce eyes and a booming voice that cowed most men. But as O'Malley, a man born in a squatter's hovel in County Mayo and now rising to wealth and political prominence in America's Irish-Catholic community, would write, he had no illusions about intimidating the muscular, nearly six-foot, two-inch jobseeker. "Highly intelligent, he did not seem a man accustomed to taking orders, but to giving them."[2]

Although O'Malley would accurately write that he sensed the man's "variance with many he came in contact with," the merchant also saw a strapping 27-year-old who would have scant trouble hauling timber to O'Malley's logging wagons and lugging barrels of pelts aboard his growing fleet of Great Lakes barges and sloops.[3] "The Irish Dragon," who rarely turned away fellow Irishmen victimized by British oppression and by famine, hired the newcomer, John Riley.

The Mackinac merchant had sized up Riley well, for John Riley was accustomed to men following his orders. He had won their respect the hard way, earning his stripes as an Irishman in the ranks of the British Empire and more than likely in battle.

Now, in 1843, after his hitch in the British ranks, John Riley was starting over, joining the flow of Irish immigrants yearning to pass through "the Golden Door," the term refugees from "that troubled Isle" coined to describe their hopes for prosperity and happiness in America, their promised land.

Riley had chosen a seemingly ideal spot from which to build a new life, as Mackinac housed a vibrant and growing Irish-Catholic "colony." The handsome British Army veteran won friends through his facile wit, his "general intelligence," his "very fair character," and his colorful anecdotes of his military service; many writers would depict him as an embodiment of Ireland's legendary "Wild Geese," hard-boiled men who, with their own nation prostrate beneath England's proverbial heel, fought for other lands' armies—even that of England—in dreams of one day unleashing hard-won martial skills against the hated redcoats. As Riley would write, he dreamed of "someday raising that glorious Emblem of Native Rights, that being the Banner which should have floated over our native Soil many years ago . . . [the banner] of St. Patrick, the Harp of Erin, the Shamrock upon a green field." [4]

Such sentiments stirred the soul of Charles O'Malley, and Riley discussed them with him, "Pat McNally, Thomas and William Chambers, Helen Kelly," and many others among Mackinac's 400 or so Irish Catholics. [5] In O'Malley's "Irish colony," Mackinac's immigrants gathered together on Saturday evenings to sup, to share the odd jar or two of poteen (whiskey), to sing, to dance to traditional reels of uileann pipes and a bodrhan (a goat-skin drum), and, most of all, to reminisce about their native soil.

Each Sunday, most of Mackinac's Irish Catholics climbed the narrow path of a 300-foot bluff to the island's church. The little church, its dull, whitewashed stone walls battered by wind and spray from Lake Huron, sloped slate roof graced with a diminutive oak cross but with no steeple, bore a strong resemblance to other churches John Riley had known. They were perched near cliffs an ocean away.

Parish records of County Galway record the births of two John Reilys [*sic*] in 1818 to two poor Catholic families. Either the son of John and Bridget Hession Reily or Stephen and Mary Reily is likely the future soldier. The destruction of parish records in a 1922 Dublin fire makes it impossible to determine with utter certainty which baptismal record is correct. But strengthening the case for John and Bridget Hession Reily as the parents is the fact that John Riley bears the first name of both the father and a John Hession who was born in 1802 in Carnoonan, Galway, and served in the British Army from 1821 to 1826. A West Galway genealogist speculates that, given John Riley's obvious affinity for military life and the fact that his mother's maiden name, Hession, was not nearly so common as Reily and other local names, John Hession may well have been John Riley's uncle and could have stoked the boy's interest in the army. If, indeed, John and Bridget Reily were his parents, the future soldier was the fourth of six brothers: Michael (1813); James (1815); Patrick (1816); Thomas 1820 (soon deceased); and a second Thomas (1823).

Riley's father was undoubtedly a tenant farmer and laborer—few Roman Catholics of the county were otherwise, except a handful listed as actual householders or tradesmen, and in 1818, none of them in the Clifden region were named Riley. Life for either John or Stephen Reily's family was one of endless labor, thatched-roof, one-room hovels, and a diet largely of milk and potatoes. At some point in the 1820s, John Riley's family had moved in or near the Galway town of Clifden.

Huddled near stark, scenic cliffs plunging to an Atlantic strand, Clifden stood in a locale notable for smugglers, deserters, and rebels. Riley men, as with the other Catholic farmers of the region, trudged each dawn with scythe and sod buster in hand to tend fields of corn, wheat, and oats for absentee landlords, Protestant nobles who owned the land but lived in London or in English or Scottish country manors. To feed their families, tenant farmers were allotted by the "Big Lord" a half-acre patch on which to grow "tubers," inferior potatoes that local landowners would not even feed to toss to their pigs.

In late 1817, the year of their son's birth, the Rileys and their Catholic neighbors had less than ever to put on the family's table, for the "Forgotten Famine" was spreading throughout Ireland, especially wracking County Galway. In a portent of the "Great Hunger" of 1845–47, the famine of 1817 began when peasants' potato beds went bad, a blight turning the crop into a reeking, gelatinous black mush. Churches set up soup and bread kitchens but were soon overwhelmed by the numbers of the needy swelled by tens of thousands of Irish soldiers returning home from the Napoleonic Wars. Rather than feed starving tenants, many absentee landlords sold their corn, wheat, and oats as cattle feed in England and Scotland; decided that future profits lay not in grain but in sheep and cattle; and began to evict tenant farmers from their cottages to open land for pasture.

The Forgotten Famine ravaged Ireland for the first seven years of John Riley's life. The paths around Clifden were "peopled with walking ruins—tattered and derelict wrecks of humanity, deformed or diseased, half-naked or clad in stinking rags: the repulsive flotsam and jetsam of a decaying social order."[6] The corpses of men, women, and children whose tongues were stained green from eating grass, littered the roadsides of the county. The wealthy mother of a Presbyterian cleric wrote, from Galway in 1817, that the famine "created watchful nights, cheerless days and a sort of reluctant shame at sitting down to a table amply spread."[7] But such "reluctant shame" did not open the hearts of many landlords to the tenant farm families, or "croppies," as they were derisively known.

In the brutal social and economic struggle to which Darwin's future adage "survival of the fittest" applied all too well, John Riley survived. A charitable commission set up by Parliament to study the famine related that the Catholic peasantry in which Riley dwelled confronted straits in which "it would be impossible adequately to describe the privations which they habitually and silently endure." The officials stated: "In many districts, particularly in Connacht [which included Clifden], the Catholics' only food is the potato, which has gone bad, their only beverage water... their cabins are seldom a protection against the weather... a bed or a blanket is a rare luxury... and nearly in all, their pig and a manure heap constitute their only property."[8]

According to Galway historians, the Rileys and other locals would have pooled their meager stores of provisions with those of relatives living also on the outskirts of Clifden and would have supplemented a scanty diet with scrapings from the nearby sea. The sight of peasant women harvesting kelp from rocky Atlantic strands to boil into a barely edible soup became a common one during the Forgotten Famine.

Tenant farmers and desperate laborers wandered farther into the county than they ever had, clearing boulders from fields; wading into bogs to hack out patches of peat for the turf fires of merchants, sheepherders, and cattlemen; and taking any other odd jobs available. The itinerant farmers, known as "spalpeens," took their payment in sacks of grain or bushels of potatoes that barely helped sustain many families from 1817 to 1826.

Famine filled John Riley's early life with scenes that shocked some of the 19th century's most renowned writers and social historians. William Carleton, an acclaimed novelist who harangued his fellow Anglo-Irish Protestants for their abuse of impoverished Catholics, wrote that in 1817, the year of Riley's birth, famine- and disease-stricken "Ireland was one vast charnel-house."[9] English poet Lord Byron asserted that even in his travels through the Ottoman Empire, nowhere had he seen "such wretchedness as in Ireland, particularly Connacht."[10] From the pen of Byron's fellow poet, Shelley, in 1820 came the observation that in Ireland, "the rich grind the poor into abjectness, then complain that they are abject. The rich goad them to famine and hang them if they steal a loaf."[11] The third of England's immortal poets of the era, John Keats, added that no scenes on earth were worse than "the nakedness, the dirt, and the misery of the poor common Irish."[12]

Nowhere in Ireland appeared scenes harsher than in Riley's County Galway. Gustave De Beaumont, the famed French writer and friend of historian Alexis de Tocqueville, visited Riley's region and noted: "I saw the very extreme of human wretchedness; but I did not know then the condition of unfortunate Ireland.... Millions live in absolute destitution.... The only splendid buildings are prisons and barracks."

The prisons and the barracks throughout Galway and elsewhere stood not only as the cornerstones of British policy, but also as a necessity, for in the crags and bogs of Galway and in the rest of Ireland, many Irish Catholics refused to accept, without a fight, starvation sanctioned by the government's indifferent stance. Filled with rage against landlords and redcoats alike, dispossessed tenant farmers formed secret societies throughout rural Ireland; bands of outlaws called the Ribbonmen, the Whiteboys, the Blackfeet, the Tubers, and the Magpies stole Protestant landlords' cattle and grain, sometimes murdered landlords' rent collectors, and ambushed British soldiers.

The courts, or assizes, of Clifden teemed with Ribbonmen hauled by redcoats before magistrates to face death on a gallows or deportation to a penal colony in Australia. The convicts were heroes to Galway farm families, driven from their hovels by landlords and soldiers and chased "onto the road of beggary and ruin," as the redcoats literally tumbled the cottages' walls behind the suddenly homeless peasants.[13]

In Clifden and in the rest of agrarian Ireland, the Catholics viewed the courts, the soldiers, and all vestiges of authority as the enemy. Alexis de Tocqueville defended the Irish peasants' fury toward the legal system: "Justice for the poor Catholics was a preparation of government-

sanctioned vengeance. It is difficult to form an idea of the tone of contempt and insolence in which the members of the Anglo-Irish Bar speak
of the people and the lower classes."

Various Rileys, Reillys, and Riellys appeared often in the Galway
assizes, which would lead a few historians to speculate that some of
those misfortunate rebels were related to John Riley's family. Although
Riley would never cite specific examples of the scenario, he did whole-
heartedly, in his own words, embrace the struggle of Catholic Ireland.
Coming of age in a social climate where "hatred of the law was almost
universal" and where "the result of this alienation of the people from justice was the sympathy felt everywhere in Ireland for the criminal and the
fugitive," Riley developed antiauthority convictions differing little from
many among the millions of the Irish who would flee their homeland.

In another conviction, which Riley defined by the Catholic religion of
his ancestors, he reflected the collective view of countless Irish immigrants. The belief lay embedded in the centuries-old strife between
England's and Scotland's Protestants and Ireland's Catholics. Both sides
could offer an equally bloody litany of the abuses they had suffered at
the other's hands. But in young John Riley's Ireland, no one could question that Catholics lay virtually prostrate beneath their Anglo-Irish
Protestant lords.

The religious chasm ripping apart 19th-century Ireland seemed
unbridgeable from where the Rileys and their fellow Catholics subsisted.
"Nearly two centuries after the Cromwellian Wars [of the 1640s]," wrote
De Beaumont, "I passed through the country once traversed by Cromwell
and found it still full of the Catholics' terror of his name." [14]

Writing in 1821 about the tortured, sanguinary relationship between
Ireland's Catholics and Protestants, De Tocqueville noted: "All of the rich
Protestants whom I see speak of the Catholics with extraordinary hatred
and scorn. The latter, they say, are savages and fanatics led into all sorts
of disorders by their priests." [15]

In fairness to the many lower- and middle-class Protestant merchants and farmers who strove to coexist with their Catholic neighbors
and who decried the indifference of rich Anglo-Irish landlords and the
British government to the famine-stricken Papist peasants, any history
of early 19th-century Ireland must record that religious strife did not

preclude all notions of humanity. The fact remains, however, that Protestants ruled the proverbial and hard-won turf of Ireland.

In such a setting, John Riley and most other Irish-Catholic youths faced bleak, desperate prospects: lives as tenant farmers or as wandering spalpeens in a country in which landlords were turning farmland into grazing land. No official schools existed for the education of poor Catholic children, the government allowing priests to say Mass but not to run classrooms.

In John Riley's case, a bit of luck entered when someone, likely a local priest, noticed the boy's intelligence and taught him to read and write.

As Riley approached his adolescence, Catholic Ireland, for the first time since 1798's revolt, leveled a threat that rocked both the Anglo-Irish ascendancy and Westminster alike. Daniel O'Connell, a brilliant Catholic lawyer from County Kerry and "the most gifted orator of his day," traveled the length and breadth of Ireland and enlisted millions of dispossessed peasants in the Catholic Emancipation Movement. He had pledged to win his coreligionists the vote and to seat Irish Catholics in Parliament. Condemned by the British as the "King of the Beggars" and revered by his hordes of followers as the "Liberator," O'Connell flung the gauntlet of "peaceful" rebellion in the Crown's face; in 1829, King George IV signed the Catholic Emancipation Bill, "weeping, raging, and protesting." [16]

O'Connell's crusade, the blueprint of passive resistance that Gandhi embraced a century later, politicized the Irish Catholics as a body for the first time and imbued them with an identity that most would carry to America. Nowhere in Ireland did O'Connell's campaign for Catholic emancipation rouse the populace more fervently than in Galway. The Liberator's stirring rhetoric not only imbued his nation's downtrodden with pride in their history and in their Catholic religion, but also con-vinced them that, for the first time in three decades, they could stand up to religious persecution and ethnic bigotry and stare the lord or landlord square in the eye if properly organized. "The point is," notes Kerby Miller, author of *Out of Ireland,* "that all of O'Connell's political crusades involved millions of Catholics throughout the island and gave Catholics a degree of political consciousness and a degree of political education and organizational experience that was very unusual in Western Europe at that time. Ireland's Catholics brought this consciousness and experience with them when they emigrated to the United States." [17]

John Riley, one of those future emigrants, came of age at that moment when Catholic Ireland attempted to break the political, cultural, social, and religious fetters imposed upon it by its British conquerors in the 17th and 18th centuries. Embracing O'Connell's nationalism, Riley honed a fierce pride in his Catholic religion and his Irish heritage. His letters years later brimmed with O'Connell-like references to "the glorious Harp of Erin," "the Holy Banner of Saint Patrick," and similar images. [18]

In the 1830s, Riley saw Parliament gut the triumph of O'Connell's Catholic Emancipation Bill by levying property qualifications of ten pounds sterling upon any Catholic who wanted to vote in Parliamentary elections. Few Irish Catholics possessed the sum, a small fortune; in the elections of 1831, only 19,000 Catholics in all of Ireland proved able to cast votes.

Having crushed Ireland's gains at the ballot box, Parliament turned its scrutiny to O'Connell's second major crusade, a repeal of the Act of Union, in which Britain had dissolved Ireland's Parliament in 1800, two years after Lord Charles Cornwallis's redcoats had crushed Irish rebels during the Rising of 1798. O'Connell's dream to restore self-government to Ireland with a Parliament open to both Catholics and Protestants faded from 1830 to 1840, when British legislators squashed his Repeal bills in the House of Commons and the Crown reinforced its military garrisons throughout Ireland. The latter move mirrored Britain's fear that O'Connell would rouse his millions of supporters to "justly resist the British by force." In the House of Commons, he announced that "in such resistance" to British injustice, he and "Catholic Ireland were ready to perish in the field or on the scaffold." [19]

Parliament's answer appeared in the ever-increasing deployment of troops to garrisons in Ireland. And in the early 1830s, with many Irish firebrands too young to recall the horrors of the Rising of 1798 and eager to answer a call to arms from the Liberator, O'Connell blinked. Unwilling to pit ill-armed peasants against veteran redcoats, O'Connell declared that he would continue Catholic Ireland's struggle through parliamentary means. His position saved untold numbers of lives but won him the rage of "Young Ireland." Thousands of his followers in their teens or their twenties retained O'Connell's tenets of religion and nationalism but rejected his doctrine of peaceful rebellion. Embittered young Irishmen arrived at the belief that only armed rebellion offered any hope of freedom.

For John Riley and millions of other Catholics, O'Connell's Emancipation Bill and his peaceful-resistance campaign did not put food on the table; agrarian distress was still a blight throughout Ireland. And in Galway of the 1830s, John Riley possessed neither the right to vote nor the means to make a decent living. In his teens, probably adding a year or two to his age, he walked into a British army garrison in Galway and signed his name to the muster rolls, his words in a later letter indicating that he had already married and fathered a son.

Riley's decision, born of desperation, would have been unthinkable to many Irishmen just a generation or two before. Irish-Catholic soldiers had formed Irish brigades in the ranks of France and Spain throughout the 18th century and had fought the British on battlefields from Europe to Canada. But with the anticlerical fervor that gripped France during the French Revolution and the rise of Napoleon, the papacy condemned the French army as the enemy of Catholicism and urged Irishmen to help Britain defeat "the Anti-Christ Bonaparte." At Waterloo, in 1815, more than a third of Wellington's victorious army was Irish.

Despite the recent precedent of Irish Catholics donning the hated red coats of the British army, an Irishman's enlistment in a Crown regiment of the 1830s generally reflected a hard-pressed man. John Riley was all of that.

Many historians would assert that Riley served in the 66th Queen's Foot, deserted the unit in Canada in the early 1840s, enlisted in the U.S. Army, earned his sergeant's stripes, served as a recruiter, and trained West Point cadets how to service artillery. This "career" was presented in an 1847 *Niles National Register* story. Riley, however, never saw duty in a recruiting office or at West Point and never wore a sergeant's stripes in the U.S. Army. He did wear stripes in the British army and was an expert gunner but never deserted to Canada.

With literally hundreds of John Rileys, Reillys, Riellys, and other spellings of the surname appearing in British regimental muster rolls for the 1830s and 1840s and with the gaps in some of the men's files, candidates emerge from heavily Irish regiments that were packed with Galway men. Chief among them were the 8th, 18th, 45th, 86th, 88th, and 89th Foot Regiments. Two men from these units had seen duty in colonial warfare and both wore sergeant's stripes. Sergeant John Reilly (John Riley himself signed his surname Riley, Reilly, and Rielly, and O'Riley) of the 88th received his stripes in September 1839 and was noted in 1841 as a Regimental Pioneer, a man who worked under engineers' orders to scout and prepare lines of march. Experienced soldiers with sterling records often served as pioneers and knew how to serve cannons. The last listing of the 88th's Sergeant and Pioneer Riley is in 1843.

Sergeant John Riely [*sic*] of the 86th Foot was also a combat veteran who had served as a pioneer and was last listed in the early 1840s.

John Riley swallowed his distaste for Ireland's rulers and discovered his innate aptitude for drill, long marches with cumbersome field packs, and cannons and artillery tactics. Winning his British stripes proved not only a source of pride to him, but also a source of frustration. As was the case with many Irish Catholics in the British ranks, a sergeant-major's stripes and sash and the respect that went along with them presented a prize within Riley's reach. He knew, however, that despite the plaudits he had won the hard way, he would rise no higher in Britain's army. "Shanty Irishmen" such as Riley did not sip brandy and port and puff on costly Cuban cheroots in the plush accommodations of British officers' clubs.

In 1843, Riley was mustered out with little more than his noncommissioned officer's kit bag and his memories of duty done well. Leaving his family behind in Galway, he crossed to Canada or the United States to start over, with the likely intent of sending for them when he was settled. He soon boarded a Great Lakes skiff and headed to Mackinac, Michigan, to "the Golden Door of America."[20]

Riley had yet to learn that the United States was not throwing open its collective arms to embrace the rising influx of immigrants to American shores. Not even in Charles O'Malley's Irish-Catholic enclave of Mackinac did refugees of "the ould sod" escape the virulent anti-Papist, antiforeigner movement gaining sway in all strata of American life.

2

"Paddy and Bridget" in the Promised Land

MANY HISTORIANS would trace the origins of the spreading new strain of ethnic and religious bigotry to Samuel F. B. Morse, the inventor of the telegraph. "A New England Puritan," Morse was watching a papal procession in St. Peter's Square, in Rome, in June 1830.[1] One of the pope's Swiss guards spied Morse's hat still on the man among a sea of heads bared in deference to the pope. The soldier strode in front of Morse and knocked off his hat. Catholic immigrants to America, scholars would assert, soon paid a high price for one man's headgear knocked askew, for in that brusque action, the political force to be known as the Nativist Movement materialized in the ire of the inventor.

As soon as Morse returned home to New York City from the scene of his "humiliation," he launched a personal literary campaign against the Catholic Church and "its insidious Papal designs upon the United States."[2] Of his experience in St. Peter's Square, he wrote that he had been "accosted by a poltroon in a soldier's costume, and the 'courteous' maneover [sic] was accompanied with curses and taunts and the expression of a demon in its countenance."[3] In a two-volume diatribe against immigrants and Catholics entitled *Foreign Conspiracy Against the Liberties of the United States,* Morse asserted: "The blame lies after all not so much with the pitiful wretch who perpetrates this outrage, as it does with those who gave him such base and indiscriminate orders—the Pope and his Church."[4]

In 1834, about the same time that Morse's polemic became a best-seller and that John Riley signed the enlistment paper of the British army, British pamphlets, magazines, and newspapers railing against the Catholic Emancipation Act and its potential to unleash ragged "Paddies" eager to settle scores with any Protestant flooded America. In a combination of religious conviction and shrewd commerce, many American publishers and writers seized upon the popularity of the anti-Irish literature and churned out antipapist screeds of their own.

A group of influential New York businessmen and politicians soon formed the Protestant Association, which proclaimed the need to preserve America's unique Anglo lineage from "Popery in this land of ours."[5] The association printed *The Protestant,* a fiery weekly newspaper, and published books nationwide with such lurid anti-Catholic titles as *Female Convents: The Secrets of Nunneries Disclosed.* Replete with sexually explicit and bizarre details of imaginary orgies behind the walls of convents and Catholic rectories, the books and pamphlets presented, by most Americans' literary or moral sensibilities, pornography—but the works were acclaimed because they exposed the alleged secrets of papist "deviates" swathed in the robes of nuns and priests. A rumor that Ursuline nuns were molesting young Protestant pupils at a convent in Charlestown, Massachusetts, a Boston neighborhood, sent a torch-bearing mob spilling into the nunnery in 1834. The rioters ransacked the place, chased several nuns, and burned it to the ground.

A book that did even more to mislead a large minority of Protestants and to enflame them against Catholics sold over 100,000 copies between 1836 and 1845 and was excerpted in newspapers across America. *Awful Disclosures,* the tale of Maria Monk, was the "true account" of the bizarre sexual practices that allegedly went on in Catholic convents; Monk wrote not only of graphic sexual relations between priests and nuns, but also of blood-drinking ceremonies and ritual sacrifice of infants by crazed Catholic clerics. When the public learned that Monk was a fraud—a prostitute and a former resident of an asylum for the insane—the revelations made no difference to hordes of firebrand antipapist foes. Notwithstanding documented proof of Monk's true background, they warned their adherents that her story was proof that Catholicism was a monstrous evil that must no longer be endured.[6] Her book and its equally salacious sequel, *Further Disclosures,* continued to sell as fast as they came off publishers' presses.

One papist attuned to the bigotry behind *Awful Disclosures* was Charles O'Malley, the Irish Dragon of Mackinac, always ready to rail against anyone criticizing Irish Catholic immigrants. At the same time, O'Malley, a man who did business with and enjoyed the company of many Protestants in Michigan, knew that *Awful Disclosures* and similar works did not reflect the inherent fairness of some Americans. O'Malley's employee, John Riley, never mentioned Monk's ravings, but knowledge of the book and what it represented proved widespread among the nation's Irish immigrants as their priests assailed the tract's lies for over a decade.

Even after responsible Protestant journalists unmasked the madness of Maria Monk, the nation's appetite for anti-Catholic, antiforeign polemics increased, with over 400 mass-circulation Nativist newspapers and magazines reaching Americans of the early 1840s. Several of John Riley's Mackinac friends had lived in the centers of anti-Catholic America—Boston, New York, and Philadelphia—before heading to the Irish Dragon's fiefdom. In the bustling Eastern seaports, the points of entry for the rising numbers of immigrants, fear and contempt for the Irish seethed in such weekly publications as Philadelphia's *Downfall of Babylon* and New York City's *American Protestant Vindicator.* The newspapers vowed to eradicate "Jesuitical abomination."[7] They harangued that "the ill-clad and destitute Irishman is repulsive to our habits and our taste."[8]

The Nativist dogma soon spread from Eastern ports to Mississippi outposts. Carried not only in books and pamphlets, but also by "lecture agents" hired by the New York Protestant Association and by the Protestant Reformation Society, the xenophobic movement gained near-messianic steam when the *American Home Missionary Society Journal,* the most respected and influential Protestant publication in America, ran Reverend Lyman Beecher's essay "Plea for the West" in

1835. Beecher, the father of Harriet Beecher Stowe, whose novel *Uncle Tom's Cabin* would decry the evils of slavery and further polarize the North and the South, "revealed" the "Papist Plot" in a matter-of-fact manner lacking the fire and brimstone of other Nativist writers but confronting the crisis of Catholicism and immigration in equally hateful contentions. According to Beecher, the pope was plotting with despotic Catholic monarchs to crush American democracy by flooding the United States with hordes of Irish immigrants who were actually "papal minions" trained by parish priests. When the Irish had arrived in sufficient numbers, Beecher warned, they would use the ballot box of democracy to establish "these twins of oppression—despotism and Romanism."[9]

To Americans, whose ancestors had battled Catholic powers France and Spain in colonial wars of survival and had endured Catholic atrocities every bit as brutal as those perpetuated by Protestants upon Catholics, Beecher's arguments, rooted in selective and mass memory, made sense. In many ways, 1840s America, imbued with the historical and cultural traits of its pilgrim, puritan, and Anglican founders, was still England's child.

Lecture agents and anti-immigrant polemics sparked violence from New York and Philadelphia to Michigan. In Detroit, not far from Charles O'Malley's Irish enclave, Irishmen and native-born Americans battled each other in a July 4th melee fueled by Catholics and Protestants who had drunk too much. Similar episodes between foreigners and Americans erupted in Massachusetts, Connecticut, Maryland, Florida, and Indiana, the Nativists denouncing the immigrants as murderous and un-American.

John Riley worked on Mackinac's dock in 1843, and, while he, unlike O'Malley, did not write about Dodd's ill-conceived attempt to preach Nativist doctrine to a crowd of Irish Catholics, Riley may well have stood in the audience.

Historians would ascertain that at the Nativists' zenith, from 1835 to 1855, the political movement numbered 25 percent of the nation's Protestants. Although most native-born Americans of the 1840s had tolerated the limited presence of Irish immigrants, the rising numbers of Irish immigrants arriving in Eastern cities during the decade's first four years unsettled even relatively unbiased segments of American society.

The unease of millions of Americans about the immigrants soon waxed into pure fright, for by the autumn of 1845, as possible war against Mexico dominated concerns from New York to the Mississippi, a catastrophe was seeping throughout Ireland. The calamity would forever change America's ethnic, cultural, and social landscape.

That summer, a farmer in County Cork wrote: "A mist rose up out of the sea. . . . When the fog lifted, you could begin to see the potato stalks lying over as if the life was gone out of them. And that was the beginning of the great trouble and the famine that destroyed Ireland." [10]

By September 1845, the roads from Cork to Dublin "were flanked by a wide waste of putrefying vegetation." [11] Father Matthew, a renowned Irish temperance advocate, recorded: "In many places, the wretched people were seated on the fences of their decaying gardens, wringing their hands and wailing bitterly the disaster that had left them foodless." [12]

Ireland's Catholic peasantry, utterly dependent upon the potato for sustenance, could only gape at their ruined crop. "All [the crop] now is black." [13]

In John Riley's home county, Galway, where his wife, his son, and relatives remained, "the stench from the fields was intolerable: the odour from decaying flesh could not be more offensive." [14]

The blight had ruined over half of Ireland's potato crop by November 1845. The Irish knew that they could count on little aid or even sympathy from Britain after centuries of oppression from Parliament. "The English, is it?" asked a starving Donegal farmer. "Depend on yourself and don't mind the English. From the English we'll get plenty of legislation, but little food." [15]

Faced by London's indifference—or tacit genocide, as many scholars would assert—and by a blighted crop, many of the Irish saw but one choice: "God have mercy on us," a Galway man wrote. "There will be nothing for us but to lie down and die." [16] Over a million would perish of hunger or disease by 1848.

Nearly two million others fled the Great Hunger aboard coffin ships bound for America from 1845 to 1848. The unprecedented waves of "barbarian" Irish and Germans reaching New York, Boston, and Philadelphia in the fall of 1845 alarmed mainstream Americans and convinced many native-born citizens to join the already sizable legions of the Nativist movement.[17] Among the most strident Nativist recruits stood Protestant U.S. Army officers, believing that any influx of new Irish-Catholic immigrants into the nation's regiments would sully the American character of the ranks despite the fact that Irishmen already served them.

Newfound fears fueled by the waves of "luckless Irish" did not plague Protestants alone.[18] America's assimilated Catholic immigrants, including Irish who had arrived in the 1830s, feared that hard-won gains refugees had grasped in the United States could dissipate in a national backlash against the exiles streaming from coffin ships into American ports. Catholics in the original 13 colonies had begun as a persecuted minority, and only after Irishmen such as "Fighting John" Barry, the father of the U.S. Navy, and General Stephen Moylan served valorously in the Continental ranks during the Revolution had Catholics won the right to practice their faith. By 1840, native-born Catholics were legally accorded full citizenship, having established themselves in commerce, politics, and the patterns of American life. And even Catholic immigrants who arrived between 1800 and 1840 and who still spoke with a brogue had garnered tacit acceptance by many Protestant Americans. In a similar vein to the manner in which racists would brand African-Americans as "good" or "uppity," many Americans of the 1840s dubbed the Irish as "right-thinking" or "shanty." The latter appellation, usually followed by "Mick," "potato-head," "boghopper," or "croppie," applied especially to the half-starved, raggedly clad, and often ailing Irish who began to pour into America in 1842, when, for the first time, immigration numbers soared past the 100,000 level, the result of poor economic prospects in Ireland and Germany. John Riley entered Mackinac in that first major groundswell of immigration, one that would reach several hundred thousand within five years.

Many of the assimilated Irish, afraid of being lumped in with the influx of shanty Irish, extended little help to the new arrivals. Ravaged physically and mentally by years of famine and unbroken political oppression in the Old World, having survived Atlantic storms in leaky, rat-infested, disease-riddled coffin ships in which passengers had rarely been allowed out of the vessels' fetid, crowded holds, the Irish immigrant of the 1840s often arrived with sole glimmer of hope—the name of a relative who had fled Ireland years earlier and had carved out some measure of success after passing through the Golden Door. Such hope often died quickly with a brusque epithet or a slammed door at the home or the business of the relative who had "grabbed the golden goose."

Instead of a warm bed in a relative's comfortable home, most of the immigrants of the 1840s jammed into the nation's first tenements, ramshackle wooden rat holes that swayed at the merest hint of a breeze, in Boston, New York, and Philadelphia. Unlike John Riley, who had received an education, many newcomers were illiterate refugees of tenant farm families who were ignorant of urban life.

In America's port cities, Irishmen and growing numbers of German Catholics also fleeing crop failures and political oppression competed with free blacks for the menial and back-breaking jobs of society's bottomfeeders: dockworkers, porters, stevedores, wood choppers, and street sweepers. Older Irishwomen worked six-day, 80-hour weeks in dim, dank sewing factories, and young Irish girls derisively labeled "Bridgets" by Americans took work as scullery maids and charwomen.

Historian Kerby Miller asserts: "Irish Catholics of the 1840s were regarded by Americans as subversives, the advanced army of Papal aggression." [19] Much of American society delighted in newspapers' and magazines' cartoons of "Paddy and Bridget" as alcohol-besotted brutes with grotesque, simian features. In countless plays, pamphlets, political speeches, and everyday conversations, Nativists derided "all of the Irish, who reek of Popery, poverty, corruption, and whatever is dirty, whiskey-loving, unruly, and improvident." [20]

Some immigrants turned to their church for solace. Many turned to liquor. Adding to the Nativists' "proof" of the social menace posed by papist newcomers, many desperate Irish and German women, without family and unable to find even menial work, turned to prostitution; various equally desperate foreign-born men formed criminal gangs whose depredations provided lurid headlines for America's newspapers. Nativist writers declared that a papist crime wave would engulf all "real Americans"; the journalists neglected to mention police blotters proving that most of the nation's rising levels of robbery, rape, and murder blazed mainly in the tenements, immigrant-on-immigrant crimes. In the 1840s, rarely did an Irishman or a German accost a native-born American. Even "respectable" American men with a taste for Irish or German brothels encountered little trouble from the pimps, the thugs, and the madams running the illicit establishments.

As the Nativists linked papist immigration to crime and rising moral decay, in 1844 they struck a theme that unnerved even Protestants who had found the dogma of the twin evils of Catholicism absurd. When Catholic Bishop John Hughes, of New York, lashed out at the effort of the American Bible Society to place a Protestant Bible in all of the nation's classrooms and at the daily Protestant prayer led by all public school teachers, his words that "it might be better if Bible reading were eliminated altogether" from schools ignited a religious firestorm. Nativists, whose ranks included future President Millard Fillmore (1850–54), charged that Hughes' comments offered proof that Catholics intended to erase Protestant Bibles from the landscape and to replace them with the "Popish version."[21]

Hugh Clark, a political heavyweight in Kensington Township, a Catholic neighborhood just north of downtown Philadelphia, echoed Hughes' words in late April 1844. On May 3, 1844, Nativist mobs of several thousand men armed with clubs, knives, and pistols and carrying torches surged into Kensington and into Philadelphia's Catholic slums. The mobs burned three Catholic churches, two rectories, two convents, and over 200 Irish shanties to the ground. For five more days and nights, the rioters returned; the city's police merely watched.

After the initial shock of the first night's melee ebbed, bands of Irishmen fought back with clubs, pickaxes, and shovels during the mob's following assaults over the next four days. Few of the immigrants unveiled firearms, for if the police discovered any Irishman holding a gun, several years in jail loomed automatically for the offender.

The Philadelphia Nativist Riots claimed at least 30 dead and nearly 150 seriously injured and were stemmed only by troops sent to restore order five days after the riots erupted. Various accounts postulated that the death toll was actually higher, as some families, fearful that the police would learn their names, dragged away bodies for secret burials.

Rural Mackinac lay far from the Nativist flashpoints of Philadelphia, New York, and Boston, but, for John Riley, his outlook for prosperity appeared as bleak as those Eastern cities' immigrants who grasped at menial jobs few and far between as the nation's first "Irish Need Not Apply" placards sprouted in factories, shops, and construction sites.

Mackinac offered Riley and other Irish Catholics a haven of sorts from rampant Nativism, but even among the lakefront cottages and bustling docks of the island hung a frustrating reality for an ambitious immigrant such as Riley. Charles O'Malley ruled the proverbial roost locally, and while he usually proved willing to provide a fellow Irishman a job, the Irish Dragon brooked no attempt by his employees to climb any higher than he deemed suitable. Scores of unmarried and otherwise footloose Irishmen labored a few months or a few years for O'Malley and then drifted from Mackinac in search of other opportunities.

Riley, as with the other unattached men in O'Malley's employ, likely lived in one of the island's Spartan oak bunkhouses. By 1845, Riley chafed beneath the monotonous routines of dockside labor. The veteran soldier, accustomed to giving orders, became, according to O'Malley, "increasingly at variance with those whom he [Riley] came into contact with." [22] He scanned for other opportunities, bristling with ability and ambition.

The origins of an opportunity to which Riley was well suited simmered in late February, in a political cauldron of which he knew virtually nothing. In that month, a joint resolution of the United States Congress endorsed the annexation of the Republic of Texas. For nearly a decade after the legendary stand at the Alamo in 1836 and the rout of Mexican dictator Santa Anna's army at the Battle of San Jacinto—a short while after Davey Crockett, Jim Bowie, and the other defenders of the Alamo had fallen—Texans had lobbied the United States to admit the Rio Grande republic as a state before Santa Anna crossed the river to reconquer the former Mexican territory.

The furor over the potential annexation of Texas had dragged on nearly a decade because of the increasingly rancorous issue of slavery: Southerners and Texans had demanded the territory be admitted to the Union as a slave state; abolitionists had blocked annexation out of justified fears that Texas would be carved up into several regions and be annexed as at least three or four slave states, throwing Congress' balance of power to the South.

The political scale had tipped the annexationists' way with the appearance of yet another player in the controversy: Great Britain. Terrified by the very real specter of Mexican invasion, Texas had looked for another powerful ally after Congress repeatedly voted down all appeals that the United States confer statehood upon the fledgling Rio Grande nation. Texas President Sam Houston dispatched envoys to London, where they were accorded a warm welcome, for the government of young Queen Victoria wanted to ensure that Texas remained a sovereign state—and a barrier to the southward and westward expansionist dreams of the United States.

When Great Britain hinted its willingness to defend Texas from Mexico, panic-stricken American President John Tyler, once a vehement foe of annexation, reversed his stand. He did so not on behalf of Texas or out of enmity toward Mexico, but out of raw fear of British designs to the West. Parliament had its eye on California, the Pacific Northwest, and the Southwest, most of which belonged to Mexico. American settlers in Mexican California flooded Congress with letters alleging British intrigues to seize California and even Texas.

Inheriting the controversy was Tyler's successor, 50-year-old North Carolina Democrat James K. Polk, an Andrew Jackson protege dubbed "Little Hickory" in reference to Jackson's sobriquet "Old Hickory" and to Polk's thick, shoulder-length silver hair, which he wore in the same backswept fashion as his mentor. Polk had defeated the Whig Party's candidate, Henry Clay, of Kentucky, on a proslavery, blatantly expansionist platform; having flung a campaign slogan of "54–40 or Fight" at Great Britain, he had pledged to fight for a treaty forcing Parliament to accept the border of America's Oregon Territory at 54 degrees, 40 minutes latitude, which would have extended the United States's boundaries into British-held Canada and all the way to the Russian colony of Alaska. The threat of a third war with Great Britain loomed.

On the issue of British expansionism, an uneasy alliance of abolitionists, slaveholders, and mainstream Americans supported Polk's "54–40 or Fight" maxim. Polk's staunchest supporters numbered not only fellow slaveholders, but also the Nativists. Although the latter shared Britain's contempt for Irish Catholics and took pride in America's "Anglo-Saxon heritage," the Nativists parroted Polk's declaration that "the people of this continent alone have the right to decide their own destiny."[23] The anti-Catholic, anti-immigrant forces believed that native-born Americans held the God-given right to conquer the continent from the Atlantic to the Pacific and to "cleanse the dominions of Romish and foreign blight."[24] And, as the annexation of Texas forced the nation's collective gaze southward toward the Rio Grande, the Nativists joined the slaveholders to eye eagerly a new and logical foe—Catholic Mexico.

"Providence intended the New World for the Anglo-Saxon," proclaimed the *Philadelphia Nativist.* "If Mexico should oppose the decree of Heaven—so much the worse for Mexico!"[25]

An essayist for the *American Review* traveled throughout the United States in the summer of 1845 and commented that Americans were "restless, fidgety, discontented, anxious for excitement."[26] Mired in economic recession, the "Western borders" teemed with "great numbers of bold and restless spirits, men gathered out of all the orderly and civilized positions of society as its most turbulent members, and ready for any enterprise that can minister to their reckless manner of life and love of danger and change."[27]

In July 1845, the restless spirit sweeping America found its true voice in the words of firebrand journalist John L. O'Sullivan, editor of the *United States Magazine and Democratic Review.* O'Sullivan, an assimilated Irish American who envisioned a war with Mexico as a perfect arena for recent immigrants to prove their loyalty to their new country, wrote an article haranguing America's "weak posture" toward Mexico on the issue of Texas and asserting America's "right" to seize all Mexican territory between the Mississippi and the Pacific.[28] In words that actually embraced Nativist themes, the Irish Catholic writer defined the national spirit of the 1840s: "It is our Manifest Destiny to overspread the Continent allotted by Providence for the free development of our yearly multiplying millions."[29]

Many of the nation's most influential publications soon trumpeted O'Sullivan's battlecry of Manifest Destiny. In August 1845, the *New York Herald* declared, "The multitude cry aloud for war."[30] *The New York Journal of Commerce,* the bible of Eastern businessmen, figuratively salivating at the economic possibilities of an America stretching from Atlantic to Pacific, proclaimed: "Let Us Go to War!"[31]

As early as August 1843, Mexico's government, headed by Santa Anna, whom Texans and Americans loathed as the "Butcher of the Alamo," had informed President Tyler that Mexico would "consider equivalent to a declaration of war... the passage of an act for the incorporation of Texas."[32] But in December 1844, a coalition of moderates and Federalists—democratic Mexican leaders backed by the army—forced Santa Anna into exile in Cuba and elected Jose Joaquin Herrera as acting president.

Herrera, titular head of a nation ravaged by its bloody but successful War of Independence from Spain in the 1820s, by Santa Anna's repulse of a French invasion, and by nearly two decades of civil war, craved peace. Herrera backed off from Santa Anna's martial stance on Texas, indicated through diplomatic channels a willingness to discuss an American purchase of California and New Mexico, and wanted to settle another thorny issue: Mexico's refusal to pay reparations to American businessmen financially battered by his nation's wars. Britain had threatened invasion to force Mexico to pay the claims of European merchants. Mexico had acceded to Britain's demands.

Even as the proverbial drums of war rattled across America, President Polk, despite his own belligerent campaign platform against Britain and Mexico, still preferred a negotiated Western land grab to a military one. He dispatched Louisiana attorney and political operator John Slidell to negotiate a treaty steeped in the intransigent dictates of Manifest Destiny. Bluntly put, Slidell's mission was that of a diplomatic bully.

Few Americans offered better credentials for the job. Cunning and politically ambitious, 52-year-old John Slidell was a transplanted New Yorker who had garnered wealth and position in New Orleans' legal circles and a reputation as a duelist and a ladies' man. The handsome, silver-haired Democrat espoused a view of the Mexicans shared by Polk. "I have no very exalted idea of the caliber of the Mexican intellect," Slidell wrote shortly after he boarded a ship for Veracruz, Mexico, in the fall of 1845.[33]

Polk, a shrewd hand in the political play of both sides against the middle, hoped that Slidell's coercive rhetoric would terrify Mexico into submission. Polk knew that Herrera's government, which, because of the United States' annexation of Texas, still refused to reestablish full diplomatic ties with Washington, had unofficially agreed to receive Slidell as a commissioner but not as a full-fledged minister. Not only did Polk designate Slidell a minister extraordinary and plenipotentiary, but the president also instructed his envoy to throw down a harsh diplomatic glove to Herrera's government. Slidell first harangued the Mexican government for largely fictitious "injuries and outrages committed by... Mexico on American citizens."[34] In the true spirit of Manifest Destiny, he presented Polk's demands that Mexico accept one of three geographic choices: a boundary along the Rio Grande and half of New Mexico in lieu of restitution to the financial claims of aggrieved American citizens; all of New Mexico, in exchange for American assumption of claims and a payment to Mexico of $5 million; or the sale of the entire Southwest and California to the United States for $25 million.

Before Polk devised the unpalatable treaty offer in August 1845, Herrera was under intense political fire by Mexicans enraged at his tactics of appeasement. Although many historians would paint the United States as the absolute aggressor and Mexico as the absolute victim in the unfolding events of 1845, in truth, a small faction of Mexican army officers and politicians, headed by the aristocratic General Mariano Paredes, were demanding an attack on Texas and the United States as early as August 1845. Confident that the Mexican army, schooled in 20 years of fierce clashes against Spanish and French troops and Texan rebels, could handle the "Yankee hereticos," America's southern neighbor girded for war. Commented a Mexico City newspaperman: "The idea of peace was not popular."[35]

Nor was the idea popular in many corners of the United States as a martial brew of exhilaration and foreboding seeped in all directions from Washington in the months following the Annexation Declaration. Fort Mackinac, a small, white stone bastion erected by the British during the War of 1812, now garrisoned by Company K of the 5th U.S. Infantry Regiment and long known as a quiet-duty billet, suddenly rang with the daily din of sergeants' shouts, the thuds of marching men, and muskets' cracks on a hastily built firing range. The soldiers of Company K, men who had rarely worn garb other than their visored blue forage caps, informal linen shirts, and gray trousers, donned new cloth-topped caps with shiny black visors and the white cap-band of the infantry; white-braided, sky-blue fatigue jackets and similarly hued trousers; and stark white belts and cross belts holding a black cartridge box, a bayonet scabbard, and a tin canteen. Officers clad in dark-blue, stylishly tailored frock coats with silver-laced rank bars and buttons and in caps similar to the ranks', but far superior in cut and quality, strutted along Mackinac's paths with eyes on admiring women and one hand on the hilt of a straight-bladed steel sword.

Sometime during the summer of 1845, John Riley met one of the jaunty officers, Captain Moses Emory Merrill, the 41-year-old commander of Company K. Merrill, a muscular graduate of West Point's class of 1826 and a career officer with a distinguished record of frontier duty, enjoyed the respect of his men as a soldier's soldier. He was a Regular army martinet noted for his bristling side whiskers, bushy eyebrows that framed stern features, and his intolerance of the slightest breach of military conduct. And in the former sergeant major, Merrill encountered a kindred martial soul, "a master of arms, a well-groomed, genial, well-spoken, restless man of action," and a man who, like Merrill, had likely distinguished himself in battle. Merrill soon found Riley to be an intelligent and highly capable soldier.

The former sergeant major, hauling crates and heaving lumber into wagons each day, sweating in the summer haze, and tormented like all the islanders by the clouds of mosquitoes swarming down from Mackinac's forests, heard the rattle of drums, the trills of fifes, the heavy tramp of marching men, and the bugle calls that marked the soldiers' hours from reveille at 5:30 A.M. to tattoo (lights out) at 10:00 P.M.—the familiar sounds of Riley's old profession echoing across the Mackinac waterfront in a martial siren's call.

The United States Army wanted men such as John Riley to hear that siren's call as the nation drifted toward "Mr. Polk's War." The army needed bodies to fill its undermanned peacetime ranks, and pragmatic recruiting officers recognized a source of experienced soldiers: European army veterans streaming from coffin ships into America. In his journal, a dragoon noted that battle-hardened "Irishmen who had left the Queen's service" comprised ideal candidates "to wear the blue of the U.S. Army."[36] As soon as the War Department ordered the expansion of each company from 64 to 100 men in midsummer of 1845, recruiters went to work on the immigrants.

The army faced a formidable task. Confronted by estimates of Mexico's forces as numbering anywhere from 30,000 to 50,000 regulars, the American army totaled 8,613 enlisted men and officers in eight infantry regiments, four artillery regiments, and two dragoon regiments scattered in over 100 posts from New York City to Oregon.

Amid the squalid tenements and alleys of Boston, New York, and Philadelphia, regular army recruiters, usually sergeants, lieutenants, or captains, promised droves of young and middle-aged "Micks" and "Dutchies" "booty, adventure, good food, and women" for any man who would sign an enlistment paper. The recruiters convinced cash-strapped immigrants that over a 5-year hitch, they could save up to $700 of wages, enough for a fresh start in civilian life. To any potential enlistees concerned about the harshness of military life, the sergeants and officers spoke of comfortable barracks, fine uniforms, the best medical treatment, and advancement for ambitious men. With classic understatement, a historian would note that the recruiters' assurances were not "always scrupulous."

The regular army's half truths and lies appeared honorable in comparison to the later pitches of volunteer regiments. "Roast beef and two dollars a day, plenty of whiskey, golden Jesuses, pretty Mexican gals"— volunteer recruiters promised men all of these, as well as offering patriotic appeals to more decent sorts. Some men intoxicated on that "good whiskey" formally charged that they had been impressed, "shanghaied," into volunteer units. Despite such charges, patriots and misfits alike would flock to the volunteers' colorful banners.

The promises of glory and dark-eyed women worked best with young, restless Irishmen and Germans. For older, savvier immigrants, however, the army devised equally effective inducements: a bonus of three-months' pay, 100 acres of farmland in the West, and a waiver of the five-year naturalization process required for American citizenship in the 1840s. To many Irish tenant farmers with hungry families, the promises of land and enough money to feed their broods for a year offered powerful motives to wear the blue; the War Department tapped into the agrarian Irishman's hunger to own his own acres and into his dream to find prosperity through the Golden Door.

Even the meager $7-a-month pay for army privates, a figure holding slight allure to the poorest native-born Americans, appealed to Irish and German immigrants, who were either unemployed or scraping by on the three or four dollars a month paid to foreigners working on docks or sweeping streets. "Immigrants of the 1840s often found the army the solution to their most basic and immediate problems," writes historian K. Jack Bauer. "Frequently less concerned by regimentation, less attractive to factory bosses in the bigger cities, less aware of the army's relatively low wages, and less capable of reaching the frontier on their own, they were attracted by the prospects of the army. The result of all this was an army of enlisted men who by and large viewed their service as a distasteful alternative to the life they wished to lead."[37]

In the cases of Irishmen evincing an especially pronounced hatred of Great Britain, army recruiters told them that a look at any newspaper proved that America and Great Britain would soon be at war in Oregon and all along the Canadian border for control of the Pacific Northwest. The chance to settle scores with the "ould sod's" ancient oppressor sent many Irishmen scrambling to scratch their signatures—an "X" for illiterate men, whose names were written out by recruiters—on the muster rolls of the American army.

In the turbulent summer of 1845, the immigrants and most native-born Americans did not know that President Polk had opened clandestine negotiations with Great Britain over the Oregon Question and that Polk's maxim that "the only way to treat John Bull was to look him straight in the eye" was slowly working.[38] A diplomatic solution in which Britain would hold onto all of the Pacific Northwest above the 49th parallel and in which Polk would back down from his pledge to occupy the region right up to Alaska was slowly unfolding.

Despite the secret sessions with British minister Lord Packenham, Polk and his cabinet continued to use nationwide fears of John Bull to stir up war fever. The administration leaked reports that British regiments were arriving in Canada to reinforce border garrisons for an invasion of the United States. To John Riley, Charles O'Malley, and the other residents of Mackinac, one glance from the island's bluffs seemingly confirmed imminent war with Britain. Across Lake Huron, Mackinac's British counterpart also rang with the sounds of troops marching, firing muskets, and, most ominously, unlimbering artillery on a waterfront cliff. Whenever talk in Mackinac, Detroit, and other northern outposts turned to the problems along the Rio Grande, fears that Polk might strip Fort Mackinac and other local bastions to deploy troops on the Mexican border arose. The president intended to do just that—and to ship troops from every other fort to points south. Some recruiters plying Irish-Catholic immigrants with food, drink, and promises, however, kept the focus on Great Britain, not on Catholic Mexico.

When Nativists discovered that the army's first major recruitment drive since the War of 1812 was targeting immigrants who included Irish veterans of the British army, the anti-Catholic and antiforeign press unleashed a torrent of denunciations of Polk and his army's commander, General Zachary Taylor, "Old Rough and Ready." Congressman Lewis Levin of Philadelphia spearheaded a Nativist campaign to restrict all enlistments to native-born Americans and presented a bill not only advancing that premise, but also raising the naturalization process from five years to 25 for all Irish and German immigrants. As Levin ranted incessantly from the speaker's well of the House of Representatives, his face shiny with perspiration, his head bobbing with every loud syllable, his hands gesticulating, immigrants continued to make their marks on enlistment papers.

Typical of the foreign-born recruits was light-haired, blue-eyed Patrick Dalton. A native of County Mayo, he was no stranger to military life as he walked from the Lower East Side tenements of New York City and into Madison Barracks on August 2, 1845. To Lieutenant Lyon of Company B, 2nd Infantry, Dalton gave his age as 21, his occupation as farmer, and his birthplace as Quebec. He was lying on all counts, Professor Robert R. Miller notes.

Patrick Dalton, as he would prove in Mexico, was a soldier, trained like Riley in the British army. As he signed his enlistment form, he was hiding his background with good reason: the U.S. Army had been ordered to turn down any deserters from the British army. Dalton had slipped away from his barracks in Canada.

His hidden past notwithstanding, Dalton possessed leadership qualities, reflecting a man who had worn stripes in his previous military career. Unlike impressionable and desperate youths fresh off the coffin ships, veterans like Dalton placed more importance on the steady though meager $7 private's wage than on recruiters' descriptions of the coming conflict as "an adventure full of fun and frolic and holding forth the rewards of opulence and glory." He did, however, harbor ambitions of rank.

When Dalton decided to enlist in the American army, he did not stroll into one of the rowdy tents set up on New York's waterfront or amid the Irish and German tenements. He took a ferry to Fort Hamilton, an island bastion guarding the mouth of the Hudson River and garrisoned by a company of the 3d Infantry Regiment. The War of 1812-era fort's crumbling granite walls, its buckling casements, and its antiquated naval cannons reflected the neglect of a nation that had feared no foreign invasion since the Treaty of Ghent in 1815 had ended America's second war with Britain. In early 1845, as Polk's concerns about a third conflict with the British escalated over the Oregon Question, the War Department assigned the army's finest engineer to refurbish Fort Hamilton, the cornerstone of any defense of New York from a seaborne invasion. The engineer's name was Captain Robert E. Lee.

The 38-year-old Virginian, who had inherited the dark-haired good looks of his Revolutionary War-hero father, cavalry commander "Light Horse Harry" Lee, and had married George Washington's great-granddaughter, Mary Ann Randolph Custis, had graduated second in the West Point class of 1829 with an enviable academic record in the study of engineering. West Point engineers composed the elite of the nation's technical ranks; so pronounced were his engineering skills that he won worldwide scientific acclaim for his dredging innovations in the enlargement of the Mississippi port of St. Louis. But his well-deserved reputation for engineering expertise led his superiors to believe that he was too valuable to risk in the frontier wars and in the Seminole Wars of the late 1830s. Lee anguished beneath the label, and as Fort Hamilton's American veterans and its foreign recruits began to drill in earnest in the summer of 1845, the Virginian hoped he, too, could prove his mettle in combat if America did go to war.

Lee found the Irish, German, and other European veterans enlisting in the army fine material for the coming fray. Perhaps because many Irishmen in the ranks had fought in Afghanistan, India, and Florida, because some of the older immigrant recruits had served with Wellington against Napoleon himself, Lee treated the foreigners with aloof respect. His attitude reflected that of Captain Moses Emory Merrill, an upperclassman at West Point when Lee had arrived there as a lowly plebe in 1825. As the immigrant recruits would learn, both captains' attitudes vastly differed from many peers in the officer corps—especially fellow West Pointers.

In August 1845, as Captain Lee stared down at Fort Hamilton's parade ground from construction scaffolds, the recruits drilled in their new campaign caps and sky-blue tunics and fired their standard-issue flint-lock muskets in close-order maneuvers. Scaffolds of a different sort awaited some of the immigrants in the events to come.

To the Irish-born recruits, the prospects of possibly fighting Britain; of an escape from the squalor, the unemployment, and the Nativist prejudices of America's cities; and of the government's three-pronged offer of land, cash bonuses, and citizenship offered ample incentives to enlist. Testifying to the effectiveness of the perks offered to foreign-born enlistees, Adjutant General Roger Jones, the architect of the War Department's recruitment tactics, informed President Polk that "the greatest number of men have been recruited [and] are situated in our large commercial cities, where vast numbers of that class of men who enter the ranks of the army reflect their desperate need for employment and where, also, vast numbers of emigrants are constantly arriving."[39]

Potential recruits such as Patrick Dalton and John Riley—no naive immigrants but veteran soldiers—required another guarantee as an incentive to affix their names to the army's muster rolls. In a conversation with friends in Mackinac, Riley remarked that if he were to join up, he would do so only if afforded the chance "to attain my former rank."[40] He sardonically commented on his unwillingness to serve for long as a mere private, given his proven capacity for command in the British army, the world's finest in the 1840s.

Recruiters promised that a thick brogue or a heavy German accent posed no impediment to advancement in the ranks of the American army. Portraying the army as committed to judging a man only on his merits, the recruiters could refer to the example of Sergeant Major Maurice "Mick" Maloney. A man whose exploits against the Seminoles in 1840 was the stuff of stirring penny novels, Mick Maloney "represented a familiar type of Catholic Irishman who loved soldiering." [41] He had emigrated from County Limerick in 1830, a few years before the Nativist movement had gained full social steam; in 1834, he had enlisted in the U.S. infantry at the age of 24. Maloney, "tall, broad-shouldered and with the freckled, ruddy complexion typical of his countrymen," had risen from the ranks through his ability in drill and in battle alike. [42] He had earned his sergeant's stripes in 1836, his commander touting him as officer material.

Another Irish success story recruiters could relate to immigrants rang in the martial-sounding name of Artillery Lieutenant John Paul Jones O'Brien. One of the first Catholic graduates of West Point, class of 1836, the short, bull-framed O'Brien sported shoulder-length chestnut hair, a razor-thin mustache and goatee, and blue eyes that glinted fiercely when anger gripped him, which, with his notoriously hair-trigger temper, it often did. In 1843 in Newport News, Virginia, he had "stirred the dovecoats of the Army" by his refusal to force several fellow Catholics in his artillery company to attend a Sunday service in a Protestant church. [43] When his commanding officer threatened him with a court-martial, O'Brien retorted that because the Constitution guaranteed freedom of choice, he and his handful of Catholic troops possessed "the right not to enter a Protestant service if they pleased." [44] O'Brien's superior dropped the threat—but O'Brien had earned several formidable enemies among high-ranking officers for his stand.

His staunch Catholicism notwithstanding, O'Brien bore little cultural resemblance to the immigrants he commanded. Born in Philadelphia to an assimilated family, he epitomized the social inroads made by a handful of Philadelphia's Irish. Aside from his religion and his surname, he had less in common with the ragged, hungry, and destitute coffin-ship Irish of the 1840s than he did with Boston Brahmins, New York City society nobs, and aristocratic Southern planters, three social wells filling part of the United States Army's officer corps in 1845.

Along with the names of O'Brien and Maloney, recruiters could trot out the "crown jewel" of the army's "Irishmen"—Colonel Bennet Riley. Of this Riley, Second Lieutenant Ulysses S. Grant would write: "Bennet

Riley was the finest specimen of physical manhood I had ever looked upon ... 6′2″ in his stocking feet, straight as the undrawn bowstring, broad shouldered with every limb in perfect proportion, with an eye like an eagle and a step as lithe as the forest tiger."[45]

Bennet Riley grasped the plight of the shanty Irish better than O'Brien did, for Riley had grown up in dire poverty, born in America to a second-generation Irish-Catholic farm family in St. Mary's County in Maryland. Various apologists for the Nativists would offer the "rags to respect" career of the tough career officer as "proof" that Irish Catholics exaggerated the prejudice they encountered in America of the 1840s. Invariably, such scholars failed to mention that their cultural yardstick, Bennet Riley, was not an immigrant, but a full citizen who spoke without a tinge of a brogue.

He had climbed from poverty to an honored niche in the army, and when, late in his life, a friend suggested that the old warrior have a coat of arms drawn up to honor his military feats, Riley replied: "No, sir, I will not—because, sir, I never had a coat of any kind till I was a 21-year-old in the Army."[46] He would prove a key figure in the lives of John Riley, Patrick Dalton, and the pair's future comrades-in-arms.

One of those future comrades-in-arms had enlisted in the 3d Regiment at Newport, Rhode Island, on September 18, 1844. Born in Dublin in 1816, Rodmand Batchelor stood nearly six feet tall, and while the dark-haired recruit had probably served a stint in the British Army as a noncommissioned officer, he was a schoolteacher by trade. Whether he just loved soldiering or just could not find a suitable classroom posting, Batchelor would prove that he knew his way as well around a musket or a cannon as he did around a book.

Another man to meet up with Batchelor, Dalton, and Riley in America's ranks was 33-year-old Auguste Morstadt, a German immigrant. A brown-haired, broad-shouldered veteran of his native Baden's army, in which he had reportedly been a noncommissioned officer, he enlisted in the 7th U.S. Infantry in 1841. Morstadt, a well-educated product of his homeland's public schools, spoke thickly accented but grammatically precise English and had no trouble in picking up the commands and European-style routines of his new army. He soon caught the approving notice of his company commander, Lieutenant

Gabriel R. Paul, West Point class of 1829. Paul even began to consider recommending Morstadt for a noncom's stripes, although the chances of a "Dutchie" getting a promotion were virtually nonexistent.

With names such as Morstadt, Batchelor, and Dalton sprouting in the muster rolls, *Niles National Register,* one of America's most popular magazines, noted: "Strangers to the soil, emigrants without home or hearth, constitute the greater portion of the enlisted men." [47]

On September 4, 1845, another "stranger to the soil" headed toward a recruiting station at an American fort. With each step, the fort's "picturesque blockhouses . . . the pretty balconied residences of the officers came into view, having the banner of the 'Stars and Stripes' waving over them." [48] The man recognized a daily scene in front of him: "Suddenly a brilliant flame, and volumes of white smoke arose above the fort, while a booming sound told us they were firing their mid-day salute in honor of the day." [49] Never had the cannon's noontime blast pealed with such import as on that September day of 1845. The locals understood that the same gun could roar in actual battle at any moment. And most believed that the foe would be Great Britain.

The "emigrant without home or hearth" walked into the recruiting station. Captain Merrill and Sergeant James Everstine greeted him. Merrill wrote the man's name, age, birthplace, and physical description on a standard enlistment form. In a bold, firm hand, the newest recruit of Company K of the 5th U.S. Infantry signed his name: John Riley.

A short while later, Riley told Charles O'Malley and other acquaintances that he had enlisted "to attain my former rank or die." [50]

3

"Buck Him and Gag Him!"

O N JUNE 29, 1845, General Zachary Taylor received Polk's orders to move the American Army of Observation to Texas "for the Lone Star Republic's protection."[1] Most of the 3d and 4th U.S. Infantry soon marched through New Orleans to the cheers of flag-waving throngs and bands' plaintive piping of "The Girl I Left Behind Me," boarded the steamship *Alabama* and other vessels, and landed on the east coast of Texas at Kinney's Ranch, the future Corpus Christi.

From garrisons all across America, soldiers tramped onto transports and sailed down rivers or on the Atlantic to Taylor's campsite along the Gulf of Mexico. Marching orders for Company K and John Riley came two days after he signed his enlistment paper.

Riley had sworn that "I will bear true faith and allegiance to the United States of America and that I will serve them honestly and faithfully against all their enemies or opposers whomsoever; and that I will observe and obey the orders of the President of the United States, and the orders of the officials appointed over me, according to the Articles of War."[2] After a Mackinac surgeon "carefully examined the above-named recruit [Riley]" and pronounced him "free from all bodily defects and mental infirmity, which would in any way disqualify him from performing the duties of a soldier," Riley donned his fatigue blues, shouldered his new flintlock musket and full field pack, and marched with most of

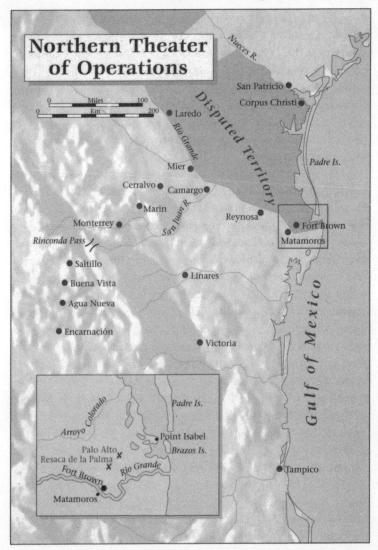

Northern Theater of Operations

Company K aboard a transport bound for Detroit.[3] There, the 5th Infantry was assembling for the long journey to Texas and would mobilize as a full regiment for the first time in nine years.

Discipline on the 5th's trip down the Ohio River by canal boats and down the Mississippi to New Orleans by side-wheeler steamers proved looser than on land. Noncoms broke up a few brawls by clamping offenders in chains but allowed the men to mill along the gunwales or play card games such as Faro and Old Sledge belowdecks.

Throughout the river journey, Captain Merrill and the officers quietly scrutinized the 5th's ranks, and a lieutenant noted that fully 50 percent of the men were Irish or German. On September 29, 1845, Captain William Chapman wrote that his company had lost "two by desertion since we left Mackinac."[4]

A handful of officers such as a 39-year-old captain worried about the anti-Irish leanings of many fellow officers of the 5th. West Pointer Ephraim Kirby Smith, whose solid physique intimidated enlisted men and whose military pedigree boasted three generations of regular army officers stretching back to the Battle of Bunker Hill, noticed the resentment flaring in Irishmen's eyes whenever officers screamed such slurs as "Mick," "Paddy," or "croppie," a particularly insulting British term.

Not until the 5th left New Orleans and arrived at Corpus Christi aboard the steamer *Alabama* did noncoms' and officers' antipathy toward foreigners in general and Irish Catholics in particular veer from verbal to physical. Much of the change was rooted in the need to ready the troops for war through tight discipline.

The regiment's first order of business was to clamber into the steamship's "lighters," or longboats, and be rowed to the Texas shore. Merrill's men had traveled 2,500 miles from Mackinac in less than a month. Somewhere to the southwest lay the Rio Grande—and the Mexican army.

Shimmering white sand and lush meadows of tall coastal grass billowing in the Gulf breeze greeted Riley and the others. From the crescent-shaped shore of Corpus Christi Bay, Merrill led Company K past Kinney's Ranch, 30 or so weather-beaten wood and adobe dwellings clinging to the finger of coastline. Neat rows of canvas tents stretched a few hundred yards inland; a quarter of a mile from camp, troops had hacked out a 200-acre drill field from a tangle of mesquite and brush.

Company K and the rest of the 5th pitched their tents alongside those of the 7th Infantry, including Auguste Morstadt, the two regiments comprising the army's 2d Brigade. Soon after stowing their gear, the erstwhile Mackinac garrison was reviewed for the first time by its brigadier, 58-year-old Lieutenant Colonel James S. McIntosh. "Old Tosh, a rough, unread Georgian...prayed and swore with equal diligence and... kicked the posteriors of privates," especially Irish-born privates.

In the following days and weeks beneath often broiling sunshine, the officers marched and drilled Riley and the other men across the open field for hours on end. Scores of men collapsed. Officers' kicks or their blows with the flats of swords prodded some men to stagger back into line; a handful never regained consciousness. With many officers, anti-Irish, anti-Catholic epithets punctuated every order despite Zachary Taylor's well-deserved reputation as that of a leader who judged soldiers not by their accent but by their merit.

The newly arrived troops soon took the measure of their highest-ranking officers. The commanders had already been dismissed as mere Indian fighters by European military experts. Taylor and his officers, however, would startle their critics and prove them wrong in the upcoming war.

Sixty-two-year-old Zachary Taylor was the antithesis of European and Mexican generals. "Old Rough and Ready" was a stocky, sunburned veteran who dressed in blue jeans, a long linen-duster coat, and common-issue army shoes. He chewed tobacco, rode a nag called Old Whitey, eschewed regimental drill, and disliked Nativists. To the troops, he was "a very pleasant old man sociable not only to officers but to buck privates."[5] His harshest critics, West Pointers, questioned his methods but never his nerve, tested and proven in the War of 1812, the Black Hawk War, and the Second Seminole War.

Taylor's highest-ranking officers were, like their commander, older men accustomed to small-scale warfare. Handsome Colonel William Worth preached the gospel of Manifest Destiny. "Built like Hercules," hard-drinking Colonel William Whistler was a 45-year army "lifer."[6] Colonel David E. Twiggs was a gruff but fair officer, and McIntosh was a stern disciplinarian.

The chief strength of the army lay in its nucleus of young West Pointers, men such as Braxton Bragg, Pierre Beauregard, George Meade, James Duncan, James Longstreet, Samuel Ringgold, and Ulysses S. Grant. Dapper in their dark-blue frock coats, visored campaign caps, and "red-leg trousers," the Academy men were eager to apply on the battlefield the lessons they had learned in West Point's classrooms.

The first lesson the "Academy Turks" imparted to the troops was the importance of drill. Incessant marching, target practice, and repetitions of the manual-of-arms did not daunt Riley and others who had served in the British army. But most officers had never maneuvered units larger than companies.

For Riley and other European veterans, the camp's routines were easy enough. The bugles blared reveille across Kinney's Ranch at 4:00 in the morning every day except Sunday and sent soldiers scrambling from their two-man tents for the first fatigue call. The flats of officer's swords awakened any who lagged.

After "the police of camp" at 5:00, the troops formed company messlines for "peas upon the trenchers," breakfast, at 6:00. Actually, peas were absent from the trenchers: each soldier's daily fare for breakfast and "roast beef," dinner, consisted of 3/4 pound of "Southern pork," bacon; one pound of beef; and one pound of hardtack, stale and seething with little white worms. The beef proved equally hard to choke down: "It was very bad," a soldier wrote. "So poor that to throw it against a smooth plank, it would stick." Private George Ballentine, a Scottish veteran of the British army, wrote that, in his years of service in Britain's ranks, never had he encountered such wretched fare. The complaint proved common among other European veterans. To chase down the rancid rations, the troops gulped strong, syrupy coffee heavily sugared and "nasty, brackish water" with "a gall-bitter taste." Many privates eagerly parted with their scanty seven-dollar-a-month pay to buy rotgut whiskey and brandy from "medicine tents" run by pimps and other opportunists on the camp's fringes.

Immediately following breakfast was the 7:30 "surgeon's call." A small horde of soldiers, reeling with dysentery, would fill the medical tents, and as autumn's warmth gave way to wind-driven winter deluges called "blue northers," the doctors grappled with hundreds of cases of pneumonia and assorted fevers.

The soldiers who did not answer the surgeon's call formed ranks on the vast drill field at 9:30, and there, the U.S. Army of Observation slowly began to take shape. From 9:30 in the morning to 4:30 in the afternoon, the sun beating down remorselessly, Taylor's 3,900 men marched and learned to maneuver in regimental strength. Life was "nothing but drill and parades," wrote a soldier. "And your ears are filled all day with drumming and fifeing."[7]

European veterans were shocked at the officers' unfamiliarity with battalion and regimental formations. "As the officers had no occasion to practice [large-scale maneuvers], they have forgotten all of their tactics."[8] To the embarrassment of many officers and noncoms alike, some immigrant recruits, speaking a virtual babel of Gaelic, German, and other European tongues, knew the larger-scale Napoleonic-model formations and tactics far better than their commanders. Nativist officers seethed whenever Irishmen or Germans automatically corrected flawed commands and nudged American comrades into the proper step or turn.

As John Riley, his ruddy complexion darkening by the day in the Texas sunshine, tramped and wheeled across the dusty parade ground, he scrutinized not only the infantry around him, but also the cavalry and the artillery. Like British horsemen, the American dragoons rode heavily muscled mounts whose hooves shook the prairie as horses and riders practiced the charge again and again. Decades of duty on the frontier had honed the cavalry into men capable of spending days in the saddle across the most grueling terrain, snatching any sleep on the move. The 2d Dragoons, with their wide assortment of beards and mustaches and with hair streaming past their shoulders, composed "the hairiest of the lot" in what one chronicler would label the most hirsute army in American history. But one look at the 2d's flashing sabers, barking horse-pistols, and tight formations evoked favorable comments from viewers, though not for spit-and-polish. Amid the men of the 2d rode Private John Little, of County Kildare, and Prussian Heinrich Venator, among the Irish and German veterans whose skill with horse and saber their mostly American comrades grudgingly respected, but whose brogue and "Dutchie" accents and Catholicism reaped insults. Both dragoons kept their mouths shut and their resentment hidden—for the moment.

As Riley surely noted, like British cavalrymen, the U.S. Army's riders were also trained to fight on foot, but hated to do so. He was to use the knowledge later with deadly effect.

Of all that the Irishmen and other European veterans saw on the drill ground, the American artillery proved a genuine marvel, for the gunners unveiled maneuvers and innovative tactics that the ex-artillerist from the British army had never encountered. Riley was not alone in experiencing the artillery maneuvers for the first time: young West Pointers commanding Taylor's limbers, caissons, and fieldpieces were creating "flying batteries" that forever changed warfare.

Largely the brainchild of General Winfield Scott and 46-year-old Major Samuel Ringgold, a brilliant Academy man, the flying batteries featured six-pounder bronze fieldpieces whose drivers and gun crews were trained to limber and unlimber (hitch the cannons to their teams of horses and unhitch the guns into firing formation, "in battery") quickly and to deploy wherever enemy infantry or cavalry threatened to pierce American formations.

A handsome man with dark hair and stylish sideburns and hailing "from an intellectual and inventive Maryland family," Ringgold commanded one of Taylor's four flying batteries and oversaw their drill at Corpus Christi. Riley and other exgunners gaped at the speed with which each battery deployed its four to six six-pounder cannons and at the deadly accurate blasts of grape and canister the flying batteries poured into such distant targets as clumps of mesquite.

In their gleaming forage caps and their sky-blue breeches sporting a vivid scarlet stripe on each leg, the men of the flying batteries swaggered amid the dusty dragoons and the sweating infantry. Wearing their powder stains as a badge of honor, the gunners considered themselves among the army's elite, second only to the West Point-trained engineers.

As he tramped through the endless paces of infantry drills, John Riley could do little but hide his envy for Irishmen ramming canister or round-shot down the smoothbores' hot, gleaming muzzles, setting the range precisely, and yanking the lanyards that fired the pieces. In Battery G rode Andrew Nolan, a native of County Down and a man who would cross paths with Riley. So too would Irish gunners Alexander McKee, Battery H, 3d Artillery, and Richard Hanley, Battery A, 2d Artillery.

Back in the states, Battery G, 4th U.S. Artillery, honed its skills under the iron-fisted drill of Captain John Macrae Washington, West Point class of 1814 and, at 50, the oldest of the Academy men training flying batteries.

Although all of the flying batteries displayed a spit-and-polish that marked them as the chief attraction of the parade ground and drill field, the battery of a 22-year-old North Carolinian eclipsed the others at Corpus Christi. Sullenly handsome Lieutenant Braxton Bragg drilled his gun crews incessantly, and his diligence paid off. "The soldiers loved to

watch him at battery drill, where his horses whirled the guns and caissons over the plain with wonderful rapidity and ease . . . his piercing, big
black eyes shining under heavy brows." But Bragg earned renown in
camp for another character trait, one tinged with Nativist fury. Those
penetrating eyes bored into his men and were accompanied by "his nervous, tremulous voice . . . forever dressing [down] their ranks." Laced
with Nativist epithets directed at foreigners serving not only in the
artillery, but also Irish and German cavalrymen or infantrymen whose
slightest, often unintentional breach of drill or conduct caught his eye,
Bragg's high-pitched harangues and his propensity to order offenders
flogged or beaten on the spot earned him the hatred of the ranks. The
Southerner's growing reputation as "perhaps the best disciplinarian in
the Army," fueled by a personality part Puritan, part Spartan, would lead
to two assassination attempts by his men later in the war.[9]

The need for discipline in Taylor's ranks was pronounced, for no
army, before or after, could function without it. With war imminent
against a battle-tested, numerically superior foe, one that no less an
authority than the Duke of Wellington asserted would trounce the
Americans, Old Rough and Ready required unquestioning obedience
from his men. More concerned with his troops' "fight" than with their
elan, however, he left the enforcement of discipline to his subordinate
officers, as did any general. Those officers, largely the last decade's
ambitious Academy graduates, chafed to earn reputations on the drill
ground and the battlefield alike.

The West Pointers had their work cut out for them. Not only were
even their most veteran soldiers—with the exceptions of Riley and other
European veterans—unaccustomed to regimental maneuvers, but they
were also mistrustful of officers untested in combat.

Many young officers compensated for lack of battlefield experience
with harsh and instantaneous discipline. Lieutenants and captains routinely slapped, punched, and kicked privates who misstepped during
drill or who had failed to button their shirt or jacket properly. Men
winced as the flats of officers' swords hissed against shoulder blades
and backsides.

On the dusty parade ground and amid the canvas rows of the camp,
youthful officers relied upon traditional disciplinary measures dating

back to George Washington's army. One of the most frequent and traditional offenses was inebriation, a problem fueled by the licentious community springing up on the fringes of Taylor's encampment. Gamblers, prostitutes, con artists, and sutlers hawking liquor beckoned "to separate the soldier... from his money." Captain Ethan Allen Hitchcock lamented that drunkenness was "the order of the day," and Lieutenant Richard H. Wilson denounced Corpus Christi as "the most murderous, thieving, gambling, God-forsaken hole in the Lone Star State or out of it." [10]

Dealing daily with privates staggering from the effects of the previous night's liquor and assignations in camp followers' tents, company commanders meted out swift punishment. They barked out orders for noncoms to seize reeling offenders from the drawn-up ranks. Within minutes, drunkards found themselves straining to stand utterly still and straight upon a wobbly barrelhead every alternate two hours for five successive days from reveille to retreat. First-time offenders also found themselves short of one-month's pay. All over the parade ground, units marched and wheeled past those barrelheads every day. Sentries stood alongside to force offenders back on if they fell or to run them through an arm or a leg if they tried to run. Several made the mistake of trying to run. Every night, fellow privates gathered the miscreants from their perches and helped the sweating, groaning men to their tents.

In a measure that appalled Riley and fellow British army veterans, many officers ordered that privates caught drinking several times be branded on the forehead with the letters "HD," for "habitual drunkard." The punishment was carried out with the culprit's company drawn up to witness it. Hands and feet bound, the man was held down on the parade ground by several comrades. Then, at the officer's command, a corporal or a sergeant removed a cattlebrand from a small fire and seared the letters upon the shrieking victim. Some officers also applied the "W" brand to privates deemed worthless.

In the British, French, and Prussian armies, branding was unheard of, and chronic drunkards were jailed or dishonorably discharged. Officers' use of mutilation as a punishment for inebriation at Corpus Christi not only horrified immigrant soldiers, but also infuriated them, because "they [officers] go out and get drunk every night and raise the very devil." [11]

Another traditional punishment inflicted upon the ranks was "riding the horse." For the most trivial offenses—a shirt cuff torn by a mishandled musket during drill; a minute coffee stain from breakfast; a slight stumble in line—officers routinely sat men atop a high wooden sawhorse. The offenders sat on the narrow wooden beam for hours with their hands bound behind their backs and with iron weights chained to their feet. If they crashed to the ground, as many did, guards forced them to remount. Some, according to an immigrant, could not: the fall broke their necks.

A genuine, intolerable breach such as sleeping on guard duty merited even sterner responses, and the specter of imprisonment, hard labor with a 24-pound weight chained to a leg, and complete forfeiture of pay—in addition to several hours each day atop the wooden horse—hammered home to the men that no leniency would—or could—extend to the offense.

By mid-October 1845, the hard mix of drill and discipline was bearing tangible results. Inspector-General Matthew Mountjoy Payne, having arrived early that month to assess for Polk the army's readiness for war, spoke at length with Taylor, his command staff, and the junior officers actually training the troops. "The men are ready and expect war to arrive soon," a captain remarked.[12] Payne heard similar assurances from other officers. But the eagerness of many young officers to fight Mexico belied a pronounced antiwar current rippling through another cadre of Academy men, most of them Whigs opposing the Democratic president's martial version of Manifest Destiny. These men believed that the United States could gain the Southwest and California through diplomacy and cash, the approach Thomas Jefferson had used for the Louisiana Purchase.

Among officers disturbed that the motives for war were those "of a strong nation preying upon a weaker foe" stood Ulysses S. Grant. He wrote to his fiancee, Julia Dent, that a war with Mexico would be "unjust and immoral."[13] Captain Ephraim Kirby Smith, of the 5th Infantry, and Lieutenant Colonel Ethan Allen Hitchcock, of the 3d Infantry, mirrored Grant's misgivings. Under scrutiny by Payne was Taylor himself, an ardent Whig who saw "no good reason for a war with Mexicans."[14]

Young officers' moral qualms notwithstanding, Payne soon assessed that Grant and the others would submerge their personal feelings and carry out their orders and their duties to the letter. On October 15–16, 1845, the infantry, the dragoons, and the artillery marched onto the parade ground in full battle gear, fixed bayonets and bronze fieldpieces shimmering in the sunlight. Payne, riding with Worth alongside Taylor, who was perched atop Old Whitey, first inspected the troops' appearance. Then, Payne cantered to the far edge of the drill field, where, for hours, he studied the infantrymen as they formed traditional defensive squares, long skirmish lines, and dense assault columns. With each shouted command the infantry displayed an astonishing grasp of large-scale formations for the scant time they had been drilling.

The cavalry performed equally well. Mounts' hooves shaking the plain, the blood-curdling cries of the "devils of the 2d Dragoons" echoing in the warm air, the troopers kicked up dust in every direction as they first rode shoulder to shoulder, then drew their sabers and broke into a thunderous charge.

Amid the infantry squares and the charging dragoons, the flying batteries stole the proverbial show. The horse-drawn caissons rattled from both flanks to the army's center and points between and unlimbered, loaded, fired, and hitched up their six-pounders with dazzling speed. Payne, a veteran of the War of 1812 and, like Taylor, an officer accustomed to antiquated charge-and-shoot tactics, gaped at the maneuvers of Ringgold and his fellow West Point gunners. Not surprisingly, Taylor's favorite among the flying batteries' officers was Captain James Duncan, who, like Taylor, was annoyed by the "graceful bearing and showy dress" of fellow Academy artillerists such as Bragg and O'Brien, reasoning that a powder-blackened face and a sweaty, scorched uniform revealed the true gunner. When it came to his six-pounders, however, Duncan "kept his guns burnished as a mirror and woe to the man whose cannon did not gleam." Even infantrymen resenting the airs of the artillery remarked that, in Duncan's case, "there was a man whom the Mexicans should fear." [15]

Zach Taylor knew "very little of drill and maneuvers," but, as Payne reported to Washington, the Academy men were proving quick studies.[16] All in all, Payne recorded, he was "generally pleased" with the progress of the Army of Observation.

How long the diminutive force, "ridiculously small to serious offi-cers," would await orders to march to the Rio Grande stirred constant speculation among the men.[17] On October 13, 1845, Captain William S. Henry wrote: "It is generally believed that there will be a movement to the Rio Grande in short time."[18]

Henry's belief, shared by the bulk of the army, led officers to push—and to punish—their men even harder in preparation for the clash with a numerically superior foe. In a letter to a friend, a Pennsylvanian infantryman would write:

> We are under very strict discipline here. [Some of] our officers are very good men, but the balance of them are very tyrannical and brutal toward the men. They strike the men with swords and abuse them in the most brutal manner possible for a human being to be treated. And if a poor sol-dier should be caught drinking a glass of liquor, he is bucked and gagged, and if he says one word protesting his innocence, they have him taken to the lake and water thrown in his face by pails full until he is nearly drowned. Many a poor soldier has been discharged after a long and severe illness [caused] by this water being thrown on him. There is now one in a hospital . . . raving crazy and lashed to his bed . . . [because of] this water. There is another poor being cramped so he walks half bent by this water and several cases I could mention and all by the accursed water.
>
> Another way of punishing men [is that] they [officers] have a hole dug underground, tight and dark with the eception [*sic*] of a small particle of light [that] comes through a crack in the door. The [victims] sleep on the cold ground as they [officers] allow them no blanket in there. In short it is a backhouse [outhouse] and altogether the prisoners are allowed three crackers and water a day. One man, a lifer, was sentenced for thirty days after having four hundred pails of water thrown on him, and all his crime was running through the guard. Many instances of this kind occur daily and tonight on drill an officer laid a soldier's skull open with a sword, and the poor man is now suffering from it in the hospital in camp.[19]

Private William Tomlinson concluded his letter with a chilling warning:

> I wish a man of good standing would inform them men in Washington of the brutality of these officers now in Mexico, but there is no use of a soldier writing to them as no notice would be taken on it, but these are facts if they do come from a soldier. They have never had any hold of me yet and I have no reason to lie about it, but I have a heart and feeling for my brother Americans who came out here in defence of their country and in a foreign country not congenial to our health. But the time may come and that soon when officers and men will stand on equal footing. The men seem to form an opinion that some of the officers will soon depart from this world.[20]

John Riley, Mick Maloney, and other immigrant veterans recognized the necessity of drill and discipline for regiments girding for war. But at Corpus Christi they learned that the same hatred that had ignited the Philadelphia Riots of 1844 and the rise of Nativism blazed among the army's officer corps. While most officers and noncoms applied iron-fisted discipline of the sort that had distressed Private Tomlinson and other native-born regulars, "the foreign-born soldier, especially if he happened to be Irish or German, automatically received a harsher sentence than a native American would for the same offense." [21]

One of the favored modes of punishment, mentioned by Tomlinson, was bucking and gagging, in which a soldier was seated on the ground with his knees drawn up and his arms clasping them. His wrists were bound in front of his legs; a stick or a pole was slid under his bent knees and over his arms. Then a gag was stuffed into his mouth. The man unable to move or talk, the disciplining officer would order him left that way for hours of joint-searing agony. All over camp soldiers were bucked and gagged in front of their tents, their messmates banned from consoling them at the risk of sharing the punishment. On the parade ground, companies drilled around men bucked and gagged "for trivial offenses." [22] And the longer the army remained at Corpus Christi, the more a brutal fact emerged: officers routinely singled out foreigners, especially Irishmen, for bucking and gagging.

Samuel Chamberlain, a dragoon, later described an officer seething with Nativism. Thirty-three-year-old Lieutenant Thomas West Sherman, a Rhode Islander raised on Yankee disdain for Catholicism and immigrants, had graduated 18th in the West Point class of 1832 and was proving himself an excellent flying battery officer. As with Bragg and scores of other Academy men, Sherman was also earning a reputation in the ranks as a sadistic fury. A dragoon would write that the Rhode Islander was "an eccentric . . . tyrannical officer." [23] As the campaign went on, his use of the buck and gag upon the Irish would escalate, including an appalling scene later in 1846. (See Chapter 14.)

While the buck and gag fell under the aegis of traditional U.S. Army discipline, officers' penchant for inflicting it upon immigrants far more than native-born troops led an anonymous Irishman to pen a ditty popular among his countrymen:

Come, all Yankee soldiers, give ear to my song,
It is a short ditty, 'twill not keep you long;
It's no use to fret on account of our luck,
We can laugh, drink, and sing yet in spite of the buck.
Derry down, down, down, derry down.

"Sergeant, buck him and gag him," our officers cry
For each trifling offense which they happen to spy,
Till with bucking and gagging of Dick, Pat, and Bill,
Faith, the Mexican' ranks they will help to fill.
Derry down, down, down, derry down.

The treatment they give us, as all of us know,
Is bucking and gagging for whipping the foe;
But they are glad to release us when going to fight.
They buck us and gag us for malice or spite
Derry down, down, down, derry down.

A poor soldier's tied up in the sun or the rain,
With a gag in his mouth till he's tortured with pain;
Why, I'm blessed if the eagle we wear on our flag,
In its claws shouldn't carry a buck and a gag.
Derry down, down, down, derry down.[24]

Although officers were supposed to administer military justice with no regard to religion or ethnicity, many presiding military judges punctuated verdicts with diatribes against offenders' nationalities and Catholicism. Court-martial records show that immigrants filling nearly half of the Army of Observation's regiments faced disciplinary sentences more than three times the number of those handed down to American-born men; the punishment levied upon immigrants proved far grimmer than that of their American comrades-in-arms.

A typical example of the two disparate codes of justice within the U.S. Army's Articles of War was that of Irish Sergeant James Bannon, hauled before a court-martial on charges of drunkenness and mutinous conduct. The charges against him did not differ in any way from those against American-born Private George Miller at the same court-martial: both men stood accused of verbally threatening officers, but not striking them. In Miller's case, the military judges sentenced him to 50 lashes, a stiff fine, imprisonment until war's end, and a dishonorable discharge. Bannon was stood in front of a firing squad.

In another case, sentries caught Sergeant J. J. Adams, Private William

Radfield, and Private Peter Murphy red-handed as they robbed a Mexican woman's home. A court-martial busted Adams from sergeant to private and fined him a month's pay; Radfield earned 10 days' imprisonment and forfeited a month's pay. Peter Murphy, the only immigrant among the trio, was sentenced to two-months' hard confinement, was fined three-months' pay, and was dishonorably discharged.

Riley, Maloney, and most fellow immigrants understood that the Peter Murphys deserved swift and hard punishment; however, the contrast between sentences infuriated foreigners powerless against the discrimination.

Immigrants composed nearly 50 percent of John Riley's unit, Company K. Captain Merrill, while no Nativist, enforced rigorous discipline in his men, and Sergeant Major James Everstine booted the company's backsides for the slightest errors in formation and target practice. For more serious violations, Merrill applied the horse and the buck and gag, which, given the heavily Irish composition of the company, meant that Irishmen most often incurred their commanding officer's wrath.

Riley's experience spared him the parade-ground ire of Merrill and other officers. "The tough, handsome Irishman" earned a compliment as "a quiet and very good man" from Captain William Chapman. Merrill's praise went further: "[Riley's] character was very fair"—rated officer material.[25]

The quietness to which Chapman referred belied Riley's gregarious, bold nature. Realizing that his familiarity with drill, tactics, and weapons precluded parade-ground mistakes that reaped floggings, bucking and gaggings, and other punishments for less experienced immigrants, Riley gleaned that the surest way he could incur Nativist wrath lay in any flicker of resentment or incredulity toward an officer's order. No matter how many times Nativist slurs assailed him and his fellow Irishmen of Company K, he kept his eyes forward and his mouth shut. He did not want to end up like his messmate and friend Richard Parker, a Dubliner who had served a hitch in the British infantry. When the veteran Parker "raised his eyebrows" at a confusing command issued by a "callow" lieutenant, the Irishman's hesitation cost him a ten-hour stint on the horse in blazing heat.

In the ranks, Sergeant Major Mick Maloney and immigrant noncoms bearing names such as McMaley, McCauley, Farrell, McFarlen, and O'Sullivan, men who had proven themselves in the U.S. Army's bloody campaigns against the Osceola and the Seminole Indians during the 1830s and 1840s, drilled the new immigrants hard but strove to act as buffers against Nativist officers. The noncoms pointed to the example of fellow Indian campaigner Zachary Taylor as hope that Nativism might wane at Corpus Christi. Not only did Old Rough and Ready halt countless floggings based on junior officers' specious charges, but he also cut short punishments when he suspected that Irish and German soldiers had merely misunderstood orders from a faulty grasp of English rather than defiance toward their superiors.

Taylor's forbearance toward immigrant recruits enraged Nativist officers. In an incident winning the admiration of Grant and startling to many, a giant Irishman "recently arrived" failed to obey an order from Taylor. Old Rough and Ready slid off of Old Whitey's back, walked over to the man, reached up, and grabbed the private's ear, a practice called "wooling."

The private bellowed and, "red with anger," decked the general.

For a moment, as Taylor laid sprawled on the dusty drill field, officers and enlisted men gaped. Then several officers drew their swords. Irishmen and Germans in the assembled ranks were certain that the man was finished.

Before the blades could slash the private, Taylor lurched to his feet and raised his right hand. Old Rough and Ready, discerning that the man had not understood the order, halted the officers. "Let him alone!" Taylor shouted. "He'll make a good soldier." [26]

The incident had a powerful effect upon George Meade and Sam Grant, both of them noting that episodes like this made even immigrants who hated the army like their commander.

Grant, Merrill, Smith, Hitchcock, and numerous other officers emulated their general's forbearance. But for every attempt to treat the immigrants fairly, too many blows from the flat of William Harney's saber, too many blows from Thomas Sherman's fists, too many buckings and gaggings at the order of Braxton Bragg, and too many anti-Irish, anti-German, anti-Catholic tirades erupted across the encampment. To the gall of Maloney, Batchelor, and other Irish veterans, recent Academy graduates lumped them into the same category as "famine Irish" fresh off coffin ships. The officers, few of whom had seen action themselves, cared nothing that Maloney and company had "fought for the blue" and that Dugans, O'Rileys, Bogans, O'Danaghs, and Egans had given their lives against the Seminoles at Lake Okeechobee and Fort Micanopy and in the fever hospitals at Tampa.

Scotsman George Ballentine, of John Magruder's battery, wrote that Nativist officers singled out foreigners "operating on a sensitive and excitable temperament" and inflicted particularly "harsh and cruel usage upon them."[27]

"One cannot believe the insolent and impertinent tone assumed by Native Americans to all foreigners," Ballentine noted.

> The barbarous treatment which foreign soldiers . . . received from igno-rant and brutal officers, and non-commissioned officers on that cam-paign, were I to relate it in minute detail, would seem almost incredible. I have frequently seen foolish young officers violently strike and assault sol-diers on the most slight provocation, while to tie them up by the wrist, as high as their hands would reach, with a gag in their mouths, was a common punishment for trivial offenses. In fact, such a bad state of feeling seemed to exist between men and officers throughout the service that I was not surprised that it should lead to numerous desertions.[28]

Second Lieutenant Gustavus W. Smith, a 24-year-old West Pointer and rich Kentuckian whose standing as an engineer placed him in the army's elite, embodied the officers whom Ballentine loathed. Smith often boasted of his "cure" for a "thick-witted foreigner."[29] A German private who barely understood English misconstrued one of Smith's orders, and the engineer marched him several miles from camp, far from a more tolerant officer's view. Then Smith, on horseback, drew his sword and threatened to run the immigrant through unless he per-formed the manual-of-arms while focusing his eyes on a wood chip on the ground. Few in the ranks doubted that Smith would have kept his word if the soldier had bobbled his empty rifle.

Smith also bragged that he had kicked a sergeant down a gully because the soldier balked at the brink of a twisting path.

Far worse examples of Nativism in the officer corps stunned Abbe Domenech, a French traveler. He stared at officers hanging Irishmen by their thumbs from tree limbs for sloppy salutes. He saw an immigrant private charged with inebriation bound hand and foot, tossed into a pond, hauled out just before drowning, and thrown in several more times in the same fashion.

Most disturbing to the traveler was the case of a young private so abused by his company commander that the immigrant committed suicide by slashing his throat with a bayonet.[30]

Similarly astonished as Domenech, a university-educated Prussian private wrote home in despair at the "numerous indignities" he suffered from Nativists. Complaining that he had found only menial work as a civilian and that recruiters' "flattering and encouraging accounts" of immigrants' prospects in the army were "the contrary of what I expected," he wrote the Prussian minister in Washington a futile letter begging a discharge and passage back to Germany.[31] He would receive no reply from the Prussian embassy and would continue to suffer from officers such as Captain James Duncan.

While officers and men alike languished in camp, November 1845 approached, heralding the winds and rain of the Gulf winter. An air of "wait and watch" drifted through the Army of Observation, replacing the state of high alert that had governed the parade ground. The men, about to shift their routines to the traditional ennui of a winter encampment, would find more time to reflect upon what lay ahead. And, while few had doubts that war loomed, many were already questioning their impending roles.

Among the Irish and other foreigners, those doubts would soon take a more disturbing tone stoked by ongoing Nativist abuse and personal frustration. "In time of peace," pronounced *The Pilot*, a Boston newspaper addressing the concerns of the nation's Irish Catholic immigrants, "we Irish are not fit to enjoy 'life, liberty, and pursuit of happiness,' but when the country needs our aid, we are capital, glorious fellows."[32]

The Pilot's harangue underscored the deepening bitterness along ethnic and religious lines in American society and the army alike. And as knots of immigrant soldiers sat around flickering campfires at night along the sands of Kinney's Ranch, swigging coffee and constantly looking over their shoulders for Nativist officers, the men griped in hushed tones about their treatment in Old Rough and Ready's ranks.

In distant Washington, Polk and the War Department, oblivious to the dissension along the Gulf, planned to call up 50,000 men once hostilities erupted along the Rio Grande. Again, Adjutant General Jones targeted desperate Irish and German immigrants as the likeliest recruits for "Mr. Polk's War." The administration still failed to comprehend the inherent problems of sending immigrant Catholic troops into battle against Catholic Mexico at the behest of a Protestant nation.

John Riley was already mulling the religious and ethnic contradictions. His ego festered with his realization that his dreams of rank and honor were futile. Despite his gunnery experience, he was not even allowed to transfer to the artillery. Naturalized citizens like Mick Maloney and Sergeant Abraham Fitzpatrick had "found their way in the Army" before Nativism had infected so many officers. Second- and third-generation Irish Catholics like Bennet Riley and John Paul Jones O'Brien had earned their officers' bars as assimilated Irish. But for John Riley and other shanty Irish, recruiters' assurances of honor and promotion had dissolved, supplanted by the buck and gag and the rawhide whip. He and other new recruits had "given up the idea of winning that [officer's] Sword as . . . impossible, for although I should, unaided and alone, surround the whole Mexican Army and take them all prisoners, it would not be deemed a deed worthy of promotion." [33]

Tired of Nativist officers and noncoms' "bullying and blustering tone," "ignorance or bad temper," and savage punishments, immigrants were "tempted to desert the service." [34]

Riley suppressed his anger and frustration for the moment, tending to his duty. Other immigrants, however, reached their breaking points.

4

"A Sullen Torpor"

NOVEMBER 1846 unleashed torments testing the physical breaking points of virtually every man at Kinney's Ranch. The hot, sunny weather of early fall turned unpredictable, one day balmy, the next frigid and rainy. By month's end, several blue northers had lashed the camp. Soldiers huddling in their tents found little more protection inside than outside them, for the heavy, duck canvas tents that Quartermaster Trueman Cross had ordered from the War Department had never arrived. The troops languished in gauze-thin tents that the army had used during the Seminole campaigns. Sleet froze the canvas, which cracked and sometimes shattered when gusts slammed the rigid cloth. Pails of water turned into ice inside the tents. Although officers and the ranks piled brush and dirt against the tents' northern sides, the wind shrieked through the canvas.

"As the winter advanced," wrote an officer, "the encampment now resembled a marsh, the water at times being three and four feet in the tents of whole wings of regiments. All military exercises were suspended; the black, gloomy days were passed in inactivity, disgust, sullenness, and silence. The troops, after being thoroughly drenched all day, without campfires to dry by, lay down at night in blankets on the well-soaked ground.... Without occupation, without excitement, without the prospect of meeting the foe, to sit day after day, week after week, shivering in wet tents. . . ."

He lauded the deportment of the Irish and other immigrants in the ranks under the abysmal conditions: "If, under such painful and trying circumstances, the 'foreign' soldier murmured not and was prompt and zealous in the discharge of duty, of what stern stuff must his revilers be made! If the men who at tattoo lay gasping for breath in the sultry night air and found, at reveille, their wet blankets frozen around them and their tents stiff with ice uttered no complaint, we certainly must confess that the 'bone and sinew' [native-born Americans] could scarcely have excelled these 'hireling' soldiers in manly conduct." [1]

The revilers the officer mentioned failed to detect any virtues of the immigrants. Although the wind and downpours prevented organized drill, Bragg, Captain George A. McCall, and other officers continued bucking and gagging foreigners for minor infractions, leaving the trussed men in deep puddles on the parade ground. Soldiers still rode the wooden horse for hours in the rain.

With the erratic weather and hard discipline breeding a "sullen torpor" already, disease swept through the ranks and officers alike. Lieutenant Daniel Harvey Hill, a future Confederate general, condemned, in a letter to his wife, "the sickness, suffering and death from criminal negligence" of the War Department in issuing "worn out and rotten" tents in a climate "passing from the extreme of heat to the extreme of cold within a few hours." "During those terrible months [November–December 1845]," Hill wrote, "the sufferings of the sick in the crowded hospital tents were horrible beyond compare or conception. The torrents drenched, and the fierce blasts shook the miserable couches of the dying. Their last groans mingled in fearful concert with howlings of the pitiful storm."

"Every day added to the frightfulness of the mortality," Hill recalled. "The volley over one grave would scarce have died on the air when the ear would again be pierced by the same melancholy sound. One procession would scarcely have been lost to sight when the solemn tread of the 'dead-march' would announce another. At one time, one-sixth of the entire encampment were on the sick report, unfit for duty, and at least one half of the Army were unwell. . . . Dysentery and catarrhal fevers," along with venereal diseases contracted in the "laundresses' tents" on the camp's outskirts, "raged like a pestilence."[2]

Even in the hospital tents, Irish and German (and, later in the war, Mormon) soldiers found no refuge from Nativism. Junior officers stormed among the cots in search of immigrants who had failed to report for guard duty or other tasks, and, unless the men lay unconscious beneath their thin blankets, hauled them groaning from their beds and to their sentry posts, sometimes in the midst of northers. Ailing troops also learned that some surgeons treated patients not according to their symptoms' severity, but according to their birthplace. Dysentery-wracked immigrants often lay untended for a day or more in their own excrement, raving and shaking with fever. Many died hours before a doctor or even an orderly arrived at their bedsides.

The only aspect of the surgical caste system that heartened many immigrants hampered the health of stricken subalterns. In a case of "just desserts," in the eyes of immigrants, "sick officers are not as well off when ill as the men are, for the latter are provided with hospital tents, which, in a great measure, afford protection from the weather, whereas the officer in his wall tent . . . little better than gauze, is completely shelterless."[3]

Irishmen discovered one welcome and long-absent source of solace from the weather, the hospital tents, boredom, and Nativism at Kinney's Ranch. There, in a small, wind-battered home, an itinerant Mexican priest sometimes held Catholic mass. Along with the Latin prayers and responses that conjured memories of stone churches from Galway to Kerry, images of "the ould sod" flared with the men's introduction to their two hosts: "an Irishman [a local trader and possibly a smuggler] and his lady, who was a fair specimen of the Emerald Isle."[4]

When each service ended, the couple served tortillas, other local foods, and generous amounts of whiskey and pulque, a corn-based liquor. Riley, by all accounts, abstained from drink, but others tossed back healths to their homeland and gambled that they could return to their sodden tents before an officer detected spirits on their breath. For some of the worshipers, the short trip from mass and their congenial

Irish hosts to the camp and its Nativist officers became ever harder. Some officers tried to deny Catholic soldiers even those Sunday sessions, but Taylor generally forbade denial of passes to any soldier, Catholic or Protestant, who wanted to attend services at Kinney's Ranch.

At the Sunday masses and in the tents, where the foul weather confined men for seemingly endless hours, foreign-born Catholics pondered their "status," in the words of young Engineer George B. McClellan, as "these wretched Dutch & Irish immigrants" and, in Irishmen's age-old words, as "cannon fodder" in the coming war.[5] The issues of religion and nationality also escalated with the newspapers and magazines arriving weekly aboard supply ships. With no censorship of reading material by Taylor and his staff, immigrants contemplated antiwar Whig tracts and Democratic polemics extolling Manifest Destiny and "the moral and religious superiority of the Anglo-Saxon" and excoriating "the Indian idolatry, superstition, and flummery of the Catholic Church" and the "simian Irish refuse infecting our shores."[6]

Various writers would stereotype Irishmen in the Army of Observation (later Occupation) as a mass of ignorant rustics with no sense of national, ideological, and even religious identity, incapable of formulating viewpoints upon the right or wrong of war against Mexico. But, as Kerby Miller, a leading authority on Irish immigration, points out, such assertions defy the experiences John Riley and his fellow immigrants of the 1830s and 1840s carried from Ireland to America. They were "political warriors" of Daniel O'Connell's nonviolent crusade to seize civil liberties for Irish Catholics. "The point is," Miller contends, "that all of these political crusades involved . . . millions of Catholics throughout the island and gave Catholics a degree of political consciousness and a degree of political education and organizational experience that was very unusual in Western Europe at that time. And Ireland's Catholics brought this political consciousness and experience with them when they emigrated to the New World."[7]

Mick Maloney and many other naturalized Irish immigrants of the 1830s still thought of themselves as Irish first, American second. They embraced Manifest Destiny, which they believed would open up land and opportunity for immigrants and pry them from the tenements of

New York, Boston, and Philadelphia, the bastions of Nativism. As the winter of 1845–46 wore on, however, even the Maloneys were troubled by the combination of prejudiced junior officers and the anti-Catholic press. Immigrant veterans willing to embrace Stephen Decatur's axiom "my country, right or wrong" were disturbed by reams of print preaching a holy war of virtuous Anglo-Saxons against "the Black Catholics of Mexico."[8] Reflective of those screeds was the *Democratic Register's* position that "the Mexicans and all Catholics, in fact, are reptiles in the path of democracy.... [and] must either crawl or be crushed."[9]

John Riley condemned "prejudice against Catholicks [*sic*]" and wrote of his growing alienation from the army and Nativist officers.[10] Still, he reined in his emotions and stayed out of trouble through the winter of 1845–46.

In late 1845, Whig newspapers that reached camp reprinted a controversial Daniel O'Connell speech that had driven a rift among America's assimilated Irish, the recent refugees of the famine-struck island, and "proper Americans." Originally delivered on May 9, 1843, O'Connell's speech had blasted America's proposed annexation of Texas, slavery, and Northerners and Southerners alike for anti-Catholic bigotry. He exhorted Irishmen never to volunteer in an American campaign for annexation on behalf of slaveowners. "It was not in Ireland you learned this cruelty," he said. "Your mothers were gentle, kind, and humane.... How can your souls have become stained with such a darkness?"[11] This speech, however, had little effect on assimilated Irish-Americans, many of whom either owned slaves or tolerated the evil. The words had even less effect on recent immigrants pitted in eastern seaports against free blacks for the nation's most menial jobs.

O'Connell's rebukes most distressed the Irish who had been in America the longest and had prospered. A group of eminent Philadelphia Irish who included few recent arrivals wrote a letter of protest against O'Connell. "The natives of Ireland," they claimed, "bear true allegiance to the country that has adopted them and are ever ready to serve her." They feared that O'Connell's statements incited suspicion toward the Irish "by our native American citizens" and hoped that their remonstrances against O'Connell would "remove from the natives of

Ireland . . . the odium which . . . has been cast upon them." [12]

For the Irish and other immigrants in Taylor's camp, far removed from the fine brick homes of the handful of Philadelphia Irish who had "made a show" in America, Nativist epithets and unrelenting, brutal discipline furnished little proof that America had "adopted them." Scores of those men were questioning whether they were "ever ready to serve her." Riley and other immigrant soldiers could not even vote in America, but, having signed the enlistment paper, could die for Americans who despised them. [13]

Although Grant, dour George Meade, James "Pete" Longstreet, and the minority of other junior officers with little use for Nativism sensed the stewing unrest among the troops, Taylor and the bulk of the officers ignored or played down the problem. "Once they [the ranks] are buoyed up by the hope of a fray, they will be cheerful," wrote Lieutenant Hill. [14]

In late February 1846, career diplomat John Black, acting United States consul in Mexico City, had nearly packed up his office in preparation to leave Mexico. Slidell's farcical "peace mission" ending, war edging closer each day, nothing could have prepared the silver-haired envoy for the sudden commotion outside his office over two days. He encountered ten men in grimy, torn clothing—the remnants of American army uniforms. Mexican regulars in shakos (tall, visored hats) and glittering tunics had herded the band into the city.

Two of the men told the gaping Black that they were deserters who had fled Taylor's camp because of "ill usage" at their officers' hands, but were not traitors, and begged him to send them back to Kinney's Ranch. Babbling a litany of thirst, hunger, and forced marches they had endured as prisoners of the Mexicans, the pair expressed their willingness to face a court-martial for their "mistakes." [15]

As soon as the two finished their pleas, Black turned to the remaining eight deserters and asked for their names. With each terse reply, the diplomat realized that a crisis was materializing in Old Rough and Ready's regiments.

The following day, Black dispatched a letter to U.S. Minister Plenipotentiary John Slidell, who was at Jalapa and was preparing to leave Mexico via Vera Cruz.

Sir [Slidell],

I embrace this opportunity to write a few lines by the English courier, Mr. Bankhead having been so kind as to offer me his services to that effect.

Two deserters from our Army in Corpus Christi have presented themselves to me. Stating that they have repented of their crime in deserting the service of their country and wish to be sent back to their post. They are to leave here in the morning for Vera Cruz in the wagons. I shall write to Mr. Diamond to have them placed on board one of our armed vessels on their arrival at Vera Cruz in order that they may be seaward and sent to their post. One is a private in Company B, 2nd Regiment, U.S. Dragoons, and the other a private in Company F, 7th Regiment, U.S. Infantry; one named Peter Smith and the other James Miller. I wish to have them sent back to their post as soon as possible in order that their return may deter others from deserting.

Yesterday, eight more arrived, and I understand they would also like to return to their post. In case they should present themselves to me for that purpose [a return to the army], shall I also send them to Vera Cruz? As there is no provision made by our government except for seamen and this a peculiar case.

Then, in a portentous line, the diplomat wrote: "There is but two Native Americans among them." He concluded: "The two [Smith and Miller] which I send, I send on my own responsibility and risk, but shall wait your answer before I send the others."[16]

Slidell's reply did not reach Black until March 1, 1846. In the case of Smith and Miller, Slidell concurred that the pair "be returned and punished as a salutary effect" upon would-be deserters.

Of the eight foreign-born deserters, Slidell responded: "As the men who have deserted their flag almost in the face of the enemy must certainly be worthless as soldiers or citizens, I shall not recommend the incurring of any additional expenses to relieve them from the misery and hardships to which their crimes have exposed them."[17] Black was willing to give the two American-born deserters a second chance, but not the eight "worthless" immigrants.

Several of those eight foreign-born men would see their former messmates again—down the barrels of Mexican muskets and cannons.

Under armed guard, the two American deserters were loaded aboard a ship at Vera Cruz. But they never faced punishment in front of Taylor's army. They were sailed instead to a military prison at New Orleans.

Unknown to Slidell yet, Secretary of War William Marcy, at Polk's order, had sent a communiqué to Zachary Taylor:

"Sir [Taylor]: I am directed by the President to instruct you to advance and occupy, with the troops under your command, positions on or near the east bank of the Rio Grande."[18]

The order arrived at Corpus Christi on February 3 or 4, 1846. Taylor replied that he would "lose no time" in marching first to Point Isabel, the small port he had targeted as his main supply depot, at the junction of the Gulf and the Brazos Santiago, and then toward the Rio Grande town of Matamoros, Mexican soil. Although he was about to lead fewer than 4,000 regulars into the path of a force rumored near 10,000 at Matamoros, Taylor liked the chances of his little army of frontier soldiers, European veterans, and eager West Pointers.

For nearly two weeks, Taylor and his colonels kept Polk's orders secret. Riley and other veterans of an army's transition from camp to campaign sensed the sudden shift in their commanders' demeanor, "tight-lipped tension and flushed excitement." On February 9, 1846, in a deluge, George Meade led a wagon train 60 miles out and back from camp along a rutted traders' and smugglers' path leading southeast toward Point Isabel. Rumors that the army's marching orders had come swirled through camp as soon as Meade's creaking ox carts faded from view.

The ill-kept secret evaporated by February 24, when Taylor assembled the troops on the parade ground and informed them "to be prepared for a field movement at short notice" to the Rio Grande, 150 miles across territory claimed by both Texas and Mexico. "We were going to Mexico," wrote a soldier.[19]

In the "hurry-scurry, preparatory for the march," officers rushing the troops through their final rounds of parade-ground drills lost their tempers even more often as the prospect of "the first red drops of the battlefield" beckoned.[20] Although hundreds of European veterans understood the coming trials far better than junior officers schooled in West Point's classrooms, not yet in combat, some Academy men still "look down with ineffable contempt upon the Irish....In [their] estimation, 'Paddy' hardly belongs to the human family."[21]

Riley had avoided physical abuse from officers since his enlistment, but, either before or after the march, several sources would claim an officer loosed a stream of curses and ethnic slurs upon him for a "nonexistent offense." Riley's face reportedly flushed, but he said nothing. Then, the officer allegedly struck Riley in the face. One fact was uncontested: as the army prepared to move, Riley "smoldered with anger." [22]

Grant wrote of his admiration for immigrants who were reviled by his brother officers as "dumb foreigners" and endured the abuse "without a murmur." [23] Beneath that stoicism, hatred and grudges churned. Riley would carry his rage every step of the impending march. He was one of many.

5

"To Provoke a War"

A T 10:00 IN THE MORNING on March 8, 1846, a Sunday, 378 riders of the 2d Dragoons saddled up to the cheers of the infantry. Ringgold's flying batteries assembled behind the cavalry, the artillerymen also mounted and their six-pounders hitched to their horse-drawn caissons. To the fifers' airy version of "The Girl I Left Behind Me," the jangling of spurs and sabers, and the rhythmic clomp of hooves, the Army of Observation's vanguard headed southwest.

The next morning, March 9, the 1st Brigade, with Brevet Brigadier General William Worth riding a giant gelding at the head of his infantry columns, streamed from camp. Several ox-drawn caissons, lugging 12-pounder cannons and two massive siege mortars, and a long train of supply wagons, each carting 1,500 pounds of food and ammunition, plodded behind the infantry. Mick Maloney marched in the middle of the column, sweating with the rest of the infantry in the strong sunshine.

No one in the column that day welcomed the advance more than the commander, who itched for action and glory. Pleased with "this really well-appointed and high-spirited force," Worth wrote: "Why [does] Mexico matter? Have not our Anglo-Saxon race been land stealers from time immemorial and why shouldn't they? When their gaze is fixed upon other lands, the best way is to make out the deeds." [1]

A man who believed that the Anglo-Saxon had stolen his homeland struck his tent and filed into formation with his company at dawn on March 10. A 60-pound field pack containing entrenching tools, several tins of crackers and salt pork, and a wool blanket roll pulled at his broad shoulders and back. New white crossbelts pressed against his woolen sky-blue fatigue jacket. In his cartridge box, 24 rounds of "buck and ball"—the musketball and three bits of buckshot forming the standard load—weighed three times as much as the previous single-ball target rounds. With his flintlock braced against his right shoulder, John Riley trooped onto the Corpus Christi parade ground for the final time with Company K, led by Captain Merrill. As with most infantry officers, Merrill rode a horse on the march.

In the ranks of the 7th, Auguste Morstadt formed up with Company I and the rest of the heavily Irish and German regiment. Lieutenant Paul led Morstadt and the rest of the company to their place in the column.

By noontime, the 5th, along with the rest of the 1st Brigade, had followed Lieutenant Colonel McIntosh from camp, "bound for the Rio Grande."[2] The 3rd Brigade, Taylor leading the way in his floppy palmetto hat and settled, as always, on Old Whitey, broke camp on March 11.

"We were delighted at the prospects of the march," wrote Captain William Selph Henry, "having become restless and anxious for a change; we anticipate no little fun and all sorts of adventure upon the route."[3]

At the march's outset, "tip-top health and spirits" filled the men.[4] But after scarcely ten miles—one day's march—beneath the unrelenting sun and across prairie where the double-file columns kicked up clouds of black ash from recent brush fires so that they soon "resembled Africans," the soldiers "were in Hell."[5]

The army's route that Meade had mapped out covered about 150 miles, and the length of each day's march depended on the distance between scarce waterholes. Up the Nueces River, across Hogwallow Prairie and the Agua Dulce and San Fernando Rivers, Taylor's regiments trudged. Scores of men collapsed in sunlight "like living fire."[6] Officers and noncoms kicked some back into the march; others were left in the dust until the surgeons' wagons rattled up to them. At one point, the troops went 36 hours without water. At night, the troops slept warily on ground infested with rattlesnakes and tarantulas. By day, peeling skin and sun-blistered lips assailed the men.

For veterans from Taylor to Riley, the torments of the march were simply the soldier's lot. They followed orders—period. They also understood that each torturous step across the prairie brought them closer to the Mexican army.

On March 19, 1846, the Army of Observation caught its first glimpse of Mexican troops. Taylor had ordered that all three of his brigades meet a few miles before the Arroyo Colorado, a sluggish, salty river 125 miles from Corpus Christi and 30 from Matamoros, because he believed that an attack could come at any point beyond the arroyo.

As the sweat-stained, exhausted infantry halted for a rest, or "blow," Taylor dispatched a contingent of the 2d Dragoons to reconnoiter the river and its banks. Officers' shouts to halt pulled up the double column of riders on the eastern bank of the river.

On the opposite shore, Mexican irregular cavalry were strung out along a chaparral-cloaked bluff, keeping the Americans from being able to assess the other riders' numbers. In clear, precise English intelligible even to many German immigrants' limited grasp of the language, a Mexican officer warned that any attempt by the Americans to ford the arroyo would be an act of hostility.

After a brief conference among themselves, the dragoon officers turned their men around and dashed back to Taylor's resting column. The tense features of the reconnaissance riders as they galloped up to Taylor sent "a wave of excitement through the ranks—something was up."

"Everyone in the army," wrote Ephraim Kirby Smith, "from the General-in-Chief to the smallest drummer boy felt certain that we were on the verge of a fierce and bloody conflict, yet I saw no one who was not cheerful and apparently eager for the game to begin."[7] That night, Taylor, Worth, and McIntosh devised a plan to cross the river in force and engage the Mexicans.

As dawn broke on March 20, 1846, bugles sent Taylor's men, few of whom had slept with action so close, scrambling into formation. Those whose stomachs did not flutter with fear bolted down a few morsels of hardtack and salt pork. Officers ordered their men to gulp at least a few mouthfuls of water against the already stifling heat. Then, from the west, a plaintive din washed across the Army of Observation: Mexican buglers were sounding the assembly.

Through the Americans' massed blue ranks, Taylor's words to his staff officers the previous evening were passed down the line: "If a single Mexican is seen after my men enter the river, I will open artillery fire on him."[8]

At 7:00 in the morning, the order to advance reverberated in the sultry air. The army tramped to the arroyo, the clamor of the Mexican buglers growing louder with each step.

As the river appeared less than a mile into the advance, orders barked in Spanish rang above the thickets of the opposite bank. The Americans could not see the Mexicans but visualized thousands of muskets and grapeshot-laden cannons leveled at them. Grant, later admitting he was unnerved by the noise and the apparent nearness of his first battle, remembered something Taylor had said at Corpus Christi: "Don't judge an enemy's strength by his noise."[9]

The flying batteries, yearning to make some noise of their own, rolled to a halt behind the cavalry and the infantry at a 30-foot escarpment on the northern bank of the arroyo. Meade and a party of engineers screened by two companies of sharpshooters, who gripped their long-distance percussion rifles and eyed the opposite bluff for any hint of Mexican movement, had hacked out a roadway to the river before dawn.

Taylor pointed toward the path and ordered Captain Charles F. Smith to lead four companies of infantry across the river. John Riley and Company K, to the right of the artillery, watched Smith's men stumble down the narrow, sandy trail and reassemble ranks at the water's edge.

On the bank behind them, Ringgold, Bragg, and Duncan's gunners unhitched their six-pounders, shoved them in positions directly across from the concealed Mexicans, took the range, elevated the cannon barrels slightly, rammed home loads of grapeshot, and waited for Taylor's order with lanyards—the cords used to fire cannons—ready. Arrayed just behind the batteries were the dragoons and Worth's infantry. The 2d Brigade, Riley included, deployed into double firing lines, the men in front on one knee, the column behind them standing. "Fingers itched on triggers," a private recalled, as the Mexican bugles and commands swelled.

At the edge of the arroyo, Smith shouted, "Commence crossing!"

As Riley and the rest waited, Smith's men waded "in perfect order" into the muddy, four-foot-deep water, holding their muskets and cartridge boxes above their heads. Stretched out in four single columns, the companies slogged forward in what one soldier called "the longest walk of my life to that point."

Behind them, Taylor and his army waited for the first blasts of Mexican muzzles. "We watched them [the advancing infantry] in breathless silence as they deepened in the water, expecting that at every step they would receive a withering fire."

Unable to restrain himself, Worth galloped down the path, splashed into the river, and, brandishing his saber at the thickets above, took the lead of the column from the startled Smith. The four companies reached the halfway point. No shots erupted from the high thickets in front. The Mexican bugles had fallen silent, and no Spanish commands were heard.

The Americans sloshed forward, the eyes of Riley and the rest fixed on the brush 30 feet above the river. Suddenly, the vanguard poured onto the opposite bank, surged up the bluff, and plunged into the thickets out of the sight of their comrades on the other bank for several long moments.

Then, Smith emerged from the brush and waved his arms in an "all clear" signal. His soggy companies stood at the far edge of the bluff and watched as the Mexican cavalry—estimated widely from 25 to 300—galloped away in a shower of chaparral ash.

A deafening cheer burst from the massed ranks on the northern bluff, and the bands struck up "Yankee Doodle." As the army roared, however, for the courage of Smith and Worth and all of the 200 or so soldiers who had forded the river, "the disappointment of the men was shown from right to left in muttered curses." Captain Ephraim K. Smith would facetiously note: "The great battle of Arroyo Colorado was terminated." [10] For Mick Maloney and others, "the first speck of war" [11] proved merely wet.

The Mexican bluff and retreat notwithstanding, Taylor's men now understood that battle might be joined at any moment. Rumors that a Mexican army of at least 10,000 soldiers with heavy artillery had gathered at Matamoros and that skilled British and French officers were serving as hands-on "advisors" unsettled some of the outnumbered Americans, who had no reinforcements in sight until war broke out and Polk could call for 50,000 recruits. But most of Taylor's officers were supremely confident, echoing Lieutenant John Sedgwick's assertion that "there never was so fine an American army." [12] Grant, although believing that Mexico was "the aggrieved party," also contended that "a better army, man for man [than Taylor's], probably never faced an enemy"; and one of the army's chief assets, Grant credited, was its nucleus of Irish and other European veterans.[13]

Taylor allowed those veterans and his other troops to rest near the Arroyo Colorado for two days after the "battle." As the infantry nursed their blistered feet and sought ointments from the surgeons for sunburn, Taylor revealed his next gambit to Twiggs, Worth, and McIntosh: on the following morning, March 24, 1846, Taylor would send Worth with the three infantry brigades and the artillery up a road to Matamoros; Taylor himself would lead Twiggs's 2d Dragoons ten miles east to Point Isabel to establish his army's supply depot. One of the infantry companies he chose to accompany him was Texans.

Worth's men left the arroyo first on March 24, and as they marched in columns of four toward the Rio Grande, the terrain changed from harsh chaparral to a lush, verdant landscape where blue lupine cast its fragrance everywhere and budding acacia bloomed near oak trees. Soldiers marveled at lustrous white blossoms crowning elongated stalks called Spanish bayonet, or, to locals, yucca plants. At sunset, Worth halted the brigades and batteries near a small pond by a stand of oak trees called Palo Alto, "tall timber."

As Worth's men pitched their tents and gathered wood for cooking fires, Taylor's column camped several miles from Point Isabel. One account claims that early on March 25, he ordered two companies of dragoons and a band of Texas Rangers to ride out first. Volunteers who refused to wear army blue and who were instantly recognizable in their slouched hats and their pistols on each hip, the Rangers had been waging a border war for years with the Mexicans, a struggle marked by atrocities on both sides. Even veteran soldiers found the Texans' collective demeanor and visage ferocious.

As buglers played "To Horse," the two companies of dragoons and the Rangers reportedly clattered down the coastal road. Three hours later, Taylor and the rest followed.

Wisps of black smoke rose on the eastern horizon several miles closer to the coast. No one paid much attention at first, but as they went on, the smoke thickened. The men's eyes began to water, and each breath left a sulphurous taste.

When the familiar blue-green waters of the Gulf of Mexico came into the troops' view, Taylor called a halt. Three American warships—the *Porpoise*, the *Lawrence*, and the *Woodbury*—swung at anchor several hundred yards offshore, far enough away to escape the flames crackling across El Fronton, the village on Point Isabel.

Fire engulfed the port's customhouse, a few dozen homes, nearby farms and fields, and the town's church. Taylor had ordered his riders into El Fronton with his command "to observe with the most serious respect the rights of all the inhabitants who may be found in peaceful prosecution of their respective occupations."

"Under no pretext," Taylor had decreed, "nor in any way will any interference be allowed with the civil rights or religious principles of the inhabitants." [14]

At the approach of Taylor's riders, most villagers had fled north and south. A few, too terrified or infirm to scatter, gathered in the little plaza, infants and adults alike sobbing and screaming. They were certain that the "Norte Americanos" would murder them.

Disregarding the flames, Taylor marched the main body into town and ordered his few Spanish-speaking officers to assure the civilians that they would not be harmed. One of those officers, Lieutenant George Deas, a West Point man and the adjutant of Riley's regiment, would write: "How unjust! All [here] were Mexicans, acknowledging none but Mexican laws. Yet we . . . drove those poor people away from their farms and seized their custom-house at Point Isabel." [15] The chaos prompted Lieutenant Colonel Hitchcock to declare that "we have outraged the Mexican government and people by an arrogance and presumption that deserve to be punished." [16]

In Washington, the controversy later led Illinois Congressman Abraham Lincoln to fire a verbal salvo at Polk's approach to Manifest

Destiny. "It is a fact that the United States Army in marching to the Rio Grande marched into a peaceful Mexican settlement and frightened the inhabitants away from their homes and growing crops," he declared. "Possibly *you* consider these acts too small for notice. Would you venture to so consider them had they been committed by any nation on earth against the humblest of our people?" [17]

According to various Mexican historians, the blame for the acts Lincoln decried rests squarely on the alleged advance party of dragoons and Texas Rangers. Many American sources contend that Mexican General Francisco Mejia, an aggressive commander at Matamoros, ordered irregulars to torch the town in a scorched earth policy, denying Taylor his intended depot. If so, Mejia's tactic failed, for Point Isabel would prove the U.S. Army's supply lifeline in the evolving campaign. The only fact that the two camps of thought agree upon is that El Fronton was set on fire.

Several Mexican scholars also contend that the panorama of terrified Catholic peasants and of their church's immolation enraged another onlooker of the 5th Infantry. Like his adjutant, Deas, John Riley would later write of the "unjustness" of the scene.[18] A noted Mexican historian believes that what Riley heard of El Fronton stirred memories passed down to him by relatives who had survived the religious savagery of the Rising of 1798.

The fires of Point Isabel dismayed Taylor, but not for long. Assigning the blame to Mejia—as likely a candidate as a Ranger—he left behind a team of engineers and quartermasters to build the depot and rushed the dragoons back up the coastal road to Palo Alto.

Taylor's columns rejoined Worth's men at Palo Alto early on March 28, 1846. Old Rough and Ready assembled the entire force and, with the dragoons in the lead, and the infantry, the flying batteries, and the siege and supply train following, marched his army four abreast the final few miles to the eastern bank of the Rio Grande. A blue haze swirled about them most of the way. Then, suddenly, they spotted the "gun-metal shine" of the river.[19]

Shortly before noon, with Old Glory and regimental flags snapping smartly in a cool breeze and with the regimental bands booming "Yankee Doodle," the Army of Observation halted on the riverbank of the river.

One hundred yards away and "across the far-famed and much talked-about waters [that] rolled beneath us," wrote Captain Henry, "the city of Matamoros rose like a fairy vision before our enraptured eyes.... The Mexican colors were flying from the quarters of the commander, General Mejia."[20]

Throngs of townspeople lined rooftops and balconies. Along the opposite riverbank marched columns of Mexican infantry clad in dark blue tunics and black shakos.

In full view of the American troops, Mexican priests in white vestments would soon splash holy water upon emplaced cannons whose crews knelt with heads bared. Then, several dozen church bells pealed above the city and echoed across the river.

Irishmen in Taylor's regiments stared at the crosses crowning graceful bell towers. Sent "to provoke a war," many of the immigrants questioned whether they served the right army. "Sons of the Green Isle" had fled a Catholic land conquered by another army trumpeting Anglo-Saxon superiority and reviling papists.[21] Now, Nativist officers expected them to march against a foe that spoke a foreign tongue in daily life, but the same language—Latin—in those churches across the river as the Irish did in theirs. Men like Private Sawney, "one of the bhoys [sic]," reflected: "If a poor devil wants to be ever so religious, it's no use of trying it here [the army]. I suppose that's what you call liberty of conscience in this blessed free republic of ours."[22]

A handful of Taylor's officers, mainly Whigs, also evinced doubts about their mission. Ulysses S. Grant wrote: "I had a horror of the Mexican War... only I had not moral courage enough to resign... I considered my supreme duty was to my flag."[23]

Some soldiers had no doubt about which flag to serve.

6

"Put None But Americans on Guard Tonight"

Wᴵᴛʜᴵɴ ʜᴏᴜʀs of Taylor's arrival opposite Matamoros, Engineer Captain Joseph K. Mansfield began surveys for a massive, five-sided earthwork dubbed "Fort Texas." The redoubt, begun by April 8, and facing the town, rose slowly, inexorably, with sweating, shirtless soldiers digging tons of dirt and, with engineers bawling instructions, shaping dense earthen walls to smother Mexican siege shot. Although the construction detail promised the laborers sore limbs and sunburn, many troops actually volunteered for the task, for Taylor had ordered a gill (four ounces) of whiskey to each man "engaged on Engineer Fatigues." [1]

Around Fort Texas, the Americans cleared a field of six-inch corn plants along the Rio Grande and pitched rows of tents. Bravado engulfed many of the younger officers for a day or two. Lieutenant John P. Hatch wrote: "The actions of the two armies are perfectly comical. They are both engaged in erecting batteries on their respective sides of the river and so near the other that we can almost converse between them, but not a shot is fired; the men work without any attempt to conceal themselves. Many of the officers and the men bathe in the river. Sometimes parties from each side will be bathing opposite each other." [2]

Bathing in the river soon became a preoccupation for many of Taylor's men—and not for hygienic reasons. Each day, scores of Mexican peasant girls gathered on the opposite bank to wash clothes and, as they had done for generations, to shed their skirts and chemises and slip naked into the water. American officers and enlisted men alike gaped at the crowds of young women "chasing each other... diving into the depths of the stream or swimming along its surface with their long, loose, raven tresses flowing behind them.... They laugh, shout, sing, wrestle with each other, and display their graceful forms in a thousand agile movements."[3] According to Nathan Jarvis, a surgeon, the lovely women and the presence of the Mexican army along the Rio Grande made the U.S. Army's first nights there full "of great excitement."[4]

On the Americans' second morning on the bluffs facing Matamoros, the men awoke to a scene reminding them of the true "excitement" awaiting them. While Taylor's men had huddled in their tents all night long beneath a pounding rain, General Francisco Mejia's troops had erected a new earthworks for 800 men. Two other redoubts, looming 800 yards from Taylor's camp, placed the Americans under the threat of an artillery crossfire. For John Riley and other experienced hands, the sight of those well-engineered bastions confirmed what young, untested officers did not yet fully grasp: the "well-developed and magnificent figures" in the river notwithstanding, this expedition was taking a grimmer turn by the hour.

Soon after the U.S. Army's arrival, Taylor, hoping to find out the conditions of two dragoons who had been captured by the Mexicans before the American army's arrival and to size up the intentions of Mejia, had sent General Worth across the Rio Grande under a flag of truce. On the riverbank, Mejia, who "was breathing fire at the prospect of battle," refused to meet with Worth. The Mexican general had sent General Rómolo Díaz de la Vega to deal with the "Yanquis." Since he claimed that he did not speak English and since none of Worth's party spoke Spanish, the "negotiations" proceeded in French. When he later reported back to Taylor, Worth said he believed the Mexicans ready for a fight. Taylor agreed that the Mexicans would strike "as soon as they receive enough troops to attack us."[5]

To assess Mejia's current strength, Taylor turned again to Worth. Old Rough and Ready considered him devious—just the man to send a spy into Matamoros.

Worth selected an unnamed soldier from the 8th Infantry. On March

29, the man swam the Rio Grande, "surrendered" to Mexican troops, and announced himself as a deserter. His captors led him to Mejia, and so glib was the alleged runaway that Mejia not only believed him, but also offered him a captain's commission to persuade other Americans to join him.

Free to wander Matamoros and study the Mexican redoubts, he "served" his new army for one day, stole back to the river that night, and swam back to Taylor's camp without Mexican pickets spotting him. He reported: "The Mexicans have 3,500 troops, 500 are cavalry and are fine troops, the remainder are good for nothing, a miserable, half-starved set of wretches. They have about thirty pieces of artillery, none larger than a nine-pounder, and many twos and threes and fours."[6] Other sources claimed that Mejia had only 2,000 troops. Reinforcements under General Pedro de Ampudia, however, were marching to Matamoros. The Mexicans would soon outnumber the Americans.

The spy's assessment of the Mexican infantry as "wretches" fed the prejudices of officers who espoused "the popular American idea of a Mexican . . . a fat face, a double chin, a muddy complexion, a bloated body, coarse appetites, a crude organization generally, and no brains to speak of above the ears—only enough to talk with."[7] But many American officers had also read newspaper quotes from British, French, and Prussian military authorities who pronounced that Mexican officers and regiments hardened in civil war and in battle against Spain and France would teach the "young Colossus of the North" a hard lesson. A British officer had warned: "A Mexican is like a mule—if you push him to the edge of the cliff, he will take you with him."[8] And Napoleon's adage that "the first quality of a soldier is constancy in enduring fatigue and hardship" applied particularly to the army gathering against Taylor.[9]

European veterans heaping the earth walls of Fort Texas, drilling in the cornfield, or standing picket duty along the river peered daily at "well-dressed [Mexican] officers . . . soldiers in full uniform," sandbagged batteries, and thick redoubts, and suspected that their foes were hardly wretches.[10]

Amid the disparaging descriptions of the Mexicans by Worth's spy, he unwittingly recounted an alarming development for the U.S. Army. Mejia's offer to commission the man to raise a company of deserters heralded an evolving Mexican strategy aimed at Taylor's men most affected by the tolling of church bells, by the sounds of hymns that wafted from Matamoros's churches, and by the priests who sprinkled holy water upon cannons and fortifications.

Through a network of spies, Mejia and other Mexican generals knew of the rancor between Nativist officers and immigrants in Taylor's ranks. The Mexicans realized that 47 percent of Taylor's men hailed from Europe, mainly Irishmen, along with many Germans. So, too, did Mexican leaders recall the Nativist mobs that had murderously rampaged through Catholic neighborhoods in Philadelphia and other American cities in 1844. And Taylor's foes were about to tap into the hard feelings permeating their enemy's camp.

The hope of immigrant troops that the nearness of battle would divert officers' Nativism dwindled. "The donkeys are part and parcel of the Mexican," an American captain stated, "as much so as the pig of the Irishman." [11] Angered by the daily sights and sounds of Matamoros's Catholic rituals, many of Taylor's officers similarly ridiculed "popery" and "papist mummery and flummery" [12] and professed their zeal to free Mexico from the "dead hand of the Roman Catholic Church." [13]

On the evening of March 29–30, 1846, just after Taylor's buglers sounded tattoo, the general alarm sent soldiers scampering out of their bivouac and clutching their muskets. Scouts had reported that at least 600 Mexican cavalrymen had crossed the Rio Grande and would fall upon the camp before dawn. American dragoons clambered atop their mounts to the bugle call of "To Horse" and galloped off into the darkness to engage the Mexicans, the jangle of spurs and sabers echoing as the riders vanished.

All through camp, "the watch-word was given out.... the train was placed in the center of camp and if firing had commenced," remembered Captain William S. Henry, there would have been a stampede of some "six hundred animals." [14]

Officers ordered their men to sleep with their weapons, but sleep that long night came to few soldiers, open eyed, listening for the first distant cracks of the dragoons' pistols and carbines.

"Nothing came to pass," wrote an officer. But, as the bleary-eyed troops pushed themselves from their bedrolls and mustered for assembly, they noticed that the Mexicans had emplaced another cannon in a sand-bagged battery.

When the dragoons clattered back into camp, wearing the dust of hours on the road all the way to Port Isabel and back, they reported that they had found no Mexican lancers. The war of nerves had begun.

The following morning, March 31, a jittery American officer noted: "Two men, foreigners, swam the river and deserted."[15]

Grant and others worried that officers' "harsh and cruel usage" on "these poor fellows" had driven them across the river.[16] Captain Philip Norbourne Barbour and Lieutenant George Meade echoed Grant's growing concern about the lure of Matamoros for immigrant soldiers.

On April 1, 1846, as "the whole city turned out" to wish them good luck, the Mexicans released the two captured dragoons, and the pair regaled their American comrades with accounts of the Mexicans' "kindness," fandangos (dances), and the beauty and charm of the women.[17] The pair's glowing accounts of life among their Catholic captors proved an immediate problem for Taylor and his commanders, for, in Meade's words, the excaptives' stories, combined with the enemy's church bells and priests, "induced a great many desertions from our side."[18]

In response to the two desertions on the evening before the dragoons' return, Old Rough and Ready issued "orders . . . verbally given to the several commanders on or about the first of April [1846] that all men seen swimming across the river should be hailed by our pickets and ordered to return; and, in case that they did not return, that they should be shot."[19] Taylor had taken the unprecedented and illegal step of ordering that deserters be shot while no state of war existed—a blatant violation of the Articles of War.

Scarcely had Taylor issued his shoot-to-kill order before scores of men defied it. Surgeon Jarvis recorded in his journal that 36 soldiers swam the river during the night of April 1–2 under the noses of the sentries, at least 14 deserters hailing from the mostly Irish ranks of the 1st Brigade. Riley's unit, the 5th, accounted for many.

On the evening of April 2–3, more men stole from camp, hid along the riverbank until pickets had passed by, and slipped into the Rio Grande. Captain Barbour wrote on the next day: "We have lost about thirty men . . . by desertion. . . . Several slaves belonging to officers have left their masters and gone over to Matamoros." The Kentuckian Barbour worried: "If we are located on this border, we shall have to employ white servants."[20]

That same day, Barbour and his fellow soldiers awoke to find leaflets strewn like piles of snow in front of their tents and the redoubt and across the campground. From the missive's first lines, trouble loomed for Taylor:

> The Commander-in-Chief of the Mexican Army to the English and Irish under the orders of the American General Taylor:
>
> Know ye: That the Government of the United States is committing repeated acts of barbarous aggression against the magnanimous Mexican nation; that the Government which exists under the flag of the stars is unworthy of the designation of Christian. Recollect that you were born in Great Britain, that the American Government looks with coldness upon the powerful flag of England, and is provoking to a rupture the warlike people to whom it belongs, President Polk boldly manifesting a desire to take possession of Oregon as he has already done Texas. Now then, come with all confidence to the Mexican ranks, and I guarantee to you, upon my honor, good treatment, and that all of your expense shall be defrayed until your arrival in the beautiful capital of Mexico.
>
> Germans, French, Poles and individuals of other nations! Separate yourselves from the Yankees, and do not contribute to defend a robbery and usurpation which, be assured, the civilized nations of Europe look upon with utmost indignation. Come, therefore, and array yourselves under the tri-colored flag, in confidence that the God of Armies protects it, and it will protect you, equally with the English.[21]

The letter bore the signatures of General Pedro de Ampudia and Francisco R. Moreno, "Adjutant of the Commander-in-Chief," and was dated April 2, 1846, the pair having composed it "upon the road to Matamoros."[22]

Although Ampudia and Moreno's references to England's flag and America's "coldness" toward Britain roused no anger in Irish immigrants, the appeal for them to oppose the "barbarous aggression" of a Protestant nation against a Catholic one was a shrewd gambit, appealing to their history, their faith, and their lack of ties to America.

John Riley certainly read the pamphlet, but, for the moment, tucked it away. He and the rest of the men went about their duties that morning, policing the camp, laboring on Fort Texas. Pickets selected for their marksmanship patrolled the riverbank and scanned the water from the bluff and the fort.

Suddenly in the afternoon "a rapid discharge of musketry was heard below the camp and on the riverbank." The troops scrambled for their muskets as the cadence of the long roll (drum command) boomed and shouting officers quickly formed them into regimental strength. Closest to the river was the 1st Brigade. They had dropped their shovels and picks, snatched their stacked weapons, and rushed to the "river with a yell." The Mexican civilians and soldiers lured to the opposite bank by the gunfire "scampered . . . and thought we had commenced upon them."

Then, the men on both banks spied a figure bobbing in the greenish waters. For a few minutes it floated past the crowds. Finally, the Rio Grande closed over it.

"The whole affair was one of some little excitement," wrote an American captain, "and proved with what alacrity our men would fly to their arms." As the details of the sudden call-to-arms spread through the ranks, excitement gave way to more somber emotions.

Sometime during the morning of April 4, Private Carl Gross, a Frenchman serving in Company I of the 7th Infantry, had decided to desert. He had plunged into the water that afternoon and splashed toward Matamoros. Pickets spotted him and ordered him to stop. He kept swimming. Several muskets barked, and Captain Henry tersely noted that "he [Gross] was shot and sank."[23]

That evening, as the men gathered at their evening mess and discussed Gross's death—a warranted act to some, an execution to others—two Irishmen, James Mills and Thomas Riley, both of Company H in the 3d Infantry, sneaked down to the riverbank, eluded the pickets, dove into the river, and reached the Mexican lines. Riley, "a giant Irishman," was no relation to John Riley.[24]

On the evening following Mills's and Thomas Riley's desertions, the cracks of pickets' muskets rousted the troops from their blankets. This time, however, the drums did not pound the long roll. The men returned uneasily to their tents. "Another attempt at desertion, and another death," wrote an officer.[25] This time, the slain deserter was Private Henry Lamb, a Swiss national who had attempted to flee Company D of John Riley's regiment.

Taylor, faced with a growing problem he had never anticipated, described his dilemma in a dispatch sent to Adjutant General Jones on April 6, the day after Lamb was gunned down in the Rio Grande. "Efforts are continually making to entice our men to desert," Old Rough and Ready wrote, "and, I regret to say, have met with considerable success. Four, however, have been drowned in swimming the river, and two have been killed by our pickets while attempting to desert." He hoped that his shoot-to-kill policy would "check the practices." [26]

Taylor's order chiefly deterred desertions by day. But as Captain Henry noted on the same date of Taylor's letter, "more of our men deserted last night," one of them County Mayo native John Murphy, of the 8th Infantry. [27]

As soldiers drifted away from Taylor's camp, Mexican reinforcements streamed into Matamoros. A "grand military display" by the Mexicans with bugles blaring and "a regiment marching and maneuvering smartly" impressed several American officers. [28] At the review's end, a priest sprinkled holy water over a newly completed fieldwork.

Intelligence that General Ampudia, the coauthor of the leaflet, was nearing Matamoros to take command from Mejia convinced most Americans that he carried orders from Mexico City to start the war. An officer wrote: "When Ampudia arrives . . . nothing can hold him back from a fight." [29]

Taylor ordered round-the-clock work on Fort Texas, and Engineer Captain Joseph Mansfield ensured that "all men off-duty will be constantly employed until it [the fort] is finished." [30] Sodden from spring rains one day, blistered by the sun the next, the men labored stoically or sullenly and tense officers meted out hard discipline to any shirkers and watched for would-be deserters. In daylight, the officers and noncoms could easily spot a man slipping away from his detail and inching toward the river. Taylor could rely upon assimilated immigrants such as Sergeant Mick Maloney to approach foreigners mulling desertion and to dissuade them through reason or discipline. Company officers also scrutinized their units' Irishmen and other foreigners liable to "go over the hill." In Company K, Captain Merrill viewed John Riley as an Irishman unlikely to be seduced by the sounds of church bells and young women's laughter. [31]

On the evening of April 7, 1846, southwestern breezes redolent with those languid, already familiar sounds carried other familiar tones—the voices of deserters. As Taylor's men peered through the darkness, they discerned several of the deserters standing on the Mexican bank, cupping their hands, calling former tentmates by name. They urged them to leave the U.S. Army behind and sample the "wine, women, and song" across the Rio Grande. Several of the deserters, still in their American uniforms and speaking with the brogues of their old counties, hollered that the Mexicans treated all Irishmen and foreigners as friends and equals.

From the American positions, some men hurled insults at the deserters; many of Taylor's troops, however, yelled greetings until officers bawled orders for silence. Pickets chafing to bring down the gray, distant shapes could merely watch, as Taylor had ordered that only men in the act of desertion were to be shot.

Eventually, the voices ebbed in the soft wind. But they would return several times in the following weeks, with more joining the chorus, reminding immigrants that "their faith was deeply rooted in their heritage," and urging them to escape from the Americans.[32]

To grapple with the "general disaffection" seeping through his ranks, "especially foreigners . . . some of them not even naturalized citizens," Taylor declared that "the most efficient measures were necessary to prevent the spread of the contagion."[33] Nativist William Butler wrote that "the sectarian treachery of the Irish deserters" could prove "overwhelming" for Taylor and threatened "the destruction of the whole American force."

To combat "the . . . class of men deserting and crossing the river to join their coreligionists on the other side," Butler contended that American officers, if not Taylor himself, issued a "celebrated order": "Put none but Americans on guard tonight."[34]

April 8, 1846, proved a busy day for the guards scanning the river. As Mansfield and his engineers pushed the fieldwork details ever harder, four or five men dove into the water in broad daylight. Sentries drew a bead on them, but never squeezed triggers. The Rio Grande, running fast that day, wrestled them all to the river bottom.

Still, others attempted to cross. One leaped from a bluff into the water, and, as pickets took aim and work details stared, battled the current. He thrashed toward the opposite shore, the guards' rifles silent. Then, he neared the bank, clutched some brush, and crawled from the river.

Suddenly, a picket's musket barked, and the deserter crumpled to the

ground. "It was a capital shot for a musket," wrote an American officer,"
being about two hundred yards, and must give them no contemptible
idea of our shooting."

Mexican soldiers gathered around the body, wrapped it in a sheet,
and buried the man.

The day's toll for deserters notwithstanding, "every inducement...
offered [deserters] by the enemy" drew others to the river that night.[35]
Among them was dragoon Private John Little, of Kildare, joining the
scores of Irishmen greeting countrymen every night in Matamoros.

Pickets' shots rang out throughout the next few evenings, but none
hit their marks. Deserters scrambled up the Mexican bank and vanished
toward the town. Both armies continued work on their fortifications day
and night, reconnoitered, and patrolled the Rio Grande. With rumors of
action escalating daily, eagerness and fear filled both camps. The wait
became almost unbearable.

Despite swelling tensions, Colonel Trueman Cross, Taylor's popular
quartermaster, decided to ride from camp on a sightseeing jaunt, and
on the morning of April 10, 1846, he did just that—alone. Dragoons had
detected hoofprints and other signs of Mexican "rancheros," or irregulars, a few miles outside of camp. When Cross did not gallop back by
nightfall, worry washed across his friends' thoughts. "Great fears are
entertained for his safety," wrote Captain Henry. "Parties have been sent
in every direction in search of him; and thinking he might be lost,
Generally Taylor directed some cannon to be fired, to guide him to
camp. I fear he is either a prisoner or has been murdered."[36]

As the American officers hoped for news of Cross on the morning of
April 11, church bells tolled wildly in Matamoros, and a 20-gun volley
crackled through the warm air. Bands struck up patriotic tunes. To the
thunderous cheers of the townspeople, the Mexican troops marched
into the town plaza to greet their new commander, General Pedro de
Ampudia, who had ridden at breakneck speed the 180 miles from
Monterrey with about 200 cavalry.

Three days behind Ampudia, 2,200 regulars under Brigadier General
Anastasio Torrejon tramped up the dusty track to Matamoros.

Planning an attack as soon as Torrejon arrived, Ampudia sent Taylor
an ultimatum:

To Don Z. Taylor:

I require you in all form, and at the latest in the peremptory term of twenty-four hours, to break up your camp and return to the east bank of the Nueces River while our Governments are regulating the pending question in relation to Texas. If you insist on remaining upon the soil of the Department of Tamaulipas, it will certainly result that arms, and arms alone, must decide the question; and in that case I advise you that we accept the war to which, with so much injustice on your part, you provoke us.[37]

Taylor gave a civil but menacing reply: "I regret the alternative which you offer; but, at the same time, wish it understood that I shall by no means avoid such alternative."[38]

Some on the Mexican side of the river not only welcomed war, but also believed that the "gringos'" strength would ebb through desertion with each day before the first shots. On April 11, 1846, American soldiers thumbed through a translated copy of the *Matamoros Gazette* that claimed: "There have been forty-three desertions from the 'barbarians,' six slaves."[39] That figure, as Grant, Meade, Barbour, and other officers soberly attested, was too low and was rising daily. While the writer's jibe that the Mexicans "momentarily expect 'Old Taylor,' body and soul," to desert "afforded us [the U.S. Army] no little amusement," the article reflected the enemy's growing confidence that the desertions would continue.[40] Mejia "expected most of Taylor's Seventh Regiment" to go over the hill, as the unit "was largely composed of Irish and Germans."[41]

That night, an Irish veteran in Taylor's ranks pondered the prejudice he had encountered in American army blue, weighing the proverbial devil he knew against that he did not on the opposite bank. He had nearly three years to go before becoming a naturalized citizen; he had no family in America, only in Ireland. Catholic to his core, he mulled over the religious themes raised in the Mexican pamphlet and present in his own experiences.

As rain slapped against his tent all night, he made a choice.

Part Two

"I Accepted of It"

7

"The Advice of My Conscience"

O N SUNDAY MORNING, April 12, 1846, a private slogged from his tent to that of his commanding officer, Moses Emory Merrill, and asked for a moment of the captain's time. John Riley, the rain of "a dismal . . . very cold day" dripping from his cap and fatigue jacket, requested a signed pass to attend a Catholic mass.[1] The Irishman stated that he had been "seized with the desire to go to church" when hearing that a priest from Matamaros would hold services in a farm building just north of the American camp.[2]

As Merrill considered Riley's request, the officer saw "a very good man," every inch the professional soldier. Merrill himself did not "recollect ever having to punish him in any way." Despite the rash of desertions, including many from the 5th, and despite any misgivings about a Mexican priest addressing Catholic immigrants, Merrill trusted his judgment in Riley's character.[3]

Merrill later said: "I signed the pass for him."[4]

Riley snapped a salute, turned, and strode from Merrill's sight with the pass tucked safely in a pocket. Reportedly, Riley's pocket contained something else—a dog-eared copy of Ampudia's leaflet.

Riley and Merrill would meet again, 17 months later, under vastly different circumstances.

The Irishman splashed past the rows of tents, the fieldworks, and the nine-foot walls of Fort Texas, where two massive 18-pounder cannons bristled at Matamoros. At the camp's northern perimeter, he stopped for the sentries' challenge and produced his pass for one, Corporal Charles Franski. Then Riley walked away from the camp.

With each muddy step northward along the riverbank, Riley risked shouted challenges from patrolling dragoons and the wary eyes and quick trigger fingers of Taylor's outermost pickets, watching the river for any hint of movement. He also risked ambush from rancheros who might shoot a stray American soldier before he could pull out Ampudia's leaflet and plea desertion, praying that one of the irregulars spoke English.

Riley kept walking. At some point out of the pickets' sight, he edged closer to the river, waiting for the right moment to slip into the roiling brown waters and to swim to the opposite bank. Across the river, church bells' echoes called worshipers to Sunday services.

By nightfall, John Riley had plunged into the Rio Grande. The War Department would record: "He failed to return to duty at the expiration of the pass and was recorded as having deserted April 12, 1846."[5]

Accounts by fellow soldiers, the era's press, and future writers would discuss Riley's desertion and motives. One version contends that shortly after the U.S. Army reached the Rio Grande, Captain Merrill loudly cursed and reprimanded Riley in front of Company K for an unspecified minor infraction. The smoldering Irishman reportedly hid a copy of the Mexican pamphlet and lit out at the first chance. In later testimony, Merrill asserted he never disciplined Riley—that Riley never gave him any trouble.

German-born private Jacob Oswandel, other soldiers, and several newspapers offered a slightly different version of Riley's simmering anger at the Army. They claimed that a young officer had erupted with oaths and insults at Riley for no discernible cause. The officer "mocked and reviled him" every day "until it was impossible for [Riley] to take any more."[6] He snapped just before he requested his pass from Merrill.

A third version states that Riley had failed to salute a "shave-tail lieutenant" on the morning of April 12 and had strained to keep "his Irish temper in check" as the officer unleashed a verbal tirade at him.[7] Scant hours later, Riley had deserted.

Riley not only resented junior officers' daily scorn, but also was "irked by the strong anti-Irish sentiment then prevalent in the United States."[8]

In no way did Riley consider himself a traitor, for, with no family in America, no naturalized citizenship, and no chance to regain his stripes, he had never been assimilated to life in the United States. He never called himself an American and always referred to himself as an *Irishman* who had endured prejudice because of that fact and because of his religion.

Many among Riley's later legions of detractors would claim that his ego drove his desertion. "He [Riley] had only one apparent flaw," writes historian Fairfax Downey. "He could enforce discipline, but found it hard to take." [9] Other scholars contend that winning personal glory and someday wearing an officer's "pair of epilitts [epaulets]" led Riley over the hill. [10] Linking him to the traditions of the Wild Geese, many believed that Riley was a soldier-for-hire, "a true professional, not in the sense that he sold his services for money alone, but in his prideful ambition for rank as an officer commanding men, regardless of the flag under which he fought." [11]

Riley's ego did ring in his letters. From his desire to wear an officer's bars and sword to his more modest determination to at least regain his former sergeant's stripes, he never wavered in his belief that he was born to lead. Each day in Taylor's ranks had hammered home the fact that he was cannon fodder in a private's uniform—with no chance to rise through the ranks. "Obsessed with rank and honor," a "dastard" devoid of any redeeming quality except martial ability, "the notorious Riley," many American writers claim, was a turncoat, a "miserable . . . fellow" who had broken his signed pledge to the United States and who would do far worse to his former comrades in arms. [12]

Such a "damned rascal," Nativist officers and writers would assert, held no ideology, no religious ideals, and no national identity. Ego, greed, and disloyalty—these substituted for conscience in "the notorious Riley," his foes charged. [13]

Riley's own words painted a stark contrast to the image of a soulless soldier-for-hire. Mexican historians, including Professor Rudy Acuna, counter that Riley early decided that the U.S. Army was no place for an Irish Catholic to serve. Another scholar postulates that "the flame and fear the private [Riley] saw in Santa Isabel rekindled the tales told in Ireland by those who had lived through the horrors of the Rising of 1798," when Lord Charles Cornwallis's redcoats had savagely crushed Irish rebels. [14]

Riley would warn a Mackinac acquaintance "be not obscured by the prejudice of the United States toward a foriner [*sic*] and especially to an Irishman."[15] He denounced the United States for treating Irish and other immigrants "with contumely and disgrace" and offering them "a slavish hireling's life."[16]

In the 19th century, breaking a sworn oath was a grave matter. But Riley and other immigrants countered that their officers had violated their word of honor first. An immigrant artilleryman voiced the foreigners' "conviction that they are not treated justly." He wrote: "No great amount of logic is required to perceive that [an enlistment] contract to be binding must bind both parties; but it would take a good deal to convince the soldier that he is bound to observe an oath which he has taken under conditions which he finds are not observed."[17] In Riley's mind and in those of other Catholic immigrants, they had been sold a proverbial bill of goods by the U.S. Army, its own pledge a Nativist fraud.

Broken pledges by government officials on both sides of the Atlantic littered the lives of Irish immigrants in the army. In their native land, their rulers used legal oaths not to protect, but to persecute; when sworn to tell the truth before Protestant judges and juries little interested in a Catholic's defense, many Irish deemed the oath tainted and nonbinding. Presenting gnarled, often fallacious defenses had become not only an act of desperation by Irish facing imprisonment, exile, or a gallows, but also an act of defiance against officials who had no intention of honoring their pledge to dispense justice. To many Irish Catholics of the 1840s, any oath broken by the other party held no sanctity and no validity. Irishmen could walk away from that pledge with minds clear.

"In the month of April 1846," Riley wrote, "listening only to the advice of my conscience for the liberty of a people which had war brought on them by the most unjust aggression, I separated myself from the North American forces."[18]

Shortly after climbing from the Rio Grande on April 12, 1846, Riley, in his own words, "was captured by the Mexicans, brought back as a prisoner to Matamoros."[19] The Irishman took in his first close-up glimpses of a Mexican town as well as curious stares greeting any prisoners or alleged deserters, as his captors hauled him along streets toward the plaza. They passed two-story brick and stone houses with latticed windows, gardens lined with tropical trees, and white walls emblazoned with red flowers.

As the guards nudged Riley into the plaza, a thick-walled structure guaranteed to unnerve any captive emerged. The city prison, stenches drifting from the cells, marred the vista of the tree-lined square and the unfinished cathedral opposite the jail.

With his pass and the leaflet, Riley was led across the plaza to Ampudia's headquarters and an audience with the pamphlet's author himself.

Beneath dark, dense eyebrows, General Pedro de Ampudia peered at the latest deserter. Ampudia, 42 years old, looked every bit the career soldier, impeccably groomed in a medal-adorned blue tunic showing off his wide shoulders and barrel chest, a barbed goatee framing his square jaw. In Mexico's service over the past 25 years, he had fought in the revolution against Spain and against French invaders. As an artillery officer in 1836, he had blasted away at the walls of the Alamo and, over the next decade, had earned Texans' loathing for his ruthlessness in border warfare. His host of military and political rivals called him "the assassin," for, in 1844, he had executed rebellious General Francisco Sentamant and had fried the victim's head in oil to preserve it for display in the plaza of San Juan Batista.

"Stern, self-centered . . . with a cosmopolitan polish," Ampudia, at first glance, had little reason to gauge anything out of the ordinary in Riley except his height, his muscular frame, and his engaging looks. With an English-born aide named Captain Furlock, or Furlong, interpreting, Ampudia asked the Irishman "several questions concerning the camp of General Taylor and his men."[20] Riley's replies convinced Ampudia that the deserter was no mere private despite having that rank in the U.S. Army. Able to draw upon his days in the British Army and present himself with his characteristic "high intelligence," the Irishman proved to the always suspicious general that neither fiction nor braggadocio colored his words.

With the exception of Worth's fraudulent deserter, the Mexicans had not offered any of the genuine deserters a commission. News of that offer had spread through Taylor's ranks, and Riley, brimming with self-confidence, viewed himself as just the man to deliver a company of fellow deserters. He sold Ampudia on that premise. The Mexican general quickly tendered the Irishman a first lieutenant's commission.

Riley stated: "I accepted of it." [21]

An American veteran would write that the U.S. Army had lost "the greatest artillerist of the day" and would suffer "greatly on his [Riley's] account." [22]

8

"A Company of . . . Irishmen"

SHORTLY AFTER ACCEPTING his commission, Lieutenant John Riley shucked his sky-blue American uniform and donned the darker Turkish blue, scarlet-collared cloth coat and white canvas pants of the Mexican officer. The Irishman cut an imposing figure in Matamoros, his blue eyes shaded by the visor of a black kepi, or campaign cap. He received not only his sword and epaulets, but also a monthly pay of 67 pesos, equivalent to $57. His monthly wages as a U.S. Army private had been $7.

Billeted with a contingent of engineers, or *sappadores,* Riley reported that he was treated with "hospitality."[1] He wrote: "From the moment I extended to them the hand of friendship, I was received with kindness."[2]

The Irishman's warm reception may have initially surprised him, but Mexico had a tradition of welcoming foreign-born soldiers into its army's ranks. Englishmen, Frenchmen, Irishmen, and even American adventurers had fought for Mexico in its bloody war of independence against Spain from 1810 to 1821. During Mexico's disastrous campaign against Sam Houston and his fellow Texan rebels in 1836, at least four foreigners saw duty as Santa Anna's generals. At the moment of John Riley's desertion, 16 foreign-born generals served Mexico, including French and Italian Catholics. And junior officers included numerous

Irish immigrants and assorted expatriates, none of whom had worn American blue but had, like Riley, marched with the armies of Britain, France, or Spain. Riley was to befriend several resident Europeans—Irishmen, a Scot, a Swede, Germans, and a Belgian.

From his first days in a Mexican uniform, the gregarious Irishman cultivated friendships with his military superiors and prominent citizens. Unlike in the U.S. Army, where Nativists reviled and abused immigrant soldiers while expecting them to die for the Stars and Stripes, Riley discovered that, as long as Taylor's deserters agreed to fight for Mexico, the Mexicans immediately accepted them. To his amazement, a man whose brogue and religion had evoked only scorn from even the lowest strata of native-born American society and centuries-old contempt from the Protestant landowners of his native Galway, the aristocrats, or *puros*, of Mexico embraced him. Men and women swathed in the latest silks, laces, and velvet finery of Europe greeted him in cafes, on leisurely evening strolls around the plaza, at dances, and at Catholic mass. "A more hospitable or friendly people," Riley offered, "there exists not on the face of the earth . . . to a foriner [*sic*] and especially to an Irishman and a Catholic."[3]

To many of the deserters, the friendly attention of Mexican women proved a potent force. For a handful of the men, the women overshadowed ideology, religion, and scores to be settled with American officers. An admiring young soldier remembered: "The ladies wear no bonnet, but a scarf [*rebozo*] that they sometimes slip over their heads—skirts of different qualities, from cotton to satin—no waist to their dress—the chamise [*sic*] made so low in the neck as to leave the chest uncovered—sleeves short, and worked or embroidered—their skirts nearly to the ancles [*sic*]—their toes stuck into small slippers—the heel left loose—the dress of the women is principally white. . . . very social . . . the women."[4]

The soldier's words described young peasant women in their Sunday best. With his officer's uniform, his affability, and his good looks, Riley could also mingle with upper-class beauties, "graceful and exotic." They would gallop "astraddle like men" on their horses and would puff thin, brown Cuban *cigarritos* in mixed company, a pastime that would have scandalized upper-tier American and European women, but that, accompanied by elegant gestures of the Mexican women's fans and by "intimate conversations with their dark eyes . . . alone," captivated their male audiences.[5] Later, several American soldiers claimed that one such refined beauty, a countess described as a lovely widow, conquered Riley.

Riley also learned another fact of life for deserters turning up in Matamoros: those seeking only senoritas but unwilling to fight for Mexico received the proverbial cold shoulder from grandees and peasants alike.

Riley soon learned "the way of it" in the Mexican Army from drill routines to proper salutes and the issue of orders. He adjusted from bland U.S. Army beef, Southern pork, and hardtack to the tortillas, chile, frijoles (beans), tacos, enchiladas, and tamales of Mexico. The sudden change to foods far spicier than any the deserters had known in Europe or America tormented the stomachs of some at first.

Along with changes in diet and drill, Riley quickly discovered that his new army operated on a caste system even more pronounced than that of Britain. The pecking order of the Mexican military mirrored in many ways the nation's three main classes. The small upper class, rich, educated, with many claiming pure Spanish bloodlines, controlled not only the government, but also the army. Most high-ranking officers came from means, and, while many of these officers were excellent, others were young rakes whose wealthy families had purchased them commissions. If an ambitious officer backed the winning revolutionary faction, he garnered rank and clout. In many cases, the younger Mexican officers' gold- and silver-embroidered tunics, riding breeches, glossy boots, burnished spurs, costly swords, and plumed hats masked their inexperience on the battlefield. A cadre of notoriously cruel and corrupt generals—of whom Ampudia was one—commanded little respect from their men but were obeyed out of fear.

The glue of any army, the noncommissioned officers, were, in the Mexican regiments, the sons of middle-class families, mestizos. The mestizos served in civilian society as clerks, merchants, government officials, lawyers, often physicians, and other invaluable professionals. Many of the noncoms, especially those in battle-hardened companies of regulars, were first rate.

The Mexican enlisted ranks offered a study in contrasts to Riley and other foreigners. Infantrymen in the regulars wore stylish, braided blue jackets, white crossbelts, shakos, and blue pants with single red stripes; the regulars marched with huge brass bands, "while the Americans had but little music over and above the necessary fifes, drums, and bugles." An American captain remarked that "the Mexican Army was equipped in a very handsome manner—many of their uniforms . . . superb." [6]

The martial abilities of some regiments notwithstanding, savvy soldiers such as Riley could detect glaring problems. As in the American and the British armies, impoverished, desperate men from society's lowest rungs filled Mexico's ranks. Many companies, particularly territorial militias, were composed of Mexico's lowest class, Indians. Ill-fed, ill-trained, poorly dressed and equipped, they endured the contempt of their officers. Morale in these units was low. Manuel de Balbontin, a Mexican officer, described the dilemma of class at Matamoros and elsewhere in the army: "Although many of the officers could boast of having Spanish blood, the ranks consisted mostly of Indians recruited from among a criminal element or impressed for service by tough military detachments that roamed city streets and countrysides." [7]

"Following such an induction, the recruits learned in and around the barracks the manual of arms and the routine of military life, taught under the stick of a stern corporal." [8] Yet, as Ulysses Grant would observe, the Mexican regulars' blend of puros, mestizos, and Indians turned out some good soldiers. They carried the famed smoothbore British "Brown Bess," but many of these flintlocks were at least 20 years old. To increase the range of the weapon's one-ounce ball, the troops used a heavier charge of powder that produced such a heavy recoil that many infantrymen shot from the hip to protect their shoulders. The adjusted aim often sent shots high and wide of their marks.

The Mexican cavalry also carried the Brown Bess, but in a sawed-off version called the *escopeta*. The riders, especially the Hussars and the dreaded lancers, prided themselves not on their marksmanship, but on their swordsmanship, their riding skills, and esprit-de-corps. In their gleaming dress helmets and colorful tunics, the Mexican cavalry looked like their European counterparts, which impressed English, French, and Prussian observers far more than the hirsute, rough-and-tumble men of the U.S. dragoons. The Mexican riders' shiny six-foot lances leveled at their prey would, Europeans surmised, scatter the Yankees in terror.

With 32,000 troops available and many of the regulars disciplined and well trained, Mexico believed that, despite the army's flaws, it would handily defeat the invaders. Officers at Matamoros derided "seedy old Zachary Taylor, an absolute nullity." In Mexican eyes, the unruly American dragoons shot poorly and rode even worse. The enemy infantry, believed Ampudia, Mejia, and their aides, stood out only for their officers and included a horde of foreigners sick of Nativist abuse and ready to desert, as had Riley and others. The "West Pointers'... often ... harsh and tyrannical natures," a Mexican general claimed, would prod 1,500 Irishmen to abandon Taylor's army.[9]

Outnumbering the Americans, dismissing them as "citizen-soldiers," not professionals, and buoyed by European experts' harsh critique of the Americans, the Mexicans expected to teach the gringos a hard lesson. Experts knew that "the Mexican soldier could be a very hard man when he geared his mind to the task."[10] And repulsing the invasion of the Protestant *hereticos* was a question of national honor from the Rio Grande to Mexico City.

As Riley watched both the Mexican cavalry charging on open ground in view of Americans gathering wood and brush and Ampudia's infantry marching in review, he knew that he wanted no part in either of those branches of the Mexican army. He convinced his superiors to let him serve in the artillery. When he broached the notion of forming other deserters into a company of gunners, the Mexicans eagerly assented.

Riley's choice, versed not only in his skills with cannon, was a shrewd one. In the infantry or the cavalry, he would have been just another junior officer among many. But in the artillery he could operate with a far greater degree of autonomy as a battery commander. He had also identified the branch of the Mexican army in the sorest need of help.

Foreign military experts believed that the Mexican army had long ignored the use of modern fieldpieces and tactics. President Paredes had begun to revamp the artillery, and at Matamoros some of the brass ordnance, as Riley learned, was in excellent shape, though a little honey-combed, or worn. The bulk, however, were relics of the 1820s or earlier, loud but packing inadequate punch. The Mexican gunners' grapeshot, the lethal metal bits essential to rake enemy infantry, was of such infe-rior quality that its range was too short.

The major problem for the Mexican batteries at Matamoros lay in the low weight of their shot: their biggest cannons were 12-pounders. One glance by Riley at the nine-foot earthen walls of Fort Texas confirmed that the Mexican roundshot could not penetrate them. And the bomb-proof shelters Mansfield's men had constructed would likely hold against the Mexicans' two siege mortars. Unless their batteries could silence Taylor's four 18-pounders, well-protected in the bastion, Matamoros lay defenseless beneath them.

Another fact discovered by Riley came with the Mexican artillery's reliance upon hired ox drivers and muleteers to lug cannons, their anti-quated Gribeauval carriages, and ammunition. During action, the dri-vers, oblivious to or ignorant of gunnery drill and tactics, generally moved the cannons twice—onto the battlefield and off of it. The maneu-vers of the Americans' flying batteries or even the ponderous but proven deployment of European batteries in battle lay far beyond Mexico's civil-ian teamsters.

Despite the Mexican artillery's lack of mobility, their gunners fired their emplaced cannons with deadly effect.

In John Riley, the Mexicans gained a soldier chafing not only to prove his worth to his new commanders, but also to pit his hard-earned gun-nery skills against those of the cocky West Pointers commanding the flying batteries. He gathered John Little, James Mills, John Murphy, and the gargantuan Thomas Riley, all except Mills born in Ireland, and con-vinced them to become gunners. Although Little had been a dragoon and the others foot soldiers in the U.S. Army, they seized the chance to man fieldpieces rather than serve as nameless, faceless cannon fodder in the Mexican infantry. Riley's recruits may have also attended British bat-teries, as had their new leader, for many men who had logged their Irish birthplaces on U.S. enlistment papers had served in the Royal Artillery.

In full sight of the Americans, Riley put his men through the tradi-tional paces of 19th-century artillerymen. His crews clambered around several brass muzzleloaders, rushed in front of their guns, rammed powder and shot down the barrels, leaped aside as the guns boomed at their practice targets and recoiled, and dashed back to swab the sizzling barrels and reload. Riley and his fellow veterans knew that once war began, artillery crews ranked only below officers as snipers' choice targets. Still, more deserters signed on with Riley. Of his first recruits, he wrote: "At Matamoros, I formed a company of forty-eight Irishmen."[11]

9

"An Immense Sensation"

Riley and his company trained hurriedly, for events along the Rio Grande took a bloody turn. On April 17 or 18, 1846, Lieutenant Theodoric Porter, a friend of Grant in the 4th Infantry, led a patrol of ten soldiers in search of Colonel Cross the quartermaster, who had been missing since April 10th. That afternoon, the patrol walked into an ambush. Rancheros gunned down Porter and one of his men, and when the nine survivors staggered into camp with the news, Porter became the Americans' first hero of the war. Meade wrote that Porter "had made three of his enemies bite the dust before he fell" and had met "a soldier's fate in so gallant a manner" at the hands of a "cowardly" enemy.[1]

An American patrol searching for Cross stumbled upon his corpse three days later. He had been shot in the head by a ranchero. Outrage at the genial quartermaster's murder engulfed the officers. "I am sorry to tell you," Meade wrote to his father, "the remains of Colonel Cross have been found . . . foully assassinated by a party from the other side who were hovering around our camp." Meade, embracing a false rumor, charged that

> at the very time that General Ampudia replied to General Taylor's letter, denying any knowledge of his disappearance, it is now known that he [Ampudia] was wearing the watch of the unfortunate victim, and some other officers riding his [Cross's] horse. . . . This dastardly act and the mean

lie of the commanding-general on the other side, have inspired us all with a burning desire to avenge the Colonel's murder, and have destroyed all the sympathy that some few did still entertain for a people they deemed unjustly treated.[2]

On April 23, 1846, at 4:30 in the afternoon, a horse-drawn caisson drew Colonel Cross's coffin, draped in the Stars and Stripes and flanked by an honor guard, past silent American soldiers. A band piped the doleful notes of "The Dead March," and the procession halted in front of a grave overlooking Matamoros. A detail lifted the casket and lowered it with ropes into the grave as a bugler blew taps. Then, three musket volleys saluted Cross.

On the same day that somber volley cracked above the Rio Grande, President Paredes had declared a "defensive war." With orders to take command at Matamoros and engage Taylor, General Mariano Arista was only one day away, leading a host of reinforcements. He not only carried Paredes's war orders, but also a leaflet for Taylor's Irish and German soldiers.

On April 24, Arista sent General Anastasio Torrejon, whose foes in the army derided him as a man with "one excellent quality—the instinct of self-preservation"—and 1,600 cavalry, sappers, and light infantry splashing across the Rio Grande a few miles upstream from Taylor's camp.[3] Rumors that the Mexicans had crossed the river in force led Taylor to dispatch 63 dragoons under Captain Seth Thornton on reconnaissance. Thornton, "a slender, sickly Marylander always looking for danger," led his troopers upriver at a gallop, thirsting to duel Mexican rancheros or regulars alike.[4]

At 10:00 in the morning of April 24, church bells pealed and cheers burst from the plaza of Matamoros. As regimental bands blared, the Mexican troops paraded in review for their newly arrived leader, Arista. Ampudia, furious at his removal from command, could do nothing but salute—and plot his return to the top post in the Army of the North.

Taylor's new foe, 42-year-old Major General Mariano Arista, an enemy of the deposed Santa Anna, inspected the troops from horseback, the sun bringing a flush to the freckled visage of the red-haired commander. A stable, careful officer who enjoyed the trust of the common soldier, he had spent several years in exile in Florida and Cincinnati to escape Santa Anna. Arista had developed a liking for Americans and respected their aggressive energies. Unlike Ampudia and other high-ranking officers who scoffed at America's citizen army, Arista dismissed such confidence "as castles in the air." He did, however, believe that his army had reached a decent state of discipline and "could fight like devils when aroused." The Americans across the river had "aroused" them, and Arista, too, was spoiling for battle. But first, he intended to soften up his foe by employing Ampudia's tactic of April 2.[5]

Within hours of Arista's arrival, pamphlets turned up all over Taylor's camp. The leaflets posed an even more potent appeal to Taylor's immigrants than had Ampudia's tract:

> Soldiers! You have been enlisted in time of peace to serve in that army for a specific term, but your obligation never implied that you were bound to violate the laws of God, and the most sacred rights of friends! The United States government, contrary to the wishes of a majority of all honest and honorable Americans, has ordered you to take *forcible* possession of the territory of a *friendly* neighbor, who has never given her consent to such occupation. In other words, while the treaty of peace and commerce between Mexico and the United States is in full force, the United States, presuming on her strength and prosperity, and on our supposed imbecility and cowardice, attempts to make you the blind instruments of her unholy and mad ambition and *forces* you to appear as the hateful robbers of our dear homes, and the unprovoked violators of our dearest feelings as men and patriots. Such villainy and outrage I know are perfectly repugnant to the noble sentiments of any; and it is base and foul to rush you on to certain death, in order to aggrandize a few lawless individuals, in defiance of the laws of God and man! It is to no purpose if they tell you that the law for the annexation of Texas justifies your occupation of the Rio Bravo del Norte; for by this act they rob us of a great part of [territory] ... and it is barbarous to send a handful of men on such an errand against a powerful and war-like nation. Besides, the most of you are Europeans, and we are the *declared friends* of a majority of the nations of *Europe*. The North Americans are ambitious, overbearing, and insolent, as a nation, and they will only make use of you as vile tools to carry out their abominable plans of pillage and rapine. I warn you, in the name of justice, honor, and your own interests and self-respect, to abandon their desperate and unholy cause, and become *peaceful Mexican citizens.* I guaranty [sic] you, in such case, a half section of land, or 320 acres, to settle upon, gratis [free]. Be wise, then, and just and honorable, and take no part in murdering us who have no unkind feeling for you. Lands shall be given to officers, sergeants, and corporals according to rank, privates receiving 320 acres, as stated.

If in time of action you wish to espouse *our* cause, throw away your arms and run to us, we will embrace you as true friends and Christians.

It is not decent or prudent to say more. But should any of you render any important service to Mexico, you shall be accordingly considered and preferred.

Headquarters at Matamoros, April 20, 1846,

M. ARISTA[6]

Several romanticized accounts about John Riley claimed that he and several other Irish deserters donned their old American uniforms, swam back across the river, and sneaked the pamphlets into Taylor's camp.

On the evening of April 24, pickets and patrols ringed the camp at Taylor's order. The troops "slept on their arms," but few men actually closed their eyes for long.[7] For men like Rodmand Batchelor, bivouacked near the river, Arista's pamphlet appealed to a variety of emotions and experiences. His offer of 320 acres to even a private offered any land-hungry Irish immigrant *ownership* of his acreage. To men victimized by Ireland's oppressive tenant farm system, rack rents, callous, absentee landowners, remorseless estate agents, and brutal evictions in which families' cottages were "tumbled" by constables and British soldiers, ownership was a potent concept. Land and property meant everything in Ireland—particularly because few Catholics of the era had ever held them. Nativists would try to dismiss the lure of Mexican land offers to the Irish; however, such denials flew in the face of agrarian Ireland's history and culture.

Along with Arista's promise of land to deserters, his assurances of immediate citizenship and "friendship" for *Europeans* targeted Taylor's immigrant soldiers, men like Riley, years away from naturalization and generations away from true acceptance in America. And because "cigar-smoking . . . young officers . . . the would-be aristocrat specimens of equal rights" never let up on "shanty Irish" and "rather refined Germans," many immigrants took a long look at Matamoros.[8] Taylor's newest veterans had signed on for their five-year hitch with recruiters' assurances of solicitous officers and good treatment. On the banks of the Rio Grande, men choking down rancid beef and bacon, moldy hardtack, and "weak, unpalatable coffee" seasoned with the only available condiment—

vinegar—recalled recruiters' guarantees of "good and wholesome diet."

Foreign veterans could handle privations in diet and camp conditions with the professional soldier's good-natured gripes and general stoicism. But the relentless abuse of Nativist officers was a different matter. An immigrant artilleryman and British army veteran wrote: "[Desertion] was . . . occasioned by the foolish and tyrannical conduct of a number of the young officers in the American service, who abused their authority greatly, and who were never sufficiently checked by the senior officers of the service."[9]

Mick Maloney, with his stripes, his citizenship, and his ten years in infantry blue, could shrug off the entreaties of the Mexicans and had learned to endure the invective of Nativist officers. But as another immigrant noted:

> The various degrading modes of punishment often inflicted by young, headstrong, and inconsiderate officers in their zeal to discipline for the most unimportant offenses were exceedingly galling to the fiery, untamable spirit of the sons of the Green Isle [Ireland]. And I have not the slightest doubt that those barbarous modes of punishment in common adoption, and the want of sympathy generally existing between the officers and their men, were the principal causes in the majority of these cases of desertion which were so lamentably frequent.[10]

On the eve of battle, Irishman Mick Ryan would say of his officers, "Is it the night before a fight, by the holy fist of the blessed Saint Patrick, the mean schaming [sic] villains that are so ready to ill use a poor devil at other times are might kind an' civil." On the evening of April 24–25, "the near prospect of war" loomed.[11] For many immigrants in the U.S. Army, so did the concern about their officers, their loyalties, and their own self-interests.

While immigrants in camp slept or perused the latest Mexican leaflet that night, Thornton and his dragoons cantered double file some 15 miles upstream. To the column's left, the first pink rays of sunrise revealed a huge field surrounded on three sides by a high picket fence. Perched on the riverbank stood several haciendas.

Thornton raised his gloved hand and barked the order to halt. All night the dragoons had ridden but had detected no sign of Mexican regulars. Hoping that civilians in those haciendas might be cajoled or bullied into revealing their army's whereabouts, Thornton ordered his riders forward and led his entire command through a draw-bar gateway, the only entrance and exit to the ranch.[12]

The dragoons tore across wide open prairie to the adobe houses. Thornton bawled the order to dismount and dispatched several long-haired, dust-covered troopers with drawn sabers and pistols to roust the inhabitants from their homes.

While most of the dragoons lit up cigars, swigged from canteens, or nibbled on hardtack, the search party prodded several shaking men, women, and children in front of Thornton. The gaunt captain, who, several years before, had survived the explosion of the steamer *Pulaski* off North Carolina; had hauled several women and children to one of the few, overcrowded lifeboats; had lashed himself to a hencoop; and had been rescued "a raving maniac" three days later, softened a bit at the civilians' fright.

Suddenly shouts erupted to his rear. The dragoons snatched up their carbines and crouched alongside their mounts.

The shakos of Mexican regulars popped up above the picket fence. Musket barrels and cavalry *escopetas* peered everywhere between the spaced posts, and several soldiers barred the gate from the outside.

"There was but a moment for reflection"—Thornton ordered his bugler to sound "To Horse" and the dragoons leaped into their saddles.[13] At Thornton's signal the bugler blared the charge. The troopers thundered toward the gate.

The Mexicans, in "overwhelming numbers," waited, holding their fire for the moment when not even their untrustworthy old Brown Bess muskets could miss.[14] The dragoons came on, and when their bearded, dusty faces were visible down the muskets' barrels, a deafening volley crashed into the cavalrymen from three sides. Riders including Thornton were blown from their saddles, and their screams mingled with the shrieks of horses. The Mexicans blasted away and cut down the surrounded dragoons "like fish in a barrel." Barely able to see through the dense smoke, Captain William Hardee ordered them to ride for the river. They wheeled to the rear and dashed past the haciendas as musket balls whizzed from the rear and sides. Several more men toppled from their saddles.

Hardee realized they could not reach the river alive. A white handkerchief went up, and the Mexican fire slackened, then stopped.

Within the enclosure, 14 dragoons lay dead. Among them was an up-and-coming, "valuable officer, Lieutenant Mason." [15] Other dragoons had been seriously hit; Thornton lay unconscious from his fall from the saddle.

With no idea of what awaited them, 47 survivors were helpless as the enemy swarmed around them.

At reveille on April 25, Thornton's Mexican scout rode into Taylor's camp and delivered the news of the ambush.

"It was the first blood shed in the Mexican War," wrote Lieutenant George Deas. "And it created an immense sensation in the United States." [16]

The next day, April 26, 1846, Taylor sent a terse communiqué to Washington: "Hostilities may now be considered as commenced." [17]

The *Washington Union* broke the news of the melee that very night: "American Blood Has Been Shed on American Soil!" [18]

Before word of Thornton's disaster stirred up "an immense sensation" in Washington, Taylor's earlier dispatch describing the shootings of Privates Gross and Lamb as they had deserted ignited a political firestorm. In Congress, legislators demanded that Polk and Secretary Marcy clarify whether the nation was at war or not. Expresident John Quincy Adams stood in the speaker's well of the House and blasted Polk and Taylor. Adams introduced a resolution "that the President of the United States be requested to inform this House whether any soldier or soldiers in the army of the United States have been shot for desertion or in the act of desertion, and if so, by whose order." [19]

Adams and a small, strident band of congressmen united in their Abolitionism and opposition to war on the Rio Grande painted the two deserters' deaths as government-sanctioned murders. Under the Articles of War, Taylor had no authority to shoot deserters, the politicians shouted. They were correct, but Polk and Marcy, who both anticipated full-scale war at any moment, stonewalled Adams, refusing to answer his charges, relying upon the American people to respond with patriotic fervor once the conflict began and to dismiss Adams's opposition.

Like Adams, a small number of Taylor's officers, Whigs and Abolitionists, were opposed to the onrushing conflict. Northerners and Midwesterners for the most part, they agreed with Boston writer James Russell Lowell's charge that war with Mexico was the aim of the South, "them nigger-driven states."

"They just want this Californy, So's to lug new slave-states in," he charged.[20]

From the Rio Grande, Sam Grant wrote that the war would prove "the most unjust thing that ever was."[21] Hitchcock and other officers voiced similar sentiments. Captain George Deas opined: "No consideration was given to the fact that the march of the American Army to the banks of the Rio Grande was, of itself, an act of hostility. To be sure, that boundary had been claimed by the United States, by sustaining the pretension of Texas to the same effect. But how unjust."[22]

Personal qualms aside, Deas, Hitchcock, Grant, and all of their brother officers would carry out their orders and duties to the letter. Most were about to "see the elephant"—battle—for the first time. Major Philip N. Barbour wrote a letter reflecting both the bluster and the fear gripping the troops after Thornton's debacle:

> In a military point of view, General Taylor has committed a blunder, I think, in coming here with so small a force; although I do not apprehend we can be whipped by the Mexican force now on this frontier, yet it is but reasonable to expect that their people will rush in to defend their own fire-sides, and they might raise an army of 10,000 men in a short time, while we are cut off, not only from retreat, but from all succor. Considering this, it is truly surprising to see with what indifference, not to say contempt, our Officers and men look upon the Mexican batteries frowning upon us. No one seems to think a disaster to our Army is possible, and most in the Army are impatient and disappointed that General Taylor does not create a pretext for taking the town.[23]

For most officers, Thornton's clash with the Mexicans demanded retaliation. Although the dragoon captain had sent back word of "the courtesy and kindness which Arista and even Ampudia lavished upon them" and although the Mexicans had "sent an ambulance to the [U.S.] camp with some of Thornton's wounded soldiers," the courtesies masked nothing.[24] "The matter was very plain," Deas wrote. "A fight must follow; but *where* and *when* were the question. Had we strength enough to combat the large Mexican Army that we knew was around us. . . . we could have wished for a few more regiments."[25]

Deas's aside that "there was no one to be depended upon" unwittingly described the ongoing desertions as April 1846 ended. At least 200 men swam the river, American officers and enlisted men declaring that the majority of these deserters were Irish, along with many Germans. An immigrant private flatly stated that "the cause commonly assigned by the officers for their [Irish] desertion was that they were fighting against their religion by fighting the Mexicans. . . . There was truth in that statement."[26]

On the afternoon of May 1, 1846, desertions abated for the moment because Taylor's army struck its tents, hitched the oxen to its 300 wagons, formed ranks, and streamed back down the track toward Point Isabel. Rumors of a Mexican attack on Taylor's supply depot had reached the general.

The 500 men of the 7th Infantry and Braxton Bragg's gunners lined the ramparts of Fort Texas as their comrades tramped from sight. Taylor had ordered the 7th's commander, 58-year-old Major Jacob Brown, to hold the bastion until the army's return, leaving the garrison two weeks' worth of food and ammunition.

Brown's weather-burnished features and gray-tinged hair testified to his 30 years in the field, a career in which he had risen from a private's stripes to a major's oak leaves through courage in frontier action and attention to duty. He had spent his entire career in the 7th, arguably the army's most vaunted regiment, nicknamed the "Cotton Balers" for their valor during the Battle of New Orleans in the War of 1812. Now, however, so many foreign-born recruits filled his companies that the Mexicans expected them to desert en masse or to surrender quickly.

Brown knew that he could rely on Captain Mansfield, left behind by Taylor to oversee any on-the-spot repairs of damage to the fort from Mexican cannons. Mansfield had crafted its nine-foot-walls—15 feet thick at their base—to stand up to 12-pounder cannons.

A brilliant engineer who had graduated second in his West Point class in 1822 and who was noted for wrinkling his brow and rubbing his chin as he pondered every detail of his designs, Mansfield had never laid out a more vital site. Now, as he surveyed the dirt walls, their six redans, and the eight-foot-deep moat surrounding the fort, he could only hope that the Mexicans were not rolling heavier guns into range. Nor could he predict how long his earthworks would hold.

Also left behind, Lieutenant Braxton Bragg inspected his three gleaming six-pounders and mortar, taking the range of the Mexican batteries around Matamoros. For him, the shooting could not start fast enough.

Soon, only distant dust to the east marked their comrades' march. Slowly, the cloud dissipated, the empty campground the sole trace of 2,500 men.

Another cloud of dust rose across the river, to the southeast, on May 1. Arista's army was on the move.

Brown's men spent a long, sleepless night peering at the Mexican guns and calming the laundresses and other camp followers who had stayed. On the morning of May 2, the batteries remained silent. Lookouts trained brass field telescopes on the Mexican positions all day, but the only smoke rising above the cannons swirled from gun crews' pipes and cigars.

As a glorious sunset's last flare cast a golden glow across Matamoros's stucco and adobe walls, American sentries called out a sudden alert. Bragg's men bustled about their six-pounders, and crews scrambled to the four giant 18-pounders trained on the town's red-tiled roofs. Soldiers and the women dashed into Mansfield's bomb shelters.

From Matamoros's main plaza, a column of men framed in torchlight paraded toward the Mexican batteries. Incense spewed from braziers that several marchers swung and wafted across Fort Texas. Several long crucifixes swayed above the procession, and as it reached the first Mexican battery, the artillerymen removed their shakos and knelt. Clad in white vestments, the line of priests blessed each soldier and sprinkled holy water across each muzzle. Slowly, they filed from battery to battery, repeating the ritual.

Alongside their cannons, Lieutenant John Riley and his Irishmen awaited their benediction.

10

"To Draw the Claret"

JOHN RILEY PEERED through the darkness at Fort Texas. He and the other men in the Mexican redoubts on May 3, 1846, looked for the first tinge of sunrise.

As the gray streaks crept across the horizon, Arista's artillerymen rammed roundshot down their muzzleloaders. The lanyards were ready, quivering in a westerly breeze that drifted from the river.

At 5:00 in the morning, officers leveled swords at Fort Texas and cried: *"Fuego!"* Up to 30 cannons belched and recoiled as gunners jumped aside. Roundshot screeched across the Rio Grande and slammed against the walls and bomb shelters of the American fort.

The men of the 7th and the ten camp followers hugged the trembling ground. Again and again the Mexicans and Riley's crew swabbed their cannons—the brass muzzles heated up with each blast—reloaded, and pounded away at Mansfield's walls. Dust and debris soon covered the huddling Americans, many covering their ears against "the singular and diabolically horrific sound which a large shell makes when passing a short distance." An ex-British soldier recalled: "There is no earthly sound bearing the slightest resemblance to its [a shell's] monstrous dissonance; the shrillest screech of the railway whistle or the most emphatic demonstration of an asthmatic locomotive would seem like a strain of heavenly melody by comparison."[1]

Shells rained upon the bastion from three directions, embedding themselves into the walls or ricocheting across the roofs of the shelters. Bragg and his men crawled to their guns, stood hunchbacked behind the parapets, and reached for ramrods and roundshot. Within minutes the Americans' six-pounders hurled balls at the closest Mexican battery. The deep-throated crashes of the 18-pounders soon joined in and shattered two Mexican fieldpieces and their crews within a half hour.

While the Americans' four heavy cannons kept firing, Bragg realized that his smaller guns did not have the range to hit the Mexicans' farthest emplacements. He ordered his crews to halt to save precious ammunition and sent them scrambling for the bomb shelters. He remained with the 18-pounders, exposing himself to Mexican metal as he strode from gun to gun, checking and adjusting the range, impressing even gunners who loathed him—most of his men—with his utter coolness under fire. The West Pointer had seen action in the Seminole War but had never faced an enemy's batteries.

After several hours of Mexican bombardment, Brown ordered his artillerymen to set Matamoros ablaze. The gunners heated balls in a furnace, and the 18-pounders hurled the "hot shot" until 11:00 that night, three and a half hours after the Mexican guns ceased fire. As the Americans' shells tore through tiles, brick, and mortar, the Mexican stone did not ignite—the gunners had been unable to heat the shells to a high enough temperature. Casualties in Matamoros proved light, as most of the townspeople had fled.

Although the Mexicans' 14 ½-hour bombardment had wounded a handful, it had killed none. Major Brown believed that no Mexican assault upon the fort would come if all their cannons could do was to kick up a lot of dust. At the end of May 3, Brown's greatest concerns were how well his men would stand up mentally beneath the next day's bombardment and the days following. Even the 3rd's Captain Henry, a man of marked bravery, wondered if he could have coped with the endless hours of Mexican metal to come, writing that he "would rather have fought twenty battles" than duck and pray as the shells screeched, the earth ceilings of the bomb shelters shuddered, and the ground quaked.[2] And even though Mansfield's fort had stood up to the 12-pounders, the surrounded American garrison did not know whether the Mexicans were wheeling 18- or 24-pounders into range in the predawn hours of May 4, which echoed with the rings of Mexican shovels, officers' shouts, and the creaking of artillery caissons with their bellowing ox teams. The din sounded closer shortly before dawn. Sweating and grunting to emplace a battery, John Riley and the deserters had returned to the opposite bank of the Rio Grande.

At 5:00 in the morning on May 3, 1846, the Mexican artillery's first blast at Fort Texas had rumbled "like distant thunder" down the Rio Grande to Point Isabel.[3] Taylor's troops spilled from their tents along the Gulf. Ulysses S. Grant and other young men wondered whether the din heralded a storm. One look at the faces of European veterans turned toward Matamoros, including some who had served under Wellington or Napoleon, unnerved comrades who had yet "to see the elephant."

"This was the cannonade and bombardment of Fort [Texas]," a nervous Lieutenant George Deas commented.[4]

A young lieutenant wrote to his wife that the bone-jarring thuds of the cannons to the west "made me sorry I enlisted."[5] His name was Ulysses S. Grant.

Several thousand volunteers from Louisiana and other states along the Mississippi were boarding steamers to Point Isabel, but Taylor could not wait for them. He also could not accede to staffers' urgings that he march back immediately to Matamoros. Not only were the troops still exhausted from their forced march to the Gulf, but Old Rough and Ready also needed several days to complete earthworks to protect the depot, Fort Polk, from an attack by Arista. A captain wrote: "The hope was that Fort [Texas] would hold out."[6]

Worried about Brown's plight, Taylor sent Captain Samuel Walker and 17 of his Texas Rangers toward the besieged fort. As the thin, hunch-shouldered Walker, whose mild blue eyes belied his ruthlessness and daring, galloped at the head of his band up the coastal road, he was seething from a reconnaissance gone wrong on the evening of April 29. Rancheros had bushwacked the Texans and gunned down ten, leaving Walker only the 17 scouts. Nothing, he vowed, would prevent him from reaching Fort Texas, speaking with Brown, and riding around or through Mexican lines back to Taylor.

As Taylor's men toiled in round-the-clock shifts to finish Fort Polk, they worried about sketchy intelligence "that Arista's men were vastly superior to ourselves, especially in cavalry." They wondered whether the 7th could hold out. Most of all, men like Grant, "who had never heard a hostile gun before," wrestled with the quiet fears of death, maiming, or cowardice common to soldiers since the dawn of warfare. Many affected the jauntiness of George Deas, who assessed: "The men were in splendid condition. Hardy, strong, and admirably drilled, they presented a force fully equal to every reasonable emergency." But even he acknowledged that "few persons in the Army"—except various immigrants and American veterans of 1812 and the Indian wars—"had ever before been under fire, so that the sensation had a peculiar charm of novelty." "Here," Deas admitted, "was anxiety." [7]

Tensions rose further among Deas and the troops at the Gulf with the first distant rumbles of Mexican cannons early on May 4. As Brown's gunners loaded their 18-pounders to return fire, they had discovered the source of the previous night's noises: the Mexicans had thrown up a redoubt on the American side of the river. A battery of 12-pounders hammered away from a mere several hundred yards to the northwest, increasing the impact of their shot.

As Brown's gunners returned fire, their eyes, sore and scarlet from the previous day's smoke, burned anew with each blast. Suffering equally were the Mexican artillerymen in that nearest battery. Bragg and a few other officers trained their telescopes on the Mexican 12-pounders to take the range and squinted through the grayish-white haze. The officers gaped at the faces of several enemy gunners. Flinging shot from the glowing brass muzzles and swabbing the smoking guns before each blast, John Riley and "some of our deserters were employed against us," Taylor would record, "and actually served guns in the cannonade and bombardment of Fort [Texas]." [8]

To the rank and file of the garrison, the news that men who had eaten, drilled, laughed, and suffered with them at Kinney's Ranch now manned Mexican guns spread quickly. Rage filled most, but others who huddled in the shelters, which shook from the deserters' fire, felt otherwise.

Privates Dennis Conahan, Martin Lydon, James Spears, Auguste Morstadt, and many other immigrants in the fort were among them.

Riley matter-of-factly stated about the bombardment: "I participated in the action at Matamoros with 48 Irishmen."[9]

With the cannonade ebbing in the evening of May 4, Samuel Walker crawled through the dry moat surrounding the fort, clambered up to the walls, and hailed the guards. Fortunate that a sentry had not shot him, he was greeted by and taken by back-slapping guards to Major Brown; the Texas Ranger spun the officer an incredible but true tale of how Walker had found Arista's entire army blocking the road to the fort, had left the Rangers hidden, and had sneaked alone past the whole enemy force. Taylor would march soon, the Texan assured Brown, but needed another few days to secure the army's supply lines. Walker asked him whether the garrison could hold out that long. The bull-necked major, his face caked with dust and sweat, guaranteed his command would not fall. Walker immediately left the besieged fort, sneaked past the Mexicans a second time, rejoined his men, and galloped "hell bent for leather" to deliver Brown's message to Old Rough and Ready.

By 10:00 in the morning of May 6, the Mexicans had been pounding the fort since dawn. A shell streaked into the bastion and tore into Major Brown as he inspected his defenses. His stunned aide, Captain Edgar S. Hawkins, took command; Brown died three days later.

At 4:30 in the afternoon, the enemy batteries fell silent. American sentries expecting Mexican infantry to mass with scaling ladders saw nothing for a long moment. Then, several Mexican officers carrying a flag of parley rode from the northern redoubt and galloped up to the American moat. The 7th and their camp followers rushed from the shelters to watch. The Mexicans demanded that the garrison surrender; Hawkins tersely refused. They galloped back to the redoubt, and moments later the Mexican guns opened up again as the defenders ducked back into their shelters and again wondered when Taylor would march.

The defenders of Fort Texas were not the only ones awaiting Old Rough and Ready. While Riley and Arista's other gunners bombarded the 7th early on May 8, 1846, the Mexican commander marched 2,100 infantry and 1,600 cavalry to a site called Palo Alto, "tall timbers," directly in Taylor's anticipated line of march on the coastal road. On the same morning, 2,200 American soldiers tramped in the heat along that very route from Point Isabel; their march to relieve Fort Texas had begun the previous afternoon.

The echoes of the barrage enveloping Fort Texas grew louder with each mile covered. Tormented by sun and thirst, coughing in clouds of dust, sweat soaking their wool jackets, the sky-blue columns marched 16 miles. Then, some nine miles from Matamoros, "just after two in the afternoon," the army slowed and stopped. Arrayed in line of battle two miles ahead stood the Mexican army. In a popular American army phrase of the day, the moment "to draw the claret"—to shed blood—loomed.

Shoulder-high grass and flowers carpeted the plain between the armies, and shallow water holes dotted the ground. Behind the Mexicans rose the stand of oak trees that gave the spot its name. Arista's columns stretched in an east-west line for more than a mile, cavalry on the flanks and 12 brass fieldpieces spaced along the line.

As the Mexicans held their fire, two young American engineers, Jacob Blake and Lloyd Tilghman, cantered between the armies and, less than a hundred yards from the Mexicans, leisurely conducted a reconnaissance of Arista's entire line and rode back with their report to Taylor. Clad in his familiar palmetto hat and leaning forward atop Old Whitey, Taylor deployed the 5th Infantry on his right flank. Next in line, from right to left, he placed Ringgold's flying battery, the 3d Infantry, two 18-pounders nicknamed the "Bull Battery," the 4th Infantry, Duncan's battery, and a battalion of foot artillery and the 8th Infantry on the left flank. Taylor parked the wagons behind his line, his dragoons covering the supply train. To the Mexicans' amazement, the flying batteries of Ringgold and Duncan unlimbered and loaded in less than a minute.

Shortly before 2:30, Arista, ramrod straight in his saddle, his medals flashing, rode from one end of his line to the other, exhorting his troops to hurl back the "gringos." A Mexican officer wrote: "Banners floated to the wind, the soldiers stood to their arms, the horses pawed the ground, the bands played, and shouts of 'Viva la Republica!' filled the air." [10]

European observers to the rear of Arista's line expected his men to overwhelm the outnumbered Americans. Blasting away upstream at Fort Texas, John Riley anticipated Mexican victory—a short war with rank and land awaiting him for his part in Arista's triumph.

As the Mexicans' "vivas" swept across the chaparral, Taylor sent one platoon from every company to fill the army's canteens before the battle. With shaking hands, many of Taylor's men swigged from their canteens. For some, it proved the last time.

Flying battery officer Samuel French recalled that, on Taylor's command, the American drummer boys "sounded the long roll, hearts beat, pulses kept time, and knees trembled and would not be still."[11] The infantry fixed bayonets with a metallic rattle. The Mexicans waited. They "stood, ready to receive us, the bright sun lighting up their gay caparisons [saddle blankets and trappings], their horses neighing, penons fluttering. . . . They presented a most formidable obstacle to our advance."[12]

Taylor sent his infantry forward. Trampling the high grass, the foot soldiers pushed across the plain. They squinted from the light flashing from the Mexicans' brass fieldpieces, bayonets, and cavalry lances. Sergeant Major Mick Maloney, marching with his company in the 3d, had tasted battle against the Seminoles; but those campaigns of hit-and-run warfare had provided little training for the classic set-piece battle looming now. Like his rankest recruits, the tough Irish noncom had never marched at the muzzles of cannons nor had he faced the leveled lances of a cavalry charge. Graybeards who had served in the Napoleonic Wars encouraged their comrades to remain steady.

Seven hundred yards from the Mexicans, Taylor's columns halted. Ringgold and Duncan's six-pounders rattled just ahead of the infantry, and the gunners loaded their muzzles with canister shot, deadly bits of lead designed to cut down massed men.

A cannon boomed. Mexicans would claim Taylor's batteries fired first, but the Americans contended that "the first gun was fired . . . from the Mexican right and taking effect upon our left."[13]

Both armies' cannons erupted. Mexican grapeshot fell just short, and, while some of their roundshot reached the Americans and shattered a six-pounder and crew, most landed in front of Taylor's men, who side-stepped ricocheting balls. Some soldiers criticized Mexican marksmanship, but inferior ammunition was the real problem for Arista's cannon crews.

With Lieutenant Churchill's Bull Battery joining in, the American cannons "tore a perfect road through the Mexicans," who nonetheless held their positions as their artillery futilely tried to take out the flying

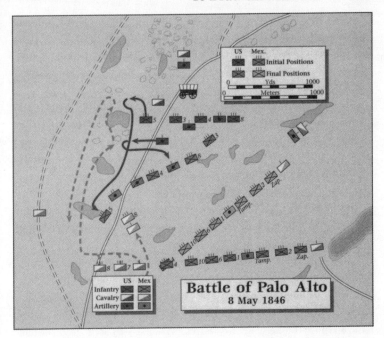

Battle of Palo Alto
8 May 1846

batteries.[14] Ringgold and Duncan's return fire was "so rapid ... that it seemed like exaggerated musketry."[15] Taylor, Arista, European observers, Napoleonic veterans—no one had ever seen horse artillery so mobile and so lethal.

Just after 3:00 in the afternoon, as the flying batteries' onslaught mounted, Taylor spotted "the whole of the Mexican left ... composed of Cavalry and two cannons," sweeping in a wide arc toward his right. If they turned his flank, the Mexicans could swoop down on his wagons and encircle his infantry. He rushed the 5th and 3d to meet the Mexican thrust.

The 5th raced 300 yards to the rear as the 3d moved even farther back to guard the wagons. John Riley's former unit, Company K, with a precision hammered home on the parade ground of Kinney's Ranch, formed a defensive square with the rest of the regiment. As Captain Moses E. Merrill stood with his men, throats constricted and fingers clenched flintlocks at the spectacle descending upon them.

"On came the Mexican cavalry in splendid order." The colorful riders formed a wide column, dipped their lances, and moved slowly forward several lines deep. The men of the 5th, "expecting, by the show of such superior numbers, to be entirely enveloped," took aim. Behind Merrill and the 5th, the soldiers of the 3d also formed a square, bracing themselves for those flashing lances.

The first line of Mexican cavalry suddenly stopped, drew their escopetas, snapped off a volley, and galloped to the rear of the pack. The second line rode forward a short distance, fired, and wheeled to the back. Each line repeating the tactic, "these gallant horsemen" advanced "to the surprise of all [the Americans] in this peculiar manner." Several men of the 5th crumpled, dead or wounded.

Merrill and the regiment's other officers shouted for the men to hold their fire. The Mexicans closed the gap, one volley after another raking the front of the square.

When the riders approached point-blank range, holstered their escopetas, and reached for their glittering six-foot lances, the order to fire swept through the square. The 5th's muskets cracked, and lancers toppled from their saddles. As the 5th unleashed one withering volley after another, the head of the Mexican column was sent "into serious confusion." Still, they did not break; instead, they unhitched two cannon and opened up on the square.

Captain Ridgely galloped up with two six-pounders and crews and, "coming instantly into Battery," pumped blasts of "spherical case-shot" into the lancers. Shredded by the metal shards and hampered by their own artillery's inaccuracy, the lancers' bugles sounded the retreat. "Amazing the Americans with their deliberate, orderly withdrawal," Torrejon's cavalry turned back to Arista's line. The flying battery had saved Taylor's flank and his wagons.

Late in the afternoon, a grass fire ignited by a flaming wad from one of Duncan's guns swept the plain and briefly forced the armies to disengage. Both Taylor and Arista used the billowing smoke to conceal flanking movements, and, as the smoke lifted, the left flanks of both armies fell under assault. The flying batteries and the Bull Battery once again shattered a Mexican foray, of infantry this time; Arista's artillery finally found the range and chased off a flank attack by Taylor's dragoons.

At 7:00 in the evening, the firing stopped. As night came, the groans of the wounded rose everywhere. Although up to 500 dead and wounded Mexicans littered the grass and water holes of Palo Alto, and only 55 Americans, Taylor had lost the irreplaceable Brevet Major Ringgold, whose flying batteries had been the day's decisive factor. With both legs mangled by a Mexican cannonball, the brilliant artilleryman bled to death over the next three days.

Both armies slept on their arms at the edges of the battlefield that night. Despite the far heavier Mexican losses, few American officers viewed Palo Alto as a bona fide victory. They had survived their first encounter with "the elephant" but realized the Mexicans were far from beaten. Deas wrote: "The close of day found both Armies on the field of battle. Neither had retreated."[16]

At Matamoros, John Riley and Fort Texas's besiegers had heard the din downstream but knew little of the battle except rumors of a second engagement to come.

With the "sinister splendor" of the still-burning grass fire flickering less than ten miles away, Riley and the artillerymen knew only their orders: to resume the bombardment at dawn.[17]

Early on May 9, Arista withdrew from Palo Alto and moved his troops five miles upstream to Resaca de la Palma, still between Taylor's army and Fort Texas. Having witnessed the deadly accuracy of the American artillery, Arista chose a sound strategy: he would fight behind cover to negate the flying batteries' toll upon troops massed in the open.

In the *resaca*, Arista selected a superb defensive position. He deployed his infantry in a three- to four-foot-deep, 200-foot-wide dry riverbed lined with shrubs, thorn bushes, and small trees; pools of brackish water dotted the ground that the Americans would have to cross. He employed his artillery to sweep the coastal road.

The American regiments moved along the road, which shook from the barrage against Fort Texas, now only three miles away. Around 2:30 in the afternoon, skirmishers spotted the entrenched Mexicans, and a half hour later Taylor's main columns arrived on the scene. The American artillerymen stripped off their shirts in the heat and rolled the guns forward while Taylor sent his infantry crawling into the dense thickets.

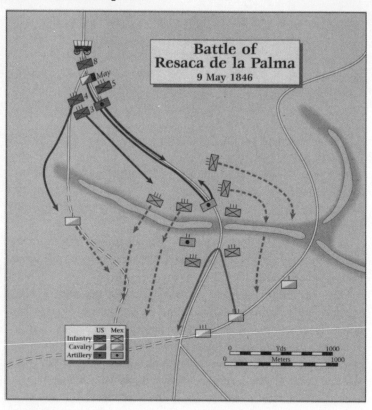

Mick Maloney, gashed by thorns, able to see but a few feet ahead in the brush, led his men toward the hidden riverbed. Mexican muskets opened fire at point-blank range, but Maloney and his howling troops kept coming and tumbled into the *resaca*. All along the riverbed, other American companies repeated the scene, men becoming separated from their comrades in the bush. Hand-to-hand melees swirled through the depression, bayonets and swords lunging, screams and curses mingling with the cracks of pistols and muskets.

With fellow Irishmen and Seminole War veterans Corporals Farrel and McFarlen and six privates, Maloney stumbled into a throng of Mexicans in the riverbed. The sergeant major and his men cut their way to a cannon and chased off the crew. Later, in his official report, Taylor would note that the Irishman and his band had captured a gun defended by 150 Mexicans.

Along the coastal road, Arista's artillery raked the advancing Americans. When Ridgely's six-pounders failed to dislodge the roaring Mexican guns, dragoons under Captain Charles May, a rugged Kentuckian with flowing black hair and a beard to match, charged the Mexican batteries. Arista's gunners scattered the yelling, saber-wielding riders, but, before retreating, May and his men captured General Rómolo Díaz de la Vega, Arista's chief of battlefield operations and a fine artillerist.

May's wild foray bought the 5th Infantry time to inch closer to the Mexican batteries and to rush them. The cannons poured grapeshot at the infantrymen, and scores writhed on the ground or lay limp as their comrades pressed forward. Joined by the 8th Infantry, which surged straight up the road, the 5th spilled into the Mexican emplacements, routed the gunners, and turned eight cannons on the fleeing artillerymen.

On Arista's left flank, the 4th U.S. Infantry lit upon a narrow path winding south to the Rio Grande. Crouching, expecting any second to walk into Mexican fire, the 4th kept moving—and realized no one guarded the path. They quickened their pace and broke into the Mexican rear, where kettles of beans were simmering atop the cooking fires of Arista's camp.

As Arista's men in the *resaca* heard the gunfire to their rear and realized that they had been flanked, pockets of defenders tossed down their weapons, climbed out of the riverbed, and raced toward the Rio Grande. At several points along Arista's line, Taylor's infantry, sensing victory, swarmed over the Mexicans, bayoneting men all over the *resaca*. Arista's army, which had fought so bravely and so well throughout the afternoon, buckled. By 5:00 in the afternoon they were fleeing "all pell mell" to the river and left the *resaca* "strewed with their dead and wounded . . . ghastly evidence of the fierce fighting." Taylor, from start to finish, had watched from atop Old Whitey, "as calm as if at a tea party."[18]

From the ramparts of Fort Texas, cheers rose. In the batteries encircling the fort, Riley and the artillerymen could only gape as thousands of Mexican soldiers surged down the road toward them, fled past the fort and the redoubt where Riley and his deserters stood, and clotted the riverbank. The scarcity of boats at the river's edge panicked the troops;

hundreds dove into the swift current and thrashed toward the town, many drowning. Several boats foundered from the weight of too many men and horses. A priest aboard one flatboat held up his crucifix as the churning waters forced him under.

At the first glimpse of blue-clad Yankees up the road, Riley and the men in the redoubt abandoned their cannons and bolted into the chaos on the riverbank. Better that, they knew, than capture by their former army.

11

"The Spread of This Contagion"

ON MAY 13, 1846, the United States Congress declared war on Mexico. Only John Quincy Adams and 13 other congressmen, all hard-core Abolitionists viewing the conflict as the work of expansionist slave-owners, voted against it. The politicians authorized the War Department to raise the regular army to 17,800 and called for 17 volunteer, or militia, regiments: 13,208 men.

Five days after the declaration of war, Taylor led his troops across the Rio Grande, occupied Matamoros, and began to plan a thrust into Mexico's interior.

Arista's army had abandoned the town the previous afternoon, the courtly Mexican having failed to wrangle a temporary truce from Taylor. Stretched out in thin columns several miles long, nearly 4,000 soldiers and 1,000 civilians and assorted camp followers shuffled ten miles upriver. Then, officers ordered all unnecessary baggage—except their own belongings—cast aside by the troops. Along the riverbank, Taylor's scouts would find heaps of clothing, field packs, and valises; five brass cannons, spiked by their gunners and surrounded by crates of ammunition, bore mute testimony to an army in flight. Hundreds of sick and wounded Mexicans had been left behind, and Taylor, over the objections of a few staff officers, ordered his medical corps to aid them.

The wounded's comrades, long gone, lurched southwest on dirt trails overgrown with cactus and mesquite. Staggering along, Riley and the other deserters struggled to keep up with the Mexican soldiers, who were capable of marching up to 30 miles in one day in comparison to the 15-mile average of the American and European armies.

A few days into the retreat, water and food dwindled and scores of soldiers and camp followers collapsed as vultures hovered. The column trudged on, individuals' tongues swelling from thirst. Many marchers crawled off the trail to die in the brush; Riley and most forced themselves southward, seared by the sun, staring ahead for any hint of a water hole.

A sudden downpour several days out brought relief to parched throats but turned the trails into a morass. With food gone, soldiers began shooting pack animals and eating the meat raw on the march; hundreds vomited the rank meal, which sapped their endurance further. At night, when the column slept on the trail for three to four hours, dozens of men pressed their muskets to their temples and pulled the triggers.

The citizens of Linares awakened on May 28, 1846, to find the grimy, skeletal ruins of Arista's Army of the North staggering into the main plaza, where hundreds fell to their knees at a large fountain and gulped spring water. The army had tramped 200 miles across some of the harshest terrain in Mexico, averaging an astonishing 20 miles a day. Although Riley and the other exhausted deserters could not have envisioned a worse march, several equally grueling treks awaited them in Mexico's service.

The American public at large did not yet know about Riley and the other deserters who had served cannons during the siege of Fort Texas. Although various family members and friends of Taylor's men had received letters mentioning the Mexicans' attempts to entice Irish, German, and other immigrants into desertion, the press had not latched onto the news.

With the first pointed accounts of Taylor's actions at Palo Alto and Resaca de la Palma and with the War Department's call for recruits, a patriotic fever burst across America. Assimilated Irishmen joined the nationalistic chorus by extolling the "distinguished behavior" of Sergeant Major Mick Maloney, the gallant conduct of Corporal O'Sullivan, who had captured a Mexican cannon at Resaca de la Palma, and many other Irishmen lauded in reports of the battles. In *Spirit of the Times*, a Philadelphia newspaper, an Irishman wrote: "In the official dispatches from 'Old Rough and Ready,' giving the particulars of our recent brilliant success of the Rio Grande, I find that the name of every non-commissioned officer sounds awful *Irish*, if not *Catholic*. What can it mean? Surely men with such names cannot have acted so bravely!" [1]

For the moment, Irish who had arrived in America in the 1820s and 1830s used Palo Alto and Resaca de la Palma to assuage their own concerns about the loyalty of recent immigrants and to rebut Nativist smears. In the *Buffalo Express*, correspondent William F. Robinson's publication of casualty lists from the Rio Grande defied Nativists to question foreigners' loyalty. At the battles of Palo Alto and Resaca de la Palma, Robinson wrote, 152 noncoms and men had been killed or wounded, and among that toll were 43 Irishmen, 17 Germans, 7 Englishmen, and 5 Scots, nearly half the casualties.

In the Albany *Evening Journal*, an editorial assailed Nativists questioning Irish soldiers' commitment to their signed oaths of loyalty: "If anything was needed to wipe out this vile calumny [Nativism], we have it in the long and fatal list of Killed and Wounded. It is only necessary to read the names to see that two-thirds if not three-fourths of all who shed their blood in that gallant action were Irishmen." [2]

The Boston *Pilot* chimed in with a challenge to renowned Nativist General Dearborn, who had urged the government to stop enlisting the Irish and huffed that native-born Americans "will do our own fighting." "Where, now, is the valiant General Dearborn?" the *Pilot* asked. [3]

In the first flush of victory on the Rio Grande, the popular magazine *Freeman's Journal* assured readers that, despite rampant Nativism, Irish Catholics would uphold the American cause "so long as our country is dwelling, under tents, on the field of battle." [4]

President Polk, Secretary of War Marcy, and Adjutant General Jones had read the Irish and German names on another growing list—that of deserters—and knew that the Nativist press would ignite a new furor as soon as those names appeared in the *National Police Gazette* and other publications. The president and his cabinet, alarmed by Ampudia's and Arista's appeals to immigrants, keenly aware that hordes of indigent

Irish, Germans, and other foreigners were flocking to recruiting stands, received a chilling dispatch from General Taylor a few weeks after the opening battles. He opened with a defense of his "shoot-to-kill" order:

> Sir—In reply to your communication of the eighth [May] instant, calling for information relative to deserters who were shot near Matamoros, I have to state that soon after my arrival on the Rio Grande the evil of desertion made its appearance and increased to an alarming extent; that inducements were held out by the Mexican authorities to entice our men from their colors, and that the most efficient measures were necessary to prevent the spread of this contagion. As our deserters, by merely swimming the river, were at once in the enemy's lines, pursuit and apprehension with a view to trial were out of the question. I therefore deemed it my duty, and warranted by the hostile attitude of the Mexicans, whose commanders assumed that a state of war existed, to give orders that all men seen swimming across the river should be hailed by our pickets and ordered to return; and, in case that they did not return, that they should be shot.[5]

In a sarcastic jab at John Quincy Adams and other critics, Taylor wrote: "How far I should have been justified in seeing our ranks daily thinned by the insidious acts of the Mexican general, without resorting to the most efficient steps to stop it, I cheerfully leave to the decision of the War Department." Then, in a sentence unnerving the president and offering more fuel for Nativist rage, Taylor revealed that Riley and "some of our deserters were employed against us."

Taylor's last paragraph in the dispatch rattled the president and Marcy even further. "As connected with this subject," wrote Old Rough and Ready, "I enclose an original draught, found in General Arista's papers, of an invitation to our soldiers to desert. A similar call was previously made by Ampudia, and has already found its way into the public prints [only in New Orleans to that point]. The department may see from these documents what arms were used against us."[6]

Along with the copy of Arista's missive and Taylor's account of the "alarming extent" of desertions, many officers contacted the War Department with letters begging for chaplains to be sent to the army. Concerned that the Mexicans' appeals to Irish and German Catholic soldiers were working and would blossom further, a cadre of Protestant and Catholic officers such as Bennet Riley stressed that Catholic priests could convince many recent immigrants to ignore Mexican overtures.

"For strong reasons that are so apparent," wrote a Catholic officer, "I ask for the appointment of chaplains to the various units."[7]

Polk, fearing a holy war that could rip the army apart before it could "conquer a peace," faced an unprecedented problem: the U.S. Army had never employed Catholic chaplains, and even though allowed by a 1775 act of the Continental Congress to hire Protestant clerics, none were ministering to the troops on the Rio Grande. The president, who would have to request congressional authorization for any official appointment of Catholic chaplains, knew that legislators would slap down the notion. He understood the rage that the mere request would incite among Nativist civilians and officers but weighed the political risks against "the spread of this contagion" [desertion].[8]

Closer to home than the Rio Grande, other factors pushed Polk to consider the matter of Catholic chaplains for the troops. The War Department's promises of a $7.50 bonus and 160 acres of Western lands to all new recruits for the regulars would fill the Register of Enlistments with more destitute Irish and Germans. They, too, would encounter Mexico's appeals to religion and purse, and the farther Taylor pushed into Mexico, the greater the number of priests to whisper about "matters of conscience" to immigrant soldiers. With so many recruits virtually stepping from coffin ships into the army's ranks and acclimated in no way to American life, the War Department worried that Catholic Mexico would appear a better deal to immigrants than Protestant America.

A look at the typical composition of new regular units further underscored Polk and the War Department's dilemma. "Company I [1st U.S. Artillery] to which I now belonged," wrote an immigrant private and British army veteran, "after having received our draft of twenty recruits, consisted of sixty men, including noncommissioned officers and privates; of these, two were English, four Scotch, seven Germans, sixteen Americans, and the remainder [31] Irish."[9]

Polk and the War Department also faced the Nativist specter as the volunteer regiments mustered at armories across the nation. "Not only natives of Europe singly entered," Adjutant General Jones recorded, "but . . . entire companies of Germans and Irishmen were mustered" into the volunteers;[10] three fourths of the volunteer units, however, featured exclusively Protestant rolls whose politically appointed officers were generally incapable of forming men "into line as straight as a crooked stick" and whose chief distinction was their hatred of Catholics.[11] In the handful of religiously mixed volunteer units, trouble between Nativist officers and Catholic recruits loomed. Typical of the problem was the 1st New York Volunteer Regiment, "about eight hundred rank and file, three hundred *Americans,* the balance Dutch [Germans], Irish, French, English, Poles, etc. . . . there were not one hundred men . . . even born in the City of New York in the whole regiment."[12]

From Philadelphia, a local politician dashed off a disturbing letter to Secretary of State James Buchanan about potential problems among the city's Irish volunteers.

> I found the general joy and enthusiasm [for war] damped by the con-
> sideration that should the exigencies of the country demand the actual
> transportation of Volunteers [Irish] to the seat of War, the public peace
> might be again compromised by a renewal of the deplorable events of May
> and July 1844 [the Nativist Riots]. I discovered that men of judgment and
> sagacity considered that the serpent of religious discord was merely
> "Scotched, not killed," and that the *Sun, Eagle,* and other native [Nativist]
> organs were as virulent in their incendiary denunciation of Foreigners and
> Catholics, as just prior to these fatal Riots. In short, it is feared that the
> departure of the Volunteers will be the Signal for another outbreak.

Concerned that the local Irish "consisted chiefly of men with fami-lies" and might desert en masse to return home if the Nativists attacked again or, in the worst case, might seek vengeance in Mexico's ranks, the politician urged Buchanan to send "unmarried and ardent young men"—native born—to the Rio Grande instead.[13] The Philadelphian's plea did not sway the War Department: it needed recruits, and poor Irishmen would do.

To dissuade immigrants from following John Riley's example, Polk arrived at a decision. On May 19, 1846, just two weeks since Taylor's vic-tories, Polk sent a message to Catholic bishops John Hughes of New York, Michael Portier of Mobile, and Peter Kendrick of St. Louis. All were attending a national church council in Baltimore and were stunned to receive a request that they rush to the White House, where a Presbyterian president waited to discuss an urgent religious matter. The carriage carrying the prelates clattered up to the presidential mansion late in the afternoon of May 20 and the men were escorted immediately to Polk's office.

In his typical stiff collar and black frock coat, his shoulder-length silver hair brushed straight back, the president looked nearly as much a man of the cloth as the trio of bishops. As he paced about the office, he told the seated visitors of his desire to address several problems affecting their Catholic countrymen in the army. First, Polk acknowledged that "much indignation was rife throughout Catholic circles over the punishment inflicted by fanatical military chiefs on Catholic soldiers who had refused to attend Protestant services sanctioned by regimental officials." Secretary of State Buchanan and Secretary of War Marcy, Polk attested, shared his concern over the practice, which had led John Paul Jones O'Brien to defy his superiors in Newport a few years ago.

To better serve the prelates' uniformed brethren, the president went on, he "expressed a great wish" for "the appointment of Catholic chaplains for the army." Then he asked "the Bishops to give him the names of two priests to whom commissions would be at once issued." [14]

The startled bishops requested several hours to furnish names and, after "the very pleasant interview," drove to nearby Georgetown College. [15] They turned to Father Peter Verhaegen, the school's president, for help, telling him they needed two priests able to convince immigrant soldiers who were not even citizens that their oath to the U.S. Army was sacred no matter how much bigotry and physical abuse their officers heaped upon them.

Verhaegen suggested a pair of fellow Jesuits: Father John McElroy, the pastor of Washington's Trinity Church, and Father Anthony Rey, a Georgetown administrator. The bishops rushed the two names to the president.

The following day, May 21, 1846, a letter from Secretary of War Marcy arrived for McElroy at the rectory of Trinity Church. A native of County Fermanagh, Ireland, the 69-year-old priest had emigrated to New York in 1803 and had been ordained at Georgetown in 1817. Though an intellectual, his craggy features and his fiery, no-nonsense sermons frightened parishioners with one of his favorite themes—the wages of sin.

No stranger to reminding fractious, wayward worshipers of their duty to God, even McElroy wondered whether he or any priest was up to the task outlined in the letter he held:

> Sir—The president is desirous to engage two Reverend gentlemen of the Roman Catholic Church to attend the Army of Occupation now on the Rio Grande to officiate as chaplains. In his opinion, their services would

be important in many respects to the public interest, particularly in the present condition of our affairs with Mexico. Having sought information as to the proper persons to be employed, his attention had been directed to you, and he has instructed me to address you on the subject in the hope that you may consider it not incompatible with your clerical duties or your personal feelings to yield to his request.[16]

Marcy's phrase "your personal feelings" drove to the core of the religious issue: could McElroy, in good conscience, urge Catholic soldiers reviled by Nativists to continue fighting against Catholic Mexico? McElroy, long convinced that America offered fellow Irishmen better prospects than anywhere else, regarded the signature on an enlistment form as sacrosanct. He accepted Polk's request.

Marcy informed the pastor "that the existing laws of the United States do not authorize the President to appoint and commission chaplains, but he has authority to employ persons to perform such duties as appertain to chaplains." The distinction was classic Polk politics, cunning and bold. Through Marcy, he was inviting McElroy "to *visit* the Army and remain some time with it." [17] No one but Polk, his inner circle, the bishops, and the two priests would know for several weeks that he had appointed the first Catholic chaplains in the history of the U.S. Army. If and when those chaplains arrived at the Rio Grande, Polk could claim that they were observers or visitors when Nativists demanded an explanation. He would have a harder time explaining the salary he wanted to pay the priests for their "nonofficial" duties.

The same letter was sent to Father Anthony Rey, a 39-year-old man known for his quiet, reassuring demeanor and deep faith. Tall, slight, with the drawn mien of an ascetic, Rey, a peer would write, was fearless. He, too, immediately accepted.

Marcy summoned the two Jesuits to his office a few days later. McElroy wrote that the secretary of war, a man with longish hair and a "poker-face," "received us very affably and ordered his chief clerk to prepare letters for the Commanders of different posts to facilitate our journey." Then, the stout secretary rose from his desk chair and "expressed his desire that we should meet the President" immediately.

McElroy and Rey shook Polk's hand within minutes, the president receiving them "with great kindness and regard." The sight of the Presbyterian Polk and the two black-robed priests chatting amiably would have enraged Nativists, who especially loathed Jesuits. When the president presented the clerics' mission as "one of peace" and a refutation of the Mexicans' and immigrant soldiers' "erroneous opinions" that the United States "warred against their religion," he further risked the rage of millions who saw the war as a Protestant crusade.

In response to Polk's rhetoric about calming Mexicans' fears about the Yankees, McElroy said that "neither of us could speak Spanish" and suggested "the propriety of associating with us a third clergyman who was familiar with the language." Polk heartily agreed and ordered Marcy "to embody that in his dispatch to the General-in-Chief [Taylor]." The true nature of Polk's design lay in two languages the Jesuits did speak fluently—Gaelic in McElroy's case, German in Rey's.

Following the interview, Marcy led the priests back to his office and "asked us what we thought sufficient for our expenses." The priests had no idea, but the secretary and Polk figured $1,200 in gold for each "by virtue of his discretionary power."[18]

On May 29, 1846, Marcy sent two dispatches, one to Lieutenant Colonel Thomas Hunt, the commander at Fort Polk (Point Isabel), the other to Zachary Taylor, both letters "confidential." To Hunt, Marcy wrote: "Sir—The Reverend Mr. McElroy and Mr. Rey are the bearers of a communication from this department to Major-General Taylor; they are recommended to your courtesy and hospitality, and you are requested to take such measures as will ensure their safe conduct to the headquarters of General Taylor."[19]

Marcy explained the priests' "secret mission" to Taylor in the following fashion:

> Sir—The President has been informed that much pains have been taken to alarm the religious prejudices of the Mexicans against the United States. He deems it important that their misapprehensions in this respect should be corrected as far as it can be done, and for that purpose has invited the Reverend gentlemen who will hand you this communication, Mr. McElroy and Mr. Rey of the Roman Catholic Church to attend to the army under your command and to officiate as chaplains. Although the President cannot appoint them as chaplains, yet it is his wish that they be received in that character by you and your officers, be respected as such and treated with kindness and courtesy, that they should be permitted to have intercourse with the soldiers of the Catholic faith, to administer to their religious instruction, to perform divine service for such as may wish

to attend whenever it can be done without interfering with their military duties, and to have free access to the sick or wounded in hospitals and elsewhere.[20]

Polk's message to Taylor was clear: use the priests to keep Catholic immigrants in the ranks, and order your officers to show deference to McElroy and Rey—like it or not.

On June 2, 1846, the priests departed for the Rio Grande. John Riley was mulling a plan that would pit him against McElroy and Rey, a plan for a "foreign legion" of Irish, German, and other European deserters.

12

The Road to Monterrey

FATHERS MCELROY AND REY landed at Fort Polk on July 2, 1846, and opened their mission with a visit to the base hospital. Moving from cot to cot, the clerics comforted the wounded from the two battles near Matamoros. Of the 17 regulars McElroy and Rey consoled, 15 were Irish. Many more craved the priests' ministrations upriver at Matamoros.

McElroy and Rey immediately boarded a small steamer and reached Taylor's headquarters four days later. "He received us in the most friendly manner and begged us to give him the opportunity of rendering us all the service in his power."[1]

The same week of the priests' arrival in Matamoros, the deserters who had bombarded Fort Texas marched northwest from Linares with the Army of the North toward the city of Monterrey. Mejia now commanded them, for Arista, still popular with his troops but scapegoated by Ampudia and other officers as responsible for the disasters of Palo Alto and Resaca de la Palma, had been court-martialed and dismissed from the army. Most of the men disliked Mejia, who stared at the common soldier contemptuously through his trademark blue glasses, and they loathed Ampudia as a braggart and possibly a coward. As the approximately 3,000 survivors of the two defeats and the deadly retreat from Matamoros straggled toward the distant peaks of the Sierra Madre Oriental, their tattered, grimy uniforms symbolized the ordeals. Many men marched barefoot, having cast aside their shoes or sandals before diving into the Rio Grande after Resaca de la Palma.

The march turned into a slow ascent into the foothills of the Sierras and then into the mountains themselves. One misstep along narrow, rocky paths sent men plunging thousands of feet into ravines. Bracing themselves against sheer rock walls for support, straining not to look beyond the other shoulder and into chasms a few feet away, the soldiers tottered 100 miles across the Sierras. Men gasping in the cold, scantier air of the mountains kept up only because of the column's slow pace. Then, in late July, the line lurched to a halt.

Below them, a white-walled city shone in the sunlight. John Riley and the other exhausted deserters took their first glimpse of Monterrey, a vista of graceful white haciendas, spacious, tree-lined plazas, and the clear ribbon of the swift-flowing Santa Catarina River. On the eastern rim of the grand plaza, the spires of an ornate cathedral soared above the red-tiled roofs, and the peal from the cathedral's bell tower swelled above the city and into the mountains.

Along with Monterrey's beauty, Riley noticed its threats for any attacker. A crag topped by the thick walls of the bishop's palace, Obispado, loomed above the city's western edge; from the escarpment's rear, troops could protect the city's supply line, the Saltillo road. The Santa Catarina River would hamper any assaults at Monterrey's southern and eastern perimeters, and on the southern bank of the river, rugged Federacion Hill faced the Obispado on the opposite bank. Murderous crossfire from artillery and muskets on both ridges would confront enemy troops.

Riley soon spotted the most sinister fortification Taylor's men would have to face. A thousand yards north of the city, the dark stone walls of the citadel jutted from the foundations of an abandoned cathedral. Eight giant cannons glowered down at the Marin road, Taylor's likeliest route. The bastion contained embrasures for 22 more cannons to greet the Americans.

As Riley filed down the foothills and into Monterrey, he found that the stone homes with their narrow front windows and flat roofs offered ideal perches for snipers to rake the straight, cobblestone streets.

For the next several weeks, Mejia ordered little more than cursory work upon the city's defenses. On Sundays, Riley and the other Catholic

deserters could attend mass, head to the bullfights, sup at church bar-
becues, and flirt and dance with women at numerous fiestas and fandangos. Some of the soldiers spent many off-duty hours in the cantinas
downing tequila, *aguardiente* (brandy), and potent pulque, fermented
maguey juice. As at Matamoros, Riley could stroll at night wearing his
lieutenant's insignia amid the grand plaza's cafes and public benches and
be accorded instant friendship and respect for his rank and his brogue.

No matter how pleasant the rhythms of life that Riley and the deserters discovered in the city of 15,000, eyes turned daily toward the Marin
road for a distant dust cloud announcing Taylor's troops. As the last
week of August waned, Mejia's force, many dreading the coming clash
with the same Yankees who at Resaca de la Palma "would charge up to
the very mouths of cannon," believed they needed reinforcements to
hurl back the Americans.[2]

On August 29, 1846, Monterrey's church bells suddenly clanged. A
mass of troops marched in neat order up the Saltillo road to the brass
blare of patriotic anthems. Crowds rushed to the western edge of the
city to cheer 1,400 regular infantry, who streamed past with three eight-
pounder cannons. A second infantry brigade arrived on September 6, a
third several days later. General Ampudia, who had left Linares shortly
after the retreat and headed south to the army's main depot, San Luis
Potosi, rode at the head of the third brigade. He held an order naming
him Mejia's successor as the Army of the North's commander.

In Monterrey, another piece of news from the south spread. Santa
Anna had returned to Vera Cruz from exile and had positioned himself
to regain power through intrigue, his personal magnetism, and his calculation that beleaguered Mexico would turn to its most controversial but
greatest leader. By September 15, acting president J. M. Salas, Paredes's
successor in the fallout from Taylor's victories, officially welcomed the
exdictator. By the end of the month, "the soldier of the people"[3] was
gathering a large army at San Luis Potosi, vowing to crush Old Rough
and Ready.

The army's spirits soared with the reinforcements' arrival, and, when
a wealthy, beautiful woman named Senorita Dosamantes reportedly
galloped up to the troops during a review, dressed in the gilded captain's
tunic and high boots of a lancer, the army erupted in a deafening chorus

of "vivas." Now, many believed, with the populace behind them, they would beat Taylor.

Santa Anna did not want the Army of the North to make a stand at Monterrey, but Ampudia and Mejia both argued in dispatches that the army's honor was at stake and that the rejuvenated force would repulse the Americans. When Santa Anna finally acceded, Ampudia believed his moment of glory was at hand.

Because Mejia had possessed no government funds to hire laborers for additional fortifications and because the Americans were starting upriver, Ampudia needed to move fast. He drafted workmen from Monterrey and surrounding towns and handed them picks and shovels to shape two bastions, the Teneria (tannery) and El Diablo (Devil's Fort), near the key Marin road. Soldiers and laborers piled sandbags on top of homes' flat roofs and braced doors with iron bars, turning streets of rubble-stone dwellings into one small fortress after another. Proving how firmly the Church supported the army, priests allowed Ampudia to use the cathedral as his main magazine; he crammed the Baroque interior with powder and cases of musket balls, roundshot, and grape.

Riley and his men, anticipating the chance to pour that shot and shell at their old officers, repaired and emplanted cannons under the direction of General Thomas Requena, Ampudia's second-in-command and a superb artillerist. Requena worked the deserters hard, dividing them among several batteries to take advantage of their expertise, especially Riley's. And Riley was creating the nucleus of his future foreign legion by adding "another company" of deserters to the 48 he had formed at Matamoros.[4] In the Army of the North's muster rolls for Monterrey, military clerks officially listed "a party of deserters, mostly Irish, from the American army" as artillerists.[5]

Riley expected many more Irish and Germans to desert Taylor's army as it besieged Monterrey. So did the Mexican government: on September 3, 1846, a five-man presidential commission unveiled a program of land grants for American soldiers "who, not having been born in the United States, would abandon the North American lines and pass over to ours." Deserters were to receive "vacant or uncultivated lands . . . in any of the [Mexican] states." For men with families in either the United States or Europe, the government would offer "financial means . . . [to] assist the

said individuals . . . or bring their families here . . . or to provide tools and
other items necessary for cultivation."[6] At the end of the deserters' military service for Mexico, they would be entitled to land commensurate
with rank achieved in the army. Even the 200 acres promised to a mere
private seemed an estate to land-hungry Irishmen who had tilled tiny
rented plots in their homeland. As a lieutenant, John Riley could claim
his first 1,200 acres.

A week after the land bill, the Mexican government guaranteed instant
citizenship for all deserters who took up arms against the American
army. Many immigrants in Taylor's regiments were 5 years away from
naturalization in the United States, and Nativist politicians were
attempting to raise the process from 25 years for foreigners.

Ampudia, also envisioning a fresh crop of deserters, turned to the
weapon he had aimed at the U.S. Army in early April—his pen—and
began a new leaflet to greet Taylor's men. In mid-September, Ampudia
addressed a message to his own men: "Soldiers, victory or death must be
our only motto!"[7]

As at Matamoros, a third option—capture by their former comrades—frightened John Riley and the other deserters more than death in
battle. But with Monterrey well fortified and defended by 7,300 regulars
and 3,000 irregulars, victory seemed possible, as the Irishman and his
comrades manned their cannons each day and waited for that dust
cloud on the northeast horizon.

In late July, Riley's old unit had boarded small steamers and had faced
strong currents to the town of Camargo, about 100 miles upstream from
Matamoros. Taylor, accompanied by Fathers McElroy and Rey, reached
Camargo in early August and over the next few weeks assembled the
men he would march to Monterrey.

In camps flanking the San Juan River, a tributary of the Rio Grande,
the two priests comforted thousands of men wracked by dysentery, the
result of foul drinking water. Over 1,500 men would die from that malady
and fevers in the hospital tents, the days and nights ringing with "the
groans and lamentations of the poor sufferers."[8] Stricken Protestant soldiers with no chaplains of their own called for the priests, who even per-
formed their church's last rites to the many Methodists, Unitarians, and
Presbyterians who asked. As orderlies hauled the dead away for burial, a

soldier grimly joked that "regimental bands...so often struck up the mournful chords of the death march that mockingbirds in the trees could whistle the refrain."[9]

A regular wrote that at least the dead would no longer have to listen to the "true West Point style" of speech toward the ranks: "You God-damned son of a bitch! God damn you!" And the two chaplains quickly learned that, while officers of "intelligence and education" treated the priests with respect, at best, or with cold courtesy, at least, at Taylor's order, the clerics' presence did nothing to ease brutal discipline toward Catholic soldiers. McElroy's and Rey's duties regularly included a kind word or two for immigrants who could not reply because of the buck and gag.

To justify bucking and gagging and stringing up men by their thumbs, West Pointers and now volunteer officers spewed such bromides as "poor Irishman...[were] the best material in the world to make infantry of, but required great efficiency on the part of officers to enforce discipline."[10] A young West Point lieutenant huffed that "the officers will have to exert themselves greatly" to control lowly "Dutch and Irish immigrants,"[11] even though many Germans in the ranks had fought Napoleon and that many "sons of the Emerald Isle" could "relate stirring tales of adventures...under the cross of St. George, in the Indies fighting the Sikhs, or at the Cape Colonies battling the wild Kaffers [sic]."[12]

Lieutenant George Meade loathed Southern officers who treated regulars as virtual slaves, which proved particularly galling to Irishmen who viewed blacks as the one group even lower in America's social pecking order than the Irish. And, as the troops awaited marching orders at Camargo, greater numbers of Germans were joining Irishmen in their contempt for their officers. Alexander Konze, a German recruit, railed against officers' "disgraceful conduct" and "the idea in their heads that the common soldier is a being far below them."[13]

"The menacing unmanly deception of the officers," as described by a private, vied with McElroy's and Rey's considerable powers of persuasion to keep Catholics from going over the hill.[14] A factor aiding the priests at Camargo was that would-be deserters could not just swim the river and turn themselves over to the Mexican army. Monterrey and Ampudia lay too far away across unknown terrain teeming with bandits. For the moment, desertions had waned, but not for long.

McElroy and Rey soon found common ground with Nativist officers on one point: a contempt for Mexican Catholics. Lieutenant John Sedgwick, of the 2d Artillery, wrote: "The priests that come from the States say that they could not recognize the Catholic religion in the mummeries practiced here.... Religion is a mixture of Indian idolatry and superstition with the Catholic." [15] At Matamoros, McElroy had brushed off a Mexican priest's invitation to stay at his rectory and had slept in the home of a transplanted American merchant, a Protestant.

The *New York Express,* one of the many American newspapers reaching the troops, editorialized on the difficulties of the priests' mission: "They [Catholic troops] cannot but see and feel that the conquests we are making are Protestant conquests ... that the native-born troops are Protestants, and that the inevitable consequence of such invasion is the subjection of the Mexican religion to the Protestant religion of the invaders." [16]

Professor Kerby Miller contends that Riley and the other Irishmen who had deserted at Matamoros, and future deserters, "were in part rooted in an alienation from their officers and from the army in which they had been treated so poorly." He also asserts that the desertions reflected "their [Irishmen's] growing realization that the United States was not fighting a war of liberty, but that it was fighting a war of conquest, and it was fighting against the people who were fellow Catholics such as themselves." [17]

When John Riley wrote that the United States had launched "this unholy war," he unwittingly used a similar phrase to that penned by Ulysses S. Grant in a letter to his wife, Julia. At Camargo, Brigadier General John A. Quitman, loathed as "Polk's spy" by Taylor, blustered that the Mexicans were "a bastard and robber race, incapable of self-government, and only fit for servitude and military rule." [18] His sentiments sounded much like centuries-old rhetoric that British leaders had leveled against Catholic Ireland. What Irish immigrant, Riley asked, should fight for another nation, the United States, that offered its most recent arrivals "a slavish hireling's life ... contumely and disgrace ... [and] trampled upon the holy altars of our religion [the Nativist Riots of 1844]." [19]

On the evening of September 7, 1846, Taylor's newest company of Irishmen milled about the gunwales of a steamer anchored just downstream from Camargo. A Savannah, Georgia, company dubbed the Jasper Greens, they were Catholic immigrants led by flamboyant hotel owner Captain James McMahon. Another company of Georgians, mainly Protestants, also jostled for space on the moonlit deck.

Both units glared at each other for several minutes. Then several soldiers shoved each other, and 200 or so men rushed to their comrades' "defense." McMahon and other officers bawled orders for the men to disperse to opposite ends of the steamer. The units edged away from each other.

Suddenly, a Georgian allegedly bellowed, "Irish sons of bitches!"[20]

Oaths erupted. Punches and kicks thudded from bow to stern. Sabers and knives slashed as dozens of shrieking soldiers crowded so close that wounded men remained upright in the mob.

As the din carried ashore, Colonel Edward D. Baker gathered a squad of the 4th Illinois Volunteers and rushed them aboard the steamer with bayonets fixed. McMahon leaped at him with a sword, and Baker countered with his own blade. While the pair feinted, parried, and thrust, a pistol cracked. Baker was blown back against a railing as the ball tore through his cheek and shattered his front teeth.

A new cry—"Rip up McMahon!"—broke out. One of Baker's men plunged a bayonet through the Irishman's cheek. Moments later, more of the 4th Illinois stormed aboard and finally broke up the brawl with the threat of their massed muskets. The 4th placed the rioters under shipboard arrest and carried one dead and ten or more wounded—two fatally—from the steamer. McMahon and Baker survived.

The next day, a court of inquiry freed all of the combatants. With over 400 participants in the fracas, no one could prove who had ignited the brawl. *The New York Herald* and other newspapers' accounts of the "riot on the Rio Grande," however, squarely blamed the Irishmen of the Jasper Greens.[21]

Irish regulars had heard their share of "Irish sons of bitches" and other epithets, but, knowing the brutal price the Academy officers would have exacted for a similar riot, refrained from such actions.

The differences between the regulars and the volunteers would plague Taylor throughout his coming campaign. The "citizens' army" descended upon the Rio Grande in a dizzying array of uniforms in all hues of blue, green, gray, and white, trimmed in yellow, red, and pink. Kentucky volunteers swaggered across Taylor's camps in tricolored hats and hip-high boots of red morocco leather. Because many of the home-made uniforms fell apart quickly, Taylor ordered various militia units to don the light blue regulation issue. "Let 'em go to hell with their sky blue," protested an Indiana volunteer. "I'll be blowed if they make a Regular out of me." [22] They would never make regulars of such men, but if Taylor insisted militia wear sky blue, they wore it.

Taylor's West Pointers loathed the volunteer officers, selected by political appointments or their men's vote. Only a handful, such as Academy graduate Jefferson Davis of the Mississippi Rifles, held the immediate respect of the regulars. In the months to come, however, some of the volunteers' leaders were to prove their mettle under fire.

Regulars scoffed at the volunteer units' self-styled names—Killers, Rifles, Gunmen, Grays, and Greens. But many regular officers worried that the colorful volunteers would prove uncontrollable for the army. Meade, who narrowly escaped death at Camargo when militiamen shooting their muskets for fun shredded his tent with balls, wrote that the volunteers were "always drunk...they rob and steal...they wantonly kill for their own amusement...they are full of mutiny." [23]

In a letter to his wife, Mattie, Major Philip Barbour complained the volunteers "were playing the devil and disgracing the country." [24]

When a band of Kentucky volunteers shot a 12-year-old Mexican boy "for sport" as he worked in a cane field and several other soldiers placed "this poor little fellow, all bleeding and crying...in front of the General's tent," Taylor merely reprimanded the culprits. Meade, usually an admirer of Old Rough and Ready, wrote that the general "has neither the moral or physical force to restrain these men." [25]

Taylor would eventually take measures to control the volunteers, but at the moment, his impending march to Monterrey dominated his thoughts. Until he had taken on Ampudia, Taylor wrote, he intended to "try & get through in the best I can & with at least all the good feeling & temper I can command even should they [volunteers] drive me out of my tent." [26] And in some of the volunteer units, especially the Texas Rangers, Taylor recognized not just Barbour's "devils," but tough men who would fight like proverbial devils.

The numbers of volunteers preying, or "sky-larking," upon Mexican citizens near the Rio Grande encampments tormented Taylor. Native-born "citizen-soldiers," hating all things Mexican and Catholic, including Catholic regulars, held themselves superior to any immigrant and groused that their monthly pay made them "a seven-dollar target" no different from Taylor's "Micks" and "Dutchies."[27] Although the militias were now under Taylor's authority, many volunteers deemed regulars "a degraded caste."[28] An immigrant veteran noted Nativists' belief that "there was contamination in the touch of" soldiers, especially foreign born, who "are a fine set of candidates for the State's prison."[29]

From August 19 to September 6, 1846, columns marched out of Camargo and filed toward Monterrey: 3,200 regulars, 3,000 volunteers, and artillery; Father Rey rode along with them. Each infantryman carried 40 rounds, nearly double the usual issue, and eight days' rations. Taylor had left behind 4,700 volunteers to guard his 400-mile supply line to Point Isabel.

On Saturday, September 19, Taylor and Texas Rangers rode ahead of his army and reined in around 9:00 in the morning. Monterrey gleamed in the sunlight some three miles away, but the sight that riveted Old Rough and Ready was the dark expanse of the citadel, much closer to the riders. He could not see the deserters peering down from the "Black Fort's" parapets.

An 18-pounder boomed, and solid shot slammed into the ground several yards from the Americans. As a white puff of smoke rose above the citadel, a second muzzle roared, then a third. One of the cannon balls caromed a few feet in front of Taylor and sailed just above his palmetto hat. He stared at the citadel for another minute or two, turned Old Whitey around, and loped back to join his army.

The troops waited for him a few miles away, pitching tents near bubbling springs shaded by live oaks, pecans, and Spanish moss and a favorite picnic spot of the locals. They knew it as Bosque de San Domingo; the Americans soon dubbed it Walnut Springs, though "Pecan Springs" would have been more accurate.

Around the camp, the troops had found pamphlets, a novel sight to the volunteers but not to the veterans of Palo Alto and Resaca de la Palma.

Ampudia's second broadside, dated September 15, 1846, was blunt in its appeals:

> It is well known that the war carried on to the Republic of Mexico by the Government of the United States of America is unjust, illegal and anti-Christian....
>
> Acting according with the dictates of honor and in compliance with what my country requires from me, in the name of my Government I offer to all individuals that will lay down their arms and separate themselves from the American Army, seeking protection, they will be well received and treated in all the Plantations, Farms, or Towns, where they will first arrive and [be] assisted for their march to the Interior of the Republic by all the Authorities on the road, as has been done with all those that have passed over to us.[30]

Ampudia's words offered disgruntled men an escape route: if they showed up at any hacienda or town in the region, he promised that locals would guide them safely away from the American army. Many regulars cleaning their weapons and bracing themselves again for combat mulled Ampudia's offer.

13

"The Dastard's Cheek Blanched"

O N THE MORNING OF SEPTEMBER 20, 1846, a soft breeze drifted across the
Mexican redoubts and the citadel, where the deserters stood by
their cannons. The guns, many "beautiful pieces ... of English manufac-
ture, and of as late date as 1842," were loaded with canister shot to
sweep the city's approaches.[1]

Drums rattled from Walnut Springs at 11:00 in the morning, and from
the citadel's ramparts, defenders spotted the 5th and 7th Infantry and
two flying batteries moving at the double-quick to the west of the city by
2:00 p.m. Under Worth's command, they had orders "to gain the Satillo
road and cut off the enemy's retreat and supply in that direction."[2]

As the blue columns streamed about a thousand yards past the
citadel, the deserters and Mexican gunners briefly opened up but with
little effect—yet. Worth's men rushed toward the Saltillo road and out of
range, and American 24-pounder howitzers and a heavy mortar roared
at the citadel from a range of 500 yards. Several detachments of volunteers flanked the cannons to protect them from Ampudia's cavalry.

On the morning of September 21, another mass of Americans—
Lieutenant Colonel John Garland's 1st and 3d Infantry, John Quitman's
Tennessee and Mississippi volunteers, and the Baltimore Battalion—
surged at the eastern edge of Monterrey. The cannons of the citadel, the

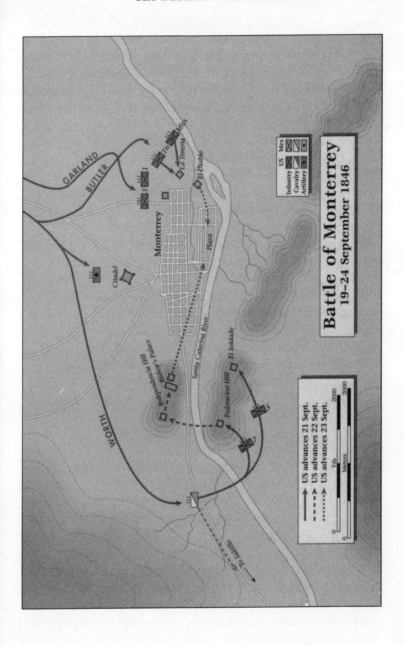

Battle of Monterrey
19–24 September 1846

	US	Mex
Infantry		
Cavalry		
Artillery		

Trinidad
La Teneria
El Diablo
Monterrey
Plaza
Citadel
Santa Catarina River
Independencia Hill
Bishop's Palace
El Soldado
Federacion Hill
GARLAND
BUTLER
WORTH
To Saltillo

US advances 21 Sept.
US advances 22 Sept.
US advances 23 Sept.

Yds 2000
Meters 2000

Teneria, and El Diablo hurled hissing canister into the Americans, but they kept coming. Five hundred yards from the city, Garland's men reformed their line of battle, and the lead companies charged at the first blocks of houses. Muskets blazed from the sandbagged roofs and loop-holed windows as canister from the deserters' cannons ripped into the 1st and 3rd. "It was as if bushels of hickory nuts were hurled at us," an officer recalled.[3] Shots slammed into the buildings and sprayed the Americans with blinding stone dust. As scores of the dead littered the narrow streets, men dragged shrieking comrades wounded in the cross-fire, propped them against house walls, flattened themselves against those same walls, and poured fire at the rooftops and windows across the street. Snipers directly above the Americans could not lean far enough over their sandbags to shoot straight down.

In groups of three and four, Garland's men crawled back to the town's outskirts. A division of volunteers joined them and soon scrambled for cover themselves. Bragg's flying battery clattered up, deployed, and un-loaded a few shots that kicked up some chunks of stone, but nothing else.

Hundreds of Mexican muskets fired at the gunners and their horses and turned "the ground about the guns slippery with their gasped foam and blood."[4] Bragg, seemingly unfazed by the enfilading fire that raked his crews, was "stripping the harness from the dead and disabled ani-mals, determined that not a buckle or a strap should be lost."[5] One of his officers, Samuel French, gaped at two of the horses calmly eating grass as their entrails spilled from them.

Taylor threw the 4th into the fray, and Sergeant Major Maloney and his company ran into one of the streets and its crossfire. They stumbled to the outskirts and huddled there with the other troops, suffering "con-siderable execution from the Mexicans."[6]

Confusion engulfed the officers from Garland on down: Because Taylor's orders had been vague, Garland did not know whether his assault should be a diversion to cover Worth or a full-bore attempt to seize eastern Monterrey.

Taylor had told Garland that "if you think you can take any of them little forts down there with the bayonet, you'd better do it."[7]

Quitman's volunteers followed that "order" as they moved forward in midafternoon to help the 1st, under heavy fire near the buildings just beyond the Teneria. Quitman, a rich Mississippi sugar planter and "political general," outthought veteran regular Garland by leading the Mississippians and the 1st Tennessee along a roundabout route that protected them from Mexican fire until they approached the Teneria.

Then the volunteers charged into a cloud of grape and musket fire. A Tennessean colonel and most regulars could hardly believe that the militia "did not run off the field like a gang of wild turkeys."[8] The first charge wavered but did not collapse, and Colonel Jefferson Davis rallied the men with a cry of "now is the time!"

Howls and oaths erupted from the volunteers. They rushed the Teneria again, as infantrymen of the 1st seized a rooftop behind the redoubt and sprayed fire into the startled garrison. At Rescaca de la Palma, the Teneria's commander had run from the Americans and now fled again in full view of his men. Many of them followed, and a minute or two later Davis and the volunteers burst into the redoubt and held it.

The 1st Ohio Volunteers rushed the other eastern bastion, El Diablo, but the Mexican garrison shattered the charge and sent the Ohioans reeling back.

Far to the west of the Teneria, Worth's attack had netted near-complete success. After his two flying batteries had smashed a thrust by 1,500 lancers on the Saltillo road, Worth's men forded the Santa Catarina and stormed the southwest face of Federacion Hill. The Texas Rangers dismounted and, with the 7th, charged through a withering fire and overran the fort. On the hill's western side, Captain Merrill and the 5th stormed the other redoubt and took it in a hand-to-hand clash.

Near dusk, Taylor withdrew most of his troops from Monterrey's bloody eastern edge. But he ordered a band of troops and Ridgely's battery to dig in at the Teneria and its flanking trenches.

As the gunfire waned and a smoke-shrouded twilight shadowed the battlefields, the church bells of Monterrey tolled evening vespers. Soaked with sweat, washing thick crusts of black powder from their faces, John Riley and artillerymen on both sides stepped away from their cannons. Rain began to fall, gentle and welcome at first, but soon hard and mixing with lingering smoke that the soldiers could literally taste every time they breathed. "In the moonless gloom," American orderlies tracked the wounded "by their groans" and carted them off to the hospital tents at Walnut Springs.[9] The deserters heard the American wagons creaking all night long, many exmessmates among the wounded, "who shrieked at every jolt."[10] Riley had helped fill those carts.

Taylor had lost nearly 400 men—*10 percent* of all Americans in action—on the first day of battle, including 34 officers. Despite Worth's success and the capture of the Teneria, the carnage had unnerved even Taylor's veterans. The guns of the citadel still commanded the valley east and west of the city, and the Mexicans had fought stubbornly and well behind their ramparts and sandbags.

Having allowed his feint at Monterrey's eastern edges to evolve into a chaotic, spur-of-the-moment assault against dug-in defenders, Taylor had committed the only major blunder of his distinguished career. A soldier's general, he anguished over his error's toll.

For the first time in the war, the valor of Taylor's regiments had not carried the day. Heightened confidence filled Ampudia's men. They had held, and the lethal flying batteries of Palo Alto and Resaca de la Palma had proven useless in the city's streets, although in the open, the American six-pounders had decimated the lancers.

On September 22, 1846, the soggy Mexicans perched on the city's eastern rooftops waited all day for the next rush of sky-blue columns. Taylor's left flank made no move. Riley and the Mexican gun crews dueled with the Americans' heavy batteries throughout the day, but neither side's cannonade inflicted any telling damage.

The day's real action exploded along the western perimeter of Monterrey. Worth's men had crept up the west slope of Independencia Hill in the lashing rain and wind and lay mere yards away from the summit as the sky lightened. They clambered to their feet and took the western redoubt with few casualties.

At the hill's opposite end, Lieutenant Colonel Francisco Berra and 200 defenders huddled behind the dense walls of the bishop's palace. As American cannons tossed shells from Federacion Hill across the river and into the palace, Lieutenant George Deas and 50 artillerymen dragged a 12-pounder howitzer 800 feet up Independencia Hill and emplaced it by noon in the western tip's earthworks. The bellow of the "witch's cauldron" (the howitzer) joined the bombardment.

For some reason, the outmanned Berra led most of his men in a wild rush at the Americans. The 5th's muskets and Duncan's grapeshot ravaged the charge. Some survivors stumbled down the hill and fled into the city; a handful scrambled back into the fort and barred the massive brass gate again.

By 4:00 in the afternoon, the howitzer had blasted the gate from its hinges. Worth's infantry climbed from their earthworks and poured into the palace's spacious courtyard to encounter stiff musket volleys from the last defenders. Duncan rolled up his flying battery and loosed grapeshot at snipers' windowsill perches. A few defenders somehow escaped and ran for Monterrey, leaving their dead and wounded and a few prisoners to the Americans.

Worth's men hauled down the Mexican banner from the palace's flagstaff and hoisted Old Glory above Independencia Hill. For Taylor, the two hills had cost 32 casualties, a far cry from the losses of the previous day.

The American flag above the bishop's palace alarmed Ampudia and some of his staff further. The Mexican commander ordered his men to abandon all positions, including El Diablo, on the city's borders on the evening of September 22–23 and to join the defenders in the buildings and streets closest to the main plaza. Units that had repulsed the Americans along Monterrey's eastern border protested, some on the verge of mutiny. Only the threat of execution prodded several companies to leave fortified houses and march to blocks near the plaza.

Shouted orders and the tramp of thousands of feet were muffled by the torrential rain but still carried from eastern Monterrey to the deserters and other troops at the citadel. Ampudia's defenses had shrunk to the inner line around the plaza and to the Black Fort.

The rain lifted before dawn of September 23, and at daylight Taylor sent Quitman's brigade to probe the city's eastern defenses as the cannons of the citadel opened up again. The volunteers encountered only sporadic musket fire as they slogged up the first few blocks. Jefferson Davis sent word to Taylor that resistance was light.

In support, Old Rough and Ready sent the 3d and 4th Infantry, the 2d Texas Volunteers, and Bragg's battery through the gauntlet of citadel shot. Taylor himself rode to the Teneria to take a closer look, calm as always as metal whined around him.

The regulars pushed forward several blocks, catching up with the volunteers. A few blocks farther, the Mexicans' rooftop musketry intensified, and once again Americans toppled to the cobblestones. Still, the troops pressed forward, chasing Mexicans from the roofs and blasting away at loopholed windows.

Only one city square from the grand plaza, Garland's ten companies, including Mick Maloney's, turned a corner and scattered as musket balls and grapeshot poured from a barricade at the street's far end. Devastated during the first day's foray into the city, having suffered dozens of casualties in the past hour, the regulars grabbed their wounded and ducked back around the corner. The other units were stumbling upon similar barricades.

Unlike the first day's debacle in Monterrey, the Americans had a tactic to escape the murderous fire sweeping the streets. Today, they carried not only muskets, but crowbars and pickaxes. The Texans, veterans of street fighting against the Mexicans, showed the regulars how it was done: batter holes in the protected side of a street's first house; hurl six-pound shells with timed fuses inside; pour through a minute after the explosions; finish off any defenders downstairs; storm upstairs to clear snipers from the roof; and start pounding holes in the common wall to the next house.

As the infantry smashed from house to house and left their own sharpshooters to blaze away in rooftop duels with the Mexicans atop the next building, Bragg's gunners and other flying batteries angled their muzzles around corners, sent blasts of grape whistling at the barricades and rooftops, yanked the six-pounders back behind the protection of corner walls, reloaded, shoved the cannons back to their original angle, and fired again. The crews kept it up until midafternoon.

West of the city, Worth chafed as the firing grew heavy and still no orders came from Taylor. Pacing Independencia Hill and peering through the smoke with a fieldglass, Worth decided that Taylor's orders to him must somehow have "miscarried." He sent the 5th, the 7th, and his Texans charging down the slope and into the western streets of the city. They too carried pickaxes and crowbars and, at the first volleys from the barricades, began smashing their way through houses.

C.J. Taylor, Taking Life Easy

A classic stereotype of the Irish immigrant, often called "Paddy," that appeared in countless Nativist publications.

Troops battle mobs rampaging through Philadelphia's Irish-Catholic neighborhoods in the 1844 Nativist Riots.

American recruiting poster for the Mexican War.

VOLUNTEERS!

Men of the Granite State!
Men of Old Rockingham!! the
strawberry-bed of patriotism, renowned for bravery and devotion to Country, rally at this call. Santa Anna, reeking with the generous confidence and magnanimity of your countrymen, is in arms, eager to plunge his traitor-dagger in their bosoms. To arms, then, and rush to the standard of the fearless and gallant CUSHING---put to the blush the dastardly meanness and rank toryism of Massachusetts. Let the half civilized Mexicans hear the crack of the unerring New Hampshire rifleman, and illustrate on the plains of San Luis Potosi, the fierce, determined, and undaunted bravery that has always characterized her sons.

Col. THEODORE F. ROWE, at No. 31 Daniel-street, is authorized and will enlist men this week for the Massachusetts Regiment of Volunteers. The compensation is $10 per month---$30 in advance. Congress will grant a handsome bounty in money and ONE HUNDRED AND SIXTY ACRES OF LAND.

Portsmouth, Feb. 2, 1847.

Future president Gen. Zachary Taylor, "Old Rough and Ready."

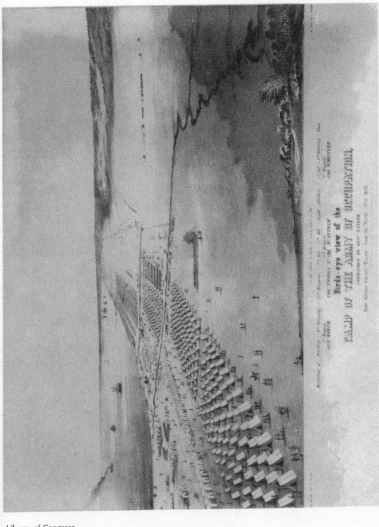

The camp of the American Army of Observation (later Occupation) commanded by Gen. Zachary Taylor near Corpus Christi, Texas, in October 1845. On the drill ground on the right, Nativist officers inflicted brutal discipline upon Irish and German troops.

On the left is Capt. William Chapman, one of Riley's officers in the 5th Infantry. He testified to Riley's good character at his trial. On the right is another officer, possibly Riley's company commander Capt. Moses Merrill, who signed the pass that Riley used to leave camp and desert.

William Dunniway

Benson Latin American Collection, University of Texas at Austin

Mexican general Pedro de Ampudia, who wrote the first appeal for U.S. soldiers to desert and who interviewed John Riley immediately after he "went over the hill."

Benson Latin American Collection, University of Texas at Austin

Mariano Arista, the Mexican general for whom Riley and forty-eight Irishmen served cannons in the siege of Fort Texas.

President James K. Polk had the Army hire Catholic chaplains to help dissuade Catholic immigrants from deserting.

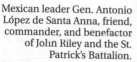

Mexican leader Gen. Antonio López de Santa Anna, friend, commander, and benefactor of John Riley and the St. Patrick's Battalion.

An Irish soldier named Doherty is whipped at the order of Capt. Thomas Sherman, while other troops, including the artist, Samuel Chamberlain, sit bucked and gagged.

BATTLE OF BUENA VISTA.

The Battle of Buena Vista. The St. Patrick's artillerymen, in the area circled, deploy their heavy cannons and prepare for the attack.

Under fire from Riley and his gunners during the Battle of Buena Vista, Zachary Taylor calmly directs his troops.

Pounded by the heavy cannons of the St. Patrick's Battalion, a 4th U.S. Artillery battery is overrun by Mexican infantry at the Battle of Buena Vista. From a painting by eyewitness Samuel Chamberlain, a dragoon who charged the St. Patrick's artillery.

San Jacinto Museum of History

Winfield Scott.

Maj. Gen. Winfield Scott, who ordered the hanging of fifty "San Patricios."

HEAD QUARTERS.

KNOW ALL MEN:

That Antonio Lopez de Santa-Anna, President of the United States of Mexico and Commander in chief of the mexican armies has been duly authorized to make the following concessions to all and every one of the persons now in the American army who will present themselves before me or any of the commanding officers of the mexican forces, viz:

1.ᵗ Every soldier in the American army who appears before me or any of the commanding officers of the Mexican armies is to receive immediately *ten dollars* cash, if coming without arms, and a larger amount if he is armed, in order to cover the cost of the arms he may bring.

2.ⁿᵈ Every person who deserts the American army followed by 100 men is entitled to receive as soon as he presents himself with his men, §500 cash, besides the §10 to which every one of the soldiers is entitled, as well as the extra allowance in case they be armed.

3.ᵗ He who deserts with 200 men has right to claim and ·shall be paid immediately §1000 cash, and so on at the rate of §500, for every hundred men; or the proportional amount if the number be under one hundred; without including the §10 allowed to every soldier, nor the cost of arms and ammunitions, all of which will invariably be paid besides.

4.ᵗ All and every one of the soldiers in the American army who will desert and appear before me or any of the Commanding officers of the Mexican forces, as aforesaid, besides the abovementioned gratifications in cash, are hereby entitled to claim and will immediately receive from me or any of the Commanding officers a document or bond by which the propriety of a grant of land consisting of 200 square acres will be ensured to them as well as to their families or heirs. The division of such grants will be made as soon as the present war is over.

5.ᵗ The Officers in the American army are not only entitled to the aforesaid document or bond but the number of acres in addition to the 200 allowed to the soldiers, will be computed in proportion to the respective grades they hold.

6.ᵗ Those who desert the American army and enter the Mexican service are to continue in it during the present campaign, and those of the same nation are to remain together if they choose and under the immediate command of their own officers, who will continue in the same grades they held in the American army.

7.ᵗ All those persons who come over to the Mexican armies shall be considered, rewarded and promoted in the same way as the Mexicans and according to their services in the present campaign.

The preceding articles shall be duly published in order that the Mexican Authorities may act in conformity thereto.

Head Quarters. Orizava the   April 1847.

Antonio Lopez de Santa-Anna.

A desertion appeal by Santa Anna to Winfield Scott's men during their advance on Mexico City.

The Battle of Churubusco. James Walker's painting of Winfield Scott's regiments storming the Santa Maria de Los Angeles monastery complex, defended by the St. Patrick's Battalion.

Brig. Gen. David E. Twiggs, who oversaw the flogging and branding of John Riley.

The execution of four St. Patrick's Battalion soldiers near Mexico City, as depicted by Chamberlain.

The San Patricios' memorial in Mexico City. Erected in 1959, it lists the names of 71 members of the St. Patrick's Battalion, 48 of which are Irish and 13 German.

A grateful Mexico carries a fallen San Patricio in an illustration from the dustjacket of *Batallón de San Patricio* by Patricia Bustamante Cox, who resurrected the saga for Mexicans.

By 3 o'clock they had stormed within a block of the main plaza, where several thousand Mexican troops were dug in with artillery and where civilians huddled and sobbed inside public buildings. Maloney's company and the other units bashing their way in from the east had closed to within two blocks of the plaza.

Late in the afternoon, Worth's artillery set up a 10-inch mortar near the Plaza de la Capella, the crew using a stone wall as cover. The squat muzzle flung shells into the plaza, and one crashed into the clock tower of the cathedral, tearing away a large chunk of masonry. Luckily for the Mexican soldiers and civilians, the shot did not ignite the tons of powder stored inside the church.

By nightfall, the firing finally stopped. Later, two rounds from Taylor's massive 24-pounder howitzers screamed through the dark and crashed into the plaza. Ampudia, holed up in a private home at the farthest end of the square from the cathedral's gunpowder, had had enough.

Ampudia called for a parley the next morning, September 25, to the fury of many Mexican officers and troops. They believed that one more day of resolute defense behind the barricades and around the sturdy buildings of the plaza would force Taylor to retreat, for another round of American casualties as heavy as those of September 21 and 23 would gut his force and soften it up for a Mexican counterattack. And with Mexican losses low—29 officers and 338 men killed or wounded—Ampudia's numerical advantage was substantial.

Another cadre of Ampudia's officers, like their commander, wanted no part of another American assault. To Taylor and, later, to Santa Anna, Ampudia contended that too many civilians would perish in a battle for the plaza and that he could not allow such slaughter. Ampudia's words had merit, but few of his detractors believed that he had anyone's safety in mind except his own.

After several sessions of negotiations on September 25, Ampudia surrendered the city to Taylor. When the rest of the terms reached Washington, D.C., politicians criticized Taylor: he had agreed to allow the Mexican troops' withdrawal from the city with all of their small arms and a six-gun battery and not to pursue the enemy for eight weeks unless he received specific orders from the War Department.

In Taylor's ranks, the volunteers, particularly the Texans, railed that Old Rough and Ready had lost his stomach for a final fight. The three-day battle, however, had ravaged his army. He admitted officially to 488 killed or wounded. With such severe casualties suffered in just three days and with most troops exhausted and many showing signs of what later armies called shell shock, Taylor made a savvy bargain in most of his men's eyes. Grant welcomed the terms, and Meade approved that Taylor had thought not of personal glory, but of his men and the civilians out of "a higher and nobler motive." [11] Taylor also had Ampudia's assurances that his government was seeking a peaceful resolution to the war.

Of all the combatants, the only ones who had anything to fear about the surrender were John Riley and the deserters: on the following morning, they were expected to march out of the citadel in their Mexican uniforms and past the drawn-up ranks of the American army. How their former messmates would react toward them and the realization that they had manned cannons against them was anyone's guess. And if soldiers whose friends had been torn apart by those guns were to seek immediate revenge against the deserters, Taylor's officers might look the other way.

Early on the morning of September 26, 1846, John Riley buttoned his blue tunic, whose collar was emblazoned with the gold bomb-burst insignia of the Mexican artillery, straightened his kepi, and joined 211 artillerymen at the rear of Ampudia's 1st Brigade. At least 100 were deserters from the U.S. Army.

All of the gunners except the officers formed a column behind the six guns Taylor had allowed Ampudia to keep. Riley and other battery commanders climbed onto the horse-drawn caissons and waited for the cavalry and the infantry ahead to move.

With a roll of drums and blare of trumpets, the column stirred and marched slowly forward out of the grand plaza and west toward the Saltillo road. Thousands of civilians watched the Army of the North file by, some weeping, some muttering, most silent as the regimental banners and lancers' pennants nodded in a warm breeze.

At the western edge of Monterrey, the Americans lined both sides of the Saltillo road, the ranks leaning on their muskets or cradling them in the crooks of their arms. Dozens of officers' hands clutched sword hilts.

The Americans' impressions of the army streaming from the city proved varied. Lieutenant George Deas, standing with the 5th, found the

Mexican infantry in their black leather shakos, blue coats, and white trousers "fine-looking" troops.[12] Other onlookers found the Mexican cavalry a "fine-looking body of men" in their steel helmets and long lances and the infantry formidable men, "brawny and thick-set." These troops, an American officer would remember, "were not a defeated army."[13] Of their ability to beat the Mexicans, Taylor's men were certain, but relieved for the respite.

Some American soldiers saw other aspects of the departing foes. Grant, a fine rider and used to the large horses of the U.S. Army, thought the lancers' mounts "miserable little half-starved creatures that did not look as if they could carry their riders out of town." In the faces of conscripted Mexican militia, he imagined that he saw "how little interest the men before me had in the results of the war, and how little knowledge they had of what it was about."[14] Yet he also admired their fight and blamed their losses on poor leadership.

Ampudia's lancers and regular infantry stared back at the sky-blue lines and wondered how American troops whose uniforms were "as dirty as they could be without becoming real-estate" had carried the three-day battle.[15] Ampudia's betrayal of his own men was the answer many Mexicans offered.

As the six-gun battery in the Mexican columns rumbled into the Americans' view, men of the 5th spotted a tall enemy officer perched on a caisson and looking somehow familiar. "His old mess mates" gaped at John Riley. The Americans recognized other "deserters...in the ranks of the enemy," and mutters swelled into a raucous chorus of curses. Desertion was one thing—but the Americans now grasped that Riley and his men had hurled grape and solid shot at their excomrades.

Pretending not to hear their former army's outcries, the deserters stared forward or at the ground. "Of our deserters," an American captain wrote, "the most conspicuous...was an Irishman named Riley, who had been appointed a captain in the artillery of the enemy. He...passed them [the Americans] amid hisses and a broadside of reproaches. The dastard's cheek blanched, and it was with difficulty he retained his position on his gun."[16]

Mick Maloney and many Irish in the jeering crowd reviled Riley and the other immigrants who had gone over to the enemy, for the deserters' actions cast suspicion upon all Irishmen and Europeans fighting for America despite Nativism in the army. Maloney and others of a similar mind intended to stay put, rise above prejudice, and earn their way as Americans even if it meant fighting against Catholic Mexico. As willingly as any Nativist, many of Taylor's Irishmen would have put a bullet into Riley.

The Mexican battery rattled down the Saltillo road, and the jeers grew fainter. Riley and the rest of the deserters knew that American officers were eager to see them dead but not at the price of Taylor's truce and his wrath. Not all of Taylor's men, however, had jeered and hissed at Riley. Many, concealing copies of Ampudia's leaflet in pockets or knapsacks, intended to join "the dastard." Fathers McElroy and Rey were about to encounter full force desertion's "contagion"; for Zachary Taylor, granting safe passage to Riley and his gunners proved a bloody mistake.

Part Three

The Banner of
Green Silk

14

"The Irish Volunteers"

AMPUDIA'S ARMY MARCHED southwest down the Saltillo road to the city of the same name in three brigades one day apart. After loading up with supplies there, Riley and the rest turned south for the 225-mile march to San Luis Potosi—and Santa Anna.

Through a flat, hard-packed desert the columns tramped, the monotonous terrain broken only by cactus, mesquite, and a few clumps of stunted palms. Riley and the others halted at several wells, where wide wooden wheels powered by mules dipped buckets into the water and filled barrels and canteens.

Three weeks later, Riley and the Army of the North had reached San Luis Potosi, about 300 miles from Mexico City. Santa Anna was waiting for Ampudia's men and a chance to size up the deserters who had shown no qualms about hurling grape and canister at their former army. He had a plan that Riley would welcome.

When Santa Anna summoned Riley, probably in late October 1846, the deserter met a commander who was the complete antithesis of Old Rough and Ready. A gray-eyed, 47-year-old *Criolo*, now portly but still handsome, Santa Anna wore resplendent uniforms and, with his imperious bearing and dark, perfectly groomed hair, looked the part of a general. To Riley the professional soldier, Santa Anna's missing left leg, replaced by a costly cork one after a French cannon ball slammed into him at Vera Cruz in 1838, would have commanded instant respect and earned the general the right to carry a cane of polished iron glittering with gems and with an immense golden eagle on the hilt.

Revered by many Mexicans as "the soldier of the people," reviled by Texans as the butcher of the Alamo and the Goliad massacre and as "the immortal three-fourths" in reference to his amputated leg, Santa Anna was charismatic, vain, opportunistic, and, contrary to his detractors' charges, a fighter. His ability to raise and equip an army was pronounced, and, as he interrogated Riley, Santa Anna encountered an experienced and fearless soldier whom the general could use in his plan to pry at least 2,000 foreigners from Taylor's army.

Santa Anna believed that a unit in which the deserters would serve as a body, rather than scattered through Mexican units, would prove a powerful attraction to immigrants and sought experienced foreigners to lead them. Riley presented himself as the ideal candidate to organize and command the foreign legion, because he could train fellow deserters into artillerymen sorely needed by the Mexicans. He had proven his talents with gun crews in the redoubts of Matamoros and at the walls of Monterrey, and, with so many foreign deserters possessing experience in European or American batteries, he could organize crews faster than Santa Anna could with untrained gunners.

Santa Anna authorized Riley to raise "an artillery company organized from the deserters of the invaders" *(compania de artilleria formada de los desertores del ejercito invasor)*.[1] In the Mexican army's payroll records for November 1846 appeared the *Voluntarios Irlandeses*, the "Irish Volunteers."

To placate any Mexican officers' anger that a newly arrived Irishman be handed a post over them, Santa Anna designated Captain Francisco Rosendo Moreno as the deserters' nominal commander. Moreno, a tall, skilled officer born and raised in Spanish Florida, allowed Riley a free hand in the unit's organization and training. Having witnessed the Irishman's gunnery skills at Monterrey and having struck up a friendship with him, Moreno, who spoke fluent English, worked with Riley to welcome new deserters to the Irish Volunteers and to persuade recruits to man the unit's cannons, wagons, and caissons.

Santa Anna also assigned Second Lieutenants Camillo Manzano, Dubliner Rodmand Batchelor, and John Stephenson—not a deserter but an Irish immigrant—to the unit. And the Mexican commander would keep his word to commission veteran deserters with experience similar to Riley's background.

Santa Anna turned over his heaviest guns, 24- and 16-pounders, to the deserters. On the parade ground of San Luis Potosi, Riley drilled his men hour after hour, the crews shoving the one-ton cannons into battery, firing hundreds of practice rounds, hitching the cast-iron behemoths to six-horse wagons, and hauling the guns to another spot to unlimber them and repeat the drill—again and again. Riley and Moreno also trained the men to ferry ammunition from the caissons to the cannons with a speed that startled Mexican artillerymen. Before long, Santa Anna had Riley and his most experienced gunners teaching their European techniques to other batteries.

An American journalist noted later in the war that Riley and many of his soldiers from "the ould sod" spoke their native Irish with each other. In 1825, a British government survey had determined that over one and a half million Irish, mainly in the remote western counties—Riley's "turf"—spoke their traditional tongue almost exclusively. Parliament's Education Act of 1831 established in Ireland a system of national schools instructing children in English and excluding the Irish language, but many men and women of Riley's generation still possessed only enough English to get by in either their homeland or America. Once in the Mexican army, the Irish also picked up enough Spanish to get by. Riley may have spoken in Irish to make a point on the drill field to countrymen with little grasp of English, but he also commanded Germans and other Europeans who shared little more language with the Irish than the English they had gleaned in the U.S. Army. The language barrier compelled Riley and Moreno, who was fluent in English, to likely issue orders in the "Anglo Saxon" tongue of Ireland's oppressors and Mexico's would-be conquerors.

Off the drill field, the deserters found San Luis Potosi a lovely haven in which they could rest sore muscles, throbbing ears, and stinging eyes. On Sundays, Riley and others could attend mass in Our Lady of Carmen

Cathedral, whose tiled domes glittered blue, yellow, white, and green in the sunlight. Inside, worshipers stood and knelt with both grandees and peasants amid gilded walls and statues of the saints. Catholic Germans among the deserters may have worshipped amid such Baroque or Gothic splendor in their homeland, but for Riley and fellow Irish immigrants accustomed to the rude stone churches of their homeland, Our Lady of Carmen, like the cathedral of Monterrey, drew awe-struck stares.

Finding a warm welcome not only in the churches, but also from the city's 30,000 citizens, the deserters attended bullfights, fandangos, and the theater and strolled along streets flanked by handsome stone homes. Locals and fellow soldiers dubbed Riley and his gunners *Los Colorados,* the "red ones," in reference to the red hair and ruddy complexions of some of the Irishmen; the unit also contained Germans, Frenchmen, and other deserters whose faces were equally flushed. Los Colorados generally heeded locals' warnings to stay away from the hovels on the city's fringes, where *leperos,* murderers, and robbers roamed.

Notwithstanding the pleasures of the mountain city, Santa Anna's frenzied military buildup consumed the deserters' days. As he cobbled together his army through a two million peso loan from the church, a sizable chunk of his own fortune, and his seizure of 98 giant silver bars from the mines and mint of the city, he planned an offensive against the Americans. Concerned that some of Ampudia's men were frightening other troops with vivid accounts of the Americans' battlefield prowess, Santa Anna issued a general order to imprison any man spreading such talk. He could not afford low morale among his 25,000 troops, for his intent was clear in the very name of his gathering force: the Liberating Army of the North.

Most of the army's units carried individual and distinctive banners. Riley sketched a design for his unit's flag and, according to Mexican sources, took his drawing to a San Luis Potosi convent and asked the nuns to sew his banner. Whether "embroidered by the hands of the fair nuns of San Luis Potosi" or by tailors in the town, the flag was to become the most famous, or infamous, of the war.[2] An American war correspondent would describe Riley's flag for readers:

> The banner is of green silk, and on one side is a harp, surmounted by the Mexican coat of arms, with a scroll on which it is painted, "*Liberatad*

por la Republica Mexicana" ["Liberty for the Mexican Republic"].
Underneath the harp is the motto *"Erin go Bragh"* ["Ireland Forever"]. On
the other side is a painting...made to represent St. Patrick, in his left
hand a key and in his right a crook or staff resting upon a serpent.
Underneath is painted *"San Patricio."* [3]

As December 1846 neared, Riley and Moreno were having little trouble
in recruiting men to serve under the green flag. Deserters, aided by civilians and guided by rancheros through the desert and into the mountains, were reaching San Luis Potosi. By year's end, the Irish Volunteers
comprised not only Riley's gun crews and wagon teams, but also supporting troops trained to cover the battery and to take dead or wounded
gunners' places. The unit's estimated strength was 100 to 150, and, while
Irishmen dominated the muster roll, Germans, other foreigners, and
even some Americans slipped south from Taylor's camps at Camargo
and Monterrey.

On September 22, 1847, even as the battle for Monterrey blazed,
Taylor had ordered his officers to arrest "false priests" working "to entice
our gallant Roman Catholic soldiers who have done so much honor to
our colors, to desert, under a promise of lands in California." [4]

Once Ampudia's army had marched south and Taylor had occupied
Monterrey, the same problems between immigrants and officers in the
camps appeared, along with a loosely orchestrated campaign by various
Mexicans to foster desertion. Just three weeks after the battle, Taylor
reported that several Monterrey priests had persuaded "some fifty more
men to desert." [5] Many were Irish, but the clerics also singled out
Germans. In November, a "Dutch" priest in the city helped John A.
Meyers, a German private in the 5th Regiment, to reach San Luis Potosi
by bringing the deserter to a Mexican colonel operating with rancheros
south of the city. When Auguste Morstadt sneaked out of the 7th
Infantry's camp on November 3 and swam across the Santa Catarina
River, a Mexican priest was waiting to show him the route to San Luis
Potosi. Herman Schmidt, of the 3d Infantry; Karl Schmitt, an artillery-
man; and scores of other Germans also turned up at Santa Anna's camp
in late 1846.

A German who did not desert wrote: "In fact, there are a great many of
our soldiers deserting...[because] the Mexicans held out inducements

of great promise to our men, to desert and join their just cause . . . they were only successful among the Catholic portion of our army who were persuaded by priests that it was wrong and sinful to fight against their religion."[6]

Along with local priests' efforts, Mexican agents such as English-born Nicholas Sinnott slipped in and out of the northern theater of operations to aid deserters on their way south. Of the first 50 deserters from Monterrey, an Ohio major huffed: "These the enemy joyfully received and speedily enrolled in their ranks, where they served with a courage and fidelity they had never exhibited in ours. Doubtless the humblest soldier of the battalion of Saint Patrick was honored with much consideration by the Mexicans."[7]

As at Matamoros, the Mexicans focused upon Taylor's foreign-born regulars, for Santa Anna wanted no part of the volunteers. In some ways, neither did Taylor himself. To protect Monterrey's civilians, he garrisoned the city only with regulars and encamped the volunteers in the countryside. But he could not control small bands of marauding militiamen around the clock. On October 5, a Texan volunteer gunned down a civilian in Monterrey. Taylor arrested him and wrote Marcy a letter requesting procedures to try the prisoner for murder. Marcy advised Taylor that no trial could take place because murder of a civilian was not addressed in the Articles of War; besides, Marcy wrote, no United States court would uphold a conviction in the case. All Taylor could do was send the culprit home unpunished.

Taylor did so and began releasing entire volunteer units from service. "With their departure," he wrote, "we may look for a restoration of quiet and order in Monterrey, for I regret to report that some shameful atrocities have been perpetuated by them since the capitulation of the town."[8]

Taylor also forbade any volunteers to enter Monterrey without a pass and ordered that any with a pass be out of the city before buglers sounded evening retreat. But, so deep in Mexican territory and with a large army gathering against him, Taylor could not send all of the volunteers home. Nor could he prevent desecrations of churches and retaliations for rancheros' killings of volunteers who wandered alone too far from camp in search of women, liquor, or just fresh air.

When Taylor invested Saltillo in early November 1846 and left General William Worth there as military governor, the latter strained diligently to protect the civilians. Worth wrote to his daughter about his frustrating post:

> I give an audience of our hours to attend to the wants and complaints of the people. The lawless Volunteers stop at no outrage . . . The innocent blood that has been basely, cowardly, and barbarously shed in cold blood, aside from other and deeper crimes, will appeal to Heaven, for, and I trust, receive just retribution. I cut matters short by administering off-hand justice although it is not always law.[9]

Various priests seized upon the crimes of Protestant volunteers to urge Roman Catholic troops to "follow the impulses of their hearts" and "pass over to our army to defend our just cause."[10] From San Luis Potosi, seven priests penned a tract that targeted Taylor's most recently arrived Irishmen. In anti-Polk newspapers reaching the army's camps from Point Isabel to Saltillo, translations of Mexican diatribes ended up in the hands of Irish regulars. The address of the San Luis Potosi priests was one; it denounced the volunteers, but not the regulars, as "Vandals, vomited from Hell who worship no God but gold" and "defile churches, destroy venerated vessels, overthrowing holy sacraments." The priests challenged: "Will you consent . . . to have the holy rites of your church abolished and the sign of your redemption exterminated? . . . Two fates are left open to you: to be vile slaves or independent Catholics."[11]

Other anti-Polk missives asked Irishmen how, in good conscience, they could serve an army whose volunteers not only reviled Catholic immigrants, but also made Mexican women—fellow Catholics—"victims to lascivious passions, even in the streets."[12] How would the Irish react to such crimes against their own women? asked translations from *Diario del Gobierno* and other Mexican publications. They contended that the volunteers were the same sort of men who had unleashed the Nativist riots and "put fire to your temples in Boston and Philadelphia."[13] A letter by Santa Anna would typify these appeals: "Are Catholic Irishmen to be the destroyers of Catholic temples, the murderers of Catholic priests, and the founders of heretical rites in this pious nation?"[14]

So too did another *Diario del Gobierno* harangue against volunteers "who have . . . clothed themselves in the ornaments of the altars, who have thrown upon the ground the body of Jesus Christ, and have made themselves drunk in drinking out of the sacred vessels."[15]

Of all the Mexican agents tempting would-be deserters, an enigmatic priest named Eugene McNamara most enraged Taylor and, later, his successor, General Winfield Scott. An Irish-born cleric and missionary working in Mexico, McNamara had floated a scheme to settle 50,000 Irish families in Mexican California as a bulwark against American expansion there. At the behest of the Mexican government, he actually met with Governor Pio Pico at Santa Barbara to set the plan in motion, but the outbreak of war gutted McNamara's venture. Captain John C. Fremont and his men declared the Bear Flag Republic at Sonoma, California, on July 4, 1846; three days later, U.S. Navy Commodore Robert F. Stockton sailed into Monterey, California. He occupied Los Angeles on August 13. McNamara fled late that month on a British vessel bound for Mexico via Honolulu.

Taylor's angry mention of Mexico's promise of lands in California to Catholic deserters referred to McNamara's failed scheme. The Irish missionary would soon reach Mexico City and work with Foreign Minister Manuel Baranda to pry Irishmen from the regulars, and the cleric's campaign eventually would earn futile appeals by American officers for his arrest and execution.

Among the regulars and the volunteers alike, officers professed outrage that Mexican priests were urging Catholic soldiers to desert the Army of Occupation. A 3d Infantry captain wrote: "On the 5th [November 1846] a priest was detected inducing our men to desert.... The reverend gentleman was placed in confinement and was shipped to Camargo. If he gets his just deserts [sic], he should be hung, in spite of his sanctity."[16]

In response to nationalistic priests' actions, Taylor issued the following declaration to occupied towns:

> Your religion, your altars and churches, the property of your churches and citizens, the emblems of your faith and its ministers, shall be protected and remain inviolate. Hundreds of our army and hundreds of thousands of our people are members of the Catholic church. In every State, and in nearly every city and village of our Union, Catholic churches exist, and the priests perform their holy functions in peace and security, under the sacred guarantee of our Constitution.[17]

Mexican tracts passed around Taylor's camps, however, reminded immigrants that *Protestant Magazine* railed against "those doctrines and practices of Roman Catholicism which are contrary to the interests of mankind."[18]

Father Rey convinced hundreds of unassimilated Irishmen and other Catholics to stay put, telling them that they would find only false promises and a "pagan" and corrupt version of Catholicism in Mexico. The Catholic bishops of America, the men were informed, supported the government, and they were bound by their enlistment oaths to do likewise.

Another reason, based less on ideology than on pragmatism, compelled immigrants to weigh daily Nativist abuse against the uncertainties of desertion: from assimilated veterans such as Mick Maloney to fresh cannon fodder from the coffin ships, many simply believed that Mexico could not defeat the U.S. Army. An immigrant artilleryman held that the only factor stopping wholesale desertions of the Irish was that joining "the Mexican service . . . was literally jumping out of the frying pan into the fire." [19]

Still, scores of men made that jump from the regulars. And Taylor and Rey not only continued to vie with several local priests for Catholic troops, but also with civilian agents. In Monterrey, several citizens, including the *alcalde*'s (mayor's) son, circulated promises of $60, civilian clothing, a horse, and a guide to escort deserters to San Luis Potosi. Several unnamed soldiers approached three of the plotters in the city, took the $60 each, and gave a signal. Another group of soldiers pounced from behind a corner and arrested the civilians.

A Monterrey man made the mistake of whispering promises of cash and high rank in Santa Anna's army to several Irishmen who served not in the regulars, but in the 1st Regiment of Ohio Volunteers. Since most of the Irishmen in the militias tended to have put down roots in their units' various regions, these men proved far less amenable to Mexican overtures. The 80 Irishmen of the 1st Ohio fell into this category, and one of their officers, Major Luther Giddings, a Protestant, bragged about the response of "his Irish" to the enemy agent. "They were all Irishmen," he wrote, "and never did ferrets pursue a rat more indefatigably than [they] did their pretended friend. He was a wily rascal and, scenting his danger, had, after many windings and turnings ensconced himself in a bake-oven in one of the back yards of the city whence he was finally dragged by the heels and lodged in the guard house."

Giddings boasted that "not a single Volunteer, either among the native or adopted [naturalized] citizens, went over to the enemy." [20] He stated that foreign-born regulars were more prone to desertion because, "as the better-disciplined troops [they] were garrisoned in important cities where they came in contact with pampered and frantic friars."[21] The volunteers, stationed in the countryside, he wrote, encountered priests who were "pious men of unblemished lives"—not to mention wary of the raucous militias.

Giddings's assertion that no volunteers deserted was inaccurate, for 6 percent did go over the hill; but they did not join the Mexicans. Disillusionment with army life, fear of disease, and the realization that Taylor, Worth, and later Scott were sternly disciplining and dismissing many who were caught stealing, raping, and murdering—these realities drove volunteers' desertions.

Giddings's assessment that desertion mainly plagued the regular army was absolutely correct: of the regulars, a staggering 13 percent— the highest figure by far in the U.S. Army's wars—went over the hill in Mexico. By December 1, 1846, Taylor reported 152 desertions, but many more had not yet been listed as deserters, merely as "missing," an all-inclusive term allowing for men who had wandered off during drunken sprees and might return. Taylor instructed his officers that any man returning from a "spree" be disciplined as a drunkard, but not as a deserter, sparing such men the rawhide lash, the noose, or a firing squad. The distinction between drunkenness and desertion was to prove a controversial one a year later, when the U.S. Army stood outside the gates of Mexico City.

As desertion swelled in late 1846 from Matamoros to Monterrey, "the cause commonly assigned by the officers for their [Irish immigrants'] desertion was that as they were Roman Catholics, they imagined they were fighting against their religion by fighting the Mexicans," wrote a veteran regular. But he added that religion, combined with "harsh and unjust treatment by their officers" upon the Irish, "operated . . . to produce these deplorable results."[22]

In Taylor's encampments, officers who, on the eve of battle, had slapped their men's backs in comradely fashion, returned to more familiar behavior. "Sure," remarked an Irish private, "there's not one of the creatures [officers] has a heart as big as a grasshopper's."[23] "Dirty, miserly rascals," "rapscallions," "ignorant," "tyrannical," "brutal," "a rat"—these terms poured even from Irishmen who did not desert. Said

Private Mick Ryan, "It's a gag they would be after putting in my mouth in the place of a pipe."[24]

The gag and the other corporal punishments separated the complaints of the Mick Ryans from the normal gripes of men against their officers. The ongoing use of the buck and gag especially infuriated veterans of the British army. One labeled the practice as "this revolting and disgusting punishment . . . often inflicted at the mere whim of an officer."[25]

Samuel Chamberlain's memoir of the Mexican War would capture Captain Thomas Sherman at his raging worst as he imposed the buck and gag. Outside Monterrey, Sherman sent Chamberlain, a dragoon serving as a corporal of the guard one afternoon, to arrest John Dougherty, an Irishman who had been wounded and honorably mustered from the ranks. Dougherty now made his living selling liquor just outside the base. Sherman, his full, handsome visage tight, his thick neck muscles twitching, accused him of illegally selling liquor to soldiers, peppering his charge with profanities.

Sherman ordered Chamberlain and seven others to strip Dougherty to the waist and to tie him to a tree. Then, Sherman sent a guard to fetch a rawhide lash from a caisson, and, when the man returned, the officer pointed at Chamberlain.

"You!" Sherman bellowed. "Apply fifty lashes to that man."

Chamberlain hesitated. Then he asked Sherman whether he had the authority to whip a civilian.

Sherman screamed the order again. Chamberlain demurred and reportedly waved a carbine at Sherman.

The captain yelled, "Buck him and gag him!"

The other guards grabbed Chamberlain, trussed him on the ground with ropes and a bulky tent pin, and stuffed a gag in his mouth. Chamberlain would recall the ordeal as excruciating.

Spewing epithets, Sherman ordered another soldier to whip Dougherty, who was braced against the tree, his eyes shut. The soldier refused and was bucked and gagged.

A crowd of other officers and men had gathered near Sherman and gaped as he ordered five other guards to flog Dougherty and they defied the command. Several of them Irishmen, they were also bucked and gagged alongside Chamberlain.

The eighth guard to whom Sherman issued the order picked up the

rawhide, stepped behind Dougherty, wound up, and snapped the knotted tails against his back. Dougherty screamed until he fainted at some
point during the punishment. Sherman ordered the guard to deliver the
final 25 lashes and to drag the unconscious civilian from camp.
Chamberlain, who endured the buck and gag for two hours in the heat,
pronounced it "the most unfortunate day of my history." [26]

Sherman filed mutiny charges against Chamberlain. Chamberlain
faced a court-martial headed by Captain John M. Washington, who had
said that he always gave more credence to an officer's word than that of
any enlisted man. At first, Chamberlain was apparently sentenced to
death, but General John Wool reduced the punishment to hard labor
with a 12-pound iron ball chained to Chamberlain's leg.

Sherman continued to buck and gag others as he had done
Chamberlain. But Braxton Bragg, one of Sherman's chief rivals as the
army's harshest officer, was about to discover that some enlisted men
were ready to settle scores with their tormentors.

On a soft, moonlit night at Walnut Springs, several soldiers sneaked to
the tent where Bragg lay sound asleep. They lit the fuse of an 8-inch-
artillery shell, rolled it through the tent's flap and ran away.

A minute or so later the shell exploded and sent men pouring to
Bragg's tent. They pulled him from the pile of shredded, burning canvas
and the pieces of his baggage and cot and carried him, his face and hair
singed, his nightshirt scorched, to a medical tent. To the disappointment of his would-be murderers and hundreds of other men, the North
Carolinian had escaped the blast with bruises, minor cuts, and a desire
for revenge.

The culprits were never identified, as the suspects' numbers included
countless immigrants and other enlisted men he had bucked and gagged,
thrashed, or deposited on the wooden horse. The *Niles National Register*
offered the army's succinct cause of the crime: "His men think he is too
severe in his discipline." [27] Bragg did not care and would apply the buck
and gag and the rawhide lash with regularity for the rest of his tour of
duty. Several months later, he would encounter another explosion in his
tent and would walk away from it again.

Desertions from Bragg's command, Battery E of the 3d Artillery, and from that of the 3d's Battery C, led by Sherman, proved especially high.[28] Dozens of foreign-born, veteran gunners, including Andrew Nolan of Down, Ireland; Henry Ockter of Osnabrück, Germany; and Irishman Richard Hanley, who was afraid of Duncan, would soon turn up alongside John Riley's cannons. Private William Keech of the 4th Artillery was punished for briefly "falling out of the company" during drill and was bucked and gagged by one of his officers. According to a battery sergeant, Keech "declared that no man in the army would have the opportunity of tying him up again.... and I [the noncom] have never seen him since."[29] Keech had deserted and joined Riley.

Ockter, who barely spoke English but who knew his way around a cannon, fell while pushing a fieldpiece from a mud puddle and shattered his collarbone. He reportedly asked his battery commander, Captain Washington, for permission to seek aid at a hospital tent, but Washington cursed him as a "lazy Dutchie" and promised he would buck and gag the German if he went anywhere near a surgeon. At his first opportunity Ockter disappeared. "The reason why I ran away was because I could not do duty, and they made me do it," Ockter said.[30] He would recover to man a gun with Riley and his crews.

Infantrymen and dragoons also slipped south to escape their officers. Private Lachlin McLachlin, a foot soldier, joined Riley's Irish Volunteers because of constant beatings "by one of the lieutenants of my company, who abused [me] and threatened to take [my] life, even though [I] was soldiering as well as I knew how."[31]

Downriver, at Camargo, an Irishman who knew something about soldiering well was Private Patrick Dalton. His unit had arrived at Camargo too late to march to Monterrey, but the men had heard about John Riley and the epaulets he now wore in the Mexican army. Dalton, having likely come to America less than a year before his enlistment in August 1845, harbored ambitions of rank and glory similar to Riley's and knew that no unnaturalized immigrant was going far in Polk's army.

On October 23, 1846, Sergeant William Marshall led Dalton and a contingent of Company B to wash their clothing in the Rio Grande. The Irishman finished his chore quickly, and, when he asked for permission to return to camp ahead of the others, Marshall, who considered Dalton "a very good man and soldier," consented. As the light-haired, ruddy-faced Mayo man ambled north along the riverbank and disappeared into a distant cornfield, his sergeant thought nothing of it.

The burly Irishman hid among the stalks all day, hoping that some soldiers would not wade into the field to "pull corn." No one did. He crawled to the bank at nightfall and slid into the rapid current. On the opposite shore, he clambered from the water and straight into two rancheros.

"They conveyed me to a place where they had some mules and some men," Dalton remembered.[32] A few hours later, he was bouncing atop a burro as the rancheros led him southwest.

Dalton's desertion was not his first. On his enlistment paper, signed on August 2, 1845, at Madison Barracks in New York, the native of Ballina, in County Mayo, had listed his birthplace as Quebec. Dalton had lied to conceal his recent flight from a British unit stationed in Canada. A mere handful of American sergeants demanded that Irish, English, Welsh, and Scottish recruits with the look of veteran soldiers produce a British army "purchase discharge" before mustering them into America's regulars. A Scot described the sort of interview in which Dalton had lied about his past: "The sergeant in charge of enlistment, having asked me if I had been in the British service, to which I replied in the affirmative, said in that case he was afraid they could not enlist me, as they had recently received an order from Washington to that effect; deserters from the British service having generally turned out bad soldiers."[33] Unlike Dalton, the Scot had produced a British discharge.

Although Colonel Bennet Riley commanded the 2d Infantry, and his desertion rates proved slightly lower than those of the other regular regiments, Companies B and I had their share go over the hill. Captain Edmund Alexander, later transferred to the 3d, heaped curses and rough discipline upon Company B, whose rolls included mainly immigrants enlisted, like Dalton, at Madison Barracks. Twenty-three-year-old Irishman John Cuttle fled from Company B after Dalton, and ten others followed soon after.

On the evening of October 23, 1846, Sergeant Marshall noted that Dalton "was absent and reported [him] a deserter." The Irishman plodded atop his mule into Montemorelas, 45 miles south of Monterrey, four days later and was brought by the rancheros to the town's *alcalde*. "He set me at liberty," Dalton would say.

The mayor and everyone else Dalton first met spoke Spanish only, and he wandered around the dusty streets to "inquire if there was anyone who spoke English in the town." To his relief, he eventually discovered an old German who did. "He advised me not to attempt to go forward without a passport and without armed guides," Dalton recalled. "The next day I got a passport and set off for the interior of the country."

Dalton reached San Luis Potosi in late November 1846, was brought by rancheros to the governor's palace, and escorted across a white-pillared portico and into the headquarters of Santa Anna. Dalton convinced the Mexican general of his experience behind a cannon.

The Irishman later stated: "He [Santa Anna] asked me whether I would join the artillery or not. I then got a commission of [second] lieutenant."[34]

Santa Anna had added another skilled artillerist to the Irish Volunteers. John Riley welcomed not only a tough, capable new gunner, but also a fellow Irishman who had been reared in that land's famine-ravaged west, had worn the hated British redcoat, and had soldiered "manfully."[35] In barracks and on the battlefield, the two men would forge a deep friendship and respect. Several future writers would see the pair less as deserters than as Irish-Catholic mercenaries in the centuries-old plight of their homeland's Wild Geese, those hardened soldiers of fortune serving in every Catholic army "save their own."

At services in and around Monterrey throughout December 1846, Father Rey reminded Catholic immigrants that their duty was to remain in the ranks and "turn the other cheek" to Nativism. Father McElroy, from Matamoros to Point Isabel, sermonized the same themes of duty and sacred oath. For hundreds of listeners, the two Jesuits' promises of eternal damnation for desertion outweighed the private hells many suffered daily at the hands of tyrannical officers. Not only were the promises of Mexican priests false, Rey and McElroy reiterated, but so was the enemy's brand of Catholicism. Riley and the others who had joined the Mexicans, the priests warned, were cursed by America and God alike.

In late 1846, scraps of information about the deserters who had served cannons at Matamoros and Monterrey first appeared in war correspondents' dispatches home. From the *Daily Picayune* of New Orleans, the first mention of "O'Reilly" spread into newspapers across the nation. The *National Police Gazette*, a widely read periodical on crime issues, ran the adjutant general's list of known deserters from

Taylor's army, and Nativists pounced on the surnames to question the loyalty of all Irishmen, pre-Famine and new immigrants alike, and to launch a new wave of anti-immigrant hysteria. The *Boston Pilot* and other Catholic publications also ran the desertion lists but pointed out that not all of the deserters were Irish and that some were Germans and native-born Americans. The latter fact did more harm than good to the *Pilot's* argument, as the Nativists lumped German Catholic immigrants into the "Popish plot."

Once again, the Nativist press harangued the War Department's ongoing recruitment of immigrants into the regular army. With nearly 175,000 Irish spilling into eastern ports from 1840 to 1844 and nearly 400,000 on the way from 1847 to 1848, the Nativists raised fears even among Americans more tolerant of immigrants. "If this [exodus] goes on," pronounced an article,

> as it is likely to go on . . . the United States will become very Irish. . . . So an Ireland there will still be, but on a colossal scale, and in a new world. We shall only have pushed the Celt westwards. Then, no longer cooped up between the Liffey and the Shannon, he will spread from New York to San Francisco, and keep up the ancient feud at an unforseen advantage.[36]

Congressman Lewis Levin and his fellow Nativist representatives introduced a bill on the House floor to compel the War Department's recruitment of native-born Americans only. In Albany, New York politicians were floating a law to curb the influx of Famine Irish and other foreigners and would pass it for a time in 1847. Nativist leaders from around the nation announced that in 1847 politicians and ministers from all Protestant sects would gather at Binghampton, New York, to address the "Catholic menace."

President Polk, Secretary of War Marcy, and Adjutant General Jones bucked the Nativists by enlisting immigrants, but not out of any affinity for them. In late December 1846, as word of the bloodshed and disease awaiting soldiers on the Rio Grande was carried home by wounded or ailing regulars and volunteers, many Americans professed support for the war but preferred to let someone else—foreigners—do the fighting and dying. The army, lagging some 7,000 men behind its target quota, stepped up recruitment of immigrants; Irish, Germans, and other foreigners alone composed one-third of the new regulars taking the oath and boarding steamers for Mexico.

Nativists in the northeast feared the soaring immigration levels as a religious threat. Southerners feared that immigrants to the northern seaports would embrace Abolitionism. Westerners dreaded the prospect of Irish political domination as more and more naturalized immigrants spread to sparsely settled regions. And even Americans condemning Nativist themes were willing to let the immigrants soldier for Manifest Destiny.

The reports of desertion along the Rio Grande and the Nativists' exploitation of them unnerved assimilated Irish-Americans, who realized that the loyalty question and the surge of new immigrants undermined the hard-won gains of pre-Famine Irish. To Nativist charges, the Catholic press responded that if native-born Americans were so loyal, they should "go to Mexico, like the Irish."[37]

Neither defensive Irish Americans nor rabid Nativists knew yet about John Riley's green banner.

15

"In High Disgrace the Holy Banner of St. Patrick"

On January 3, 1847, General Winfield Scott and his staff stepped from a steamer at Camargo. He had arrived as Polk's new commander-in-chief of the U.S. Army of Occupation and with the president's authority to launch a campaign against Mexico City, but not the southward strike Taylor had envisioned. Scott planned an amphibious assault at "impregnable" Vera Cruz and a westward strike at Mexico's capital. Taylor, rightly deemed by Democrat Polk as a potential Whig candidate for president, was to have no role in the daring campaign retracing the route by which Cortez had conquered the Aztecs. Taylor was far to the west in Victoria, having rushed there when Santa Anna made an abortive foray north with 1,500 cavalry.

Although Polk had forbid Scott from apprising Taylor of the switch in command and strategy, on November 25, 1846, Scott sent Old Rough and Ready a letter that broadly hinted at the changes. "I am not coming, my dear general," Scott wrote, "to supercede you in the immediate command on the line of operations rendered illustrious by you and your gallant army. My proposed theater is different. . . .

"I shall be obligated to take from you most of the gallant officers and men [regulars and volunteers] whom you have so long and nobly commanded."[1] Scott claimed that in the spring reinforcements would allow

Taylor to push southward. Polk, however, had decided that Taylor's days on the offensive had ended and that the hero of Monterrey must be neutralized militarily as well as politically. The president was also fuming over the truce that had allowed the escape of Ampudia's army to San Luis Potosi.

With Taylor to the south at Victoria, Scott ordered General William O. Butler to start the bulk of Taylor's army, including all his regulars except several batteries and some dragoons, moving eastward. They were headed to Tampico, on Mexico's eastern coast about 225 miles from San Luis Potosi and a staging area for the impending amphibious assault.

Winfield Scott, the man who would lead the invasion, was 60 years old, a career soldier who had earned national acclaim in the War of 1812 with his brilliant battlefield performances against British regulars at Chippewa and the savage battle of Lundy's Lane. So outspoken that he had been court-martialed in 1809 for criticizing a superior officer and had been booted from the army for a year, Winfield Scott had spent his suspension studying European tactics and returned to the service as its most knowledgeable officer. He had been named general-in-chief of the U.S. Army in 1841 and had proven instrumental in forming the flying batteries that had ravaged the Mexicans along the Rio Grande. Relegated to Washington by Polk, who disliked him just a little less than he disliked Taylor, until November 1846, Scott now grasped his chance to make military history in the footsteps of Cortez. The same European military experts who had given Taylor little chance against the Mexicans gave Scott even less.

As Mick Maloney, whose valor had just earned him the lieutenant's bars that more recent immigrants could not wear, and the cream of Taylor's 12,500-man army headed past Camargo to the mouth of the Rio Grande, many took their first glimpse of the six-foot four-inch, 250-pound Scott in his gold-braided uniform. Veterans of the Napoleonic wars saw a general akin to a French or Prussian field marshal, confidence, conceit, and ability radiating from his creased features. Sam Grant wrote: "The awesome Scott was an Army formalist, valuing ceremony, dress, and the niceties of military etiquette. He was impeccable, even frigid, in morals, taking pains to praise virgin spinsters as 'the blest [sic] of their sex.'" [2] Dubbed "Old Fuss and Feathers" by junior officers, he was the antithesis of folksy Old Rough and Ready in all respects except the most important: his ability to command.

As Scott siphoned off Taylor's troops, he sent two couriers galloping separately to Taylor with detailed plans of the new deployments. One of the riders, infantry Lieutenant John Alexander Richey, West Point class of 1845, headed toward Victoria with a small, heavily armed escort. On January 13, 1846, the detachment neared the dusty village of Villa Gran, roughly halfway between Victoria and Monterrey.

As the small column was running low on water and provisions, Richey rode into the village alone over the protests of his men. They dismounted and waited as he disappeared amid sand-colored huts. By nightfall, the young Ohioan had not returned.

At daybreak Richey's men searched the village but found nothing except glares from a few townspeople. Then, on the outskirts of Villa Gran, the dragoons discovered Richey's trussed corpse—but not the dispatches he had carried. Rancheros were tearing south to San Luis Potosi with details of Taylor's weakened dispositions.

To the north of Monterrey, another death rattled the Americans. Father Rey, trusting his clerical collar to protect him, rode alone into the countryside on a trip to Matamoros. He encountered a party of rancheros or bandits and was murdered, though no one knew exactly how. Search parties never located the priest's body, but several bands of volunteers, who did not particularly like Rey's religion but respected his valor, ransacked and burned several ranches in retaliation.

The murder distressed Taylor, who had come to like the priest and had welcomed his aid in preaching against desertion, and many of Taylor's officers believed that local Mexican priests had persuaded rancheros to kill Rey. An American major wrote:

> Father Rey...was a member of the society of Jesuits...an unpopular order in Mexico.... It was hinted by some that while his ostensible mission was to counteract the influence of the Mexican priests and their insidious attempts to cause disaffection among our Catholic soldiers, his object was to secure, in the progress of events, the interests of his order, whose vast estates and possessions had been confiscated upon their [the Jesuits'] banishment.[3]

Rey had been riding downriver to join up with the departing regulars to minister to those flirting with desertion.

As the exodus to Tampico began, many soldiers believed that peace was at hand and that they would board steamers for home. Even junior officers thought the same until they marched into Camargo and learned that they would steam south. The news sent scores of men such as the 6th Infantry's Roger Duhan, of Roscommon, Ireland, over the hill. Duhan's unit, Company F, would lose more Irish and German deserters because of harsh discipline than any of the regiment's other companies. In Matamoros, Father McElroy reminded hundreds of immigrants of their duty to finish what they had started in American blue, to march with Scott to Mexico City.

Taylor dashed off a furious reply to Scott's peremptory note to Butler, criticizing Scott's heavy-handed approach and the reduction of Taylor's force to fewer than a thousand regulars and several thousand largely untested volunteers. But, disappointing Polk, Old Rough and Ready did not resign, "however much I may feel personally mortified and outraged by the course pursued, unprecedented, at least in our own history."[4] Taylor also defied Scott's, as well as Marcy's and Polk's, suggestions "to abandon Saltillo, and to make no detachments...much beyond Monterrey."[5] Old Rough and Ready decided that "the safest course" to meet any northward thrust by the Mexicans was to move most of his stripped-down army to Saltillo and into "the heart of the country."[6]

Taylor was planning a gradual southward march to San Luis Potosi, for even though he suspected that Richey's letters sat on Santa Anna's desk, he believed the Mexicans' only option was to meet Scott's invasion at Vera Cruz. Scott concurred.

On January 26, 1847, Taylor, still believing rumors that the Mexicans would not march north, wrote of "a report...from Saltillo, sixty or seventy miles in front of this [Monterrey], where there is considerable force stationed." He noted "that one or two companies of the Arkansas mounted men, under Major Borland...sent in advance some fifty or sixty miles, to gain intelligence and watch the movements of the enemy, has been surprised and the whole captured; although it comes from an officer of high rank, yet I flatter myself it will prove erroneous."[7] Any sizable Mexican force in that region, Taylor wrote, was cavalry retreating back to San Luis Potosi. He began moving his men south, nearly 5,000 under General John Wool marching to Agua Nueva, 18 miles past Saltillo; Taylor rode there himself in mid-February 1847. He played down reports of Mexican cavalry materializing farther down the road.

On January 26, 1847, at San Luis Potosi, the Irish Volunteers and the rest of Santa Anna's 21,553 troops received marching orders. John Riley and the deserters were told to pack an extra shirt or two, besides the one worn beneath their coats, four rounds of ammunition per man, and cooking utensils. The "San Patricios," as the Mexicans now called them, were to head north. Ever the gambler, Santa Anna planned to hit Taylor with an overwhelming force and to deal with Scott later.

Several days before their orders came, Riley and his men had paraded and drilled for Santa Anna, his staff, and local dignitaries. The editor of the Mexico City newspaper *El Republicano* wrote:

> We had the pleasure Sunday last of seeing [the] American deserters, mostly Irish, reviewed by his Excellency, the general in chief. They are perfectly armed and equipped and on the point of departure.... These brave men, who have abandoned one of the most unjust causes for the purpose of defending the territory of their adopted country, will find in the Mexican ranks a frank and loyal heart, open and hospitable; and besides, a just and ample recompense for their merited services.[8]

Riley and Moreno drew up their ranks, hitched up their artillery train on the sun-splashed morning of January 27, 1847, and moved into the grand plaza. The rest of the Mexican batteries, 20 or so guns ranging from 8- to 24-pounders, the sappers, and the engineers joined them.

The rest of the army stood at attention, lining the square and the road leading northward. As thousands of citizens cheered and tossed garlands from balconies and rooftops, Riley, on horseback, and his unit clattered to the head of the column beneath their glittering green banner.

"Vivas" poured down on the deserters and swelled as Santa Anna and his generals galloped in front of the Irish Volunteers and halted. Then, "the man who was Mexico" removed his field marshal's hat and waved it several times for silence. Slowly the cheers subsided, horses' neighs and snorts and hooves scraping impatiently against cobblestones the only sounds.

"Privations of all kinds await you," Santa Anna shouted to his troops.

But when has want or penury weakened your spirit or debilitated your enthusiasm? The Mexican soldier is well known for his frugality and capability of sufferance. Today you commence your march through thinly settled country, without supplies and without provisions; but you may be assured that very quickly you will be in possession of those of your enemy, and of his riches! And with them, all your wants will be remedied![9]

Then, Santa Anna pointed to the north. Cheers cascaded from the rooftops and balconies, and regimental bands struck up the plaintive tune "Adios." Riley's horse-drawn battery lurched forward and rolled past the "rose-tinted buildings and multicolored domes and towers... that glittered in the sun" and out of San Luis Potosi.[10] Six brigades of infantry and cavalry would follow "the San Patricios...almost all of them Irish," from January 28 to February 2, 1847, with camp followers, wives, and sweethearts swarming just behind, coughing in the army's huge clouds of dust.[11]

Santa Anna, riding in a gilded carriage with several beautiful courtesans, departed on February 2 with the elite, scarlet-coated Hussar Regiment.

For the first 30 miles, Riley and the San Patricios marched across cultivated country in sunny but cool weather. Then, slowly, fields, woods, and clear streams vanished amid mountains offering no cover from the days' sunshine or the nights' icy winds. Infantrymen in the columns a day or more behind the San Patricios tossed aside extra sacks of food they had lugged from San Luis Potosi on their backs. From the front of the columns to the distant rear, daytime sweat turned to evening chills, and hundreds of men collapsed along the road, left to fend for themselves or die.

A few days out on the road between San Luis Potosi and Matehuala, Riley and his men spotted a small dust cloud to the north. Several columns of Mexican cavalry slowly appeared, their lances prodding along 19 grimy men who staggered on foot. They were Kentucky cavalrymen among the captured riders Taylor had mentioned. As their guards shoved them to the side of the road to let Santa Anna's oncoming army tramp by, the Americans gaped at the first unit and their banner. Curses rippled among the prisoners, and several jeered Santa Anna's vanguard.

"We met the great army of the 'Napoleon of the South,'" one of the Kentuckians recalled, "twenty thousand strong, and marching in four divisions. First came his splendid park of artillery. . . .

"Among the mighty host we passed was O'Reilly and his deserters bearing aloft in high disgrace the holy banner of St. Patrick."

The Kentuckians were the first American soldiers to see that flag and the organized unit marching beneath it.

A number of the San Patricios yelled back. "One of these fellows was a Dutchman [German], who said to Corporal Sharp of Captain Heady's corps, tauntingly, 'Vell, you ish goin to Shan Louish, hey?'

"'Yesh' replied the 'Dutchman' to his own question.

"'Then you ish goin to hell in ten days,' rejoined Sharp" in a mocking German accent.[12]

The San Patricios marched on to Matehuala, 140 miles behind them and another 100 to go—across the desert. But in the days before they reached Matahuela, a storm howled down on them, dumping rain, sleet, and even freakish blasts of snow, thinning the ranks by an estimated 400, who froze to death.

Into the wastes the deserters led the columns. They discovered that Santa Anna had ordered all wells destroyed, the ruins seemingly mocking the parched troops. "On this desert," wrote one of the marchers, "nothing was observed beyond sky."[13]

The San Patricios rumbled into La Encarnacion on February 17, 1847, the last of the columns arriving on February 20. Death, illness, and desertion in the mountain passes and the desert had whittled as many as 4,000 men from Santa Anna's force.

Santa Anna held a full review of his army on the 20th, and the 15,000 or so who had survived the hellish march greeted him with cheers that proved they were ready for a fight. Santa Anna informed them that Taylor was waiting 35 miles to the north, at Agua Nueva. At 11:00 on the morning of February 21, the Mexican army filled its canteens at La Encarnacion and drew two rations of jerked beef, two biscuits, and a lump of rock-hard brown sugar for the advance's final leg.

The day's march proved one of the expedition's most grueling. Early in the afternoon the temperature plunged as the long column—infantry first, the San Patricios and the other heavy batteries, ammunition wagons, engineers, cavalry, more infantry, the lighter batteries, pack mules, and, in the rear, lancers—snaked through a mountain pass.

"The cold was intense," an officer wrote. "The soldiers were half-dead with cold, looking like an army of lifeless bodies."[14] They marched all night, reaching the summit and reeling partway down the slippery pass. An hour or so before dawn on February 22, Santa Anna halted the army for a short rest. A few bursts of distant gunfire rattled all but the most exhausted men from their brief sleep. At dawn, officers' shouts rousted even the soundest sleepers, and the army rushed on toward Agua Nueva.

Dark funnels of smoke appeared to the north, and a few hours into the march, an orange glow pierced the murk. Cavalry dashed from that direction and up to Santa Anna. Word that the Americans had abandoned Agua Nueva and had set heaps of food ablaze passed down the line. Mexicans and deserters who had swallowed the last of their rations winced: the army had been counting on Taylor's victuals as its next meal, its victory banquet. Santa Anna drove them onward, not even allowing them to refill their canteens at Agua Nueva, for Taylor's men were reportedly retreating to the north and were less than 15 miles away.

Santa Anna, having shed his usual field marshal's regalia for an infantry officer's standard blue coat and white pants and a long white cavalry duster, rode up and down the line to exhort his men to think only of the enemy, not of hunger, thirst, or exhaustion. Dozens of soldiers toppled and died where they fell. But the army listened to him, staggering northward. Ten miles into the march, scouts spurred up to Santa Anna, and he halted the army moments later near a ranch called La Encantada. Riley and the other gunners slumped in their saddles or against caissons as those whose canteens still held a few drops shared them with comrades.

Santa Anna galloped ahead to train his field glass upon the American positions and found Taylor's men defending a rugged bottleneck. The main road wound through the Narrows, a valley only 40 feet wide and flanked by mountains, and east of the road a broad plateau was sliced by deep ravines stretching to a mountain. To the west lay a canyon cluttered with brush. Just to the west of the road at the Narrows stood three of Colonel John Washington's six-pounders, guarded by Captain John Washington's 1st Illinois Infantry.

To the east of the road, Colonel William McKee's 2d Kentucky Infantry, Colonel William Bissell's 2d Illinois Infantry, Colonel William Bowles's 2d Indiana Infantry, and eight cannons were deployed across the Plateau, a broad, flat expanse 50 feet above the road; a gully 1.5 mile east of the Narrows offered the only possible route against the American left.

Another possible avenue of Mexican attack, one that Wool and Taylor deemed unlikely, stretched along a winding, narrow ridge beyond the Plateau, but the Mexicans would have to march at least four miles to reach it, leaving the Americans plenty of time to react.

Santa Anna quickly devised a plan of attack and sent couriers galloping down the line with his order of battle. About 5,000 Americans stared as the distant masses assembled to bugles and drumbeats booming down the Narrows and across the Plateau. The Mexicans swarmed through the pass, and entire columns wheeled right and left in perfect order.

On a ridge to the right of the road and behind the dense lines of infantry of the Mexican center, John Riley, army chief engineer General Ignacio Mora y Villamil, and chief of artillery General Antonio Carona skittered up the escarpment on horseback and saw that from the top, the deserters' heavy cannons could sweep the road and the Plateau.

Riley and the other officers dismounted, strode to the ridge's rim, and barked orders to the men to drag the guns and shot up the escarpment with ropes and hauling pins and deploy the horses behind the slope for their safety. The deserters unhitched two 24-pounders and a 16-pounder, tied the ropes to them, and, with Gaelic and German curses and grunts surely accompanying each tug of the one-ton, cast-iron monsters, hauled them a foot at a time up the ridge. The crews worked in shifts, new teams of gunners jumping in to grab the taut ropes from men whose arms and legs were going dead. By 3:00 in the afternoon, Riley and his men had emplaced the cannons and began to haul cases of round shot, grape, and canister to the waiting muzzles. Peering down at the Americans, Riley and the San Patricios anticipated the moment to avenge their humiliation at Monterrey.

To Riley's eye, the battle could have but one outcome. His guns commanded the field, and the Mexicans outnumbered Taylor three to one. The Irish veteran saw that the Americans had chosen excellent terrain for defense but that the polyglot of uniforms across the Narrows and the Plateau signified more volunteers than the tough, battle-tested, sky-blue regiments of regulars who had broken Ampudia's will at Monterrey.

Although regulars stood behind Taylor's batteries, and several companies of the 1st and 2d Dragoons saddled up across the plain, Riley and his battery held a severe advantage in weight of metal over the Americans' four- and six-pounders. The deserters also would have clear shots at the flying batteries each time they attempted to rush to key points of the battle. The ex-British army gunner was poised to go head to head with elite West Point artillerists Braxton Bragg, John Washington, and Thomas Sherman. Also staring back at the deserters from the Plateau was Brevet Captain John Paul Jones O'Brien's battery.

As the San Patricios were lugging their cannons into battery, Santa Anna had sent Mexican Surgeon General Peter Van der Linden, a Dutchman, and several officers under a white flag to Taylor. The physician carried a surrender demand: "You are surrounded by twenty thousand men, and cannot in any human probability avoid suffering a rout and being cut to pieces with your troops. I . . . give you this note, in order that you may surrender at discretion. . . . to which end you will be granted an hour's time to make up your mind."[15]

Old Rough and Ready, in his palmetto hat and linen duster, read the note and allegedly cursed. Then he dictated a response to his aide, William "Perfect" Bliss, to send to Santa Anna: "In reply to your note of this date, summoning me to surrender my forces at discretion, I beg leave to say that I decline acceding to your request."[16]

At 3:00 in the afternoon, Santa Anna sent General Santiago Blanco's division forward a few hundred yards into the Narrows. They halted and exchanged sporadic musket fire with the 1st Illinois, but the Mexican maneuver was merely a feint to cover a move by Ampudia's 2,000 infantry onto the mountain anchoring Taylor's left flank. As the Mexicans scaled the slope, Taylor ordered the dismounted Arkansas and Kentucky cavalry regiments and a battalion of Indiana infantry to intercept Ampudia. Until nightfall, musketry crackled across the mountain, and, even though Ampudia forced the Americans to dig in at the peak's base to prevent their being outflanked, Taylor felt confident enough about his army's positions to gallop back to Saltillo to inspect his rear guard and to bring Jefferson Davis's doughty, battle-tested Mississippians to the field the next morning.

Soon after dusk, the gunfire died away, and both armies lit campfires of smoky green wood. The San Patricios, who had not fired a shot that day, and their Mexican comrades cooked the last of their rations. Shortly after they ate, Santa Anna rode along his army's positions to cheers that carried across to the Americans. Mexican regimental bands blared, and their American counterparts struck up "Hail, Columbia."

A cold drizzle began to fall after dark. Riley and his men covered their powder and shot with oilskin tarpaulins and puffed on cheroots or pipes or snatched what sleep they could in sodden blankets alongside the guns.

16

"Take That Damned Battery!"

Taylor's troops arose from their ice-encrusted blankets near dawn on February 23, 1847, to the hints of a clear, warm morning. The scene across the valley, however, quashed any relief from the promise of sunshine. The Mexicans were in full battle array, and, for the first time, the Americans spied a green banner snapping in an early morning breeze above the roadside ridge. John Paul Jones O'Brien and other officers trained their telescopes on the flag and gaped at the gilt images of St. Patrick and the harp of Erin. The officers moved their lenses along the escarpment's line and fixed it on a tall officer. The face seemed familiar—and they quickly realized that it belonged to "the notorious O'Reilly" and that "the dastard" was flanked by swarms of other familiar figures such as Patrick Dalton. They manned the most powerful cannons on the battlefield. The regulars of Monterrey knew what the deserters could do with those guns.

With Captain John Washington's cannons at Taylor's extreme right flank, a number of Irish gunners stared at that green banner, as did Irishmen in the other flying batteries. An American colonel would angrily write that the men arrayed across the ridge were "the company of San Patricio, Saint Patrick . . . composed of deserters." He huffed that "they were all Europeans, and some of them deserters from the British

189

army in Canada . . . thence passing over to the enemy at Matamoros and Monterrey." [1]

The Americans' stares soon shifted from the deserters to the panorama unfolding in front of the ridge. "I doubt if the 'Sun of Austerlitz' shone on a more brilliant spectacle than the Mexican army displayed before us— twenty thousand men clad in new uniforms, belts as white as snow, brasses [cannons] and arms burnished until they glittered like gold," wrote a dragoon. The previous night's rain had washed much of the dirt of the march from the Mexicans' uniforms.

"Their cavalry was magnificent," he continued.

> Some six thousand cavaliers richly caparisoned in uniforms of blue faced with red, with waving plumes and glittering weapons, advanced towards us as if they would ride down our little band and finish the battle at one blow.
>
> They formed one long line with their massed bands in front, and then a procession of ecclesiastical dignitaries with all the gorgeous parapher- nalia of the Catholic Church advanced along the lines, preceded by the bands playing a solemn anthem. . . . This ceremony offered a striking con- trast to conditions in our lines; there was not a Chaplain in our army! [2]

Mexican bugles cried, the drums pounded, and, to the right of the San Patricios, the 7,400 infantrymen of Generals Manuel Lombardini and Francisco Pacheco, a brave soldier, plunged into the ravines in front of the Plateau and slowly advanced. Santa Anna's elite Regiment of Engi- neers tramped into the Narrows.

On the ridge, Riley shouted the order to load the guns with canister. His men pushed cloth bags of powder into the muzzles, ramrodded the canister cylinders, which were filled with musket balls, down the bores, poured priming powder into the cannons' vent holes, readied the lan- yards, and waited.

Riley and Dalton estimated the range of the Plateau at roughly 250 yards and adjusted the muzzles. The Americans poured small-arms fire from the Plateau into the Mexican infantry stumbling through the gul- lies. In the Narrows, Washington's flying battery opened up with grapeshot on the Regiment of Engineers. Their screams rolled upward, and the column wavered and fell back, their dead and wounded strewn along the road. The Mexican batteries began dueling with Washington's guns.

Riley and Moreno waited a bit longer as Pacheco's and Lombardini's divisions inched forward through the American volleys. On top of the

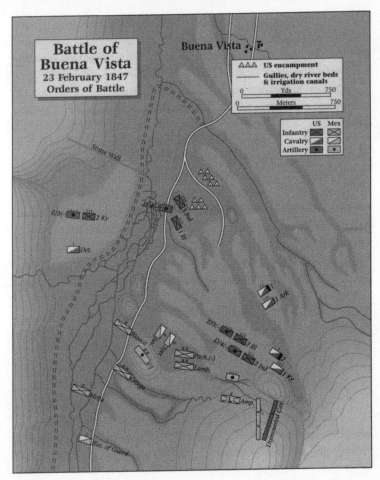

Battle of
Buena Vista
23 February 1847
Orders of Battle

Buena Vista

US encampment
Gullies, dry river beds
& irrigation canals

Yds   750
Meters   750

US   Mex
Infantry
Cavalry
Artillery

Stone Wall

E/3(-)   2 Ky

Det.

D/4(-)   2 Ind

1 Ill

1 Ark

E/3(-)   2 Ill

Blanco   D/4(-)   2 Ind

XX
Pach.(-)

XX
Lamb.

2

1 Ky

Mex

Ortega

Amp.

Bus. of Guard

Dismounted Cav.

Plateau, Lieutenant O'Brien opened up with his "Bulldogs"—two six-pounders and a four-pounder—and hurled canister and grapeshot into the infantry packed into the gullies. The bodies piled up, but the Mexicans kept pushing forward.

Riley trained his guns on the 2d Indiana Volunteers and other infantry screening O'Brien's guns and bellowed the command to fire "in battery," together. The 24- and 16-pounders crashed in a ground-shaking chorus, and canister screeched over the Mexican infantry's heads and into the massed Americans.

Striding from gun to gun, Riley directed one lethal barrage after another, and scores of moaning or silent Americans soon littered the Plateau. The Indianans, ravaged by each new blast of the San Patricios' cannons, edged backwards.

Near 9:00 in the morning, Pacheco's and Lombardini's men began streaming from the gullies and assembling for an assault against the Plateau. They formed three thick columns and charged.

O'Brien, hatless, unhurt though his jacket and trousers had been sliced by several bits of canister, urged his gunners to fire even faster, and they poured loads of grapeshot into the Mexicans and cut apart scores of men. Still, over the writhing, bloody carpet of fallen comrades, the infantrymen pressed closer. Although George Thomas's and Samuel French's cannons also pumped grape into the Mexicans, they pushed even closer and suddenly wheeled in a wide semicircle, threatening to roll up Taylor's left flank. As Riley's gunners raked the Plateau, the Americans' left flank buckled from an east-west line to a north-south one that was about to be enveloped. Farther east, General J. M. Ortega's infantry division and the cavalry brigades of Generals Anastasio Torrejon and Julian Juvera were driving the American dragoons back to Buena Vista hacienda itself, where Taylor's supply wagons were parked.

At about the same time, 9:00 in the morning, Taylor returned from Saltillo and rode onto the Plateau in full view of both armies. Peering through the smoke, leaning forward atop Old Whitey, Old Rough and Ready saw that his right flank would hold. Of his battered left, however, Taylor would report: "The Mexicans were now pouring masses of infantry and cavalry along the base of the mountain . . . and gaining our rear in great force."[3] Then, as Pacheco's division pummeled the 2d Indiana, Colonel William Bowles ordered his regiment to retreat. They broke and fled toward Buena Vista. The American left lay open.

On the Plateau, Wool turned to Taylor. "General," Wool said, "we are whipped."

As blasts from the San Patricios' guns shrieked nearby, Taylor snapped: "That is for me to determine."[4] He ordered Jefferson Davis's red-shirted, floppy-hatted Mississippi Rifles into the gap with the 3d Indiana. They shattered the Mexican advance with deadly volleys.

By noon, the San Patricios' rain of shot had littered the Plateau with dead and wounded volunteers. Taylor summoned Lieutenant Rucker of the 1st Dragoons and pointed at the distant green banner. "Take that damned battery," Old Rough and Ready ordered as "the deserters pitched their shells into every part of the field, some bursting in the road a good mile on our rear."[5]

A dragoon would write:

> Now the order was very easy to give, but rather difficult to execute, but such men as Rucker...and [John] Buford [a future Union hero at Gettysburg] are not apt to hesitate in the face of danger, so we tightened our saddle girths, and stripped ourselves of all encumbrances such as greatcoats, haversacks, nosebags, etc. With a firm grip on our Sabers, down a ravine we went at a trot, cheered by Sherman's battery as we passed under the muzzles of their guns, and were soon hid from the sight of both armies by the banks of the ravine. We passed many dead and wounded Mexicans in the gulches, and more than one poor wretch was trampled to death beneath our horses' hooves. We moved up another ravine and rising the bank, saw through the dense cloud of smoke and dust the glittering cross that waved over the deserters' guns.

Riley, waving his sword and shouting orders to his gunners, spotted the riders in the haze and realized that he could not lower his muzzles enough to fire at them. Along the line, infantrymen stepped in front of the guns, knelt on one knee, and aimed muskets at the dragoons. One of the riders may have seen Riley sheath his sword, grab a musket, and take up a position directly beneath the green flag.

"Reforming our platoons, we went for them at speed," a dragoon recalled.

The San Patricios' muskets blazed, but their shots went high. The deserters' cannons unleashed another blast at the Plateau even as the dragoons thundered nearer to the ridge's base.

"I thought we would capture the guns without much trouble," wrote one,

> as the pieces were so elevated that the shots passed high over our heads. Just as we were on them, the Bugler sounded to the "right," in the nick of time for our wheeling flank to clear a yawning chasm full ten yards wide that opened in front of the battery. We were soon under shelter in the ravine, and we kept down this to the road and struck for the pass. The road was literally blocked by heaps of dead horses and men mowed down by the fire of Washington's battery in the cavalry charge that morning.

To the fury of Taylor and to the suffering of his troops on the Plateau, the "heavy battery... manned by Irish deserters from our army.... the commander the notorious Reilly," continued to rip up their old army with seemingly endless blasts.

Davis and the flying batteries had barely thrown back the first Mexican assault, and Taylor's left flank was still exposed. To his rear and in front of the hacienda, his cavalry, Davis's Rifles, and the 3d Indiana had repulsed a horde of Mexican cavalry "using their lances freely on every side."

Another barrage suddenly shook the valley, but this had not erupted from the deserters' heavy guns. "The wind blew a gale," a soldier remembered,

> and the thunder was fearful; peal after peal burst over us as if to mock our puny artillery. For a few minutes all was darkness from the thick clouds of dust driven along by the violent blast. The firing ceased on both sides, as if by mutual consent. The rain was cold as ice, but was favorable to us as the wind was driving it with great force in the faces of our foes. The shower lasted some fifteen minutes, clearing off as suddenly as it came up, the sun came out, and a magnificent rainbow spanned the valley.[6]

Any Americans' hopes that Riley and his men had dragged tarpaulins over priming powder and vent holes too late to keep them dry sagged immediately with the cannons' roars and the hiss of shot atop the Plateau.

Sensing a shift in the battle's ebb and flow, Old Rough and Ready hurled six companies of Hardin's 1st Illinois at Ortega's retreating infantry. But the Mexicans turned and met Hardin's startled volunteers with a blaze of muskets. The 2d Illinois and the 2d Kentucky rushed toward the beleaguered companies and straight into a curtain of metal from the San Patricios' cannons. As the Americans scrambled to close up ranks around piles of wounded or dead comrades, thousands of Lombardini's infantry burst out of a partially hidden gulch and slammed into the volunteers. The Americans poured musket balls into the massed Mexicans but slowly, steadily retreated. As the Mexicans pressed forward, trampling the wounded, bayonets flashing all across the line, a handful of volunteers fled. Scores followed, and moments later their ranks crumbled toward the rear.

O'Brien was already rushing his Bulldogs forward as volunteers dashed past and as blue waves of howling Mexican infantry surged toward his men. His flying battery unlimbered a few hundred yards in front of the Mexicans and blasted away at the astonishing pace of one round a minute. But Riley fixed his guns on O'Brien's fully exposed crews and tore apart gunners and horses.

Now, each time that O'Brien, serving a gun himself, and his thinning crews fired, they moved backwards with each recoil, reloaded, fired again, and repeated from farther back. They hurled double loads of canister into the oncoming infantry but gave more ground.

Riley's blasts shredded O'Brien's men. The bleeding American gunners refused to quit, cutting up the enemy. A piece of Mexican lead tore into O'Brien's leg, and the Mexicans swarmed over his four-pounder and bayoneted its few remaining gunners. Another blast of the San Patricios' guns damaged the barrel of one of O'Brien's six-pounders. His horses all dead or wounded, O'Brien ordered several men to drag the crippled gun away.

With the blood-streaked wall of bayonets closing in and the nearest Americans a few hundred yards away, O'Brien sensed that unless he slowed down the Mexicans for at least several more minutes, Taylor's center would collapse. "I could have saved the guns," O'Brien later wrote, "but in such case the day might, perhaps, have been lost."[7]

Faces blackened by powder, O'Brien and his few remaining gunners ducked from each blast of the San Patricios but kept firing the sizzling brass fieldpiece.

Braxton Bragg's flying battery clattered east across the Plateau toward the gap. A few minutes behind, Sherman and Thomas's guns rattled forward.

As Lombardini's men surged closer to O'Brien's last blazing gun, several of his men pushed another six-pounder, his reserve cannon, alongside and opened up with grape. Both crews fired and rolled back again and again, more Mexicans toppling with each blast. Musket balls ripped into several of O'Brien's men, but the skeleton crews kept firing. Finally, as the lead Mexican column pushed within yards of the Bulldogs, O'Brien ordered his men to run. Two of the gunners grabbed their badly wounded lieutenant and hauled him away from the nearing bayonets.

Moments later, Lombardini's men, including San Patricios dispatched to the site, seized the pair of six-pounders, and a company dragged them back to Santa Anna's lines.

The advance continued, the Mexican infantry pushing back out-numbered Kentucky volunteers who were fighting a stubborn rear-guard action under Captain Henry Clay Jr. and Colonel William R. McKee. Smoke engulfed the ridge from which the San Patricio guns supported the advance. Clay, ripped by the deserters' metal and several musket balls, fell and squeezed off a last pistol round from his back before he died.

Davis's Rifles and the Illinois and Indiana infantry formed lines and poured flank fire into the Mexicans. The advance slowed but did not stop.

Bragg's battery swept up close to the spot of O'Brien's stand and whipped from column into battery. Gunners leaped from saddles and wagons, unlimbered their six-pounders, loaded canister, and unloosed a deafening barrage. Taylor rode up on Old Whitey to Bragg, the desert-ers' metal spraying nearby and several Mexican balls tearing through his white duster.

Taylor reportedly ordered Bragg: "Double-shot your guns, and give 'em hell!"[8]

Bragg did so eagerly with canister, and soon Sherman and Wash-ington's flying batteries also pumped double loads into the Mexicans. As chunks of Santa Anna's infantry were blown from their columns, their comrades tried to regroup, but the rapid bursts of metal shattered the assault. The Mexicans fled back into the ravines. Lew Wallace, an Amer-ican officer and later the author of *Ben Hur*, remembered: "The dead lay in the pent space body on body, a blending and interlacement of men as defiant of imagination as of the pen."[9]

As the Mexican attack collapsed, Bragg and his fellow battery com-manders rolled their guns forward, elevated the muzzles at the ridge in front of the Plateau, and opened up on the San Patricios. All around Riley American shot sliced into his gun crews. Screams burst from the battery, and men slipped in their friends' blood as they served the guns. Riley and his men held and returned fire. The duel of metal raged until dusk; neither the San Patricios nor the American crews pulled back. As the last echoes of the cannons faded across the valley, nearly one third of Riley's men lay wounded or dead around their guns.

A wan moon washed across the bodies heaped in the ravines and along the Plateau. The wails and moans of the wounded pealed without letup. "In sight already," a Mexican officer wrote, "were the jackals and the dogs who awaited the moment when they might begin their frightful banquet." [10]

Americans stared at the camp fires of the Mexican army, steeled themselves for the battle's second day, and wondered how their battered little army could hold again. They worried that a cloud of dust far behind the campfires signaled the approach of Mexican reinforcements.

At daybreak of February 24, 1847, the Americans discovered that the Mexican army was gone. Santa Anna knew that his men were too exhausted to repeat their near-victorious performance of the previous day. Mexican losses were 591 killed, 1,049 wounded, and 1,854 missing.

As Taylor's men realized that they had turned back Santa Anna, cheers broke out from the hacienda to the Narrows. Men wept and hugged, including Taylor and Wool.

On the ridge where the green silk banner had fluttered, Taylor's men would find at least 22 dead deserters. Riley and his men had carried off their wounded, saving them from American nooses.

The San Patricios trudged back toward San Luis Potosi, a march "worse than three retreats from Matamoros put together.... the road strewn with dead and dying.... and we ourselves barely able to walk, being attacked by illnesses." [11] Santa Anna rushed toward Mexico City, well ahead of his men. He had taken the captured Bulldogs of O'Brien with him as proof of "victory" over Taylor. Riley and the bloody columns stumbling in Santa Anna's wake knew better.

What Riley did not know yet was that his performance and that of his men at Buena Vista had awed the Mexican generals and had even earned the enraged accolades of American officers. The deserters would never face Taylor again, for the war in northern Mexico was over. But Old Rough and Ready's tart description of the green-bannered unit as "that damned battery" testified to the brutal role the San Patricios had played in the 272 Americans killed and 387 wounded—14 percent of Taylor's army—at Buena Vista. An American officer testified: "It [the San Patricios] was a fine battery, and the havoc it made in our ranks was a melancholy evidence of the skill with which it was served." [12]

As the war shifted to the south, rank, influence, and more notoriety beckoned John Riley. For the new American commander, Winfield Scott, the Irishman, his band of "desperadoes," and their "contagion" of desertion awaited. [13]

Part Four

"Jump In and Be Damned"

17

"Well, Pat, My Good Fellow"

O N FEBRUARY 25, 1847, General Francisco Mejia's Buena Vista battle report lauded the San Patricios as "worthy of the most consummate praise because the men fought with daring bravery." [1] Mejia, the unit's brigadier in the clash, singled out Riley for his courage and coolness.

When the Irishman and his gunners straggled into San Luis Potosi in the second week of March 1847, Riley found a captain's commission and a hike in pay awaiting him. He also learned that Winfield Scott had landed 8,600 troops 2.5 miles south of Vera Cruz and was bombarding the city with batteries ashore and naval guns in the harbor.

On March 14, Santa Anna declared he was taking over the government because of the national emergency and left for Mexico City to impose his new regime. He ordered 6,000 men of his weary Army of the North to march east to Jalapa, which lay on the National Highway and in Scott's eventual line of march from the coast.

Riley replenished his unit with several dozen Irish residents of Mexico and more deserters such as Cork native and veteran infantryman Francis O'Conner and immigrant foot soldier John Price. The San Patricios refurbished their heavy guns, restoring them to their pre-Buena Vista sheen. In the third week of March, the deserters hitched them to new teams of horses, rolled out of San Luis Potosi, and turned southward to join the Army of the East.

Santa Anna not only planned to use Riley as a key artillerist against Scott's army, but also as a recruiting officer in the government's plan to pull "at least three thousand Irish" and other immigrants from the American force.[2] Santa Anna believed that the pamphlets at Matamoros and Monterrey and the efforts of Mexican priests had paid off handsomely in the deserters' performance at Buena Vista. An intensified propaganda campaign appealing to religion and conscience, he asserted, would create a bona fide "Foreign Legion" under Riley's aegis and his green flag.

Among the nearly 9,000 men Scott landed without a single casualty near Vera Cruz on March 9–10 were over 3,000 Irishmen. Although many were now battle-tested veterans of the Rio Grande and Monterrey, hundreds of others had literally stepped off coffin ships in New York, Boston, Philadelphia, and ports of entry as far north as Eastport and Houlton, Maine, and Oswego, New York, in the winter of 1846–47. Manual labor in the cold season always proved scarce, and immigrants leaped at the Army's seven dollars a month and promises of Western lands at war's end. Although many of the new recruits had soldiered like Riley and Dalton in the British army, they knew nothing yet of life in the United States, for they were bound for Mexico before seeing much of America beyond a recruiting station.

Their reception from their Regular army officers proved generally as harsh as that of their predecessors over a year earlier at Corpus Christi. One of Scott's new immigrant soldiers, a weaver unable to land work in his trade and a British veteran, described his introduction to his new army. Two officers, "probably chagrined at having been detained for a minute or two" as the recruit and two others climbed into a longboat ferrying them to the Governor's Island barracks in New York harbor glared at the trio. One of the officers snapped "in a petulant tone for us to jump in and be damned."[3] An Irish recruit sized up the imperious officer and muttered to the weaver: "Faith and there's many a strong word comes off a weak [cowardly] stomach."[4]

From the moment that Scott's force landed near Vera Cruz and surrounded the city, many immigrants suffering their officers' epithets and fists did feel "damned." Officers were edgier than usual, for the landing had been nearly two months behind schedule, and with each day spent besieging the city and not marching westward toward the mountains, the closer the army came to early spring's clouds of mosquitoes, which carried yellow fever—*El Vomito.*

Vera Cruz was ravaged by bombardment and suffered over 200 civilians dead from American shells, which forced the garrison to surrender on March 29, 1847. It was at this time that the first cases of fever had appeared in Scott's ranks. Headache, chills, high temperature, and incessant vomiting racked the victims. As the disease spread to the liver, their skin soon turned yellow with black and blue splotches. Internal bleeding filled the lungs, and men choking on their own fluids heaved up coagulated black blood. Physicians knew no cure. One in five victims would die, and few survivors ever regained their full health. If an epidemic struck Scott's army, the Mexican mosquitoes would defeat the Americans.

In the week after Vera Cruz's capitulation, Scott's quartermasters purchased every horse, mule, and wagon they could find. Scott also set up military courts in the city to deal with breaches of discipline, and now many new immigrants felt full bore the Nativist prejudices of their officers. The wooden horse, the buck and gag, and the barrel sprouted outside the city walls, and the field court-martial records recorded the many foreigners who got acquainted with the devices. A new crop of West Pointers, including George B. McClellan, second in the class of 1846, heartily endorsed the measures as necessary to control "wretched Irish and Dutchies."[5] Months later, however, after he had seen them fight, "Little Mac" would do an about-face in his estimation of the immigrants.

Scott, though fully apprised of the desertions from Taylor's army and aware of the many immigrant Catholics camped around the city, had brought only one chaplain, an Episcopalian named, ironically, McCarthy. Father McElroy still ministered at Matamoros but was suffering from dysentery. Many regular officers who had long forced their Catholic soldiers to attend Protestant churches near garrisons at home marched them to McCarthy's services.

A 1st Artillery lieutenant who, like John Paul Jones O'Brien, did not compel Catholics to attend Protestant services tried nonetheless to persuade them to go and learned of the particular horror that Irish Catholics felt about the practice. The officer asked Private Dennis

O'Toole, "honest . . . a Munster man and a staunch Catholic," to "come over and hear the sermon." O'Toole replied: "Heaven forbid, sir."

"Eh, what's that you say, Dennis?" the lieutenant asked.

"Sure, Lieutenant, the Blessed Virgin knows I'm bad enough already without sinning my soul any more by going to hear a swaddling preacher mocking the holy religion."[6]

O'Toole was lucky: his officer shook his head and laughed. Others would have punished—and did—soldiers for insubordination for a similar response. In May 1846, the Catholic bishops had formally objected to Polk about Nativist officers forcing Catholic soldiers to attend Protestant services, one of the key factors in his appointment of Rey and McElroy.

In the court-martial sessions at Vera Cruz, new immigrants soon learned what Old Rough and Ready's veterans knew: foreigners usually received stiffer sentences for the same infractions or crimes committed by native soldiers. Scott appointed "two distinct military commissions: the one composed of officers of the Regular Army, having exclusive jurisdiction for the trial of its offenders, the other exclusively of Volunteer officers before whom citizen soldiers alone could be tried."[7] In a large room inside the Vera Cruz custom house, the committees heard several dozen cases, many involving insubordination and mutinous conduct. The latter was especially serious, for it could carry a sentence of death by firing squad if a man had accosted an officer. Privates Liam McCabe and Thomas Miller, the former Irish, the latter native born, were tried for drunkenness and striking a superior officer. There were no differences or mitigating circumstances in either case, but Miller garnered imprisonment and a dishonorable discharge, McCabe a firing squad. A military commission presided over by Colonel John Garland, of the 3d Infantry, heard both cases. In another case, in the 7th Infantry near Vera Cruz, Irish and German privates were branded on the hip with an "HD" for "habitual drunkard"; Privates Smith, Todd, and Rawlings were fined 12 dollars for the same offense.

In another case, sentries captured two privates, one Irish, one American, as they broke into a Mexican home. Presiding over the case was hard-driving Captain Samuel Chase Ridgely of the 4th Artillery. Both prisoners faced the same offense of aiding and abetting robbery, with no distinction between the charges for each. Neither man could offer a defense. They pled for the mercy of the court. The judges sentenced the American to ten days' imprisonment and "a fine equal to one month's pay as a private"; the Irish immigrant reaped two months' confinement, a fine of three months' pay, and a dishonorable discharge at the end of the war.[8] That both men were thieves was undeniable. So, too, was the lighter sentence of the Yankee soldier. The courts-martial were replete with two sets of punishment—one for the native-born soldier, another for the immigrant.

No Irishman nor German, recorded an Irish artilleryman, should expect fair treatment from most officers. "The rascals," he wrote. "May the Lord look down on us, for we've happened badly on them [officers] for gintlemin [sic]."[9]

Typical of many regular officers was Captain George A. McCall, who, despite his surname, loathed the "unsophisticated, untutored, and intractable sons of Erin" in the ranks, deriding them as men with neither the wits nor the ambition "to fill the higher places in the walks of life."[10]

From similarly minded officers, a German immigrant encountered such Nativist bromides as "sauerkraut" and "God Damn Dutch."[11]

Private John F. Meginness wrote during Scott's campaign that a U.S. Army private "must expect to be treated more like a vicious dog, than a civilized, intelligent human being" and that enlisted men must not be surprised "when a young Lieutenant chooses to amuse himself by Knocking them down with his sabre." Among the many abuses Meginness saw were a lieutenant's blade slicing "a gaping wound" in "a poor fellow" who made a minor error during drill, and an officer who ordered 180 lashes for a soldier who had missed roll call.[12]

A Protestant regular noted that "I have good reason to believe" that officers' disproportionate use of the buck and gag and the horse upon Irish troops was putting desertion in their thoughts.[13]

Old Fuss and Feathers Scott believed that tight discipline and prosecution of soldiers who committed outrages against Mexican civilians and churches would keep their Catholic coreligionists in his ranks, proving that America was not demanding them to fight a Protestant crusade against Catholic Mexico.

Shortly after the fall of Vera Cruz, Scott issued a proclamation designed to calm the locals' fears of the Yankee *hereticos* and to show immigrant soldiers that they were not at war against their church:

> Mexicans! Americans are not your enemies, but the enemies, for a time, of the men who, a year ago, misgoverned you and brought about this unnatural war between two great republics. We are the friends of the peaceful inhabitants of the country we occupy, and the friends of your holy religion, its hierarchy, and its priesthood. The same church is found in all parts of our own country, crowded with devout Catholics, and respected by our government, laws and people.[14]

Many men in Scott's army could recall Catholic churches burning in Philadelphia, Boston, and St. Louis. The papers reaching camp carried accounts of the Protestant convention that would gather in New York to fight the popish menace. And the printed accounts of the deserters and their green silk banner were causing some officers to question the loyalty of all Irishmen in the army. Even Lieutenant Mick Maloney encountered suspicious stares from Nativist officers. He determined he would fight all the harder to prove his devotion to the army—after ten years, *his* army—and hoped new immigrants to remember their sworn oath. From his company, few Irish were to desert.

To show his respect for Catholicism to the Mexicans, Winfield Scott led several of his officers in full dress uniform on April 4 to services at "an old and venerated Catholic church" battered by the American bombardment. One of the officers, Captain Robert E. Lee, recalled how uncomfortable he and the others, all Protestants, felt as they carried lighted candles to the altar for the priests' blessing. Most of Scott's fellow Whig officers were furious at their commander's appearance in a "heathen temple" and ranted that the spectacle would cost Old Fuss and Feathers his well-known goal to become president.[15]

So far, no leaflets offering deserters land, cash, and rank or appealing to Catholic consciences had turned up in Scott's camps. But they would, and at that time, Scott would have to rely on the Reverend Dr. McCarthy, the Episcopalian missionary who "preached a most excellent sermon peculiarly adapted to . . . officers and men who were professing Christians of any Protestant denomination." Scott had no Father Rey or McElroy to minister to the army's Catholics.

Scott could have used them to calm immigrants' anger at a "humorous" newspaper story that many officers regaled each other with when Irishmen were within earshot:

> "Well, Pat, my good fellow," said Old Rough and Ready to a brave son of Erin after a battle, "and what did you do to help us gain this victory?"
>
> "Do?" replied Pat. "May it plase your honor, I walked up boldly to wun of the inimy, and cut off his feet."
>
> "Cut off his feet!" Taylor said. "And why did you not cut off his head?"
>
> "Ah, an faith that was cut off already," says Pat.[16]

The anecdote galled Maloney and other Irishmen who had fought and bled for Taylor. It proved a particular favorite, wrote an Irish veteran, among junior officers who had not yet seen battle.

Also typical of the relish with which many of Scott's officers belittled immigrants was infantry Lieutenant Henry Judah's discovery that a German laundress and camp follower was married to a private named Clancy. As evidence of Clancy's resemblance to "Pat" in the popular newspaper story, Judah proclaimed that the "brave" Clancy cringed beneath his wife's "huge red fist." The cowardly Irishman's spouse, Judah said, was "the ugliest of her sex—Dutch [German] to extremity, a huge misshapen body, round, ugly face, and given to whipping her husband every little while."[17] The lieutenant's words mimicked the grotesque caricatures appearing in the Nativist press.

On the evening of March 21, 1847, a week before the surrender of Vera Cruz, Privates Hezekiah Akles, John Bartley, John Bowers, and Alexander McKee, all serving in Samuel Chase Ridgely's 3d Artillery, Company H, disappeared from camp. Five days later, another immigrant crept away at night. Within a week, company sergeants reported John Little, an Irish dragoon in the 2d, James McDowell, a Galway man in the 7th Infantry, and some 50 others as deserters. Among the missing troops' officers were Harney, Ridgely, and Alexander, men noted for their hatred of foreigners. Harney, of third-generation Irish-Catholic lineage, fell into that category of established Irish who resented the "shanty Irish" streaming into America and its army.

On April 8, 1847, Scott started General David Twiggs up the sandy National Highway at the head of 2,600 regular infantry, two flying batteries, six 24-pounders, two eight-inch howitzers, and a company of dragoons. Scott, with Worth's regulars and General Robert Patterson's volunteers, followed on April 9–14. Scott's 8,500-man force was striking out for Jalapa, 74 miles up the highway and 4,680 feet above the yellow fever belt. With over 1,000 men left behind with the disease in Vera Cruz, the Americans could afford no delay in reaching the healthier mountain climate.

Twiggs's vanguard halted in front of a gorge of the Rio del Plan, 20 miles east of Jalapa, on the rear edge of the fever zone. Two crags, El Telegrafo and La Atalaya, hovered above the highway, and arrayed between them and the gorge was Santa Anna's Army of the East.

Dug in south of the highway with their heavy guns, which commanded the highway as it squeezed into a narrow pass at the base of the hills, John Riley and 150 to 175 deserters had planted their flag. Unlike at Buena Vista, the regiments massing down the road were mostly the deserters' old units. Mick Maloney and hundreds of Scott's Irish craved a chance to tear down the green flag, the source of so many Nativist officers' insults. But other immigrants, including 60-year-old Ned McHeran, felt something else. Still, he prepared to do his duty behind a fieldpiece, as he had always done.

After serving as "a loyal and faithful soldier for many years in the U.S. Army," 5-foot, 9-inch Edward P. McHeran had worked as a painter in riot-torn Philadelphia.[18] On February 17, 1847, he had reenlisted in Company G of the 4th Artillery—a week after his son, David, a laborer, had joined the same company. Perhaps the father wanted to look after his son, who wore the uniform for the first time. Awaiting the religious Edward McHeran in Mexico, an officer would write, was a man who would "influence" the old veteran to make a choice about which flag he would serve.[19]

18

"The Butcher's Bill"

W HEN SCOTT FIRST studied the Mexican positions at Cerro Gordo on April 14, 1847, they appeared impregnable. Sam Grant would write: "The difficulties to surmount made the undertaking almost equal to Bonaparte's crossing the Alps." The Mexican artillery "in embrasure sweeping the road would [have made] it impossible for any force in the world to have advanced."[1]

Scott had no intention of throwing his army into Santa Anna's bottleneck. He ordered his best engineers, Lee, Pierre T. Beauregard, Joseph E. Johnston, Zealous B. Tower, and W. H. T. Brooks, on night reconnaissance to find a route to flank the Mexicans. Beauregard went first, sneaking up La Atalaya to scan possible approaches, and determined that a path could be hacked to the west of the hill, part of Santa Anna's left flank. He fell ill, however, before he could lead the effort.

Scott sent Lee with a small company of engineers to scout Beauregard's suggested route on the night of April 15, and Lee quickly concurred with his fellow West Pointer's idea. Then, following a hunch that they could cut a flanking path even farther to the enemy's rear, Lee and his men crawled through thickly wooded gullies deep into Santa Anna's flank, narrowly eluding capture near a spring. Lee and his men reported back to Scott on the 16th with their suggestion, and he ordered the

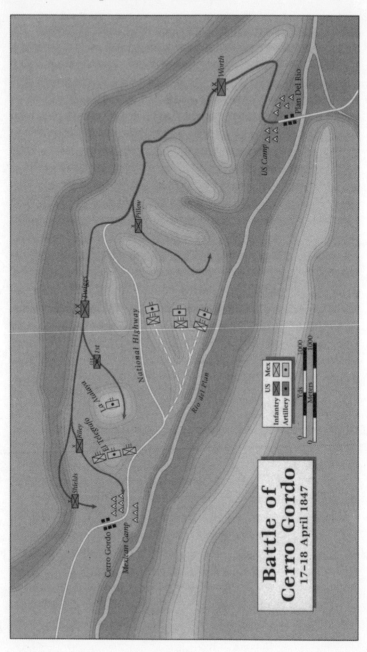

Battle of
Cerro Gordo
17–18 April 1847

Virginian to form construction parties and cut a road along and past El Telegrafo. That night, the engineers hacked a trail wide enough for infantry and even artillery. Mexican pickets never detected the American work crews, perhaps mistaking the thuds of axes and picks as last-minute preparations by Santa Anna's batteries.

At 4:30 in the morning of April 17, Twiggs's division, the 3d and the 7th Infantry, the 1st Artillery, and a brigade of Illinois and New York volunteers gulped "biscuit, beef, and coffee—the last meal for many a poor fellow—formed in file" and were ordered to Lee's narrow trail.

Covered by the tangled woods and brush, they tripped forward as branches cut hands and faces. At the head of the column, a man from the 1st Artillery stumbled on a rock, and his musket scraped against his tin canteen. A comrade remembered: "A captain rushed up to him in the utmost fury and screamed loudly enough to be heard along the entire line, 'You infernal scoundrel, I'll run you through if you don't make less noise.'" The unit, mainly immigrants, despised the officer, nicknamed "Blunderbore." He "stood flourishing his sword in a striking and theatrical attitude, [and] the poor fellow seemed terrified lest he should put his threat into execution. The scene presented such a ludicrous aspect that in spite of our proximity to the Mexican batteries, all of us within sight and hearing burst into a hearty and simultaneous laugh." Four miles and four hours later, they reached the base of La Atalaya. With Lee's report that the hill was lightly guarded, Twiggs ordered Lieutenant Frank Gardner to take it with a company of the 7th.

The company clambered up the slope, tripping in thickets. As they reached the crest, they walked into musket volleys fired off by Mexican infantry who were surging up the northwest side. Twiggs ordered the 3d and the 7th up the hill. They swarmed up the southwestern slope to the top and drove off the Mexicans.

"Beg pardon, General, how far should we charge them?" a captain asked.

Twiggs shouted: "Charge them to hell!"

The Americans lurched down La Atalaya and into a wooded ravine and pursued the Mexicans toward El Telegrafo. To Twiggs's left, the enemy batteries south of the highway opened up with roundshot. At the edge of a ravine, Riley and the San Patricios blasted away behind 16-pounders.

Two Mexican infantry regiments rushed onto the hill and fired at will into the sky-blue masses in the ravine.

"We saw the error we had committed in pursuing them," an American soldier wrote, "and we were now caught in a complete fix."

"To attempt to retreat up the hill [La Atalaya] in the continuous fire of some thousands of Mexican infantry and of their batteries, who now opened a crossfire, would have been instant and total destruction." The deserters' cannons cut down scores of Americans and sent hundreds diving behind rocks and trees. Those who dared to lift their heads in the incessant fire to squeeze off an occasional shot at the enemy might have glimpsed the green flag above the smoking muzzles at the ravine. Moans and sobs from men cut down by the deserters' metal filled the ravine. Many were as Irish as the men serving those guns.

Near sunset, the fire of the San Patricios stopped. Mexican bugles blared across El Telegrafo, and infantry officers formed their men into an attack line. Then, "with colors displayed," bayonets flashing in the fading sunlight, the dark blue lines advanced down the slope. The situation, an American pinned down in the ravine recalled, "seemed sufficiently perilous."

On La Atalaya, Twiggs's artillerymen had pulled a small howitzer to the crest and now stuffed its wide barrel with grapeshot. The men trapped in the gully "waited with some anxiety to see its [the howitzer's] effects."

The Mexican column swept to the bottom of the hill and the ravine's approaches less than 200 yards away from the crouching or prone Americans. The howitzer boomed and sprayed grape into the Mexicans.

A veteran soldier "never saw such sudden havoc and confusion caused by a single shot." He gaped as "it swept right into the head of the advancing column, killing and wounding a great number of those in advance."

As the Mexicans grabbed their wounded and tripped back up the hill, an Irishman of the 1st Artillery remarked that the howitzer "knows how to pay the piper."

"Groans of wounded men in all directions" drifted out of the ravine through the moonless night. As Twiggs's division crawled back to La Atalaya and search parties carried the wounded soldiers from the rain-swept gullies to medical tents, another sound assailed the weary troops: the screams of men losing shattered limbs to surgeons' saws.

On La Atalaya, "there was very limited conversation amongst us this night," most men "taking a few mouthfuls of biscuit, a drink of water, and a smoke" before trying to sleep.

An artilleryman reflected that evening on a scene of "this . . . diabolical spirit called religious hatred" in the American ranks. The soldier wrote:

> I was witness to an incident this afternoon during the action, which for the diabolical spirit displayed by one of its actors exceeds anything of the kind I ever saw. An ordnance sergeant named Armstrong, having received a wound, sat down seemingly in great agony. One of the men belonging to his own company came over to where he was sitting and asked him if he was wounded. On his answering that he was, very badly, ". . . then may the devil cure ye, you blackhearted rascal," was the unfeeling rejoinder. The sergeant was not popular, and I believe his conduct was not calculated to inspire much sympathy for his misfortunes; the sergeant having been an Orangeman [Presbyterian], and the [Irish] man addressing him a Roman Catholic. The sergeant died on the field that night, his watch and a purse containing some money. . . were missing, and there were several bayonet wounds in his body. . . some did not hesitate to express their suspicions of foul play and plainly intimated that some of his own company had killed and robbed him.

That same chilly night on La Atalaya, an artillery lieutenant sent a sergeant "to a man named Reilly [no relation to John Riley] with a request for a smoke of his pipe." Reilly replied: "The lieutenant is mighty condescending. Maybe you would be pleased, sergeant, to inform the lieutenant, along with Reilly's compliments, that if he will wait until Reilly has his own smoke—may the Holy Virgin be near us, maybe it's the last smoke ever the same Reilly will take—I'll not be lending him the pipe."

The sergeant stomped off, and one of Reilly's friends warned that his defiance had "sent the sergeant off with a flea in his lug" [angry] and would earn the Irishman the lieutenant's wrath after the battle.

"Bad luck to the impudence [of the officer]," Reilly retorted. He added that "if I was to ask one of themselves for a loan of the same thing," a buck and gag would be an officer's response.[2]

Roughly 500 yards away from the indignant Private Reilly and his pipe were John Riley and the San Patricios. The deserters and Santa Anna's other batteries expected to hand the Yankees a heavy "butcher's bill," casualties, in a few hours.

A third Riley, Bennet, poured over Scott's General Order III, which directed Bennet Riley's men to cut their way alongside the northwestern flank of El Telegrafo and storm the village of Cerro Gordo. Mick Maloney would march with him.

An Irishman spoiling for action and appalled by the deserters' flag read General Order III, too. Scott expected volunteer General James Shields, the very symbol of an Irishman successfully making his way in America, to flank the Mexican left with his brigade of Illinois and New York militias and to take Cerro Gordo from the north.

A staunch Democrat and a political general appointed by his friend Polk, Shields was "a stout, soldier-like man with a heavy mustache, black hair, and brilliant eyes." Unlike many volunteer officers, he had served a hitch in the regular army and had fought in the Seminole War. He hailed from a family of County Tyrone Catholics who had lost their lands and wealth during the religious wars of the 1690s and had lived in poverty ever since.

Shields was born in Tyrone on May 12, 1806. An uncle who returned to Ireland after fighting for America in the Revolution and the War of 1812 fired the boy's imagination with dreams of a military career, as did a neighbor and Waterloo veteran who taught the youth to handle a sword and a musket. From another uncle, a priest, Shields learned the classics.

Shields emigrated to America in the 1820s, before Nativism exploded in American life. He eventually settled in Illinois, was admitted to the state bar in 1832, and, by 1837, was a "mover and shaker" in the state legislature.

During the national economic panic of 1837, Shields served as Illinois's financial auditor and ordered that only silver and gold, not paper money, could be used for taxes. *The Sangamo Journal*, a Whig newspaper, attacked Democrat Shield's policy and grossly caricatured his Irish features, background, and manners. Two women, one of them named Mary Todd, had written the diatribe, and the seething Shields challenged Todd's fiancee to a duel with dragoons' sabers. Todd's intended—a gangly lawyer named Abraham Lincoln—accepted.

They confronted each other on a sandbar on the Missouri side of the Mississippi to escape Illinois's ban on dueling. Sabers in hand, Lincoln and Shields started talking and kept on doing it. Lincoln calmed his "foe," and, despite their political differences, a lifelong friendship between the pair began. Although Lincoln was a strong, sinewy man, he would have stood little chance against Shields's swordsmanship.

Now, camped with his brigade behind La Atalaya on April 17, 1847, Shields welcomed any chance to prove Irish loyalty to the American flag and to obliterate the men beneath the green banner.[3]

Shortly after dawn on April 18, grapeshot sliced into the Mexican battery and the thousands of Mexican infantrymen on El Telegrafo. Americans had lugged two 24-pounders up La Atalaya during the night. The 3d and 7th U.S. Infantry and the 1st Artillery, "red-leg infantry," crouched in a hollow near the roaring 24s and "could watch the effects of the [deserters'] grapeshot passing above us, with its peculiar harsh and bitter whistle," and "the saplings and branches [that] crashed under the withering influence of the unseen messengers."

The 24-pounders blasted away infantry massed at the opposite crest to repel an American assault. Then, Colonel Harney, in command at La Atalaya, ordered the charge. The Americans climbed from the hollow "to face the horizontal shower which for the last hour and a half had been flying harmlessly overhead."

At the sound of the bugles and with "an excited hurrah," the infantry "leaped and tumbled" down La Atalaya. Harney's curses, according to one soldier, "seemed to grate as harshly on one's ears as the missiles showering over us."[4]

Mexican muskets peppered the Americans, but slowly, as the 24s scoured the defenders without letup, their return fire slackened. Harney's men reached the lower breastworks of El Telegrafo and overran them in a bloody whirl of bayonets, point-blank fire, and screams. Hundreds of Mexicans clawed up the slope in retreat.

The Americans took a few seconds to recover their breath; then they crept upward across rocks and through prickly brush, "deploying as skirmishers, covering themselves among the bushes and briars."[5] The Mexican infantry blazed away at the Yankees but could not drive back the climbing horde.

Streams of Mexican soldiers tossed their muskets aside and "scampered in the utmost confusion down the hill."[6] Several hundred held their ground behind a stone breastwork at the top of the hill and pinned down the Americans' vanguard, but as more Yankees reached the upper slope, those defenders also disappeared down the hill.

"The sword in his [Harney's] long arm waved" his men on.[7] They spilled into the deserters' emplacement to find dozens of exmessmates sprawled limply around the San Patricios' abandoned cannons. Riley, Dalton, and the remnants of the unit dashed with their flag amid the "disordered mass running with panic speed down the hill and along the road to Jalapa."[8] Men of the 1st Artillery turned around the deserters' guns and flung their own grapeshot into the fleeing pack.

Shields's and Bennet Riley's brigades turned Santa Anna's flank as Harney's men took El Telegrafo, and the entire Mexican line disintegrated. The San Patricios abandoned their guns and fled. With the exception of volunteer General Gideon Pillow's bloody error in hurling the 2d Tennessee into the point-blank fire of the Mexican batteries near the National Highway, the rout was complete. By 10:00 that morning, the battle was over.

Scott's army captured over 3,000 Mexicans and 40 cannons, including the San Patricios' heavy pieces. They also "captured" Santa Anna's spare cork leg at his Cerro Gordo camp. Although the Mexican commander never released the tally of his dead at Cerro Cordo, the number was estimated as at least 1,200.

Of the 8,500 Americans engaged, Scott lost 63 dead and 367 wounded, among whom was Shields, shot in the lung. Because of a captured Mexican surgeon's skill, Shields would recover to meet John Riley and the San Patricios hand to hand several months down the road. For the moment, though, to the fury of Maloney and many other Irishmen, Riley and his band had slipped the judge advocate's noose again.

The flight of the deserters and the other survivors of Cerro Gordo did not end until they reached Mexico City itself, about 200 miles up the National Highway. The road to Montezuma's capital lay open—in more ways than one for some of Scott's soldiers who were to meet the "notorious O'Reilly" sooner and differently than such immigrants as Shields and Mick Maloney.

19

"Come Over to Us"

THE DEBACLE AT CERRO GORDO and his political foes notwithstanding, Santa Anna was far from finished. In Mexico City, he pushed through a decree of martial law, ordered all healthy Mexican men between 16 and 60 in the city's district to report to military units, raised new National Guard units, and forced civilians to report for fortifications details. Extorting "loans" from wealthy locals, the church, and foreign businessmen, he fashioned an army of 25,000. The army's nucleus included several crack regiments he had not marched to Cerro Gordo.

Into the depleted ranks of the San Patricios John Riley welcomed dozens more Irishmen and other foreign nationals living in Mexico City, but he needed additional recruits. Throughout May 1847, he visited American prisoners of war languishing inside the dank cells of Santiago Tlatelolco Prison, once a monastery. Several of the Yankees had deserted to escape the rigors of army life and harsh officers. Donning an enemy uniform to fight their countrymen had been the last thing on their minds. Riley moved from cell to cell and showed several dozen prisoners "an order in Spanish, by which he was empowered to take up [into the San Patricios] all the Americans who remained in the city." [1] The handsome Irishman, resplendent in a new dark blue uniform, speaking to every prisoner as if they were old friends, would ask if he could help in any way. After all, he pointed out, he shared a similar problem. When asked what he meant, Riley would say that both of them were deserters who could hang if caught by their old army.

If a prisoner protested that he had gone over the hill but had never fought against his old army, Riley could shake his head and said that the U.S. Army saw no distinction: desertion meant death. And if the Americans took Mexico City, as well they might, Riley realized, all deserters would stand on the gallows together.

At least Riley would go to his death fighting, he pointed out, settling scores with certain officers on the way, rather than trussed up like a dumb beast for the slaughter. A man might as well put on the Mexican uniform and fight Scott's army, for it was coming for him anyway and would have no trouble taking him in a cell.

Riley, often accompanied by Patrick Dalton, convinced John Bowers, Elizier Lusk, and at least 20 other native-born deserters to enlist in the San Patricios. "The gift of gab," "the blarney," "his high intelligence"—all these terms would later describe Riley's ability to turn even native-born deserters into San Patricio soldiers.[2]

One of the most potent arguments Riley could use on any deserter was that with the American army down the National Highway, most Mexicans were inclined to help only those willing to fight against the invaders. Privation and scorn greeted those who demurred from joining the San Patricios, aliens literally adrift in a hostile land. Many deserters, including both native-born and immigrant soldiers, had fled their units not only to escape hard duty or Nativist abuse, but also the war itself. Eighteen deserters, all English, Scottish, or Irish, had petitioned the British consul general in Mexico City:

> The undersigned humbly state that they are subjects of Great Britain or its dependencies who, having enlisted in the service of the United States and on their arrival in Mexico not wishing to carry arms against a country at peace with Great Britain and in which our Fatherland has a peculiar interest, deserted the army at various periods, and after many privations and dangers arrived at the City of Mexico where we are hourly subject to insults and in danger of assassination . . . added to which is the probable arrival of the American Army, in which case we must inevitably share the fate of deserters—that of death. . . . We pray that you will grant us information as to . . . whether you intend to place us in a situation where we may live secure from the above dangers, or not.[3]

Still hoping for a Mexican victory, the British consul general left petitioners such as Francis O'Conner and Matthew Doyle two choices: fend for themselves or join Riley's band.

Riley handled matters from that point. He offered the 18 their most basic needs: food, clothing, money, and shelter—the San Patricios' rations, uniform, wage, and barracks. Fourteen joined up, and Doyle, like Riley, a likely British army veteran, quickly received a lieutenant's commission from Santa Anna.

A few dozen deserters had not enlisted in the Mexican ranks but had been receiving a paltry 25 *centavos* a day to serve in the Lancer Escort Company, which guarded Mexican citizens on the roads to the capital. Riley persuaded many of these men to join the San Patricios. Hezekiah Akles and John Bowers, who had deserted the 3d Artillery near Vera Cruz, were among the new enlistees.

Once new recruits reported to the unit's billet, they found life in Mexico City far easier. After daily drill, they were free to roam the capital with the other San Patricios. Irishmen reared in rural counties who had seen New York or Philadelphia but never a city with the Mexican capital's soaring Spanish architecture gawked at the National Palace, a block long, and the graceful columns, porticoes, and spires of the Grand Plaza. The sprawling city of 200,000 citizens featured dozens of churches, but few of the Catholic deserters had ever worshiped at an edifice like the Metropolitan Church. Rising from the north side of the grand plaza, the cathedral dwarfed any other in Latin America. The churches in Monterrey and San Luis Potosi were puny echoes of the Metropolitan.

The deserters who entered the cathedral found an "interior... gorgeous beyond description—chapel succeeds chapel—the roofs groomed and gilded with massive church ornaments and wondrously ornamented altars... with richly set paintings." The vista within "fills the beholder with curiosity and astonishment." Even to a Yankee Protestant who visited the cathedral, it appeared "a melange of barbaric splendor" not without "tasteful arrangement."[4]

As the San Patricios made their off-duty rounds of the city, many took a path similar to that of a young soldier who strolled from the "great cathedral to the museum and the National Palace," where visitors viewed "the iron armor of Cortez and feather armor of Montezuma, the celebrated calendar and sacrificial stones and many interesting relics of the Aztecs and Spanish conquerors."[5]

In Ireland, Riley and others had grown up around stone dolmens, massive megalithic structures of two or more upright stone pillars with a capstone and chamber, brooding over rocky fields. But none had seen anything to rival the deserted pyramids and other ruins of Montezuma's ancient capital.

Few of the San Patricios had ever strolled through a park so lovely as the Alameda, with its giant trees, tropical mountain flowers of all hues and scents, and magnificent fountains. And as church, monastery, and convent bells announced the approach of dusk, many of the San Patricios could seek diversion in soldiers' traditional evening haunts: bars and brothels whose employees were eager to relieve military men of their monthly wages. Before seeking female companions for an evening, the men generally spent a few hours in the city's ubiquitous bars, cantinas, and *pulquerias,* whose walls were "gaudily decorated using brilliant water colors or fresco from top to bottom and with representations of landscapes, birds, animals, battles; the subject of the painting being illustrative of the name of the shop."[6]

Inside the *pulquerias* or on the city's cobbled streets at night, the San Patricios had to be wary of *leperos;* for many of these desperate men and women, robbery and even murder were tools of survival, a visitor remarking that when one saw the *leperos,* "you think of Hell."[7]

Riley and the other deserters serving as officers could frequent establishments where *leperos* did not show their faces or their blades, but for all of the San Patricios and Santa Anna's other units, the capital's diversions did not obscure a hard truth: the Yankees lay roughly 75 miles down the National Highway.

Between April 20 and May 15, 1847, Scott garrisoned Jalapa, Perote, and the beautiful mountain city of Puebla. Two thousand of his men were battling yellow fever or a virulent form of dysentery dubbed "diarrhea blue." Allowing for the troops stationed from Vera Cruz to Perote, only 5,820 Yankees occupied Puebla, with Santa Anna massing five times that number around Mexico City. Dogged by a continuing shortage of wagons and animals and by Mexican guerillas preying on all but the most heavily armed supply convoys, the American advance stalled.

In late April, another problem suddenly assailed Scott. A circular bearing Santa Anna's signature flooded American camps in and around Jalapa. To all deserters, the leaflet guaranteed a ten-dollar bonus, 200 acres "to them as well as to their families or heirs," and five dollars extra for every man a deserter brought with him.[8]

For Scott, the most alarming part of the appeal lurked in its one-page supplement entitled "Mexicans to Catholic Irishmen"; the tract marked the first step of a new propaganda campaign:

> Irishmen—Listen to the words of your brothers, hear the accents of a Catholic people.
>
> Could Mexicans imagine that the sons of Ireland, that noble land of the religious and the brave, would be seen amongst their enemies?
>
> Well known it is that Irishmen are a noble race; well known it is that in their own country many of them have not even bread to give up to their children.
>
> These are the chief motives that induced Irishmen to abandon their beloved country and visit the shores of the new world.
>
> But was it not natural to expect that the distressed Irishmen who fly from hunger would take refuge in this Catholic country, where they might have met with a hearty welcome and been looked upon as brothers had they not come as cruel and unjust invaders?
>
> Sons of Ireland! Have you forgotten that in any Spanish country it is sufficient to claim Ireland as your home to meet with a friendly reception from authorities as well as citizens?
>
> Our religion is the strongest of bonds.
>
> What! Can you fight by the side of those who put fire to your temples in Boston and Philadelphia? Did you witness such dreadful crimes and sacrileges without making a solemn vow to our Lord?
>
> If you are Catholics, the same as we, if you follow the doctrines of our Savior, why are you men, sword in hand, murdering your brothers, why are you the antagonists of those who defend their country and your own kind?
>
> Are Catholic Irishmen to be the destroyers of Catholic temples, the murderers of Catholic priests, and the founders of heretical rites in this pious nation?
>
> Irishmen—You were expected to be just, because you are the countrymen of that truly great and eloquent man, O'Connell, who had devoted his whole life to defend your rights, and finally, because you are said to be good and sincere Catholics.

Why, then, do you rank among our wicked enemies?

Is it because you wish to have a grant of land that you call your own?

But what can the most powerful armies do against a whole nation?

By conquest you can take the cities and towns, but never possess two feet of ground unmolested as long as there is a Mexican. The last of Mexicans is determined to fight without release from his country and his God.

But our hospitality and good will towards you tenders you what by force you you can possess or enjoy: as much property in land as you require, and this under the pledge of our honor and our holy religion.

Come over to us: you will be received under the laws of that truly Christian hospitality and good faith which Irish guests are entitled to expect and obtain from a Catholic nation.

Our sincere efforts have already been realized with many of your countrymen, who are living as our own brothers among us.

May Mexicans and Irishmen, united by the sacred tie of religion and benevolence, form only one people.[9]

Citing land ownership, dispossession, persecution, religious conscience, the Famine, even O'Connell, the missive's writer or writers displayed deep familiarity with Ireland's past and present. There is no proof that Riley contributed to the circular, but its content mirrors themes of religion, Irish nationalism, and Nativist prejudice that he penned. He helped draft a future pamphlet, which would raise speculation that he had a hand in Santa Anna's first appeal to Scott's immigrants.

Along with Santa Anna, the Mexican architects of the desertion campaign were Father McNamara, Minister of Foreign Relations Manuel Baranda,and two journalists: Manuel Payno, editor of the magazine *Don Simplicico*, and Luis Martinez de Castro, a captain in the Bravos Battalion. Politician Jose Fernando Ramirez served as a liaison between the others and Santa Anna.

Before General Worth led his division into Puebla on May 15, 1847, Baranda had positioned several civilian agents to entice deserters and expected local clergy to help. As soon as the hoped-for mass desertions depleted Scott's army, Baranda's scheme called for Puebla's 80,000 citizens to rise up against Scott at the moment that Santa Anna arrived with his troops. So confident of success was Baranda that he hid from Santa Anna a fund for new deserters' payment out of fear that the commander would use the money for some other measure.

With the increase in bucking and gagging and other punishments that invariably appeared in the American army when no battle was at hand, the Mexicans' scheme got off to a pronounced start. One American soldier wrote:

> For some time before we left Jalapa, the Mexican government had been busy tampering with the [Irish and German] soldiers of our army, holding out large promises of preferment and distinction to any of our men who would join their army, and giving them money and liquor as earnest of a future higher reward. Unfortunately for their dupes they were only too successful, and a great many of our men stayed behind [to desert at the first chance].

He blamed junior officers' incessant abuse of immigrants for "between two and three hundred desertions from our army while we lay at Jalapa" in just two weeks following Cerro Gordo.

"Out of the company to which I belonged," the private wrote, "nine deserted, more than an eighth of our entire company, which was not eighty strong at the time." [10]

Another private, a German, noted: "In fact, there are a great many of our soldiers deserting; even at Jalapa city, the Mexicans held out inducements of great promise to our men, (and particularly to the Catholic portion) . . . they were only successful among the Catholic portion." [11]

At Jalapa on April 20, 1847, American soldiers kicked down the door of Father Rafael Ignacio Cortez's home on a tip that seven deserters were hiding in his house. The search party found the men, several of them Irish, and dragged them and Cortez to a makeshift jail. The next day, Cortez and the seven were hauled before a military commission, and the judge advocate charged the cleric with "seducing American soldiers to desert and harboring them in his house." [12] Many of Scott's officers wanted the priest hanged. With Captain John Kenly, a Maryland Catholic, serving as Cortez's advocate, the priest claimed that the seven soldiers, all Catholic, had come to his house not to desert, but to receive confession and communion. Never, Cortez said, had he enticed the men to desert.

For three days the trial went on, but, finally, the judges could not prove the charges conclusively, and they released Cortez. The seven alleged deserters escaped the noose but were confined for the rest of the war.

American soldiers believed that the religious appeals were having a deep effect upon the Irish, but that officers' ongoing "unjust treatment" of immigrants was of equal importance "in the majority of these cases of desertion which were so lamentably frequent." [13] In Jalapa, Thomas

Tennery wrote: "It chills one's blood to see soldiers tied up and whipped like dogs in a market yard in a foreign land." [14]

In late May 1847, Scott departed Jalapa, leaving only a 1,000-man garrison, and marched the bulk of his army to join Worth at Puebla. Scott arrived on May 28, and, on June 4, he issued one of the war's most momentous orders: he directed all his troops between Jalapa and Perote to march to Puebla. Old Fuss and Feathers was taking one of the greatest gambles in American military history. He had abandoned his supply line to Vera Cruz on his calculation that his troops could live off the fertile land around Puebla and had taken the same risk as had Hernando Cortez when he had burned his fleet off Vera Cruz three centuries before.

In England, the duke of Wellington, who had heard of Scott years ago in London and liked and respected the American, had tacked up a map of Mexico in his library and, through diplomatic correspondence and *London Times* accounts of the war, was charting both armies' moves.

When the victor of Waterloo learned of Scott's gamble, he exclaimed: "Scott is lost! He has been carried away by his successes! He can't take the city, and he can't fall back on his bases." [15]

In Washington, a stunned Polk said that Scott had made "a great military error." [16]

Polk had sent high-ranking State Department official Nicholas P. Trist with a rough draft of a treaty and with presidential approval to negotiate with the Mexican government. Trist arrived in Jalapa on May 14. Old Fuss and Feathers was furious both at Polk's lack of confidence in the army and at the political overtones of the Democratic president's intent that his negotiations, not a Whig general's triumphal entry into Mexico City, end the conflict.

Eventually, when British diplomats approached Trist with Santa Anna's alleged offer of a peace if the American government "advanced" him a million dollars and when Trist opened clandestine negotiations through the British consulate in Mexico City, Scott reluctantly agreed to go along with such a deal. All the while, however, he drilled his troops at Puebla and, as reinforcements marched from Vera Cruz, Scott's ranks rose to 14,000. Believing that the Mexican commander was buying time to gather his army and build fortifications, Scott organized his army into four divisions and planned a campaign to take Mexico City.

Santa Anna, certain he could defeat the overextended Americans, suddenly informed Trist in the early summer that a new Mexican law branded any negotiated peace as treason. The talks collapsed. Santa Anna kept the $10,000 advance Trist had sent him.

Not all of Scott's men would march into the Valley of Mexico with him. In the army's hospitals, 3,100 were stricken with or recovering from *El Vomito* and dysentery. Scores of Irish and German soldiers, including dragoon Friederich Fogal, slipped past Scott's pickets and up the National Highway. Along the route, Mexican lancers were waiting to escort them to the capital, where John Riley, Patrick Dalton, and a charismatic new San Patricio officer, Captain O'Leary, reportedly a British army veteran and a former prizefighter, greeted them. Many Americans believed that O'Leary had served as a lieutenant in the Louisiana volunteers and had deserted early in the war, but, unless he changed his name in Mexico's service, no Lieutenant O'Leary appeared on the Louisiana muster rolls.

At the San Patricios' barracks, an abandoned monastery not far from the fragrant Alameda, Riley and Dalton daily met new deserters from "the ould sod." Patrick Casey, Barney Hart, Martin Miles, James Mahon, Thomas Cassady, and many other Irishmen listened as Riley explained how far they could rise in Mexico's army and how they would be landowners at war's end. He could point to his epaulets and those of Dalton as proof and escorted the new men to the monastery's courtyard, where the San Patricios drilled beneath "the holy banner of St. Patrick" as coreligionists and equals in this army. Then he led them back into the barracks to enlist.

Also arriving at Riley's barracks were the "Dutchies" fleeing from their units. George Dalwig and other veteran gunners joined Riley's battery, along with many German infantrymen. To handle the cannons, wagons, and teams with battle-hardened Irishmen, Riley added German dragoons. From the 2d Dragoons in Puebla, defections of men hailing from Prussia to Bavaria soared into the 70s, nearly 20 percent of Harney's 400 effectives.

Whenever German deserters turned up at the San Patricios' barracks, Riley could depend upon one of his officers not only to translate the Irishman's words to the newcomers, but also to show that "Dutchies" could rise as high as anyone else in the unit. In the dark blue coat and black kepi of a Mexican officer, a sheathed saber and a lieutenant's sash dangling from a gleaming black belt, Auguste Morstadt had proven his former company commander, Captain G. R. Paul, of the 7th Infantry, correct: "I [Paul] considered him a well-behaved and good soldier, so much so that I had some idea of promoting him."[17] But Morstadt knew that a "Dutchie's" chances of wearing stripes were remote, especially with a long list of veteran native-born soldiers awaiting their chance. And with the 7th Infantry noted for harsh treatment of its many immigrants, the Baden native and veteran soldier had taken his chances with the Mexicans.

Despite his military experience, Morstadt had received no more than a corporal's stripes when he had joined Riley's band at San Luis Potosi. Perhaps a thick German accent among the many brogues of the San Patricios had held him back at first. But his valor at Buena Vista had earned him a promotion to sergeant. His steadiness in the rout at Cerro Gordo had won him his epaulets. He had risen—or sunk, in his former commander's view—to a rank well beyond any a new immigrant could claim in the U.S. Army of 1847.

Although soliciting Irish desertions at Puebla remained Baranda and Santa Anna's top priority, the increase in Germans who fled Scott's ranks stemmed in large part from an agent hand-picked by Baranda. Shortly after Scott's vanguard had marched into the city, officers noticed a tall, well-dressed blond man conversing with German soldiers in cantinas and on Puebla's cobblestones. Few officers gave the local much thought at first except to remark that he stood out among his Spanish and Indian neighbors. Then, in late May, artillery Captain Robert Anderson and other officers serving on the American Council of War, Scott's military court, received several reports that the blond man had been handing out leaflets to German soldiers. The court ordered that one of the handbills be brought to it.

In early June 1847, an 8th Infantry sergeant seized watchmaker Martin Tritschler and dragged him before the Council of War. General John Quitman glared at him and charged him with distributing leaflets that were written in German and appealed to his countrymen to desert with their horses and weapons. Quitman did not mention the handbills' harangues against Nativism.

Tritschler's trial opened the day after his arrest, the court appointing an interpreter. A throng of Mexicans gathered outside the iron-gated hacienda where the Council of War heard cases, and infantrymen with loaded muskets stood guard. The civilians waited for word about Tritschler, for he was not only a popular tradesman in Puebla, but also a naturalized citizen and a captain in the city's National Guard. At Cerro Gordo, he had fought valiantly as the Americans had ravaged his unit. Left for dead near the highway, he had limped back to the city to recover from a serious wound.

Tritschler stood accused of spying and fomenting desertion, both charges carrying a sentence of death upon conviction. He denied nothing and called the 13 judges *hereticos;* they sentenced him to a firing squad.

According to a Mexican, the verdict brought cries and curses from the crowd outside, and the soldiers broke up the mob at bayonet point. When the transcript reached Scott's desk an hour or two later, he had heard about the near riot and worried that Puebla's 80,000 citizens would rebel against their occupiers to avenge the "martyrdom" of Tritschler. A trained lawyer who had chosen an army career long ago over the courtroom, Scott searched for a legal loophole to overturn his council's sentence. But any technicality he devised could not appear to usurp the authority of the judges.

The next morning, the bishop of Puebla reportedly visited Scott and pleaded for the German's life. Petitions from Tritschler's neighbors were delivered to the general over the next few days.

A week after the trial, Scott informed the prisoner and the bishop that no execution would take place. Tritschler, Scott asserted, had shown signs of partial insanity in jail, and the court, in all good conscience, could not stand an addled man in front of a firing squad. Tritschler walked out of his cell that same day and would remain under close watch until the troops left the city. An American officer noted the man's "remarkable" recovery from his malady. Tritschler remained in Puebla, living quietly and revered as a war hero; two of his sons would become Mexican archbishops.

Scott's pragmatic handling of the Tritschler affair helped cement a better relationship with Puebla's bishop and his clergy, whose antipathy toward Santa Anna Scott had quickly detected. If the clerics would do nothing to aid Santa Anna's efforts to stir up desertions and civilian uprisings, Scott offered to do everything in his power to protect the local churches, their property, and their parishioners from his volunteers. He pointed out that "my orders to that effect . . . are precise and rigorous" and that "under them, several Americans have already been punished, by fine, for the benefit of Mexicans, besides imprisonment." Alluding to a case in Vera Cruz, he wrote that "one [offender], for a rape, has been hung by the neck." But Scott did not add that the man had not been a soldier, but a black camp follower named Isaac Kirk, undeniably guilty but strung up for the same crime for which volunteers routinely escaped punishment.

"Is this not proof of good faith and energetic discipline?" Scott asked the people of Puebla. "Other proofs shall be given as often as injuries to Mexicans may be detected." [18]

In another proclamation, Scott also cajoled the bishops to keep unrest in check: "We adore the same God, and a large portion of our army . . . is Catholic like yourselves. . . .

"The Army of the United States respects, and will ever respect, private property of every class, and the property of the Mexican Church. Woe to him who does not—where we are." [19]

With Scott's courts cracking down on soldiers who had committed crimes against civilians and with Scott's respectful approach to the church's local leaders, the bishop of Puebla and his clerics did not aid Baranda's scheme for mass desertions. Nor would the priests call for an uprising in the hated Santa Anna's name, even if he marched on the city.

By June 1847, Baranda's plan had collapsed—except for its call to deserters. Hundreds, rather than the thousands of turncoats Baranda had envisioned, were stealing away from their units, but Santa Anna still exuded confidence that even without support from Puebla's priests, his leaflets and agents would push desertions to even higher levels than the 13 percent alarming Scott and his staff by early summer.

Although the city's priests would not solicit desertions, Puebla itself offered potent images of Catholicism to any immigrant soldier who grappled with misgivings about fighting coreligionists. Puebla's residents reveled in their city's reputation as "the Rome of Mexico." Sixty churches, including the 200-year-old Cathedral of the Immaculate Conception, offered worshipers everything from small stone chapels to the dazzling spires and arches of the cathedral. And for Catholic and Protestant soldiers alike, four volcanos soaring in snow-shrouded grandeur above the city appeared otherworldly—close to God, in a soldier's words.

Baranda's Puebla agents, sometimes friendly foreign nationals, sometimes lovely young women, did their part to spark desertions from May to August 1847, and so did the buck and gag and the rawhide lash. Desertions escalated among immigrant regulars. In the words of the popular ditty, "Faith, the Mexican ranks they [abusive officers] have helped to fill." [20]

Aside from Scott's relationship with powerful clerics, two factors, American soldiers wrote, kept Santa Anna from harvesting his stated goal of at least 3,000 deserters. Some potential deserters feared they might not end up with Riley's men and might be forced to fight in units of poorly trained, poorly equipped conscripts and criminals. "If [Catholic immigrants] had not known how utterly wretched was the condition of soldiers in the Mexican service," a soldier wrote, "deserting . . . would have been infinitely greater." [21] And veteran immigrants mulling Mexican promises of land, equality, and freedom from Nativism and convinced that the San Patricios were a far cry from battalions of conscripts faced a military truth: the U.S. Army, heavily outnumbered against a resilient foe, battling disease and desertion, had not lost a battle. To many foreigners, the choice came down to certain Nativist abuse if they stayed, a possible U.S. Army noose if they bolted. As one man put it, the choice for each proved a roll of bloody dice. Many still chose to fight beneath Riley's flag and "with the halter around their necks." [22]

In early June 1847, Riley and Moreno reported to Santa Anna that over 200 deserters were billeted at the San Patricios' barracks and more were arriving daily, along with dozens of foreign residents of Mexico City. Santa Anna ordered the men formed into a new unit named the Foreign Legion of San Patricio. Along with the directive came a promotion for Riley: "By my good conduct and hard fighting," he wrote, "I have attained the rank of Major, a rank which no other foriner [sic] who has fought for the Mexican government has ever attained." [23] He professed equal delight that his friend Dalton had been promoted at the same time to first lieutenant.

Santa Anna dispatched Riley the written specifications for the Foreign Legion of St. Patrick on July 1, 1847, but Riley and his fellow officers had already begun reorganizing their companies: "the Foreign

Legion will be called the...Militia Infantry Companies of San Patricio," and "each company will consist of a captain, one first lieutenant, two second lieutenants, one first sergeant, four sergeants second class, nine corporals, four buglers, and eighty privates. Their uniforms will be that designated for the Active Infantry."[24]

Although the St. Patrick's Battalion was now called infantry, Santa Anna had not taken away the cannons of his best battery. Riley's men were virtually foot artillery, the most experienced gunners serving four heavy pieces and their wagons and the rest of the unit acting as infantry-men to protect the guns or serve as assault troops. They were issued new .75 caliber Brown Bess flintlocks, the muzzleloader many of the deserters had carried in the British ranks, and needed no introduction to infantry formations from skirmish lines to squares, the standard three-rounds-a-minute musketry, and the hand-to-hand use of musket butts and bayo-nets. Still, Riley drilled the men hard, readying them to settle scores with officers who had bucked and gagged, beaten, and whipped them.

Riley momentarily turned his attention from the drill field in early July to lobby Santa Anna to honor all of his promises to the deserters. To the surprise of the dictator's foes who had never pried concessions from him, he not only looked at a document Riley may have drafted for his men's futures, but signed it. The contract read:

> FOREIGN LEGION—SAN PATRICIO COMPANIES
> We, the undersigned foreigners, voluntarily contract ourselves to serve in the said Legion for the term of six months, counted from this date [July 1847], legally serving the Mexican Republic under the following condi-tions:
> 1. The Mexican government will give us lands to cultivate at the con-clusion of the war.
> 2. Those who do not wish to remain in this country will be embarked for Europe at the expense of the supreme government, which will also give them a gratification in money.
> 3. The Mexican government agrees to give to the Legion, during the time of their service, quarters, clothing, shoes, etc.
> 4. First sergeants will receive five *reales* daily, corporals three, and pri-vates two and a half *reales* per day [eight *reales* in a *peso,* and a *peso* equal to a U.S dollar].[25]

Throughout July and August 1847, most Mexican units received erratic or no payment. The newspaper *Diario Official,* however, printed notices of regular payments from the treasury to "the Foreign Legion of San Patricio."[26] They would earn their wages.

At 2:00 on the afternoon of August 9, 1847, a 16-pounder roared from the ramparts of the citadel. Soldiers and civilians alike stiffened on Mexico City's streets and drill grounds. Several more booms shook windows. The alarm had been sounded: Scott's army had entered the Valley of Mexico. Negotiations had fallen apart, and if any Mexican still had hopes for a treaty, drums pounding out the long roll and summoning soldiers to their posts shattered all illusions.

Santa Anna's army and thousands of civilians crowded into the Plaza de la Constitucion early the next morning, the military bands filling the square with patriotic music. Thousands more people jammed the balconies and rooftops of the city, watching their army assemble and peering for any hint of sky-blue columns down the National Highway.

All morning and afternoon, the Mexicans' best regiments, colorful banners snapping in a warm breeze, weapons burnished, white crossbelts gleaming, the lancers' horses brushed and spirited, marched from the capital to the drums' cadence and deafening *"vivas"* from the roofs and the balconies. Among the Bravos Brigade, Brevet Major John Riley, Patrick Dalton, Auguste Morstadt, O'Leary, Matthew Doyle, and Colonel Francisco Moreno led the Foreign Legion of St. Patrick from the city and onto the highway. Cheers poured down on them, for, as a biographer of General Jose Joaquin Herrera wrote, "the battalion was largely made up of Irish Catholics" willing "to fight for Mexico and Catholicism."[27]

As Major Riley reviewed the 204 men marching in close, well-ordered ranks beneath their green flag, he proudly counted "142 Irishmen . . . all gathered by me."[28] They flowed from the city in new uniforms, dark blue coats with red collars and cuffs, lapels piped in yellow. Their trousers were sky blue with red piping, ironically similar to those of Scott's foot, or "red-legged," artillerymen. The officers wore their usual visored kepis, but the noncoms and privates had new headgear: jaunty, red-tasseled caps.

A new officer of the battalion rode near Riley. Patrick Maloney, an Irish immigrant, likely British veteran, and deserter from the 5th

Infantry, had gone over the hill just three days earlier, turned up at the battalion's barracks, signed his contract, and was commissioned a lieutenant.

At the 450-foot-high bulk of El Penon, crowned by a fortress and 30 cannons, Santa Anna gathered some 15,000 men to block Scott's line of march northwestward up the National Highway. He deployed 7,000 infantry and artillerymen on the hill, and 8,000 infantry and cavalry under Major General Gabriel Valencia south of the highway to counter a flanking thrust; Lake Texcoco and a narrow corridor defended by El Penon's guns guarded against an American move to the north.

On August 12, Santa Anna staged a grand review of his cheering troops. He harangued the *hereticos* and assured his men that they would crush the gringos. No past battles mattered, he cried, only the victory to come.

Scott's vanguard reached the town of Ayotla, only seven miles from El Penon, that same day. Santa Anna was preparing a familiar greeting for the Americans, but not the first crashes of Mexican cannons: in the evening appeared another broadside urging immigrants to desert because their only reward after a battle was "the contempt of the United States."[29]

Santa Anna had asked a deserter with a feel for words to shape an appeal to the Irishmen in Scott's regiments. A printer in Mexico City readied the type for John Riley's missive, which opened with the words "To My Friends and Countrymen in the Army of the United States of America":

> Actuated by nought but the purest motives, I venture to address you on a subject of vital importance. . . . The President of this Republic, in hope of giving every advantage to the foreigners in the American army, through a feeling worthy of his high station both military and civil, and through motives of the purest friendship towards the misguided inhabitants of other countries than the United States who have foolishly embarked in this impolitic and unholy war, once more offers to you his hand & invites you, in the name of the religion you profess, the various countries in which you first drew the breath of existence, of honor and of patriotism, to withhold your hands from the slaughter of a nation whose thoughts or deeds never injured you or yours.
>
> My countrymen, Irishmen! I call upon you for I know your feelings on this subject well, for the sake of that chivalry for which you are celebrated, for that love of liberty for which our common country is so long contending,

for the sake of that holy religion which we have for ages professed, I con-jure you to abandon a slavish hireling's life with a nation who in even the moment of victory treats you with contumely & disgrace. For whom are you contending? For a people who, in the face of a whole world, trampled upon the holy altars of our religion, set the firebrands upon a sanctuary devoted to the blessed Virgin, and boasting of civil and religious liberty, trampled in contemptuous indifference all appertaining to the dearest feelings of our country. . . .

My Countrymen, I have experienced the hospitality of the citizens of this Republic; from the moment I extended them the hand of friendship, I was received with kindness; though poor, I was relieved; though unde-serving, I was respected, and I pledge you my oath, that the same feelings extended towards me await you also. . . .[30]

At the bottom of the tract, Riley signed his name in large script. His words never made it from the printer's office, for events burst too fast upon the armies over the next 72 hours.

20

"A Bloody Field It Was"

BEHIND THE EMBRASURES of a 12-foot wall and the windows of an ancient monastery, the San Patricios stared at thousands of Mexican soldiers fleeing up the road and past them. John Riley stood in a fieldwork just in front of the monastery with his battery of four eight-pounders. He knew what was pursuing the Mexicans down the road.

Riley likely moved from gun to gun, checking the elevation of the muzzles, clapping the shoulders of the gunners, urging them to hold steady. For the moment, all they could do was wait.

When Scott had feinted toward El Penon two days before with Twiggs's division, marched south past Lakes Chalco and Xochilco, and turned south of the capital to the town of San Agustin, Santa Anna had shifted his forces to a new defensive line anchored on the right near the town of Padierna (mistakenly called Contreras by many accounts) and now at Churubusco. On August 19, he had ordered the San Patricios to take up positions at the Franciscan monastery, *convento,* of Santa Maria de Los Angeles at Churubusco, an Aztec word meaning "the place of the war god."

Rain slapped against the stone walls of the monastery all night on August 19–20; the San Patricio gunners shivered in the open fieldwork and surely wished they were dry with their comrades inside Santa Maria.

Less than seven miles to the southwest, General Gabriel Valencia defied an order from Santa Anna to pull back to the town of San Angel and planned to meet the Americans with his 4,000 troops and 23 cannons the next morning. To his right, ravines and ridges blocked Scott; on the left, the Pedregal, an ancient volcanic field five miles wide and three deep of allegedly impassable boulders, fissures, sharp points of calcified lava, and tangles of stunted trees and scrub. A soldier described the Pedregal as "hell with the fires out."[1]

With Santa Anna and a division of troops arrayed east of the Pedregal, Scott's ability to flank the Mexicans on either side had seemed impossible. Old Fuss and Feathers had sent Lee to reconnoiter the lava field on August 18, and after stumbling across three miles of terrain, he had returned to inform him that a rough path ran across the southern edge of the Pedregal and could be widened for artillery. On the morning of August 19 Scott dispatched Lee and 500 men from Pillow's division to chop through the "raging sea of molten rock"[2] to Mount Zacatepec, which overlooked Valencia's positions.

Later that morning, Valencia's batteries spotted the work crews and opened up on them. Captain Jeb Magruder, with an eager young West Point lieutenant named Thomas Jackson, unlimbered two flying batteries of the 1st and dueled with all 23 enemy guns. Magruder withdrew only after the Mexican metal grew too dense. Jackson's calmness in the action and the rapidity of his three six-pounders caught Scott's attention.

During the cannonade, Bennet Riley, Persifor Smith, and George Cadwalader's brigades crossed the road a mile north of Valencia's batteries, halted near San Geronimo, and stayed put. Santa Anna marched with a division toward the guns' crashes late in the afternoon, halted at San Angel, near the eastern rim of the Pedregal, and ordered Valencia to join him there. But flushed with his "success" against Magruder, certain that his cannons would smash any assault up the Padierna road or any ill-advised approach across the lava field, Valencia assured Santa Anna that the batteries would finish the Americans on August 20. Many historians would write that if Santa Anna had attacked on the afternoon of August 19, he might have cracked the three American brigades between his own division and Valencia's men. Santa Anna remained at San Angel.

All that evening, as thunder crashed above the armies and a deluge chased Valencia's pickets to the shelter of his camp, Valencia proclaimed victory to his officers and got drunk. Many men joined him.

To Valencia's west, the storm muffled scrapes and thuds reaching ever closer to the Mexicans' rear. Bennet Riley's brigade, half of Cadwalader's, and the 15th Infantry, in support, were moving through a barely passable ravine discovered by Lieutenant Zealous B. Tower.

The Americans had begun crawling through the ravine at 3:00 in the morning and had inched forward along the rock-littered path. Three hours later, Magruder's guns opened up as General Franklin Pierce's brigade assembled down the Padierna road in sight of the Mexicans.

Suddenly, the Americans poured into Valencia's camp from behind and cut down several hundred Mexicans with one volley. Then Bennet Riley, Smith, and Cadwalader's infantry fixed bayonets and charged.

Across the Pedregal at San Angel, Santa Anna scanned the action through a field glass. If he quick-marched his division, less than 2,000 yards from the melee, to Valencia's aid, he might still catch the three American brigades in a vice. He watched the smoke billowing above the road for another minute or two—and ordered his men to fall back toward Churubusco.

Valencia's troops crumbled in 17 minutes. Over 3,000 dashed up the road toward San Geronimo, where Shields's brigade captured hundreds. Some 2,500 fled toward the Rio Churubusco and the capital. Near San Angel, Santa Anna, on horseback, met Valencia's fleeing troops and lashed at them with his riding crop before galloping to the rear through the masses that ran past the monastery.

The victors of Padierna seized Valencia's abandoned guns and found John Paul Jones O'Briens's Bulldogs among them. Officers of the 4th Artillery wept as they hugged the muzzles and remembered the price their fellow officer and his gunners had paid at Buena Vista.

Scott caught up with his men at San Angel. The 4,500 troops he had deployed against Valencia had killed 700 Mexicans, had captured over 800, and had lost only 68 themselves, routing "7,000 on the spot and at least 12,000 more hovering within sight and striking distance." Scott reflected: "I doubt whether a more brilliant or decisive victory is to be found on record."[3] In his battle report, he gave Robert E. Lee the major credit for the morning's success.

As 4,000 Americans pursued Valencia's men, General William Worth marched his division north along the road leading past the eastern rim of the Pedregal and straight to Churubusco. Scott had ordered him to wait for Pillow's brigade to cut the Churubusco–San Antonio road from behind and trap thousands of Santa Anna's men. Worth, however, thinking that the road straight to Mexico City lay open, pushed ahead of Pillow and toward one of the Rio Churubusco's bridges. Twiggs's division surged from the left less than a thousand yards from the monastery.

For the first and only time in the campaign, Winfield Scott allowed emotion to cloud his military reason as his divisions charged toward the capital—"the object of all our dreams and hopes—toils and dangers—once the glorious seat of the Montezumas." He had proclaimed: "That splendid city shall soon be ours."[4] Scott hurled his men against the

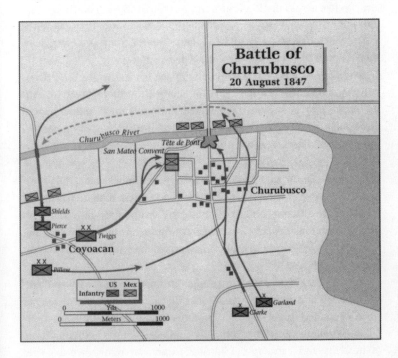

Battle of Churubusco
20 August 1847

bridge and the monastery before Lee, Beauregard, and the other engineers could reconnoiter the positions. Future Confederate general Dick Ewell would recall that near noon beneath a scorching sun, "we rushed our heads against Churubusco, and a bloody field it was."[5]

All morning, John Riley and the San Patricios had squinted down the two roads at the sky-blue regiments rolling closer. He waited for instructions from Major General Manuel Rincon, the fine officer commanding the monastery's defenders. He ordered them to hold their positions. "The Independencia battalion would cover the heights of the convent [sic] and the right flank," his report read. "The Bravos battalion and the San Patricios occupied the parapets and screens of the front and left, fortified with breastworks."[6]

Riley, pacing behind the breastworks, knew what was coming before Santa Anna issued the actual order late in the morning. Rincon's 1,400 defenders must hold the monastery to the death, buying time for the army to flee across the Rio Churubusco's main bridge. There, at a skillfully laid out tête-de-pont—a fortified bridgehead—with three cannons, a regiment of Mexican regulars loaded their weapons and waited as thousands of their comrades pounded across the span.

Around noon cries of "Here they come" echoed across the St. Patrick's Battalion's defenses. Twiggs's division charged up the highway toward the monastery, as Worth's men rushed the bridgehead. Riley ran the green flag up behind his battery in plain view of the onrushing Americans. They dashed within a hundred yards of the defenders' muzzles. Still, Riley held his fire.

When the 2d, 3d, and 7th Infantries surged within 60 yards, Riley bellowed the order to fire, and his four eight-pounders roared. "The awful cry of terrified horses and mules and men" erupted as grapeshot tore Twiggs's columns apart.[7] His soldiers dove into cornfields flanking the road and sprawled amid six-foot-high, uncut stalks as musket balls and grape whined past.

Worth's charge had wilted in a similar firestorm from the bridgehead, his men pinned down in muddy cornfields, marshes, and dikes. As smoke engulfed the bridge and the monastery, the deserters and their fellow battalions raked the "blind and confused" Americans with blasts of muskets and cannons.[8] A terrified American remembered: "The flower of both armies were now engaged in terrible combat. The rattling of musketry, the clash of arms, and the deafening roar of the cannons and the groans of the dying made the scene truly awful!"[9] Captain Francis E. Taylor, of the 1st Artillery, unlimbered his battery on the muddy road in front of the monastery and bombarded Riley's crews and the monastery, dropping deserters across the breastworks. Riley returned fire with grape that cut down 22 of Taylor's gunners and 15 horses in the most accurate cannonry General Smith had ever seen. Taylor and his surviving crews pushed the six-pounders just off the road, reloaded, and swept scores of San Patricios from the monastery's roof and embrasures.

One hour into the attack, the Americans were still pinned down, their losses piling up with each Mexican volley. "Even the artillery, backbone of the army, failed now," an American gunner would write.[10]

As the Mexican fire raged, one of Twiggs's infantrymen would recall how Riley and his unit "poured a plunging fire upon us" from "two tiers of men" firing from "the wall pierced with loopholes." The deserters' guns fired "at once from four separate positions" at a height that over-looked the entire "place of the war god."[11]

Riley's gunners, slick with sweat and black from powder, fired their cannons with such precision that Americans marveled that no sniper's rifle fired with more accuracy. Twice the 6th Infantry Regiment rushed the tête-de-pont and broke in the crossfire coming from the murderous cannonade and musketry of the bridgehead. An American officer was sickened when he came across 100 dead or wounded infantrymen strewn amid a bloody heap of corn stalks.

In front of the monastery around 2:00 in the afternoon, Twiggs's men crawled forward in small bands. "Our advance through the corn was necessarily blind and confused," Lieutenant Lyons wrote. They were always "within range of the [deserters'] guns" and "compelled to stand exposed to a fire from ... breastworks, and in the convent [*sic*]."[12] The St. Patrick's Battalion's flag, perched above the roaring battery, incensed the men writhing and crawling in the corn. As the deserters' fire ripped into horses, soldiers, and officers, Twiggs's troops blazed back at the fieldworks. Mounted Rifles fighting on foot aimed their long-barreled weapons at the embrasures and loopholed windows and downed scores of deserters.

By 3:00, the Americans had noticed that an unusually high number of officers had been hit and realized that Riley's men were singling out "the Yankee disciplinarians whom they hated so bitterly."[13] A soldier surmised that "knowing our way of drill," the deserters instinctively located dark-coated officers among the sky-blue ranks.[14] Riley's troops trained their sights on their frock-coated tormentors and dropped many of them. An artilleryman whose battery the St. Patrick's Battalion pounded would write: "For the gratification of their revenge, they aimed at no other objects [only at officers] during the engagement."[15]

An American captain ducking the sheets of the St. Patrick's Battalion's fire would bitterly record that Riley's "battalion of American deserters . . . manned the enemy's battery that did such fatal execution and inflicted the severe loss upon our brigade."[16]

To the left of the deserters' defenses, Scott had flung Shields's and Pierce's brigades against 2,200 Mexican infantry deployed in ditches behind the road. The Mexicans' musketry was steadier and more accurate than usual, and the Americans' flanking attempt bogged down. But Santa Anna, fearing that Shields and Pierce would eventually break through along the highway and cross the river, yanked a large detachment supporting the tête-de-pont and sent them to his right flank.

Santa Anna also rushed 200 infantry and a huge wagon of ammunition to the monastery near 3:00. Soldiers quickly unloaded the wagon and dashed throughout the fortifications with powder and musket balls for the defenders, but Rincon's men discovered that only the .75 caliber muskets of Riley's men could use the ammunition.

Worth, detecting a slight letup in the fire from both the monastery and the bridgehead shortly after 3:00, called up another brigade and ordered it to storm the tête-de-pont with his own division. The 4th Infantry stumbled from the cornfields, gained its footing, and led the assault with wild shouts. Mick Maloney and his company burst to the right of the enemy battery with Garland's brigade, splashed across the chest-high Rio Churubusco, and charged to cut the road behind the bridgehead.

In front of the bridge, Captain James Duncan's flying battery rolled up and pounded the Mexicans. Five American regiments hit the tête-de-pont and took it with the bayonet, and James Longstreet, of the 8th

Infantry, planted the Stars and Stripes on the bridge. The Mexican infantry behind the river fled before Maloney and Garland's men could cut off a retreat.

Duncan turned his own battery and the captured guns of the tête-de-pont on the monastery and blasted the walls and fieldworks. The 1st Artillery wheeled back into the open because of the slackening Mexican fire and, adding O'Brien's rescued Bulldogs to the action, tore into Riley's battery and the monastery's windows and walls.

Twiggs and Worth's infantry closed on the monastery from two sides. Captain Edmund B. Alexander led the 3d Infantry, which carried scaling ladders, through waning fire to the eastern ramparts. In the breastworks, Riley exhorted his gunners to keep firing as Duncan's shells plowed into the battery and shattered three of Riley's four cannons and scores of his gunners. Hatless, his face dark with powder, Riley ordered dazed men to load the sole cannon with grape. Down to their last few rounds, deserters reached for powder. A flash sizzled across the tangle of bodies and ruined guns. A spark suddenly ignited the St. Patrick's Battalion's last store of powder, and flames enveloped Captain O'Leary and three other gunners. As they screamed and stumbled blindly amid bodies and the ruined cannons, comrades knelt above them, snuffed the flames with blankets, and carried the four men into the monastery. With the Americans' bayonets scant yards away, Riley poured a round of grape into them and ordered his men into the monastery for a last stand. They carried their bullet-torn banner with them.

The 3d swarmed first into the courtyard and at the monastery. Thousands of others followed. Some clubbed open doors with their musket butts; others poured musket balls into first-floor windows. Inside, the deserters and hundreds of Mexican troops heaped furniture into piles. The first Americans crashing into the hallways met fire from San Patricio muskets. Dozens of Americans fell, but others surged over them and pushed the defenders down the corridors and to the monastery's top floor.

Cries, curses, and gunfire pealed from every corner of the building as Twiggs's and Worth's men drove the defenders into a narrow corridor on the top floor. A Mexican tried to raise a white flag, but a deserter tore it down. Dalton thrust at the sky-blue uniforms with his sword. Riley fell wounded among the pile of bodies.

Two more white flags went up. Deserters pulled them down and kept fighting with bayonets, fists, and feet. Some of the defenders slipped down a back staircase and made a dash for the river. Nearly a hundred escaped, but dozens of others were "headed off either by the victorious troops of Worth or Shields and were taken back" to the monastery.[17]

Twenty minutes into the hand-to-hand struggle, Captain James Smith of the 3d Infantry waved a white handkerchief of truce and screamed at the American troops to back away a few feet. It was over. Riley and 84 of his men, many of them wounded, sat or lay on the floor or sagged against the bullet-pocked walls. They had bought Santa Anna time, but now, in the words of an American captain, what loomed "was the eventful and deserved fate . . . of traitors to their adopted country."[18]

The battered Americans intended to make them pay right away. "It was with much difficulty that the American soldiers could be prevented from bayoneting these miscreants on the spot, so deep was their indignation against them," an onlooker wrote.[19] To Captain Smith's credit, he stepped between the deserters and their captors and prevented a massacre.

Captain George Davis wrote: "Their capture proved a greater source of gratification to our entire army than any other single event of that memorable day's victories."[20]

Sixty percent of those in the St. Patrick's Battalion were killed or captured at Churubusco. A hundred had escaped, dispersed in all directions. Prussian-born deserter Othon de Groote had fled during the final stand and wrote that "almost by a miracle [he] escaped, managing to hide in a maize field, where, unsheltered for three days, he withstood thirst and hunger, nourished only by ears of corn."[21]

The Americans dragged de Groote's less fortunate comrades from the monastery and into the courtyard, piled with the dead and wounded of both sides. Twiggs and Worth rode up to the prisoners and spat "Saxon expletives, not very courteously, on Riley and his . . . disciples of St. Patrick."[22] In an official report of the battle, Worth wrote that the prisoners were "deserters from our own army, arrayed in the most tawdry Mexican uniforms."[23] He fumed: "These wretches served the guns—the use of which they had been taught in our own service—and with fatal effect, upon the persons of their former comrades." [24]

The troops of the 14th Infantry, which had seized the battalion's green flag, reportedly waved it contemptuously as they marched out of the courtyard past Riley and the rest. Also in the courtyard was a band of Mexican robbers led by Mexican bandit Manuel Dominguez. They had abandoned their own country to serve Scott as the "Spy Company."

The deserters' former comrades had lost 1,031 dead and wounded that day to the Mexican guns in the bloodiest action of the war, the number nearly 12 percent of Scott's 9,000 troops. Of the St. Patrick's Battalion's hand in the carnage, an American soldier wrote that Riley's men had been the "principal cause of the obstinate resistance our troops met at Churubusco. . . . The large number of officers killed in the action was also ascribed to them." [25]

In Mexico City, Santa Anna lamented, "Give me a few hundred more men like Riley's, and I would have won the victory." [26]

The Mexican leader had lost more than 6,000 soldiers on August 20. If not for the men herded at bayonet point into the monastery's courtyard, his losses would have been even worse.

George Kendall, a *New Orleans Picayune* correspondent who had rushed with the troops into the monastery, grudgingly revealed to readers across America the desperate courage of the deserters' stand: "The boldest in holding out were the deserters of the San Patricio Battalion, who fought with desperation to the last, tearing down, with their own hands, several of the white flags hoisted by the Mexicans in token of surrender." [27]

That night, the deserters lay in the courtyard beneath a downpour. Sentries with bayonets and a full charge in their muskets glowered at the prisoners, hoping some would try to escape and give guards the chance to put balls and blades in them. Lightning flashed across the courtyard and cast ghostly white and fleeting glimpses of Mexico City's spires, only four miles away.

The groans of wounded deserters joined those of thousands more drifting from Padierna to the monastery, the rain and the thunder failing to mute the sound. "The wounded were still uncared for from the want of sufficient medical aid, and without sufficient protection from the heavy rain of the night; and our patriot dead unburied, simply from the want of a shovel or a spade of any kind to dig for them either a trench or a grave," wrote an American captain.[28]

Santa Anna sent Scott a request for a truce on August 21, "propos-ing... an armistice to consider the terms of a permanent treaty of peace to be settled by commissioners selected respectively by both armies."[29] Scott agreed to a temporary cease-fire, in large part to let his army recover from the battles of August 20, dubbed "Bloody Friday." With the halls of Montezuma so close, many of Scott's officers protested against the truce, but Scott, for the moment, was unswayed.

Captain George Davis rode into the monastery on August 21 with an order from Major General John Quitman to take custody of the deserters and "to make whatever requisitions would be necessary to properly feed and protect them from the inclemency of the weather, and for a suffi-cient guard to secure them against escape."[30]

Four days later, at Davis's order, guards removed the 85 San Patricios from the monastery, divided them into two columns, tethered their hands with artillery drag ropes, and ordered them to march. Guards pitched the most seriously wounded prisoners, such as Francis O'Conner, whose legs had been blown away by an artillery shell, into wagons headed to surgical stations.

As one column trudged northwest to the town of Tacubaya and the other southwest to San Angel, American soldiers jeered the San Patri-cios. Captain Alexander of the 3d Infantry spied a familiar figure shuf-fling past with Riley on the track to San Angel—Patrick Dalton—and cursed him until he passed from earshot. From thousands of other mouths at every step of the march, catcalls and curses accompanied the prisoners as men recognized former comrades who had poured grape and musket balls at them from Fort Texas to Churubusco.

On August 25, 1847, Davis wrote that he had turned over Riley and the other San Patricios for trial. "All had deserted from the Regular Army," he noted, and "as deserters... in time of war, the penalty... under the Articles of War, was death."[31]

Part Five

"No Higher Punishment
Can Be Inflicted"

"Gloomy Curtains of Despair"

As JOHN RILEY and 28 of his men languished under heavy guard inside a jail or warehouse in San Angel on August 22, 1847, Scott issued General Order 263 to Colonel Bennet Riley. He was to serve as "President of a General Court-Martial" to be convened at San Angel at noon on August 26.[1]

Farther north, at Tacubaya, an affluent town of red-tiled haciendas and flowered verandas, 43 deserters sat in another warehouse as Colonel John Garland received General Order 259, with the same message to convene a general court-martial.

Excitement and an air of revenge swept Americans who had lost friends to the guns of the St. Patrick's Battalion. An American officer wrote of the coming trials: "We must turn aside to witness another and a sadder tragedy, one in which no rays of glory light up the darkness of death, but gloomy curtains of despair and shame are drawn round the unpitied and unhonored criminal."[2]

Inside those prisons at San Angel and Tacubaya, despair seized some, resignation others. But Riley and Dalton, imprisoned together, had not yet given up. They hatched "defenses" similar in theme and language.

The trials of the 43 men at Tacubaya began first, at noon on August 23. Guards hauled the first case into the court, likely a dingy warehouse. Twelve officers sat behind a long wooden table, shuffling through neat piles of papers, inkwells and quills in front of each. Colonel John Garland, president of the court, nodded to a 13th officer, who sat at a small writing desk in front of the table. The officer turned from Garland, held up General Order 259, and read it to the prisoner and the judges. He concluded: "This court will sit without regard to hours as the cases to be tried require immediate example."[3]

Then he introduced himself as the trial's judge advocate—who would act as the prisoner's prosecutor *and* his defense counsel and would cast a vote of guilty or not guilty along with the 12 judges.

A translator explained the proceedings to Friedrich Fogal and told him that his "counsel" was Colonel Robert Buchanan of the 4th Infantry. Fogal probably needed no introduction to Buchanan, for "Old Buch," a whiskey-guzzling, profane martinet, was one of the most bigoted officers in the service. And from the judge's table, Garland, Lieutenant Colonel James Duncan, whose men dreaded the punishment he inflicted, and several other harsh disciplinarians faced Fogal. Not even the presence of judges Moses E. Merrill and Robert E. Lee offered the German any solace, for neither man, while fair and honest, would condone desertion on grounds of harsh discipline or religion. Fogal and the others had signed the enlistment paper of the *American* army.

Fogal pleaded guilty to all charges of "desertion to the enemy." Swiftly the judges scratched out their verdicts and Buchanan intoned that Fogal would "be hanged by the neck until he is dead."[4]

Over the next two weeks at Tacubaya, 42 other deserters stood in front of Garland and his fellow judges. The deserters fully understood the futility of offering Nativist abuse or religious conscience as a defense. In any event, the Articles of War considered religious or ideological arguments as inadmissable in a desertion case, and Scott's military judges would cut off any prisoner's arguments of that sort as irrelevant to his case's facts. And the facts showed that each man had been captured in a Mexican uniform, the blood-stained, grimy one that each still wore in that courthouse.

Still, in final gambits to escape the noose, 37 of the Tacubaya prisoners pleaded not guilty. Twenty-seven offered a defense of drunken "sprees" in which they had been captured by Mexicans and impressed into the St. Patrick's Battalion, proving their awareness of the general order allowing

AWOL drunkards back into the ranks. The prisoners' pleas also showed some familiarity with the Articles of War's codicil on liquor as a defense for desertion:

> Where a certain knowledge or a deliberate purpose or specific intent is necessary to constitute the offense of... desertion, mutiny, or cowardice... the drunkenness, if clearly shown in evidence to have incapacitated the accused from having that knowledge or intent... will ordinarily be treated as constituting a legal defense to the specific act charged.[5]

The prisoners who claimed coercion, with or without drunkenness attached, also offered an admissible defense. According to the *Practice of Courts-Martial* (1846), a prisoner impressed into enemy service and forced to fight his countrymen through coercion was technically a deserter but had "a legal justification," and "for his conduct in that particular... he was therefore excusable."[6] Because of precedents from the War of 1812, when Great Britain impressed captured American seamen and put them against their will behind Royal Navy cannons, Scott's courts-martial had to allow any prisoner's argument of coercion. And 32 deserters would claim at Tacubaya and San Angel that, despite Mexican coercion, they had never fired a shot against the Americans, or else had shot too high to hit anyone.

Soon after a noncom or an officer from each "drunkard's" or "impressed" man's unit had testified to the date each had deserted, Judge Advocate Buchanan summoned either John Wilton or Thomas O'Connor as prosecution witnesses. And when they revealed that each "prisoner was in the Legion with me; he fought against the Americans at Churubusco, and he was taken prisoner there with me," the proverbial jig was up.[7] Why Wilton, an English national who had served Riley as a trusted sergeant, and O'Connor, an Irish immigrant who had lived in Mexico City for nine years and had lied that he was only a "muleteer" in Riley's unit, turned on their comrades would remain a mystery, because both informers were not deserters and faced no punishment as prisoners of war. Whenever either took the stand, guards stood between the accused and the informer.

Once Wilton and O'Connor had gutted the deserters' not-guilty claims, Buchanan offered the prisoners a chance to call their own witnesses to render testimony. Many of the deserters summoned their former sergeants and officers as character witnesses, such as Captain G. B. Paul, who described Auguste Morstadt's high ability and attested astonishment at the German's disappearance. But the tactic often backfired, such as when Lachlin McLachlin called his former sergeant, H. P. Downs, to the stand.

"What was my character previous to my desertion?" McLachlin asked.

Sergeant Downs replied: "He had no character at all. He was almost always in the Guard House, and a few days previous to his desertion, charges against him for mutiny had been withdrawn."

McLachlin retorted "further in his defense" that he had had good reason to "mutiny" and to run away from the 6th Regiment: one of the unit's lieutenants had vowed to kill him. He was the first defendant to reproach an abusive officer.

McLachlin's charge rattled Garland; unlike the previous 17 trials, he ordered the courtroom cleared of everyone except the judges.

Several long minutes passed. Then the order came to return the prisoner to the court. McLachlin faced the long table, and Buchanan stood with the signed verdict. "The court," he read, "after maturely considering the evidence, pronounces the following: The court...finds Private Lachlin McLachlin of F Company of the Sixth U.S. Infantry, *guilty* of the charge...and does therefore sentence him to be hung by the neck until he be dead."

Buchanan added that "two thirds of the members [judges] concurred therein."[8]

McLachlin's accusation against his lieutenant had swayed several of the judges, but not enough of them to save his neck. The transcript did not mention the officers who had disagreed with the majority.

On September 17, an accused deserter whose use of noncoms and an officer as witnesses for the defense presented a far better "character" than had McLachlin pleaded for his life. Sergeant Abraham Fitzpatrick of the 8th Infantry had vanished from his company near Monterrey on October 6, 1846, and, according to Buchanan, "did remain absent until he delivered himself up at Tacubaya on or about the 30th of August 1847," allegedly wearing civilian clothing. A career soldier with a fine record on the frontier and in the Seminole War, he pleaded not guilty.

Buchanan called his first witness, a Sergeant Anderson of Fitzpatrick's former company, and asked him to describe the man's disappearance.

"The prisoner left, without permission, as far as I know," Anderson testified, "between the 22nd of September and 10th of October, 1846.... The next time I saw him was when he delivered himself up to Lieutenant Longstreet at this place."

Fitzpatrick asked his old comrade: "Did you ever think that I premeditated desertion at the time I left the company?"

"I positively did not," answered Anderson, "on account of his general good character... and his being a sergeant at the time."

Buchanan called another 8th Infantry sergeant, named Blankinship, to the stand to corroborate the date of Fitzpatrick's desertion; when Fitzpatrick asked whether he seemed a likely deserter, Blankinship responded: "No! I did not because of his previous conversations with me on the subject of desertion, his having friends and relations in the States... and the kindness with which he was treated by his Company Commander."

Then Fitzpatrick asked: "Did I have any [Mexican army] clothing or property when turning myself in to Longstreet."

"I do not know," replied Blankinship, who had seen Fitzpatrick arrested.

The odd response jotted down by a clerk, Buchanan closed the prosecution—choosing not to call informers Wilton or O'Connor.

Fitzpatrick called his company commander, James Longstreet, to the stand and asked: "What was my character previous to my absence from the Company?"

One of the toughest but fairest junior officers in Scott's army, the West Pointer described the prisoner as an excellent soldier. "I have not known a better noncommissioned officer."

Fitzpatrick then launched into a detailed account of his capture by Mexican lancers, his alleged imprisonment in San Luis Potosi, and his claim that "when Riley began to raise his Legion, he urged him to join, but [Fitzpatrick] refused, saying he would never take arms against the Americans." "They then offered him a commission, which he refused." [9] He never fully explained how he had survived for eight months in

Mexico City as a "loyal" American soldier or why he was not held as a prisoner of war there.

The judges convicted him despite his skillful testimony and use of solid character witnesses. In deference to his years in uniform, they sentenced Fitzpatrick to a more honorable death than a noose: a firing squad.

As guards led the veteran noncom off, the Tacubaya courts-martial ended. Garland, Buchanan, and the other 11 officers had condemned 41 of 43 deserters to die. Only Edward Ellis, a dragoon who had somehow neglected to sign an enlistment paper and was not technically in the army, and Lewis Pieper, insane, "a perfect simpleton," were spared.[10]

Throughout the proceeding at Tacubaya, John Riley's name punctuated the testimony of the deserters and the two informers, reinforcing American officers' image of him as a malevolent "pied piper" who had used his wiles and a dose of coercion to lure gullible or desperate men into his Legion. A handful of witnesses—one English and the rest native-born Americans—claimed that Riley, Dalton, and Moreno had coerced them into the battalion, Moreno having allegedly beaten some of them. But the Irish and German defendants, as well as Wilton and O'Connor, while acknowledging that Riley had recruited them, denied he had coerced them in any way. Typical of their responses was that of Auguste Morstadt, who had stood with Riley from Buena Vista to Churubusco. As he stood before the court in his Mexican lieutenant's uniform, the German claimed that after his "capture by two Lancers" and finding himself without the means of making a living at San Luis Potosi, "he was compelled to take service with the Mexicans." Then he closed his defense with a statement seemingly ill-advised for a well-educated product of the Baden state schools, but not so incongruous for a veteran and a career infantryman: "From [my] good conduct, [I] was successively promoted to corporal, sergeant, and finally was made an officer of the Legion."[11] At the end of his defense, he had dropped all pretense of innocence and resigned himself to a rope.

On September 5, 1847, the General Court-Martial at San Angel finally summoned "the notorious Riley." Scott's entire army knew the inevitable verdict but wondered whether a brazen or cowed Riley would face his judges.

Since August 26, Riley had seen his men hauled out of the prison and to the courtroom one at a time and tossed back into the jail an hour or two later with a death sentence. As with most of their compatriots at Tacubaya, all of the men imprisoned with Riley pled "not guilty" and forced the court to present a case. Dennis Conahan pleaded that he was literally "a prisoner of love"—dragged by lancers from the bed of his Mexican sweetheart near Monterrey and forced to join the battalion. Thomas Riley, one of the first to desert, contended that U.S. law did not apply to him because "I am an Irishman." [12] When Henry Octker pleaded through interpreter Private David Voise that a Nativist battery commander had refused him medical treatment for a snapped collarbone, which prevented him from doing his duty and forced him to desert, Sergeant Jacob Dearing buttressed Ockter's account: "The prisoner . . . a good character . . . had his shoulder put out of joint at the mouth of the Rio Grande."

The court called in a surgeon to examine the German's shoulder, and the physician confirmed the "collar bone has been broken." With Thomas O'Connor's testimony that Ockter's shoulder had not stopped him from firing a cannon and a musket at Churubusco, the court sentenced him to hang. [13]

Four deserters from the 4th Artillery who had blasted away at the Americans a few days before claimed they had been beaten by Moreno and forced by Riley to hurl grape at their former comrades. As a witness, they called Private James Doyne, who swore he had gone out to look for the men on the night of their desertion, March 21, 1847, and had been captured. Although Doyne had not served with the St. Patrick's Battalion, he said he had heard such things about Moreno but was unable to elaborate. The court handed down four death sentences.

On September 4, the 20th prisoner to face trial at San Angel pleaded "not guilty" to the charges of desertion. Sixty years old, a survivor of the Nativist riots in Philadelphia, with a distinguished career in the U.S. artillery behind him, Edward McHeran was one of the oldest enlisted men in the regular army. A devout Irish Catholic who had experienced no pangs of conscience in fighting Seminoles but had later told several friends in Mexico City that he could no longer fight fellow Catholics,

McHeran was too wise in the ways of his former army to raise his papism to Protestant officers. Described by his 4th battery commander as "a loyal and faithful soldier for many years in the United States Army," he hoped that his record would lead some of the "Old Army" officers, such as court president Bennet Riley, to punish him but not hang him.

McHeran also offered the "drunkenness defense" that nearly two fifths of the deserters presented. "I got to drinking very freely," McHeran said, "with some acquaintances among the [future] deserters" on a four-day binge. "Much bewildered by liquor, I wandered out beyond our pickets. I was surprised by a body of Mexican Lancers, was taken prisoner by them . . . and marched to the City of Mexico.

"I was compelled to put on the Mexican clothing, uniform, to save myself from starvation. . . . I had no intention of fighting against the United States. But I saw no chance of escaping."

Then, McHeran claimed that he was "compelled to march out with thousands of Mexicans to the breastworks [at Churubusco] where we were stationed." No one had forced the men of the St. Patrick's Battalion to the field.

"I did not fire a shot at an American soldier," he said. "I delivered myself up" as a prisoner.

In his final appeal to the judges, the white-haired gunner said: "One reason I would give to the court to show that I was not a voluntary deserter. I have a son in the [U.S.] company with me, who fought . . . and I would not voluntarily desert the company or fight against it."

Thomas O'Connor swore that with Riley's battery, McHeran *had* fired on his own son's unit during the action at Churubusco. One of McHeran's former battery commanders, Captain Samuel Chase Ridgely, the judge advocate, signed at the top of his death sentence.[14]

As with McHeran and the others, John Riley had watched helplessly as guards dragged his best friend, Patrick Dalton, to his court-martial. When Ridgely asked whether Dalton "objected to any member" of the court, Dalton glared at Captain Alexander and charged that the officer had shown bias toward him. Asked to explain, Dalton said that "when we were marched" from the monastery, Alexander had threatened him "with violent language."

Ridgely turned to Alexander. He responded that when he saw the deserters, Dalton "looked very insolent." Alexander admitted only "that he made some remark to the effect that [Dalton] deserved punishment."

Bennet Riley cleared the court of everyone but the judges to discuss the matter, and when the trial reconvened, Alexander was gone. "[Dalton's] objection was sustained," Ridgely announced. Dalton then pleaded "not guilty to all charges."

After the Irishman's former sergeant testified to the prisoner's disappearance near Camargo but described him as a fine soldier and man, Ridgely trotted out not just one informer, but both. Thomas O'Connor pointed at the accused and identified him as "Patrick Dalton, a lieutenant of the Legion of Strangers in the Mexican service."

O'Connor testified that at a bullfight in San Luis Potosi, Dalton had "told me he was a soldier in the Mexican artillery."

John Wilton also identified "Lieutenant Dalton of the Legion of Strangers."

"He commanded the company that I belonged to," Wilton said. "He gave his sword to point"—surrendered it—at Churubusco.

In his defense, Dalton rendered a far different account of his odyssey from Camargo to Churubusco, claiming that rancheros had spirited him away to San Luis Potosi and that the words of the two informers could not be trusted. He had to admit he was a Mexican officer—he was wearing the uniform—but asserted that facing starvation far from American lines, "having no means to live, I concluded that I was better to join the [Mexican] Army until I could get an opportunity to leave it." Nowhere in his statements did Dalton accuse his friend Riley of coercion; the Mayo native did not even mention his Galway-born commander.[15]

Historian Michael Hogan asserts that Dalton and other Irish soldiers' colorful excuses for their desertions and their obvious fabrications—"I did not fire a shot against Americans"—was not desperation. "Given the love of the Irish for storytelling, it was likely that these soldiers had already accepted their fate but were simply relishing the opportunity to tell one last good story, or to pull the court's leg."[16] As every combatant at Churubusco knew that among the defenders, near battle's end, only the St. Patrick's Battalion had ammunition and fired to the last round.

Dalton even related "evidence" of having saved a wounded American soldier from Mexican bayonets, perhaps hoping "a life for a life" might sway his judges to spare him the rope.

He received no such largesse from the court. As soon as the death sentence was read, Dalton requested that he be permitted to receive confession and communion from a Mexican priest and be buried in church ground. They were the only concessions granted him.

A few days after Dalton learned of his preordained fate, John Riley, his hands bound behind his back, stood before Bennet Riley, Ridgely, and the rest. Dried blood, encrusted dirt, and sweat did not completely hide the gilded epaulets and yellow insignia of his Mexican major's dark-blue coat. Off-duty American soldiers thronged the cobblestones outside the courtroom.

Resigned to a drum-head trial, one an Irish-American artilleryman labeled "a farce called a military commission," Riley was determined to infuriate his judges even further by dragging his case out as long as possible and insulting the commission's intelligence with the most facile storytelling they had heard in that stuffy room.[17]

Like all the other Irish deserters, John Riley knew Colonel Bennett Riley was a Catholic but also a native-born American with both feet rooted in the United States and its army, his impressions of "the ould sod" dusty memories of his parents. The colonel's deep voice, with a pronounced lisp startling in such an imposing figure, called the trial of John Riley to order. Indictment in hand, Captain Ridgely rose and read aloud: "In this that Private John Riley of K Company, Fifth Infantry, did desert the service of the United States on the twelfth of April 1846 . . . and was captured bearing arms in the Mexican ranks . . . at the battle of Churubusco, how does that prisoner plead?"

"Not guilty."

Ridgely called Sergeant James Everstine to attest to Riley's desertion; Riley then got him talking about the prisoner's good character. "I never saw anything bad about him," Everstine remarked.

Following the sergeant to the stand, O'Connor and Wilton bluntly portrayed Riley as the force behind the St. Patrick's Battalion. Riley, displaying Irishmen's centuries-old contempt for one of their homeland's most reviled characters—the informer—ignored both men.

When Ridgely, content with the damning testimony of the pair, rested his case, Riley called three 5th Infantry officers as defense witnesses. From Captain George Deas, so disturbed by the fires of San Isabel in March 1846, Riley elicited testimony that muddied a court document that "a tall man and an Irishman" causing desertions at Matamoros had been Riley. He forced Deas to admit that the letter, written by his brother, a prisoner in Matamoros at the time, did not make "certain that the man was Riley."

Riley's former company commander, Captain Merrill, who had condemned the Tacubaya prisoners to death, followed Deas and, "duly sworn," lauded Riley as "a man of good character and an excellent soldier." Another 5th officer, Captain William Chapman, also described Riley as a "very good" man and soldier. In a letter to his wife, Chapman wrote: "Riley is quite a celebrated character and holds a Captain's commission in the Mexican Army. You must recollect the tall Irishman named Riley who worked . . . at Mackinac and was enlisted by Merrill." [18] About his desertion, the Irishman asked them nothing, tweaking Ridgely, Duncan, and other martinets with each reference to the good character of the "notorious Riley."

To gall the court further, Riley summoned H. R. Parker, a prominent English businessman in Mexico City, to the stand to testify that he had seen Riley provide food and clothing for American prisoners and that any talk that he had coerced any man into the St. Patrick's Battalion was "damned lies."

If the judges expected Riley to close his case at that point, they soon discovered that he was just beginning. Like Dalton, though far more elaborately, Riley spun a tale any novelist of the day could have admired. He claimed that he had gone to church above Matamoros, was seized and taken across the Rio Grande by lancers, and was imprisoned 19 days with only bread and water for sustenance. Then Ampudia had given him three choices: face an American firing squad, face one of Ampudia's, or join the Mexican army. Ampudia allowed him time to think things over on the retreat to Linares, "my hands tied behind my back."

Throughout his story, Riley reiterated that he was not an American. Ampudia responded by "telling me that as being an alien to the United States and Mexico both, I should suffer death; brought me out on the plaza, with my hands tied behind my back as a prisoner and sentenced me to be shot in twenty-five minutes, to which General Arista rode up upon horse-back and said to Ampudia that no such business should take place while he was in command of the Army."

Arista, Riley continued, interrogated him about his background and about Taylor's army. In a jibe at Wilton and O'Connor, Riley "made [Arista] an answer that I did not come there for [to be] an informer." Arista replied he "had not considered me or any other foreigner entitled to take arms . . . in the ranks of the United States . . . therefore, all foreigners who should be prisoners from those ranks should be treated as traitors to the Mexican government."

Now, Riley stated, his arms were bound yet again behind his back by the Mexicans. His constant references to the Mexicans' trussing him up came as he stood in that courtroom with American ropes grating against his hands. Arista had offered him one last chance "to take arms in the defence of Mexico." In choosing the word *defense,* Riley rankled officers believing in America's Manifest Destiny to invade Mexico and those espousing Polk's claim that when Thornton had been ambushed, "American blood had been shed on American soil."

Then, in words capturing the resentment of Irish and German veterans whose military experience counted for little in the American army and whose chances of promotion were nonexistent if they were not naturalized citizens like Mick Maloney, Riley testified: "I made him [Arista] answer that I had never served as a private soldier [with no chance of promotion]—with the exception of the seven months and three days I had served in the American ranks."

"Therefore," he said, "if I was [to be] sentenced to death as a British subject, I would rather serve as a commissioned officer." A man whose Irish nationalism tinged his letters and filled the St. Patrick's Battalion's flag with images of the saint, the harp, and the shamrock, Riley had told his accusers that he would rather be a *British* subject in the Mexican army than to die for the U.S. Army.

Riley took one more verbal jab, this one at the most controversial band of volunteers. "I requested some officers of the service of the United States for to convey me to General Taylor's tent after the capitulation of

Monterrey," but they declined because "they were afraid that I would be killed by the Texan Rangers."

No one believed for a second that Riley had ever contemplated turning himself over to Taylor, just as no one believed the Irishman's claim that he had "refused to take up arms against the United States."

Riley closed his defense. He had never directly mentioned Nativism, his Irish-Catholic affinity for Mexican coreligionists, "the advice of my conscience," or "this unjust war," for the judges would have halted any such "flummery." Still, Riley had subtly touched upon all of those issues. He had also presented a clever coercion defense.

Minutes later, Riley's judges rendered their unanimous opinion of his story: "The court . . . after deliberation finds the prisoner Private John Riley, of Company K, Fifth Infantry, guilty of the specification, guilty of the charge, and do therefore sentence him *"to be hanged by the neck until he is dead."*[19]

"Intense Dissatisfaction"

ON SEPTEMBER 8, 1847, a disturbing rumor rippled through Winfield Scott's ranks. The day had proven a brutal one already: the armistice had collapsed on September 6, and early on the 8th, Scott's regiments had stormed Molino del Rey, a foundry and flour mill complex about three miles from the gates of Mexico City. By 1:00 in the afternoon the battle was over, Scott's men having killed or wounded an estimated 2,000 Mexicans and having captured nearly 700. One of the dead was a San Patricio whom a former messmate had spotted and shoved beneath the mill's grinding wheel. But Scott's troops suffered nearly 800 casualties of their own, a Pyrrhic victory. According to an American soldier, many officers had been shot by their own men to settle scores. The depleted army could hardly afford another such triumph, and the formidable bulk of Chapultepec Castle still guarded the city.

As wagons carted the wounded to Tacubaya and Scott's exhausted surgeons removed Mexican metal from hundreds of men and amputated limbs that orderlies piled up outside the hospitals for burial next morning, the American army's effective strength ebbed to a little over 7,000. Now, the weary attackers heard that rumor: Old Fuss and Feathers had decided to spare John Riley.

Earlier that week, Colonels Bennet Riley and John Garland had sent Scott the transcripts of the deserters' courts-martial for the general's "approval, modification, or rejection."[1] Old Fuss and Feathers pored over each case, bringing his legal acumen and his adherence to the Articles of War to bear as he pondered the prisoners' arguments. He knew that deserters' pleas of drunkenness had "some right to consideration," for the Articles advised that "certain or apparent disposition" to desert must be present regardless of intoxication. In the cases in which deserters used liquor as a defense, the judge advocates had not proven disposition. But Scott did have the wherewithal to negate disposition and drunkenness in cases where the "enormity" of the deserters' actions were a "shock to the sentiment of humanity." In coercion defenses, he could apply the same rationale. Most troubling, however, to Scott's deliberations was the Articles of War's ironclad maxim that only a soldier who deserted in a declared war could be executed for the crime.[2]

Along with the stacks of transcripts on Scott's desk, he received pleas from influential Mexican citizens to show mercy to Riley and his men. War correspondent George Kendall, concerned that Riley and his "precious set of scoundrels . . . might get off easily," worried further when "all the Mexican ladies from this town [Tacubaya] . . . signed a warm petition in their [the prisoners'] favor" and personally delivered it to Scott. Chief among the petitioners, Kendall noted, was the influential "Senora Cayetano Rubio . . . the wife of the rich Rubio."[3]

Another American correspondent wrote of the appeal: "Those ladies who petitioned General Scott to release the San Patricio prisoners suggested that they be paroled on the word of honor . . . they and honor parted company when they left our ranks to join in with those whom we were warring."[4]

Kendall and Scott's officers were even more alarmed that "the English, and perhaps some of the other foreign ministers have also interested themselves in behalf of the scoundrels."[5]

A letter from Mexico City's archbishop and its community of foreign residents, who had embraced Riley in their homes and social lives, begged Scott for the Irishman's life:

> We . . . Citizens of the United States and Foreigners of different Nations in the City of Mexico. . . . Humbly pray that His Excellency the General in Chief of the American forces may be graciously pleased to extend a pardon to Captain John O'Reilly [sic] of the Legion of St. Patrick, and generally speaking to all deserters from the American service.

We speak to your Excellency particularly of O'Reilly, as we understand his life to be in most danger, his misconduct might be pardoned by your Excellency in consideration of the protection he extended to this city to the persecuted and banished American citizens whilst in concealment, by notifying an order he held to apprehend them and not acting on it. We believe him to have a generous heart admitting all his errors.

Your petitioners therefore repeat that their humble prayer may be granted by your Excellency, and as in duty bound will every [one] pray.[6]

Scott was hardly in a "pardoning" mood toward the deserters, but as he labored over General Orders 281 and 283, his final word on the sentences of the courts-martial, he braced himself for his officers' outrage.

Word spread quickly on September 9 that Scott had upheld the death sentences of 50 of Riley's men but had pardoned five and had reduced 15 execution orders. He had spared 16-year-old John Brooke and 15-year-old David McElroy because they were underaged soldiers, "mere youths" whom army recruiters had enlisted without necessary parental permission.[7] In the case of German immigrant Henry Neuer, Scott went along with specious claims that Mexican officers had impressed Neuer into service but that he had never fired at Americans, serving only as a stretcher bearer in the St. Patrick's Battalion. The general ordered him returned to his unit, the 4th Artillery.

To Abraham Fitzpatrick came the news that his prior honorable service in the U.S. Army and his having surrendered himself voluntarily to Longstreet had saved him. Fitzpatrick was ordered back to the 8th Infantry, his only punishment a demotion from sergeant to private.

Scott also pardoned another veteran soldier, Edward McHeran, who had manned a gun at Churubusco. The general's rationale had no concrete basis under the Articles of War but "on the recommendation of many members of the court," he wrote, a "remission is made in the case of Edward McHeran, Company G [4th Artillery] out of consideration for a son, a private in the same company who in the hour of greatest temptation was loyal and true to his colors."[8]

In large part, McHeran owed his life to the intercession of one of Scott's staff officers, Captain George T. M. Davis, who remembered:

He [McHeran] was an old man of threescore years, and had been a loyal and faithful soldier for many years in the United States Army until he fell under the evil influence and example of Riley. In the same company with himself was his eldest son, who had attained the meridian of the allotted period of man's life, and was still in the service of his country. The son had refused to desert, or to become a traitor to his flag.

This circumstance was brought to the notice of General Scott mainly through my instrumentality, but without any expectation or design that it would in any way influence the action that followed.... The deserter condemned to death was unconditionally pardoned....

I was privileged to communicate to the father condemned to death his reprieve and its cause, and when I said to him that he had been ransomed through the loyalty of his son to the flag of his country the condemned prisoner dropped upon his knees exclaiming: "This is worse than death! I would rather have died!" I looked upon the poor wretch with pity, but without the power of speech to reply; it was the last time I ever saw him, but the whole scene in his prison, saved as if by fire, is as vivid as in the hour when it occurred.[9]

On February 1, 1848, the loyal son, William McHeran, deserted but was soon caught. He was discharged on August 21, 1848. Whether he was drummed out of the service is not apparent.

In the 15 other death sentences Scott struck down, he ordered that 12 deserters "to be stripped to the waist of their pantaloons, and to receive fifty lashes each on their naked backs, and to be branded with the letter D high up on the cheek-bone, near the eye, but without jeopardizing its sight." While all of the men had fought against their old army, Scott viewed liquor or coercion—however remote—as possible mitigating circumstances in nine cases: Akles, Bartley, McKee, Bowers, Duhan, Thomas, Daly, Cassady, and Miles.

Six escaped the noose on the technicality Scott could not ignore:

These [six] prisoners severally committed the crime of desertion in the early part of April 1846. At that date the United States were at peace with Mexico and all the world; for the present war did not break out, in fact, till a later date and was not recognized to exist by the Congress of the United States till the 13th of the following month.

No higher punishment can, therefore, be inflicted upon these atrocious deserters—[James Kelley, John Murphy, John Little] Thomas Riley, James Mills, and John Reilly [*sic*]—than that prescribed for a state of peace, viz: fifty lashes with a raw-hide whip, well laid on the bare back of each, and their punishment is commuted accordingly, with the addition that each be branded on a cheek with the letter D; kept a close prisoner as long as the army remains in Mexico, and then be drummed out of the service.[10]

Immediately after Scott issued the orders,

intense dissatisfaction, and an earnest remonstrance among the officers of the army in general, followed at the commutation of the sentences from death to whipping and branding, more particularly in the case of Riley, who was in command of the Mexican Battalion of St. Patrick, composed entirely of deserters...who, from...his general intelligence and influence, was believed by our officers to have been the principal cause of the desertion of the others.

Davis wrote:

It was urged upon General Scott that it would be far preferable that every one of the rest of the...condemned deserters should be pardoned rather than Riley should escape death, more especially as we were in possession of the knowledge of the high estimate placed upon him as an officer by the enemy. The importance attached to saving his life was attested by the unwearied efforts that had been made by the whole Catholic priesthood within our lines to procure his liberation by exchange or ransom.

Scores of Scott's officers, Twiggs, Worth, and Irishman Shields among them, beseeched Scott "to hang him [Riley] in pursuance of the military court which tried and convicted him." If Riley escaped the noose, "it would, in their [the irate officers'] judgement, be attributed by the enemy to fear on our part, and its tendency would be to produce a more stubborn resistance, and increase our difficulties in taking the City of Mexico." According to one of his aides, Scott "listened with dignified patience and courtesy to the arguments with which he was stormed to drive him from his position and induce him to abandon the modification he had made in the finding of the military tribunal that condemned Riley to death." Then, to each, the commander replied that hanging Riley "would be nothing less than judicial murder."

"Sooner than the life of Riley should be taken," Davis recorded, "he [Scott] would rather with his whole army be put to the sword in the assault he was about to make upon the gates of the City of Mexico." [11]

Scott's enraged officers could only hope that "fifty lashes, well laid on," would kill the "notorious Riley" as the rawhide tails had killed some strong men over the years in the U.S. Army.

Scott had closed General Order 281, which dealt with Riley and the San Angel prisoners, with a directive that the executions and the lashings and brandings of the group be carried "out between the hour of six and seven o'clock in the forenoon [morning of September 10] next after the receipt of this order." [12] Scott handed General David E. Twiggs the task—the honor, in Nativist officers' eyes.

23

"This Revolting Scene"

RAIN BEGAN TO FALL on San Angel early in the evening of September 9, 1847. Inside the prison, John Riley and 26 of his men lay on the dirt floor or propped themselves against the thick stone walls, hands and feet in chains. Of the 27, 23 were immigrants—3 Scots, 1 Englishman, 5 Germans, and 14 Irishmen; few of them were likely American citizens.

The rain grew heavier, beating down upon the roof, a rain not unlike the Atlantic squalls John Riley and Patrick Dalton had known in Galway and Mayo.

For several hours, rasps of saws echoed from the direction of the Plaza of San Jacinto. Then they faded away. The rain went on, its soggy cadence as gloomy as the thoughts of the 27 men.

Shortly before dawn, the showers ended. Another hour or two stretched past as the prisoners awaited the sudden heavy tread of American soldiers outside the door.

They came at 6:00 in the morning. Guards threw back the bolt on the door, shoved it open, and streamed into the prison. They removed the deserters' chains and ordered the prisoners to stand. At bayonet point, they herded them into two groups. Riley said his final good-byes to Dalton as soldiers pushed the latter into line with 15 other prisoners. They shoved Riley alongside six others. Then the guards tied the deserters' hands and marched them from the warehouse and into the street. Four prisoners were left in the jail, the reason soon to become clear to their puzzled comrades, who slipped along the wet cobblestones toward the plaza, blinking in the sunlight that dispersed the last gray clouds.

As the prisoners neared the plaza, rows of trees and a Catholic church nestled along the square's southwest edge appeared. Several hundred American soldiers and their officers filled the square, their sky-blue ranks as dirty from battle as the tattered dark-blue uniforms of the deserters. Hundreds of civilians stood behind the soldiers, shawled women weeping, people holding rosaries and crucifixes aloft as the guards marched the prisoners into the square and halted.

In a tiny park just a short distance from the church, Riley and his men spotted the source of last night's muted sounds: "The scaffold was about 40 feet in length, consisting of heavy string-pieces of timber supported by large square uprights, one at each end and a third in the middle, mortised into the stringer; it was 14 feet high," wrote an officer.[1] Sixteen nooses dangled from the stringer.

General David Twiggs, on horseback, ordered the guards to march the 16 to the gallows and the 7 to a stand of trees in front of the church's steps, where five priests in full vestments stood, one cleric holding a large wooden crucifix. Because the gallows had no platform, eight mule-drawn wagons and a teamster in each were parked beneath the ropes. As soldiers prodded John Riley, Thomas Riley, James Mills, Hezekiah Akles, John Bartley, Alexander McKee, and John Bowers toward the church, guards lifted Patrick Dalton and his 15 comrades two apiece into the wagons and forced them to stand behind the drivers. The 16 men's hands still bound, the nooses swaying just a short way above them, American officers held white caps to be pulled over the heads of the condemned. But first, they would watch Riley and the others receive their punishment.

Riley's guards cut the ropes around his hands, stripped off his coat and shirt and tied him to a tree. The other six were also bound to trees.

Twiggs read aloud the order of punishment, his face beet-red as always, white hair streaming to his shoulders from his visored fatigue cap. A Mexican muleteer moved behind each of the prisoners, measured the distance to the naked backs, drew back the whip—each containing nine 18-inch-long, knotted rawhide tails—and waited for Twiggs to begin the count. Although sergeants usually swung the lashes at convicted men, Twiggs had "deem[ed] it too much honor to the Major [Riley] to be flogged by an American soldier"[2] and had offered a sizable bonus if Riley were to die under his muleteer's lash.

Twiggs bellowed the order to lay on the first stroke, and the seven rawhide whips cracked together and tore into the deserters' backs. Twiggs counted slowly, increasing the chances that the prisoners could bleed to death or slip into shock. Then, about halfway through the 50 lashes, the general "lost" count, and before he "remembered" the correct number, nine extra strokes had ripped into Riley and the others.

"Riley, the chief of the San Patricio crowd, came in for a share of the whipping and branding," an onlooker in the plaza wrote, "and right well was the former laid on."[3] To the disappointment of an American newspaperman recording the event, Riley did not cry out or faint, as did several of the others.

A captain looking on recoiled at "this revolting scene" as each "experienced Mexican muleteer inflicted the fifty lashes [59] with all the severity he could upon each culprit." The officer wrote: "Why those thus punished did not die under such punishment was a marvel to me. Their backs had the appearance of a pounded piece of raw beef, the blood oozing from every stripe as given."[4]

Finally, Twiggs shouted for the muleteers to stop. As Riley and the others sagged against the trees, seven soldiers approached with white-hot cattle brands and held the smoking irons inches from the prisoners' faces. Twiggs ordered the branders to proceed.

They pressed the left side of each deserters' face into the tree trunk and seared the "D" into the right cheekbone just under the eye. Several screamed, but not Riley.

Twiggs moved down the line of prisoners, inspecting the branders' work. He lingered over Riley, looked at the soldier who had applied the cattle-iron, and pointed at the two-inch high "D"—the man had burned it upside down on Riley's cheek. To Riley, Twiggs said that the Irishman "was sentenced to be branded with the letter "D," and that he would keep on branding him until he made a good plain "D" if he had to burn his damned head off."[5] Twiggs ordered the soldier to brand an upright "D" on Riley's other cheekbone.

Again the iron charred Riley's face; he cried out this time and fainted. An officer scoffed that Riley "did not stand the operation with that stoicism we expected." [6]

The odor of singed flesh drifting across the plaza, soldiers tossed a pail of cold water on Riley to revive him, dragged him and his comrades across the street and the park, and tossed them down a few yards from the gallows. The five priests followed with the crucifix.

Offering absolution and extreme unction, the last rites, the clerics moved from wagon to wagon. At their heels, soldiers climbed into the carts, pulled the white caps over the heads of the 16 men, fixed the nooses around their necks, and nudged the prisoners to the tail end of the wagons.

The priests stepped back a few yards in front of the gallows as the soldiers hopped from the wagons, which left a teamster and two prisoners in each. A drum roll rent the air, drowning out the braying of mules that were hitched to the carts.

The drumbeats suddenly stopped. The drivers' whips cracked, the carts lurched forward, and 15 were "swung off without a struggle."

The 16th jerked and thrashed for several minutes. As John Riley's rapidly swelling cheeks narrowed his vision, he could still see Patrick Dalton as he "literally choked to death." [7]

When Dalton's spasms finally ceased, soldiers cut the corpses down from the stringer. Twiggs allowed the priests to cart the bodies of Dalton and six others to consecrated ground in a cemetery two miles from San Jacinto.

As the clerics' wagon rattled off, the nine other bodies lay beneath the gallows, the severed nooses still fixed around the necks. Guards thrust shovels in the hands of Riley and the other six deserters, barely able to stand. They buried their comrades beneath the stringer.

When the prisoners had tossed the last shovelfuls of dirt upon their comrades, Twiggs issued one more order. Guards surrounded Riley and the other six and forced them to their knees. Regimental pipers struck up the shrill, mocking notes of "The Rogue's March," whose lyrics every veteran soldier knew:

Poor old soldier, poor old soldier,
Tarred and feathered and sent to Hell,
Because he wouldn't soldier well....

Seven American soldiers holding straight-edged razors knelt along-side the deserters as other troops pushed them to the ground and held them there. The "barbers" then shaved the heads of the prisoners, leaving each scalp a bloody latticework.

As the fifes continued screeching, the guards dragged the seven back to jail. John Riley's war had ended.

An American soldier wrote: "I shall never forget the punishment meted out to these deserters."[8]

If not required to attend, Captain Davis wrote, "nothing on earth could have influenced my witnessing what I did."[9]

Winfield Scott wanted just those reactions from his men. On the following morning, September 11, the four deserters for whom there had been no room on the San Jacinto gallows were hanged at the village of Mixcoac. The final part of his message to potential deserters would prove even harsher.

24

"A Fearful Dance of Death"

As DAWN BROKE across a small hill outside the village of Mixcoac on September 13, 1847, 29 men with nooses around their necks stood on wagons beneath a gallows. With their hands and feet bound, the condemned of the Tacubaya courts-martial could barely move. They faced the northeast, where the strengthening sunlight turned the walls of Chapultepec Castle from ivory to stark white. The prisoners had a clear view of the bastion—their executioner had planned it that way. He would pull no white caps over the eyes of Auguste Morstadt and his comrades.

In front of the gallows stood eight more prisoners; the rawhide lash and the branding iron awaited them.

To the northwest, American 16-pounder siege guns, two eight-inch howitzers, a 24-pounder, and a ten-inch mortar opened up with solid shot at Chapultepec. They had pounded the position, site of Mexico's Military College, most of the previous day, and scores of teenaged Mexican cadets among the defenders had endured their baptism under fire. All youthful dreams of war's glory dissolved inside a castle corridor "converted into a surgical hospital [where] were found mixed up the putrid bodies, the wounded breathing mournful groans, and the young boys of the College."[1] Only 50 of nearly 100 cadets were still on their feet.

At 6:30 in the morning, Colonel William Selby Harney rode within a few paces of the gallows, his back to the distant castle. He glanced at General Order 283 and counted the names—30 to be hanged, 8 to be whipped and branded—2 Scots, 1 Englishman, 1 Frenchman, 8 Germans, 5 Americans, and 21 Irishmen. The 47-year-old Tennessean dragoon, "tall, spare, red as a fox about the head and face," then counted the men beneath the stringer—8 Germans, and 14 Irish, and seven other men—and noticed an empty noose.[2]

Harney barked at the surgeon assigned to pronounce the victims dead: "I count only twenty-nine. Where is the thirtieth?"[3]

The surgeon replied that Francis O'Conner, a deserter from the 3d Infantry, had lost both legs at Churubusco and was close to death in a nearby hospital tent.

"Bring the damned son of a bitch out!" Harney bellowed above the bombardment. "My order is to hang thirty, and, by God, I'll do it!"[4]

He dispatched several soldiers to fetch O'Conner.

Harney's order to drag the dying O'Conner from a surgical cot to the stringer surprised no one at Mixcoac that morning. None of Winfield Scott's officers relished a hanging more than William S. Harney. A career officer who, during the Seminole Wars of 1835 to 1841, "had acquired proficiency as an executioner in hanging Indians in Florida," Harney had ordered his troops to carry nooses not only as a threat to the Indians, but also to any of his men harboring thoughts of desertion.[5]

Few officers in the U.S. Army were so feared by their own men as Harney. "As brave as a lion and also as untamable," he had "penchants" for bucking and gagging and hanging foreigners by their thumbs. Scores of immigrants had deserted his 2d Dragoons; three of them—Friedrich Fogal, John Klager, and Henry Longenhamer—stood on wagons at Mixcoac.

Harney also had another penchant, one that made him the butt of many campfire jokes out of his earshot. One of his long-suffering aides related that Harney, a man with a strong appetite for hard liquor and women, "kept a vicious and notoriously abandoned camp follower [prostitute] and diverted army ambulances and wagons for the transportation of her person and baggage."[6] Although newer recruits were amazed by the camp follower's henpecking of the hard-boiled Harney, Seminole War veterans claimed that his lust for women had taken not a similarly humorous turn, but a sordid one, in the swamps of Florida. According to a number of accounts, Harney "had ravished young Indian girls and then strung them up to the limb of a live oak in the morning."[7]

In 1834, Harney had beaten a black woman, a slave, to death in St. Louis, Missouri, had been arrested, and had been indicted by a grand jury. He had posted bond and fled, the army refusing to hand him over to civilian authorities and assigning him elsewhere. Because his victim was a slave and because he had a powerful ally in fellow Democrat Andrew Jackson, who had appointed him an officer by presidential commission, Harney never faced prosecution for the murder.

Scott loathed Harney, having court-martialed him for insubordination in early 1847 but having dropped any punishment because Democratic President Polk pressured Scott, a Whig, to shelve the proceedings against the dragoon. Despite his contempt for Harney, Scott had hand-picked the "right-hard hater" of foreigners to send a message to any Irish or German soldiers still mulling desertion.[8]

Shortly after 6:30, litter bearers carried Francis O'Conner to the gallows, pitched the unconscious prisoner into a wagon, propped him against the driver's seat, and adjusted the length of the noose to account for his missing legs. Soldiers then lowered the rope around his neck.

Harney cantered a few paces in front of the stringer and faced the 30 doomed men and the other eight—seven Irish—who stood in chains, with eight shovels nearby, in front of the gallows. Shouting to be heard above the cannonade, Harney read General Order 283. He turned and pointed at Chapultepec and at the red, white, and green Mexican flag hanging above parapets nearly shrouded by white smoke. The deserters, he cried, would stand "under the gallows with the ropes around their necks and would remain until the American flag was displayed from the walls of Chapultepec."[9] Then, Harney vowed, he would swing them "into eternity."[10]

At 7:30, the condemned men had already stood beneath the stringer for more than two hours as the artillery ropes chafed the skin of their necks almost unbearably and the brilliant sunlight bored down upon their bare heads and drenched them in sweat. Clouds of black flies and other insects alighted and crawled across the deserters' hands and faces.

Ahead of them, Scott's batteries depressed their muzzles and hammered the lower defenses of the castle. For another half hour, the cannons fired. Then, at 8:00 in the morning, they stopped. Several of Scott's regiments poured from Molino del Rey toward the western flank of Chapultepec; others, including James Shields's volunteers, moved against the northeastern defenses. Grapeshot erupted from Mexican cannons.

On the hill at Mixcoac, the prisoners and their guards peered through the smoke at the blue ranks inching toward the castle. One of the doomed Irishmen addressed Harney: "If we won't be hung until your dirty old flag flies from the castle, we will live to eat the goose that will fatten on the grass of your own grave, Colonel."[11]

Harney ignored him.

The Irishman's taunt that Chapultepec would not easily fall appeared prophetic at first. So, too, did the words of General William Worth, who, on the battle's eve, had said, "We shall be defeated."[12] Winfield Scott himself had stated, "I have my misgivings."[13]

Those misgivings materialized now amid dead and dying American soldiers strewn in front of the crag of Chapultepec and the 200-foot-high white walls of the castle. Still, the divisions of Worth, Gideon Pillow, and John Quitman staggered forward. Leading their men through the withering Mexican fire were Ulysses S. Grant, Robert E. Lee, George McClellan, John Magruder, George Pickett, James Longstreet, and Thomas ("Stonewall") Jackson, each one having already shown his mettle on the proving ground of the Mexican War.

In a dense cypress grove at the foot of Chapultepec, known as "the Hill of Grasshoppers," the American assault wavered. Infantrymen scrambled behind trees and boulders scant feet away from the blazing muzzles of Mexican muskets and fieldpieces. Hundreds of yards behind the Americans, giant 24-inch American mortars belched, lofting huge shells at the walls of the castle and at Mexican gun emplacements and sniper pits on the Hill of Grasshoppers.

Ulysses Grant peered at the smoke shrouding the grove and glanced backwards now and again at the faraway gallows, where, "in the hot September sun, the doomed men of the San Patricios stood in the wagons watching the ebb and flow of the distant battle measure their lives."

On the wagon seats in front of the condemned, the teamsters watched. Around them the guards and the sightseers watched. All eyes strained as the distant smoke puffed up, sank down, and billowed upward again, sometimes hiding the hill altogether.[14]

Nearly an hour passed, and the American infantry was still pinned down beneath the metal pouring from Chapultepec. Some of the deserters cheered the Mexican defenders, especially General Nicholas Bravo, Chapultepec's commander, a man of "flawless courage."[15]

At 9:00 in the morning, some 3½ hours since guards had prodded the prisoners beneath their nooses, the condemned spied a handful of figures clambering from the far edge of the grove and staggering up the treacherous escarpment of the Hill of Grasshoppers. More figures emerged behind the first group—and were followed by a flood of other men. The Mexican troops were fleeing the grove to make a last stand within the walls of the castle. Howling American infantrymen tripped over their own dead and wounded and those of the Mexicans in the grove, burst from the trees and shrubs with scaling ladders, and surged up the cliffs, despite heavy losses inflicted by Mexican sharpshooters lining the castle's walls.

An American private at the Plaza of Mixcoac recorded that the deserters fell silent, peering at the thousands locked in a death struggle that pushed ever closer to the gates of the fortress. Several of the San Patricios began to pray, and Mexican priests clad in the chasuble and vestments of a funeral mass moved past the lines of American troops and in front of the scaffold. No one, not even Harney, made a move to halt them. Holding up small crucifixes, the priests gave absolution and read the last rites of the Catholic Church.

Then, from one of the wagons came a shout: "Colonel! Oh, Colonel, dear! Will you grant a favor to a dying man, one of the old Second, a Florida man, Colonel?"

Harney edged his horse in front of the man and asked what he wanted.

"Thanks, thanks, Colonel," the deserter replied. "I knew you had a kind heart. Please take my dudeen [clay pipe] out of my pocket and light it by your elegant red hair—that's all Colonel!"

Harney dismounted, drew his dragoon's saber from its scabbard, climbed atop the wagon, and "struck the jester a dastard blow on the mouth with his [Harney's] Saber hilt, knocking some of his [the prisoner's] teeth out."

An American soldier wrote: "As the poor wretch spit out blood, he cried out, 'Bad luck to you! You have spoiled my smoking entirely! I shan't be able to hold a pipe in my mouth as long as I live!'"[16]

Harney sheathed his saber, leaped from the wagon, climbed back on his horse, and trained his brass telescope on the parapets of Chapultepec. Hundreds of American troops were scaling the stone walls of the fortress as Worth's division breached the gates. Hidden from the sight of those at Mixcoac raged the hand-to-hand slaughter in the corridors of Chapultepec. American soldiers who had seen wounded comrades bayoneted at Molino del Rey did the same inside the castle, and six cadets, one clutching a Mexican flag, leaped from the ramparts to their deaths rather than surrender or die from Yankee bayonets. Mexico would revere the youths as *Los Niños Heroicos*, "the heroic children."

The 30 deserters, battle-tested veterans all, grasped that the fray across the valley was nearing the inevitable end. So too did they understand that their lives were waning to their last minutes. All that remained for the San Patricios was a glimpse of Old Glory above Chapultepec and the noose's snap.

The din from the fortress reached a deafening crescendo and suddenly ebbed. On a staff visible through the smoke above the parapets, the Mexican flag disappeared. Lieutenant Ulysses S. Grant spied "a flash of red, white, and blue" as the American flag "was flung to the breeze from the highest tower of the Castle."[17] At 9:30, a rumbling cheer broke from the throats of the American soldiers. Harney sat rigidly in his saddle, staring at the flag, his back to the gallows.

A second volley of cheers erupted on the hill, these "huzzahs" pouring from the throats of the deserters and perhaps saluting their leader, John Riley, for the last time. "A cheer came from them which made the valley ring," an Irish-born gunner wrote.[18] "Hands tied, feet tied, their [the deserters'] voices were still free—Hail and farewell!"[19]

Harney, "with as much sangfroid as a military martinet could put on," barked at the muleteers to lash their teams forward.[20] The whips snapped. "Thirty bodies hung whirling, swinging, kicking, and rubbing against each other in a fearful Dance of Death."[21]

A soldier asked Harney whether the bodies should be cut down from the stringer.

Harney replied: "No. I was ordered to have them hanged, and have no orders to *unhang* them."[22]

25

A War of Words

O<small>N</small> S<small>EPTEMBER</small> 14, 1847, Santa Anna and his remaining 12,000 soldiers withdrew north from Mexico City to the town of Guadalupe Hidalgo. Scott rode in full-dress uniform into the Grand Plaza at the head of Worth's division as a mounted dragoon band piped "Yankee Doodle" across the Halls of Montezuma. Colonel William Harney rode alongside Scott.

In the ranks of the 4th, Mick Maloney joined in the army's booming cheers for their general. But a treaty finalizing Scott's victory would not be signed until February 1848.

When the news of Mexico City's fall reached the duke of Wellington, he wrote: "His [Scott's] campaign is unsurpassed in military annals. He is the greatest living soldier." [1]

On Scott's order a few days after his triumphal entry into the square, guards hauled John Riley and the 14 other whipped and branded prisoners into the city and shoved them into cells on the second floor of the Acordada Prison. A report that the San Patricios "have been for a number of days chained up by their arms, so that they could not sit down, and having an iron collar with prongs around their necks, cannot even incline their heads" appeared in the newspaper *El Monitor Republicano*. "Afflicted with hunger," the article stated, "the food given them being very sparingly dealt out, they are scarcely able to sustain their fainting heads, so that their suffering is very aggravated indeed. . . . We hope that General Scott will not be deaf to our request and will consider that not even the laws of war permit inhuman chastisement. The light of the age has proscribed all cruel treatment."[2]

The *American Star,* just established in the city by New Orleans journalists John R. Barnard and John H. Peoples, retorted that the editor of *El Monitor* "richly merits the appellation of a meddler" and that "we most emphatically deny. . . that [the prisoners] are hungry."

"That those men are ironed," the Americans wrote, "and richly merit it too, we acknowledge—that they wear around their necks the iron collars of disgrace, we will not deny." And regarding the hanged prisoners, the *Star* offered "little sympathy for those who have paid the penalty of their crimes with their lives: they. . . were unfit to live."[3]

When Scott soon allowed a civilian committee to begin regular inspections of the imprisoned Irish volunteers and then granted permission for friends of the men to visit them, the iron collars, but not the chains, disappeared. "The guard over these. . . miserable apologies for humanity. . . is importuned daily by persons apparently occupying a respectable position in society, who drive to the place in their carriages, and carry to them all sorts of luxuries, while their own countrymen, prisoners also, the sick and wounded officers and privates, are utterly neglected," wrote William Tobey, who reviled Irishmen and Mexicans alike.[4] He sneered that the deserters' fetid cell was "cleaner and more comfortable than any debtor's prison" and that each prisoner's thin blanket and straw bedmat provided more than adequate protection against Acordada's always damp floors and walls.[5]

For American readers clamoring for news about Riley, "the most hated man of the Mexican War," Tobey stopped by the Irishman's cell; his appearance impressed even the vitriolic editor, who guessed Riley's age as 35—[five too many]: "He [Riley] is six feet one or two inches high, broad-shouldered and muscular, and, we should suppose, a man of great strength and capable of enduring fatigue or hardship with indifference. . . . The letters 'D' branded on his cheeks" had left scars with "the appearance of a severe burn."

Tobey had little to say to Riley but noted that "he complained that a shirt made for him by a woman of the city had been kept from him."

Tobey peeked at the other prisoners and described them as "fat rascals," thanks to their "ostentatiously benevolent women" who brought them food. "Most of [the deserters] spoke a tongue foreign to our own," he wrote with Nativist disdain.[6] His account of his visit to Acordada would run in newspapers across the United States.

In the British press, accounts of Churubusco, Chapultepec, and Scott's capture of Mexico City appeared. But English reporters and diplomats in Mexico made no mention of the St. Patrick's Battalion and the trials and punishments. *The London Times,* Britain's chief source on the Mexican-American War, was no friend of the Irish and would not have been inclined to run stories that might have inflamed Irishmen against the United States, the "dumping ground" for the British government's Famine "problem." Such articles might have raised another vexing issue: although, as Riley and his fellow Irishmen knew, the Crown's official position was "once a British citizen, always a British citizen," the British consulate in Mexico City had not even attempted to help the condemned San Patricios.

The firebrands of the Young Ireland movement, who labeled the Famine a British genocide and who, in 1848, would launch an abortive, ill-planned rebellion against the British, would probably have seized upon the executions of Irish soldiers in Mexico as yet another Anglo-Saxon atrocity. But the fate of the St. Patrick's Battalion, an ocean and a continent away, never reached the ears of Young Ireland.

To occupied Mexico, Scott's treatment of the San Patricios remained an outrage. A staff officer would claim that Old Fuss and Feathers had wanted to spare the 50 condemned deserters the noose, but that with heavy fighting ahead, he had needed to set a harsh example for the immigrants in his ranks. Although he had waited until the breakdown of the truce to sign the execution orders, his choice of Harney to carry out the final hangings and the fact that Scott had chosen disfigurement in branding prisoners on their cheeks rather than their hips had reflected that only the Articles of War had saved Riley and 14 others from the gallows.

Mexican luminaries and journalists condemned the hangings and the whippings and brandings as "an atrocious act." Senator Jose Fernandez Ramirez stated: "I was frightened and horrified by news of the terrible slaughter of our luckless Irish soldiers who fell into the enemy's hands."[7] Guillermo Prieto, a congressman, lamented: "The punishment of the Irish prisoners of San Patricio has left a very deep impression on me."[8]

Summing up the feelings of countless Mexicans, *Diario del Gobierno* devoted a special insert to the punishments of the San Patricios:

> Mexicans: Among the European volunteers whom the American Army has hired to kill us, there are many unfortunate men who are convinced of the injustice of this war, who profess the same Roman Catholic religion as we do.... Some of these men, renouncing their error and following the noble impulse of their heart, have passed over to our army to defend our just cause. From them, the president formed the Foreign Legion, known under the name...San Patricio....At Angostura [Buena Vista] and Churubusco they fought with utmost bravery, and after the enemy took this last place, they were made prisoners.
>
> This day [September 13], in cold blood these Caribs [Americans]... after the manner of savages...have hanged these men as a holocaust...[9]

Although an American correspondent acknowledged that the executions and whippings and brandings were a "terrible spectacle," he wrote that they were "justified by the enormity of the crime...provoked throughout the whole war, by the allurements with which the Mexican generals basely tempted them [the deserters]."[10]

An American lieutenant spoke for most of Scott's officers:

> These executions, which would have been proper at any time, were particularly so now...there were many foreigners in our ranks; some of them not even naturalized citizens, and the enemy was making every effort still, to entice them away. The salvation of the army might depend upon an example being made of these dishonored and dishonorable men.[11]

In the *New York True Sun*, a front-page editorial pronounced: "We feel but one sentiment in the court-martials [*sic*]...the justice of their doom.... this 'Foreign Legion' were more than deserters...they joined the enemy against whom they enlisted, and in solid column turned their weapons of death against their brothers and their country.... No good citizen will mourn their deaths.... 'God have mercy on their souls.'"[12]

The editor did not relate that of the 50 hanged and 15 whipped and branded, 41 were immigrants and many were not American citizens.

Like the newspapermen, most of Scott's officers did not see the distinction. "Desertion . . . is treason—disloyalty—in its worst, least excusable, and most dangerous form," a major wrote. "Of this crime were 'the companies of St. Patrick' palpably and undeniably guilty. They had fought in the ranks of the Mexican army, at the batteries of Churubusco; they had fought longest and hardest against those colors which they had sworn to defend." [13]

In a diatribe against John Riley, William Tobey charged:

> We can paint no man, however cursed by conscience and despised by all, so perfectly unmanned, so infamously degraded, as the deserter. To his country a traitor—the mark of Arnold upon his forehead; to his God a perjurer; and the guilt stamp burned deep into his soul. . . .
>
> There is no punishment too severe for the traitor; no infamy too blackening for his name. There is no word in the language that implies so much shame as that of the deserter. With Americans it expresses more than all the epithets of the language; for if all crimes were bundled together and stewed down into one, they could not convey the strength of the blackest of all—DESERTER! [14]

As more of the war correspondents' accounts of the St. Patrick's Battalion and John Riley reached America's newspapers, the Nativist press launched an effective print campaign capitalizing upon the unit's green flag, its Irish Catholic majority, and its commander's name to assail the loyalty of all Irish immigrants, as well as German Catholics. Adding "literary" vitriol to the furor, such popular national publications as *Niles National Register* claimed that "the notorious" Riley had also deserted as a sergeant from the British army, had lied his way into the U.S. Army, had risen through the ranks to regain his sergeant's stripes, and had served as an American recruiter and an artillery drillmaster at West Point. So fixed did these fallacies—with the exception of his rank in the British army—become that writers of the 1990s would still use them. [15]

As at least 118,000 Famine immigrants landed in America in 1847 with many more to come, the Native American parties' messages of popish plots and disloyal foreigners appealed to rising numbers of suddenly anxious Protestants. The "Protestant Crusade" was evolving from the Nativist movement into the Know-Nothing Party, which professed an even more virulent brand of antiforeign and anti-Catholic prejudice. The Know-Nothings advocated bans on all Irish and German immigration, revocation of naturalized citizenship for all immigrants whose families had not lived in the United States for 50 years, and denial of the vote and any public office to all except native-born Americans. Because the Nativists refused to discuss what went on at their closed meetings, the *Cleveland Plain Dealer* reported, they would only say: "I *know nothing* about it." By 1856, the Know-Nothing Party fielded a presidential candidate—Millard Fillmore—who lost to James Buchanan.[16]

The movement's "bible," the *Know-Nothing Almanac,* and hundreds of other publications installed John Riley and the St. Patrick's Battalion as a cornerstone of Nativist doctrine against Irish Catholics. From Matamoros to Churubusco, the Nativist papers, magazines, and books proclaimed, "renegade Irishmen who had deserted from the American ranks" with "the notorious O'Reilly" had threatened not only the war effort, but America's Protestant future as well.[17]

When the mainstream press began to run the anti-immigrant polemics, assimilated Irish-Americans countered with mistaken or misguided claims that of the captured San Patricios, 34 were Irish and 54 native-born Americans. The Boston Catholic *Pilot* charged that John Riley was a fictional creation of the Nativists: he was no Irishman at all, the *Pilot* contended, but an *Englishman* named Ryder. "Instead of stirring anti-Irish and anti-Catholic rancor by dwelling upon this imposter, why do not the nativist papers pay attention to another [Bennet] Riley, the brave and gallant colonel, who has distinguished himself so valiantly?" the *Pilot* asked.[18]

The most compelling argument the Catholic press hurled back at Nativist charges of disloyalty was that, of the more than 5,000 Irish immigrants among the 40,000 regulars who saw battle in Mexico, the majority did not join Riley. Those who stayed were the Mick Maloneys, assimilated to "the way of it" in America, and newer immigrants who chose to endure Nativist officers, disease, and other hardships of the U.S. Army despite any religious misgivings about the war. At the conflict's end, President Polk awarded Certificates of Merit, the military's highest award, to 238 soldiers. Eighty-six were Irish, including Maloney. Names of Irishmen in far greater numbers filled the casualty lists.

Among the Irish and other immigrants who did not desert, there was an understanding of why many others did. Deserters or not, some had suffered at the hands of the Harneys, the Shermans, the Braggs, the Duncans, the Buchanans, the Smiths, the Ridgelys, and all the other Nativist officers and "Yankee disciplinarians." And many victims of Nativism who did not go over the hill evinced sympathy for the former comrades who had faced them down cannons and muskets from Fort Texas to Churubusco. Officers' relentless, brutal bias against immigrants, especially "the sons of the Green Isle," stated an artilleryman, had sparked the desertions. "I have not the slightest doubt" that "overly harsh" U.S. military discipline, "as well as religion, was the problem," he wrote.[19]

To assimilated Irish and other American Catholics' distress, the Irish-Catholic majority of the St. Patrick's Battalion, nearly *70 percent* according to Riley's account, gave the Nativist press an explosive opening for its claims of Irish disloyalty. Beginning immediately after the executions as a response to Nativist rantings and continuing into the 1990s, several generations of scholars and writers attempting to debunk the Irish domination of the St. Patrick's Battalion seized upon the list of the 85 San Patricios captured at Churubusco to point out that Germans, other Europeans, and even Americans served in this Mexican "foreign legion." Slowly, as the decades passed, many tracts distorted the battalion's flag into a whim of Riley's and his troops into a loose mix of misguided or criminal types. The worst of such contentions was the stereotype of "Paddy the drunkard": several writers would twist the "drunkenness defenses" of 32 deserters into "proof" that the San Patricios were dissolute Irishmen and would overlook or ignore that drunkenness and coercion were the only defenses the men could argue under the Articles of War and court-martial procedures.

In a similar tack, a number of historians would pontificate that, because Riley and his men did not deliver ringing "scaffold speeches" full of fiery religious and ethnic rhetoric, they were worthless, amoral men. Again, there was—and is—one fact shaved from such "proof": courts-martial of 1847 did not allow defenses of religious or ethnic conscience. And the handful of deserters who had tried to raise the issue of sadistic punishments to such judges as Duncan and Ridgely—relentless practitioners of the buck and gag, the wooden horse, the covered pit, and the rawhide lash—did so in vain and were not even permitted to point out the blatant Nativism behind those torments.

With the notable exception of Miller and Michael Hogan, few American scholars examined Mexican documents recording the Irish character of the St. Patrick's Battalion. With complete ignorance of or contempt for any Mexican sources, many American historians hammered home the fallacy that such a rabble could have no cohesive identity nor any esprit de corps. The contention crumbles not only from the weight of the Mexican army's official reports of the San Patricios' stellar performance in all their battles, their commendations, their promotions, and the effusive praise accorded Riley and his men by Santa Anna and dozens of other Mexican generals, but also from the evidence of virtually every letter or other account written by U.S. Army soldiers, both native-born and immigrants, who fought against the St. Patrick's Battalion. In the words of both armies' combatants, no unit of the war possessed a stronger identity than the St. Patrick's Battalion. And no words proved it more emphatically than those of the unit's driving force, John Riley.

If Nativists, Scott's officers, and assimilated American Catholics could have read the words that the field commander of the St. Patrick's Battalion was allowed to mail from his cell on October 27, 1847, the letter might have been his last. Addressed to Charles O'Malley, Riley's former boss in Michigan, it read:

Respected Sir,

I have taken the liberty of writing to you hopeing [sic] that you are in good health as I am at present, thank God for it.

I have had the honour of fighting in all the battles that Mexico has had with the United States . . . and have attained the rank of Major.

I suppose from the accounts you have seen in the United States papers, you have formed a very poor opinion of Mexico and its government, but be not obscured by the prejudice of a nation which is at war with Mexico, for a more hospitable or friendly people . . . there exists not in the face of the earth, that is to a foriner [sic] and especially to an Irishman and a Catholic. So it grieves me to have to inform you of the deaths of fifty of my best and bravest men who have been hung by the Americans for no other reason than fighting manfully against them, especially my first Lieutenant Patrick Dalton, whose loss I deeply regret, he belonged to Ballina, Tyrawley, in the County of Mayo.

You may possibly have thought strange at my not writing to you before, but there being no communication between Mexico and the United States, it was impossible for me to address you before now, but as I am at present a prisoner of war by the Americans, it is impossible for me to state facts as they are, but in my next letter, I will give you a full and true account of the war as it has progressed. No more at present. Give my best regards to [Riley mentions 19 men and women, all Irish residents of Mackinac]. Let them know what of the Mexicans has honored me with a pair of Epaulettes and that my old acquaintances are thought of with many feelings of satesfaction [*sic*] and at the same time I regret at not having them here to share with me the honours the Mexicans have been kind enough to place upon me. If you will remember my last words to you and Thomas Chambers when last we parted, which was if God spared me I would again attain my former rank or die....

My situation is such that it is impossible for me to give you a better account at present but have patience for my next.

In all my letter, I forgot to tell you under what banner we fought so bravely. It was that glorious Emblem of native rights, that being the banner which should have floated over our native Soil many years ago, it was St. Patrick, the Harp of Erin, the Shamrock upon a green field.[20]

In January 1848, Winfield Scott received an envelope from Mackinac. O'Malley, horrified that any friendly link to the leader of the St. Patrick's Battalion might ruin a rising career in the Michigan legislature, had sent Riley's letter to Scott and included another letter in which O'Malley claimed that Riley had been a mere employee and only that. "Riley worked in my employ off and on for the space of two years with whom I had more trouble than all the other men who worked for me," O'Malley claimed.[21]

On November 30, 1847, Riley and "all the American prisoners were put in a room at night & were not permitted to leave it & a guard of one Cpl. and three men put over the door," stated Lieutenant John G. Whistler. "In the morning they were let out [for hard labor], as usual....About 7 o'clock [A.M.] the Cpl. of the Guard...informed me that one of the American prisoners could not be found....I found that two women had passed out [of the jail] about half an hour before. One of them he [a sergeant] recognized as a woman calling herself the wife of one of the deserters. I then found out that the man she called her husband was the one that was absent & the woman that was with her must have been the prisoner as he was a very small man & could easily be disguised in women's clothing."

Five-foot-three-inch Roger Duhan escaped to Guadalupe Hidalgo, where the Irishman, a deserter from the 6th Infantry, was promoted to lieutenant. Although Whistler faced a court-martial, he was acquitted from charges of "neglect of duty"; the incident was expunged from his record, the first of many U.S. Army cover-ups to come in the story of the St. Patrick's Battalion.[22]

Scott ordered that all the San Patricios be moved to Chapultepec Castle, where visits to the prisoners were restricted and any escape from the crag was more difficult than on the streets of the city. In a letter to the British consul, Riley sought a more conventional release from the fortress: "Your Excellency, with opportunity of . . . writing to you hoping that your honour will take compassion on me as a British subject as I am unfortunate to be here in prison, I write hoping that you will do your utmost with General Scott . . . on the conditions that I do not take arms against them."

As in his letter to O'Malley, Riley's thoughts were turning toward Ireland: he informed the consul that with his help, "I shall go to my home, that is the old countery [sic]."[23]

Percy Doyle, an embassy official, replied: "I would not fail to speak to the General in your behalf, were there any chance of my being of service to you, but I see none at the present moment."[24]

Scott was of no mind to let any of the San Patricios go free despite the ongoing petitions from the archbishop and prominent Mexicans and foreign residents of the city, for despite Scott's warning that "all our soldiers, Protestant and Catholic, remember the fate of the deserters taken at Churubusco"—men he called "these deluded wretches"—desertions continued, and over 100, mainly Irish and German, joined the hundred or so San Patricios who had escaped Churubusco and were camped at the town of Queretaro, northwest of Mexico City.[25] Taylor issued General Order 296, warning his officers to watch for Mexican agents urging "our gallant Roman Catholic soldiers, who have done so much honor to our colors, to desert" and set up new military courts to try captured agents and recent deserters. Scott's courts did not execute any Mexicans but did stand four deserters in front of firing squads in early 1848. Three were Irish: Privates Sullivan, Collins, and Hale.[26]

On February 2, 1848, as Riley's and the other prisoners' days of hard labor and nights on Chapultepec's stone floors stretched on, Nicholas Trist and Mexican negotiators signed a treaty at Guadalupe Hidalgo. Pending ratification by the U.S. Senate and its Mexican counterpart, the pact ceded all Mexican land from the north of the Rio Grande to the United States. Including California, the terms increased the continental United States by 529,000 square miles. Mexico also gave up all claims to Texas. For its part, the United States would absorb any of its citizens' previous financial claims against Mexico and pay $15 million for the land north of the Rio Grande.

In Washington, ratification came hard. New Englanders wanted slavery abolished in the new territories; Southerners took the opposite position. Many senators screamed that Trist had driven too soft a deal and that he should have taken all of Mexico. Finally, on March 10, 1848, the Senate passed the treaty by a vote of 38 to 14.

Mexico did not ratify the treaty until May 25, 1848, because many Mexican leaders wanted to keep on fighting, even though Santa Anna was exiled. With Indian uprisings in five provinces, however, the Mexican army was too overextended and too battered to resume the war against the Americans.

Before Santa Anna had departed Mexico, he had attempted to negotiate the immediate release of Riley and the other San Patricios, but Scott had rebuffed the plea. In Article IV of the treaty, both sides had agreed: "All prisoners of war taken on either side, on land or on sea, shall be restored as soon as practicable after the exchange of ratification of this treaty."[27] Scott, however, did not recognize the San Patricios as prisoners of war, and rumors that the U.S. Army would ship the deserters to New Orleans reached the cell at Chapultepec. With the Mexican government shaky, clerics' and citizens' appeals for the deserters' freedom denied, and the British embassy indifferent, John Riley had nowhere to send another of his letters. All he and his men could do was wait, pray, and hope that they could escape the army they had abandoned. In May 1848, they were imprisoned in the citadel.

On June 1, 1848, several notables of Mexico City importuned General William O. Butler, who had succeeded Scott when he had left for home in April at Polk's orders, to do what Scott had refused again and again: "We would humbly beg the commander-in-chief to show his clemency by pardoning these unfortunate men and remitting the rest of their term of punishment, setting them at liberty and allowing them to remain among us."[28]

By pure chance on that same day, Butler issued General Order 116, his decision on the fate of Riley and his men. Butler summoned the officer of the guard, Lieutenant Gibson, handed him the order, and commanded him to execute it at once. Gibson read it and snapped a salute. Then he rushed to the citadel. The sun was just coming up over the massive prison.

Outside the San Patricios' cell, on the second floor, the shoes of many more soldiers than those of just the corporal and three guards who usually fetched them to hard labor each morning crunched against the rubblestone floor. The door creaked open, and a platoon of infantrymen with muskets shouldered marched into the long cell. Paper in hand, Gibson strode into the middle of the room and ordered the chained prisoners to stand. They rose from their straw bed mats.

Gibson held up Butler's order and called off each prisoner's name. Of the 16 names, 12 were deserters who had been whipped and branded; the other four included Mexican resident and informer John Wilton and three nondeserters. He read aloud the general's "disposition" of the deserters: "The prisoners in confinement at the Citadel, known as the San Patricios, will be immediately discharged."[29]

Butler's order contained one more instruction. Soldiers stepped forward and held the deserters. Razors scraped against the 12 heads. Then Gibson and his men unchained the prisoners, dragged them out of the cell, down the corridor and a staircase, and out of the citadel. As a waiting military band broke into "The Rogue's March," John Riley and his men staggered away from the mocking tune.

26

"Back from the Lips of Fame"

I<small>N LATE</small> F<small>EBRUARY</small> 1849, former U.S. Navy lieutenant John Perry strolled through the streets of Puebla. A New England adventurer with a taste for "wanderings," he was keeping a journal of his travels and observations about the people he encountered from Mexico to Polynesia.

He happened upon a group of soldiers at an outdoor cafe, and when he realized that they were, like himself, not Mexicans, he struck up a conversation.

Perry found himself talking almost exclusively with one of the soldiers, a "quite social" colonel with a brogue. "He wore his hair long," Perry observed, "and stood over six feet in height." Black hair spilled from the officer's kepi as if "to hide the marks on his cheek and ear."

At first, Perry thought the marks might be shrapnel wounds from the late war; he suddenly realized that they were two "D's," one on each cheek. In his journal, he would excitedly record that he had spent the day talking to "the famous Riley."

Perry described Riley as an extremely intelligent, engaging man but noticed that his complexion was wan and his uniform hung loosely on his frame, giving him "a miserable, dissipated look." [1] What Perry thought "dissipation" was actually the pinched features of a man likely recovering from yellow fever.

John Riley's bout with the disease had proven one of his many strug-
gles in chaotic postwar Mexico. In the weeks following his humiliating
release from the citadel, he had pleaded with Mexico City residents and
officials for money for himself and his men, no easy task in a city whose
government was still tottering from months of occupation. A newspaper
editor started a campaign to raise funds for Riley and his San Patricios.

Two weeks later, Riley wrote a letter in Spanish that ran in *El Siglo
Diez* and ended with the following line: "All the individuals [San
Patricios], and I [Riley] also, give the most affectionate thanks to the persons who have honored us with a show of consideration [232 *pesos,*
roughly $225]."[2]

While waiting for orders to report back to the army, Riley and his men
spent hours of frustration in a *pulqueria* in Tlalnepantla, a northern
suburb of Mexico City, where a few of his men, but not Riley, provoked
"frequent and serious disorders" from "the excessive use of liquor." The
locals made allowances for "the valiant defenders of Mexico."[3]

As several of his men fought their fears and frustrations with pulque,
their commander made the rounds of noteworthy residents to raise
more money. Juan Carlos Franco, a judge, offered as much help as he
could: "I have aided the Irish defenders of Churubusco, giving food and
lodging in my house to them [the released prisoners] and to their worthy
captain, Don Juan Reilly. But this gentleman urgently needs money for
the daily pay of his seasoned soldiers and the new ones that frequently
arrive." Franco asked the government to provide "the necessary sum of
money... to the aforementioned Señor Reilly."[4]

In late June 1848, orders for Riley finally arrived at Franco's home. The
Irishman was to take command of the revamped St. Patrick's Battalion,
divided between Mexico City and Queretaro. Along with the directive
came a promotion to colonel for him.

New president General Jose Joaquin Herrera crushed a coup by
General Mariano Paredes in July 1848, and, because of the involvement
of one of Riley's captains, Scotsman James H. Humphrey, in the abortive
rebellion, all of the San Patricios fell under suspicion. Paredes ordered
an agent to tail Riley around Mexico City.

The Irishman walked on the evening of July 23, 1848, into a house at
11 Medinas Street, "a place known as a hangout for conspirators."[5] But

the "house," actually a cafe, was also a well-known haunt of a range of Mexican army officers. Still, soldiers arrested Riley and escorted him to a cell at Santiago Tlatelolco, a military prison.

The next day, Lieutenant Maloney dashed into the San Patricios' barracks at Guadalupe Hidalgo and shouted: "Riley [is] to be shot!"[6] A revolt nearly broke out at the mistaken report, and by the time order was restored in a few days, Herrera had come to a decision. The St. Patrick's Battalion was to be disbanded and its men offered honorable discharges with all back pay or reassignment to Mexican units. Most opted for the discharge and either settled in Mexico or boarded ships for Ireland and other countries.

Riley wrote a letter from his cell to the British embassy, disillusionment rife in his words:

> I hope that you will please present to the Supreme Government [of Mexico] the enclosed request for my military discharge. I don't consider myself a traitor to the Mexican Government, and in view of the suffering endured for the Mexicans, which is well-known by everyone, I can scarcely bear to be treated in a manner which I do not deserve. They don't treat me according to the laws of the country.[7]

With the letter, Riley also enclosed his two-page petition for a discharge:

> In the month of April 1846, listening only to the advice of my conscience for the liberty of a people which had had war brought on them by the most unjust aggression, I separated myself from the North American forces. Since then I have served constantly under the Mexican flag. I participated in the action at Matamoros, where I formed a company of 48 Irishmen; in Monterrey I did the same with another company of Mexicans; I was in [the battle of] la Angostura [Buena Vista] with 89 Irishmen; with them and more I was at Cerro Gordo; at Churubusco I presented myself with 142 Irishmen, all gathered by me. Here I was injured and taken prisoner, and my treatment by the American government is well-known and notorious, having received 59 whip lashes and two brand marks on my face, which will always remind me of what I have suffered for the Mexicans.
>
> Considering the suffering, and for the merit incurred on behalf of a nation to which I had resolved to give my life, I want only one concession. That favor is that I be given a discharge in order to retire from a career in which I will always be regarded with the mistrust which inspires all men of arms in a country torn apart by factions and civil wars, where individual guarantees promised in the constitution are scarcely observed in the

courts, and where, although I have been charged as a supposed conspira-
tor, I have not seen the conclusion [of the proceedings] after twenty-six
days of intense suffering and delays beyond what the law provides. . . .[8]

A military judge exonerated Riley on September 5, 1848, and ordered
him to report to the army. He was reassigned to regular infantry at Vera
Cruz and, in the early spring of 1849, after likely contracting yellow
fever, was sent to a garrison at Puebla "on account of health."[9]

Ailing and with pay nonexistent for months at a time in the postwar
Mexican army, Riley wrote that he was virtually "starving on the streets
of Puebla." In July 1849, he sent another letter to the British embassy in
which he stated that

necessity compels me to call on you once more for to do me the favor to
lend me four hundred dollars to send to my son, as I received a letter from
him yesterday and he tells me he is in a state of poverty. . . owing to the
poor condition of Ireland at the present time. . . . I will pay you fifty dollars
per month with interest . . . and will give you the promissory note.[10]

In a follow-up letter in November, Riley wrote beneath his signature,
"Native of the County of Galway, Ireland."[11] Again, his thoughts were
turning eastward to his son and to the "native soil."

The Mexican government's official newspaper, *Periodico Oficial*, published the army's list of recent promotions and discharges on August 14,
1850. One item announced: "Retirement to Vera Cruz, with full pay for
service disability, to permanent Major [though a colonel, his retirement
pension was a major's] Don Juan Reley [*sic*]."[12]

John Riley had headed to Vera Cruz—Mexico's chief Atlantic seaport.
Counting his back pay at $1,224, he could live comfortably for a time in
either Mexico or Ireland. The retirement notice was the last mention of
Riley in official Mexican records.

Many Mexicans believe that Riley remained in their nation, married a
beautiful *puro* (aristocrat), and lived out his life a revered hero. A number
of American soldiers, such as dragoon Sam Chamberlain, asserted the
same story.

Citing an intriguing but incorrect rumor, a German veteran of Scott's
army wrote that in an act of "colossal gall" Riley surfaced in Cincinnati
in 1849 and sued the United States government for $50,000 in damages
but that the court ruled against him and ordered him to pay the trial's

cost. Riley's alleged suit would have been quite a feat—in 1849, he was sick in Puebla, and the Mexican government had denied his request for a 15-day leave to visit the British embassy in Mexico City and lobby for his discharge.

A soldier with "the mark of Benedict Arnold" to Americans, a soldier of religious conscience to Mexicans, one of Ireland's Wild Geese—Riley wore all those historical labels. Of his anger at the prejudice of Nativists and their "unjust war" and of his love for the Mexicans who embraced him as their equal, John Riley's letters left no doubt. His words and actions also proved how the leader of the St. Patrick's Battalion saw himself: "an Irishman and a Catholic." [13]

As postwar Mexico's political woes and the United States' agonized rush to the Civil War dominated the nations in the 1850s, the name of John Riley, once "the most hated man in America," slipped "back from the lips of fame." [14]

Griffith's Valuation Lists, a survey of all Irish householders from 1848–64, listed the owner of a small house on "Bridge Street, Clifden, County Galway," in 1855. His likely occupation was farmer, and his name was John Reilly, one of the spellings John Riley used for his surname. In local parish records from 1838 to 1864 are several mentions of children who were "possibly the family of the John Reilly of Bridge Street." Sometime in 1850, John Riley (Reilly, O'Riley, O'Reilly—he used them all) had "undoubtedly" departed Vera Cruz for Havana, where ships stopped before crossing the Atlantic, and home, Galway. [15]

Today, in the cobblestone plaza of San Angel, 71 names adorn a marble monument, including 48 Irish and 13 German. Most are men of the Saint Patrick's Battalion. One—Lewis Pieper—was not a San Patricio. Abraham Fitzpatrick *claimed* he was not.

The memorial is emblazoned with a Celtic cross, a gamecock, a pair of dice, and a skull and crossbones, the last three the emblems of gamblers who lost their wager and paid with their lives. Every year on

September 13, a Mexican army color guard marches with the Mexican and Irish flags to the memorial, around which are throngs of dignitaries and citizens of both nations. Then an Irish embassy official reads off the names on the plaque. In response to each name, the crowd roars: "Murio por la patria!" ("He died for the country").

Mark Day, writer, producer, and director of *The San Patricios*, the first documentary presenting the story of John Riley and his battalion, has filmed the ceremony, capturing what he describes as "the passion of the San Patricios" and Mexico's depth of feeling for them.[16]

Mexico honors the battalion with two other annual ceremonies—one on St. Patrick's Day at San Angel and one on August 20, the anniversary of the Battle of Churubusco, at the monastery where Riley and his men made their last stand. In front of stone walls that still bear pockmarks from American artillery, one of the cannons Riley and his crews manned on that "bloody field" stands in front of the monastery's main gate.

Across the Atlantic, another ceremony unfolds at John Riley's birthplace in Clifden, Ireland, each September 13, the anniversary of the hangings of 30 San Patricios in front of Chapultepec. The Irish army's Western Command Band, officials of the Irish and Mexican governments, and a crowd of spectators gather around a plaque honoring Riley and the Irish soldiers of the St. Patrick's Battalion.

To many in Ireland, John Riley is hardly the "poor old soldier" of "The Rogue's March." He is one of their Wild Geese returned. Now, 150 years after "the notorious" Riley and the men of the St. Patrick's Battalion fought a war far from their native soil, they are returning to "the lips of Fame."

Epilogue

The Civil War and the Cover-Up

IN THE SUMMER OF 1848, General William O. Butler sent the War Department the court-martial transcripts of the St. Patrick's Battalion and all his general orders in regard to the deserters. Scott's and Taylor's letters and orders concerning Riley, his men, and the war's other desertions were already there. No one except a handful of upper-tier War Department officials would view the records for nearly a century, and they would not become accessible to the general public until the 1970s. The army and the government simply wanted to bury the fact that several hundred soldiers had not only deserted, but had fought in their own unit in the ranks of Mexico; the army also did not want the overall number of deserters to become public knowledge.

Still, though not publicly admitting that Nativism had infected the officer corps of the 1840s or that religious qualms had plagued unassimilated Catholic Irish and Germans in the ranks, the army recognized the role that brutal discipline had played in desertions. The rawhide lash, the use of which had particularly enraged ex-British army soldiers such as John Riley and George Ballentine, was banned by the U.S. Army in 1861, the year the Civil War began. Branding men for various offenses lingered until 1871, six years after Appomattox, but in Grant's and Lee's armies the practice was discouraged.

With so many volunteer regiments in the Civil War, most West Point veterans of the Mexican campaigns again realized that discipline must be enforced, but they phased out mutilation of offenders except in grievous cases. To curb drunkenness, brawls, gambling, thievery, and the other traditional vices of any army, the commanders of the North and South did not rely upon rawhide or cattle brands but upon the traditional buck and gag, the barrel top, and, to a lesser degree than in Mexico, the wooden horse. Non-Academy officers also put up with far more from their citizen-soldiers than West Point officers did: Drunken assaults upon politically appointed officers that in Mexico would have earned either a death sentence or lesser but still severe punishment were often dismissed by field courts-martial as a "minor vice...the result of pent-up emotions in those troubled times."[1]

With the issues of the Civil War helping to shove the Know-Nothings into the political background, many Union and Confederate officers who had marched with Taylor and Scott proved that they had learned from the anti-Catholic, anti-immigrant woes of that "dirty little war."[2] Tens of thousands of poor Irishmen and Germans filled the ranks of the Union armies and, to a lesser degree, that of the Rebels. In Northern blue, Grant and Meade, in Southern gray or butternut, Lee and Longstreet—they treated the immigrants as soldiers equal to any native-born Americans. While no one could completely quell epithets against foreigners, courts-martial no longer meted out harsher punishments for soldiers simply because they spoke with a brogue or a German accent. Many Yankees and Southerners still may "have hated Paddy," but new officers soon learned what Grant and other Mexican War veterans already knew: Paddy could soldier. "Other men go into fights finely, sternly, or indifferently," Union army surgeon Thomas Ellis wrote, "but the only man that really loves it, after all, is the green, immortal Irishman. So there the brave lads from the old sod...laughed and fought and joked as if it [battle] were the finest fun in the world."[3]

Of all the West Pointers who had "seen the elephant" in Mexico, none changed more drastically in his view of the "wretched Irish soldiers" than a man who had regularly uttered Nativist epithets upon his arrival in Vera Cruz in 1847. George B. McClellan's perceptions changed as he saw Scott's "potato heads" and "thick Micks" rise above Nativism; storm Cerro Gordo, Churubusco, Molino del Rey, and Chapultepec; and bury their comrades of "the ould sod" in unmarked graves beneath the Mexican sun, far from their native counties. McClellan, Grant, Meade, Longstreet, Pickett, Magruder, Jackson, and the many other future Civil War generals who had led those Irishmen, as well as Germans, into battle had discovered what British, French, and Spanish armies had long known: Irishmen made for some of the world's finest infantry, especially when on the offensive. So well did "Little Mac" treat his Irish soldiers of the Army of the Potomac that many wept and threatened to riot when Lincoln sacked him in 1862. No mutiny erupted—because Irish Catholic priests, "Holy Joes," whom McClellan had welcomed to his camps, pacified the men.

From Fort Texas to Churubusco, John Riley and the St. Patrick's Battalion had taught the U.S. Army another lesson, a harsh one: the Irish fought even more effectively when commanded by their own officers and beneath their own flag. For Confederate Generals Lee, Longstreet, and Pickett and for other Southerners who had seen Riley's green banner planted above his battalion, an eerie reminder of that unit materialized during the Peninsula Campaign and the hellish Seven Days' Battles (1862) and at Antietam, Fredericksburg, Chancellorsville, and Gettysburg; on all of those battlefields, the men of the Irish Brigade marched beneath emerald-green banners gilded with harps, shamrocks, and the words "Erin Go Bragh"—the same symbols on the St. Patrick's Battalion banner. Led until May 1863 by valiant Irish revolutionary Thomas Meagher, the Irish Brigade suffered one of the war's highest casualty rates—66 percent—and one of the lowest desertion rates in the army—1 percent. The U.S. War Department, as well as its Southern counterpart, had borrowed that sound idea from the Mexican army and John Riley: let the Irish fight in their own units and under their own officers. The Union had its Irish Brigade and Irish companies in other units; in the Confederate ranks, Irish companies served in South Carolina, Georgia, and Louisiana regiments. Still, most were in standard units.

Among the Irish-born officers who had distinguished themselves in

Mexico and added to their military laurels in the Civil War was James Shields. He turned down an opportunity to command the Irish Brigade but served as a brigadier general of volunteers in the Valley Campaign in the spring of 1862.

Mick Maloney also made his mark in the Civil War. Promoted to captain for his heroics at Chapultepec, he had remained in the army after the Mexican War. He served with Grant's army at the siege of Vicksburg, Mississippi, and distinguished himself under fire again. In Grant's post-battle report, the general cited Maloney for gallantry and recommended a promotion; the War Department bumped the Irishman up to lieutenant colonel and, by the war's end, to full colonel. Of the immigrant Irish who had fought in the Mexican-American War, Maloney had risen the furthest in the ranks of the regulars and had battled Nativism to carve out a remarkable niche in Irish-American history. Through merit and valor, he had earned a higher rank than some of the West Pointers who had abused both the assimilated Mick Maloneys and the recently arrived Famine Irish, "strangers to the soil."

Though not born in Ireland, John Paul Jones O'Brien had been one of the few West Pointers to stand up for Irish Catholic soldiers before and during the Mexican-American War. He never recovered from the wound he suffered at Buena Vista and died in 1850. His stand with his Bulldogs beneath John Riley's metal and the onslaught of Santa Anna's infantry had saved Zachary Taylor's army from disaster and would go down as one of the U.S. artillery's proudest moments. Today, at West Point, two of O'Brien's Bulldogs adorn the administration building's portals. An eagle-crested marker honors the muzzleloaders with the following inscription:

O'BRIEN
Lost without
dishonor at the battle
of Buena Vista, by a Company of the
4th Artillery.
Recaptured with
just pride and
exultation by the
same regiment at Contreras.

Two of O'Brien's fellow battery commanders at Buena Vista never reined in their Nativism nor their love of the buck and gag. In the Confederate army, General Braxton Bragg added to his well-deserved reputation as one of the most sadistic, feared, and loathed commanders of his day. Thomas W. Sherman served in the Union Army, proving both a brave, skillful officer and a raging martinet who had to be reassigned several times during the conflict because so many of his men complained to the War Department about his brutal discipline. Even an admirer euphemistically referred to Sherman's controversial "manner of exercising authority."[4]

Several other officers who had brutalized Irish and German troops in Mexico never got the chance to fight in the Civil War. Samuel Chase Ridgely, who had served at the San Angel trials as prosecutor against and counsel for deserters from his own battery, died two years before Fort Sumter. One of the heroes of Buena Vista and a Nativist who had grudgingly acknowledged the deep religious convictions of deserter Edward McHeran, John McCrae Washington drowned on Christmas Eve 1853. Another martinet, James Duncan, whose wrath Irish gunner Richard Hanley feared worse than the judge advocate's noose he wore on Harney's stringer beam, died before the War Between the States.

The man who had erected that gallows and had carried out Winfield Scott's execution order with sadistic "sangfroid" on September 13, 1847, William S. Harney had risen to the rank of brigadier general in 1858. When the Civil War began, he commanded federal troops in Missouri for a short time but was replaced after he attempted to arrange a temporary truce with the state's secessionists. He was retired from the service in 1863, and shortly after his death in 1889 another old dragoon described him as "a right-hard hater" to the end. By the time of Harney's death, few Americans except Mexican War veterans remembered the "revolting spectacle" at Mixcoac. The War Department wanted those memories to die away, and so had the general who had signed the execution orders.

In July 1850, less than two years after ordering the hangings of Irishmen who had deserted his ranks, General Winfield Scott wrote: "Truth obliges me to say that, of our Irish soldiers save a few who deserted from General Taylor, and who had never taken the naturalization oath—not one ever turned his back upon the enemy or faltered in advancing to the charge."[5] Scott's "truth" was that only his rival Taylor's "Irish" had deserted, and he included no mention of whippings, brandings, and hangings. The official denials had begun.

In April 1886, the adjutant general received a letter from a man named Albert Richardson. He had written "to ascertain the existence of a group of deserters who formed a battalion in the Mexican Army called the St. Patrick's Guards and led by a Colonel Riley."

"Is it true," he asked, "that these Irishmen proved their fidelity to the Mexican government by burning the American flag and then hoisting a Green Flag with a harp on it?"[6]

"Dear Mr. Richardson," replied J. C. Gilmore, assistant adjutant general, "we have no official record sustaining such a belief and no knowledge of any such deserters from the Army."[7]

To the War Department in 1896, Daniel Maloney wrote, "Have you any record of a number of Irish deserters named the St. Patrick's Battalion and hanged by the U.S. Army during the Mexican-American War on September 13, 1847? I hear they were led by a man named Riley."[8]

Maloney received the exact same reply as had Richardson a decade earlier. So too did scores of other letter writers.

From the 1890s to 1915, more queries about John Riley and the St. Patrick's Battalion arrived at the War Department and always garnered that same evasions. Each time such letters reached the adjutant general, interoffice memos would mention the records about Riley, the trials, the whippings and brandings, and the executions but would order officials to blur the documents' existence.

In 1915, Congressmen William Coleman of Pennsylvania and Frank Greene of Vermont spearheaded an inquiry into the War Department's silence about the St. Patrick's Battalion and the desertion woes of the Mexican-American War. The army was compelled to admit that records on Riley and the deserters did exist and issued a brief memorandum stating that "a few men did desert" in the Mexican War and fought under "the command of John Riley, a Catholic and an Irishman."[9] In the sketchiest of summaries, the note admitted that a "few" courts-martial and hangings had taken place near Mexico City.[10] Of the whippings and brandings and Harney's behavior at Mixcoac, the memo included nothing.

Ordered by Congress to turn over the records to the National Archives, the army did so in 1917, but without public mention. The documents, detailing one of the most embarrassing episodes in the army's annals, literally gathered dust in two large boxes tucked away in a corner of the archives. Only a handful of scholars and writers knew of the papers' existence, and most who did found it as convenient to ignore Riley's letters as to overlook the words of Mexican-American war veterans, Irish records, and Mexican archives. To do so is to miss the most important aspect of the saga: For like the gilded shamrock John Riley chose for his unit's "banner of Erin," the story of the St. Patrick's Battalion contains three distinct divisions—American, Mexican, and Irish.[11]

Apppendix

The St. Patrick's Battalion

Italics for Men Hanged
+ for Men Whipped and Branded

Officers

Alvarez, Ignacio
Arce, C.D.N.
. Batchelor, Rodmand
Bachiller, Michael
Calderon, Jose M.
Dalton, Patrick
Doyle, Matthew
+ Duhan, Roger
Fany, Carlos
Humphrey, James
Maloney, Patrick

Manzano, Camillo
Mejia, Enrique
Mestard, Agustin
Moreno, Francisco R.
Morstadt, Auguste
O'Leary, [Saturnino ?]
Peel, ?
+ Riley, John
Schafino, Francisco
Stevenson, John
Sutherland, John
Thompson, Henry

Ranks

+ Akles, Hezekiah
Aloif, C.
Antison, Patrick
Appleby, John
+ Bartley, John
Benedick, John
Bingham, George
+ Bowers, John
Brooke, John
Burke, Richard

Burns, Michael
Casey, Patrick
+ Cassady, Thomas
Cavanaugh, John
Chambers, John
Conahan, Dennis
Cuttle, John
Dalwig, George
+ Daly, John
Delaney, Kerr

Donaley, Thomas
Eglen, William
Ellis, Edward
Fitz-Henry
Fischer, William
Fogal, Frederick K.
Frantuis, Marquis T.
Fritz, Parian
Garreston, Robert W.
Geary, August
Green, Joseph
Groot, Othon de
Hamilton, John
Hanley, Richard
Hart, Barney
Hogan, Roger
Hogan John
Horacs, John
Hynes, John
Jackson, George W.
Keech, William H.
+ Kelley, James
Kenney, Harrison
Klager, John W.
Linger, John
+ Little, John
Longenhamer, Henry
Lusk, Elizier S.
Lydon, Martin
Lynch, John
McClellan, Hugh
McCornick, John
McDonald, John
McDowell, Gibson
McDowell, James
McElroy, David H.
McFarland, James D.
McHeran, Edward H.
+ McKee, Alexander
Macky, Lawrence
McLachlin, Lachlin
Mahon, James

Mauray [Murray ?]
Meyers, John A.
+ Miles, Martin
Miller, James
Millett, Thomas
+ Mills, James
Milord ?
+ Murphy, John
Neill, Peter
Neuer, Henry
Nolan, Andrew
O'Brien, Peter
O'Conner, Francis
O'Conner, William
O'Connor, Thomas
Ockier, Henry
O'Sullivan, Michael
Outhouse, William
Parker, Richard
Popes, Henry
Price, John
Rhode, Francis
+ Riley, Thomas
Rocher, Daniel
Romero, Elizio
Rose, John
Schmidt, Herman
Sheehan, John
Smith, Charles
Spears, James
+ Thomas, Samuel H.
Vader, John
Venator, Henry
Vinet ?
Vosbor, John
Wallace, William A.
Ward, Edward
Wheaton, Lemuel N.
Whistler, Henry
Williams, Charles
Wilton, John
Winitt, Luis

Notes

Introduction

1. George Ballentine, *Autobiography of an English Soldier in the United States Army, Comprising Observations and Adventures in the States and Mexico* (New York: Stringer & Townsend, 1853), 286.

2. Samuel Chamberlain, *My Confession* (New York: Harper and Brothers, 1856), 226.

3. Colonel George T. M. Davis, *Autobiography of the Late Col. Geo. T. M. Davis, Captain and Aide-de-Camp Scott's Army of Invasion (Mexico)* (New York: Jenkins & McCowan, 1891), 228.

4. Fairfax Downey, *Sound of the Guns: The Story of American Artillery from the Ancient and Honorable Company to the Atom Cannon and Guided Missile* (New York: David McKay, 1955), 113; *The North American* (Mexico City), November 16, 1847.

Chapter 1: "To the Golden Door"

1. George Ballentine, *Autobiography of an English Soldier,* 21.

2. Letter from Charles O'Malley to General Winfield Scott, National Archives, Record Group 94 (hereafter RG 94), February 5, 1848; George T. M. Davis, *Autobiography,* 225.

3. Letter of Charles O'Malley to Winfield Scott, RG 94, February 5, 1848.

4. Letter from John Riley to Charles O'Malley, RG 94, Miscellaneous Papers, box 7, October 27, 1847.

5. William D. Griffin, *The Book of Irish Americans* (New York: Times Books, 1990), 22.

6. Giovanni Costigan, *A History of Modern Ireland, with a Sketch of Earlier Times* (Pegasus, 1969), 171.

7. Diary of Mrs. Archbishop Richard Trench, quoted by Giovanni Costigan, *A History of Modern Ireland,* 168.

8. Investigations of the Devon Commission, 1843, quoted by Giovanni Costigan, *A History of Modern Ireland,* 172.

9. Giovanni Costigan, *A History of Modern Ireland,* 168.

10. Ibid., 169.

11. Ibid.

12. Ibid.

13. Ibid., 170.

14. Ibid., 171.

15. Ibid.

16. Ibid., 149.

17. Kerby Miller, *The San Patricios* (documentary by Mark R. Day, San Patricio Productions, 1996).

18. Letter of John Riley to Charles O'Malley, RG 94, October 27, 1847.

19. Giovanni Costigan, *A History of Modern Ireland,* 151.

20. A commonly used phrase of Irish immigrants of the 1840s.

Chapter 2: "Paddy and Bridget" in the Promised Land

1. Ray A. Billington, "The Know-Nothing Uproar," *American Heritage* 4 (1954), 58.

2. Ibid.

3. Ibid.

4. Ibid.

5. *The New York Observer,* January 14, 1834.

6. Ray Allen Billington, "The Know-Nothing Uproar," 59.

7. Ibid., 60.

8. William D. Griffin, *The Book of Irish Americans,* 49.

9. Ray Allen Billington, "The Know-Nothing Uproar," 60.

10. Thomas Gallagher, *Paddy's Lament: Ireland 1846–1848, Prelude to Hatred* (New York: Harcourt Brace Jovanovich, Publishers, 1982), 6.

11. Ibid.

12. Ibid.

13. Ibid.

14. Ibid.

15. Ibid., 7.

16. Ibid.

17. A term commonly used by the Nativist press.

18. Ray Allen Billington, *The Protestant Crusade,* 154.

19. Kerby Miller, *The San Patricios* (documentary by Mark R. Day, San Patricio Productions, 1996).

20. Mark R. Day (quoting Dale Knobel), "The Passion of the San Patricios," *Irish America Magazine* (May–June 1993), 45.

21. "Popish" and "Popery" were common Nativist epithets.

22. Charles O'Malley to Winfield Scott, RG 94, National Archives, February 5, 1848.

23. President James K. Polk, "Inaugural Address, 1845."

24. *Vindicator,* March 1845.

25. *Philadelphia Nativist,* August 1845.

26. *American Review,* Summer 1845.

27. Ibid.

28. John O'Sullivan, "Annexation," *United States Magazine and Democratic Review,* vol. 27 (July/August 1845), 5–10.

29. Ibid.

30. *New York Herald,* August 1845.

31. *The New York Journal of Commerce,* August 1845.

32. Justin H. Smith, *The War with Mexico,* 2 vols. (New York: Macmillan, 1919), vol. 1, 84.

33. Beckles Willson, *John Slidell* (New York: Minto, Balch, & Co., 1932), 15.

34. Ibid.

35. *Diario del Gobierno de la Republica Mexicana,* September 1845.

36. Samuel Chamberlain, *My Confession* (New York: Harper and Brothers, 1856), 76.

37. U.S. Army Recruiting Handbills, 1845–1846, Library of Congress; George Winston Smith and Charles Judah, *Chronicles of the Gringos: The U.S. Army in the Mexican War, 1846–1848* (Albuquerque: University of New Mexico Press, 1968), 15; K. Jack Bauer, *The Mexican War, 1846–1848,* 41.

38. Polk, "Inaugural Address, 1845."

39. Dispatch from Adjutant General Roger Jones to President Polk, September 1845, National Archives, Department of State, Records Group 59.

40. John Riley to Charles O'Malley, RG 94, October 27, 1847.

41. George W. Potter, *To the Golden Door: The Story of the Irish in Ireland and America* (Boston: Little, Brown, & Co., 1960), 476.

42. Ibid.

43. Ibid., 478.

44. Ibid.

45. Charles S. Hamilton, "Memoirs of the Mexican War," *Wisconsin Magazine of History* 14 (September 1930), 63–92.

46. Dabney H. Maury, *Recollections of a Virginian in the Mexican, Indian, and Civil Wars* (New York: Charles Scribner's Sons, 1894), 43.

47. *Niles National Register,* September 11, 1846.

48. *Miscellaneous Selections,* Mackinac, Michigan, Historical Collections, 595.

49. Ibid.

50. Letter of John Riley to Charles O'Malley, RG 94, October 27, 1847.

Chapter 3: "Buck Him and Gag Him!"

1. Secretary of War Marcy to General Zachary Taylor, Executive Document 60, June 15, 1845.

2. The U.S. Army's standard 1845–48 enlistment oath; Robert R. Miller, *Shamrock and Sword* (Norman: University of Oklahoma Press, 1989), 28.

3. Ibid.

4. William Chapman, "Mexican War Letters, 1845–48," West Point, United States Military Academy Library, September 29, 1845.

5. Lloyd Lewis, *Captain Sam Grant* (Boston: Little, Brown and Company, 1950), 133, 100.

6. Ibid., 100.

7. Letter of Lieutenant John Hatch to His Sister, October 28, 1845.

8. Ibid.

9. Cadmus M. Wilcox, *History of the Mexican War*, ed. by Mary Rachel Wilcox (Washington, D.C.: Church News Publishing Co., 1892) , 118; Luther Giddings, *Sketches of the Campaign in Northern Mexico by an Officer of the First Regiment of Ohio Volunteers* (New York: George P. Putnam & Co., 1853), 76.

10. Letter of Lieutenant Richard H. Wilson to Judge Advocate's Department, 1845–1848, National Archives.

11. Letter of Private William Tomlinson to His Brother, Beinecke Library, Yale University.

12. Ulysses S. Grant, *Personal Memoirs of U. S. Grant*, 2 vols. (New York: C. L. Webster & Co., 1885–86), vol. 1, 40–41.

13. Ibid., 37, 45.

14. George Gordon Meade, *The Life and Letters of George G. Meade*, 2 vols. (New York: Scribner's, 1913), vol. 1, 26.

15. *The American Star*, May 2, 1848.

16. Letter of Inspector General Payne to the War Department, RG 59.

17. Major Philip N. Barbour, *Journals of the Late Brevet Major Philip Norbourne Barbour, Captain in the 3rd Regiment, United States Infantry, and His Wife, Martha Isabella Hopkins Barbour*, ed. by Rhoda van Bibber Tanner Doubleday (New York: G. P. Putnam's Sons, 1936), 23.

18. William S. Henry, *Campaign Sketches*, 39.

19. Letter of Private Tomlinson to His Brother, Beinecke Library, Yale University.

20. Ibid.

21. Dennis J. Wynn, *The San Patricio Soldiers: Mexico's Foreign Legion* (El Paso: Texas Western Press, 1984), 45.

22. George Ballentine, *Autobiography of an English Soldier*, 285.

23. Samuel Chamberlain, *My Confession*, 193.

24. George Ballentine, *Autobiography of an English Soldier*, 247.

25. National Archives, RG 94; RG 153, EE 531, Case 27, John Riley; Fairfax Downey, "The Tragic Story of the San Patricio Battalion," *American Heritage* 6 (1955), 20.

26. Lloyd Lewis, *Captain Sam Grant*, 117–118; Henry W. Webb, "The Story of Jefferson Barracks," *New Mexico Historical Review* 21 (1946), 197–198.

27. George Ballentine, *Autobiography of an English Soldier*, 285, 331.

28. Ibid., 285–286.

29. Gustavus W. Smith, *Company A, Corps of Engineers, in the Mexican War* (Willetts Point, NY: Battalion Press, 1896), 10–12; 13–15.

30. Abbe Domenech, *Missionary Adventures in Texas and Mexico* (London: Longman, Brown, Green, Longmans, and Roberts, 1858), 69–72.

31. Letters Received by the Adjutant General, 1845–1848, National Archives, RG 94.

32. *The Boston Pilot*, May 21, 1846.

33. Letter of Samuel Starr to His Wife, Missouri Historical Society, April 5, 1847.

34. George Ballentine, *Autobiography of an English Soldier*, 22.

Chapter 4: "A Sullen Torpor"

1. Letter of Lieutenant Daniel H. Hill to His Wife, December 1845.

2. Letter of D. H. Hill to His Wife, December 1845; K. Jack Bauer, *The Mexican War, 1846–48* (New York: Macmillan, 1974), 34.

3. Ibid.

4. William S. Henry, *Campaign Sketches*, 26.

5. George B. McClellan, McClellan Papers, May 3–13, 1846.

6. Excerpts from the *Nativist*, 1845–1846.

7. Kerby Miller, *The San Patricios* (documentary), by Mark R. Day, San Patricio Productions, 1996.

8. The expression, "the dead hand of the Catholic Church," the "Black Legend," and others filled the Nativist publications.

9. *Democratic Register* (Illinois), Summer 1845.

10. John Riley to Charles O'Malley, RG 94, October 27, 1847; John Riley to the President of Mexico; British Public Office Records, Foreign Office 203, File 93: 367.

11. *The Liberator* (full text of O'Connell's speech), November 17, 1843.

12. *Freeman's Journal*, October 1843.

13. John Riley to Charles O'Malley, RG 94, October 27, 1847.

14. Letter from Daniel Harvey Hill to His Wife, January 1846.

15. Letter from John Black, United States Consul, to John Slidell, Minister Plenipotentiary of the United States to Mexico, National Archives, RG 59, Department of State, February 27, 1846.

16. Ibid.

17. Letter of John Slidell to John Black and James Buchanan, Secretary of State, RG 59, March 1, 1846.

18. Marcy to Taylor, January 13, 1846, Executive Document No. 60, 90.

19. George Ballentine, *Autobiography of an English Soldier*, 46.

20. George Meade, letter to his wife, March 2, 1846.

21. "Native Americanism," *Brownson's Quarterly Review II* (January 1845), 80–97.

22. Fairfax Downey, "The Tragic Story of the San Patricio Battalion," 20.

23. Letter from U. S. Grant to John Lowe, *Chicago Tribune*, January 27, 1885.

Chapter 5: "To Provoke a War"

1. Letter from Brevet Brigadier General William J. Worth to Surgeon General Thomas Lawson, Thomas Lawson Papers, November 1, 1845.

2. This phrase was used in many publications of the era to describe the advance to the Rio Grande.

3. William S. Henry, *Campaign Sketches*, 51.

4. Ibid.

5. Letter of U. S. Grant to John Lowe, August 14, 1845.

6. Ibid.

7. Letter of Ephraim Kirby Smith to his wife, March 25, 1846.

8. Lloyd Lewis, *Captain Sam Grant*, 136.

9. U. S. Grant, *Memoirs*, 56; Thomas Bangs Thorpe, *Our Army on the Rio Grande* (Philadelphia: Cary and Hart, 1846), 13–14.

10. Letter of Ephraim Kirby Smith to his wife, March 26, 1846.

11. George Deas, "Reminiscences of the Campaign on the Rio Grande," *Historical Magazine* 7 (January–May 1870), 21.

12. John Sedgwick, *Correspondence of John Sedgwick, Major General*, 2 vols. (New York: Stoeckle, 1902–1903), vol. 1, 18.

13. U. S. Grant, *Memoirs*, vol. 1, 101.

14. Lloyd Lewis, *Captain Sam Grant*, 136.

15. Zachary Taylor, "A Proclamation," Executive Document No. 60.

16. George Deas, "Reminiscences," 22.

17. Ethan Allen Hitchcock, *Fifty Years in Camp and Field; Diary of Major General Ethan Allen Hitchcock, U.S.A.*, ed. by W. A. Croffut (New York: G. P. Putnam's Sons, 1909), 212.

18. Abraham Lincoln, Anti-War Address in U.S. Congress, December 22, 1847.

19. John Riley to Charles O'Malley; "Desertion Appeal," August 17, 1847, Box 2 E 288, George W. Kendall Collection, Univ. of Texas; Riley to president of Mexico, British Public Records, Foreign Office 203, 93: 367.

20. Lloyd Lewis, *Captain Sam Grant*, 137.

21. William S. Henry, *Campaign Sketches*, 65.

22. Ballentine, 19.

23. U. S. Grant, *Memoirs*, 37, 45.

Chapter 6: "Put None But Americans on Guard Tonight"

1. Justin Smith, *The War with Mexico*, vol. 1 (New York: MacMillan, 1919), 148; Zachary Taylor, General Orders, March–April 1846, National Archives.

2. John P. Hatch, Letter to his sister, April 1846, John Porter Hatch Papers, Library of Congress; Ephraim K. Smith, *To Mexico with Scott: Letters of Ephraim Kirby Smith to His Wife* (Cambridge: Harvard University Press, 1917), 33–34; John B. Robertson, *Reminiscences of a Campaign in Mexico by a Member of the "Bloody First"* (Nashville: J. York & Company, 1849), 116.

3. Ibid.

4. Dr. Nathan Jarvis, "An Army Surgeon's Mexican War Notes" (*Journal of the Military Service Institution of the United States* 40 [1907]), 445.

5. Letter of Zachary Taylor to Adjutant General Jones, March 25, 1846, National Archives.

6. George Meade, *The Life and Letters of George Gordon Meade*, vol. 1 (New York: Scribner's, 1913), 54; Philip N. Barbour, *Journals of the Late Brevet Major Philip Barbour, Captain in the 3rd Regiment, United States Infantry, and His Wife, Martha Isabella Hopkins Barbour* (New York: G. P. Putnam's Sons, 1936), 25.

7. Justin Smith, *The War with Mexico*, notes to Chapter 5.

8. Lloyd Lewis, *Captain Sam Grant* (Boston: Little, Brown and Company, 1950), 130.

9. *The London Times*, December 4, 1846.

10. William S. Henry, *Campaign Sketches of the War with Mexico* (New York : Harper and Brothers, 1847), 70.

11. Ibid.

12. Philip N. Barbour, *Journals of*, 27–28; William S. Henry, *Campaign Sketches*, 72; John P. Hatch, letter to his sister, April 1846; John Sedgwick,

Correspondence of John Sedgwick, Major General, 2 vols. (New York: Stoeckle, 1902–03), 37; Letter of U. S. Grant to John Lowe, October 1846.

13. A common Nativist expression appearing in dozens of the era's periodicals including the *Illinois State Register,* July 1845.

14. William S. Henry, *Campaign Sketches,* 69.

15. Ibid., 70.

16. George Ballentine, *Autobiography of an English Soldier,* 285–286.

17. William S. Henry, *Campaign Sketches,* 71.

18. George G. Meade, *Life and Letters Of,* vol. 1, 53; Nathan S. Jarvis, "An Army Surgeon's Notes," 447.

19. Zachary Taylor, April 1, 1846, National Archives, Executive Document 60, pp. 302–304.

20. Philip N. Barbour, *The Journal Of,* 27–28.

21. John Frost, "Desertion Appeal of General Ampudia, April 2, 1846, verbatim in *Life of Major General Zachary Taylor* (New York: D. Appleton & Co., 1847): 48–49.

22. Ibid.

23. William S. Henry, *Campaign Sketches,* 72.

24. *Niles National Register,* October 9, 1847.

25. William S. Henry, *Campaign Sketches,* 72.

26. Zachary Taylor to Adjutant General Jones, April 6, 1846, Executive Document 60, 133.

27. William S. Henry, *Campaign Sketches,* 72.

28. Philip N. Barbour, *The Journal Of,* 29.

29. William S. Henry, *Campaign Sketches,* 71.

30. Ibid., 72–73.

31. RG 94, John Riley File.

32. "Desertion Appeal" of John Riley, George Kendall Collection, University of Texas, August 1847.

33. Zachary Taylor, Executive Document 60, 302–304.

34. Thomas F. Meehan, "Catholics in the War with Mexico," *U.S. Catholic Historical Record* 12 (1918), 40.

35. William S. Henry, *Campaign Sketches,* 73.

36. Ibid.

37. Ampudia to Taylor, Executive Document 60, 140.

38. Taylor to Ampudia, Executive Document 60, 139–140.

39. *Matamoros Gazette,* April 11, 1846.

40. Ibid.

41. Letter of Francisco Mejia to Mariano Arista, RG 94, National Archives, May 4, 1846; K. Jack Bauer, *The Mexican War, 1846–48,* 42.

Chapter 7: "The Advice of My Conscience"

1. William S. Henry, *Campaign Sketches,* 74.

2. National Archives, RG 153, EE 531, Case 27, John Riley.

3. Captain Moses E. Merrill, RG 94; Case 27, John Riley.

4. Ibid.

5. RG 94, File on John Riley.

6. *Niles National Register,* October 9, 1847; Fairfax Downey, "The Tragic Story of the San Patricio Battalion," *American Heritage* 6 (1955), 20; Byron Stinson, "They Went Over to the Enemy," *American History Illustrated* 3 (1968), 31; Stan Federman, "Battalion of the Damned," *Army* (July 1979), 43.

7. Ibid.

8. Ibid.

9. Fairfax Downey, "The Tragic Story of the San Patricio Battalion," 20.

10. George Potter, *To the Golden Door,* 483.

11. Ibid.

12. Potter, *To the Golden Door,* 483; William S. Henry, *Campaign Sketches,* 223–24.

13. *Niles National Register,* October 9, 1847.

14. Mark Day, *The San Patricios* (documentary), San Patricio Productions, 1996.

15. John Riley to Charles O'Malley, October 27, 1847, RG 94.

16. "Desertion Appeal" of John Riley, George Kendall Collection, University of Texas, August 17, 1847.

17. George Ballentine, *Autobiography of an English Soldier,* 28.

18. Letter of John Riley to the President of Mexico, British Public Records, Foreign Office, 203. 93: 367.

19. RG 153, EE 531, Case 27, John Riley.

20. Ramon Alcarez, *The Other Side,* 39; Justin Smith, *The War with Mexico,* vol. 1, 117.

21. RG 153, EE 531, Case 27, John Riley.

22. Thomas Nugent, Letters, Kendall Collection, University of Texas.

Chapter 8: "A Company of . . . Irishmen"

1. John Riley to Charles O'Malley, RG 94, Riley File, October 27, 1847; "Desertion Appeal" of John Riley, August 1847; John Riley to the President of Mexico, British Public Records, Foreign Office, 203, 93: 367.

2. "Desertion Appeal" of John Riley, August 1847.

3. John Riley to Charles O'Malley, RG 94, Riley File, October 27, 1847.

4. John A. Perry, *Thrilling Adventures of a New Englander; Travels, Scenes and Sufferings in Cuba, Mexico, & California,* 28.

5. Richard McSherry, *El Puchero; or, A Mixed Dish from Mexico* (Philadelphia: Lippincott, Grambo, 1850), 157; *Niles National Register,* September 26, 1846, 55, and April 10, 1847, 87–88; William S. Henry, *Campaign Sketches,* 70.

6. Major George Deas, *Reminiscences,* 20.

7. Ibid., 103; Manuel Balbontin, *La invasion, 1846 a 1847,* p. 26; *Niles National Register,* September 26, 1846, p. 58; George McCall, *Letters from the Frontiers,* vol. 2, 103.

8. Balbontin, 26.

9. Francisco Mejia, Letter to the President of Mexico, RG 94, May 4, 1846.

10. Letter of U. S. Grant to his wife, June 5, 1846.

11. John Riley to the President of Mexico, British Public Records, Foreign Office, 203, 93: 367.

Chapter 9: "An Immense Sensation"

1. George Meade, *The Life and Letters Of,* 66.

2. Ibid., 67–68.

3. Manuel Balbontin, *La invasion,* 49.

4. Lloyd Lewis, *Captain Sam Grant,* 140; *Niles National Register,* October 1847.

5. Ramon Alcarez, *The Other Side,* 42–44.

6. Arista's Desertion Appeal, April 20, 1846, Executive Document 60, 303–304.

7. George Deas, *Reminiscences,* 22.

8. George Ballentine, *Autobiography,* 11, 14, 16, and 25.

9. Ibid., 235.

10. Ibid., 332.

11. Ibid., 271–72.

12. George Deas, *Reminiscences,* 22.

13. Ibid.

14. Ibid.

15. Ibid.; Lloyd Lewis, *Captain Sam Grant,* 141.

16. George Deas, *Reminiscences,* 22.

17. Taylor to Adjutant General Jones, April 26, 1846, Executive Document 60, 141.

18. *The Washington Union,* April 26, 1846, 1.

19. RG 94, Adjutant General's Office.

20. James Russell Lowell, "Biglow Papers," *The Boston Courier,* June 17, 1846.

21. U. S. Grant, *Memoirs,* 37, 45.

22. George Deas, *Reminiscences,* 22.

23. Philip N. Barbour, *The Journal Of,* 23.

24. George McCall, *Letters from the Frontier,* 491–542; Nathan Jarvis, *An Army Surgeon's Notes,* 450–451; George Deas, *Reminiscences,* 22.

25. George Deas, *Reminiscences,* 22.

26. George Ballentine, *Autobiography of an English Soldier,* 332.

Chapter 10: "To Draw the Claret"

1. George Ballentine, *Autobiography of an English Soldier,* 140–141.

2. William S. Henry, *Campaign Sketches,* 104.

3. U. S. Grant, *Memoirs,* 58.

4. George Deas, *Reminiscences,* 100.

5. U. S. Grant, *Memoirs,* 58.

6. George Deas, *Reminiscences,* 100.

7. Ibid., 100–101.

8. Zachary Taylor to Adjutant General Jones, Executive Document 60, 302–304.

9. John Riley to the President of Mexico, British Public Records, Foreign Office, 203, 93: 367.

10. Manuel Balbontin, *La invasion,* 53.

11. Samuel G. French, *Two Wars, An Autobiography* (Nashville: The

Confederate Veteran Press, 1901), 52.

12. George Deas, *Reminiscences*, 101.

13. Ibid.

14. Letter of Grant to John Lowe, May 1846.

15. George Deas, *Reminiscences*, 101.

16. Ibid., 101–102.

17. Ramon Alcarez, *The Other Side*, 49.

18. George Deas, *Reminiscences*, 102.

Chapter 11: "The Spread of This Contagion"

1. *Spirit of the Times*, May 1846.

2. *The Albany Evening Journal*, May 1846.

3. *The Boston Pilot*, May 1846.

4. *Freeman's Journal*, May 1846.

5. Zachary Taylor to Adjutant General Jones, Executive Document 60, 302–304.

6. Ibid.

7. Letter to the Adjutant General, May 1846, RG 94, National Archives.

8. Taylor to Jones, 304.

9. George Ballentine, *Autobiography of an English Soldier*, 40.

10. George Potter, *To the Golden Door*, 475.

11. Albert Lombard, *The High Private, With a Full and Exciting History of the New-York Volunteers* (New York: n.p., 1848), 10.

12. Ibid., 8.

13. Letter of Morris Longstreth to James Buchanan, May 31, 1846, Buchanan Papers, Historical Society of Pennsylvania.

14. Blanche McEniry, *American Catholics in the War with Mexico* (Washington D.C.: Catholic University of America, 1937), 59.

15. Ibid.

16. Letter of Secretary of War Marcy to Fathers McElroy and Rey, May 21, 1846, RG 94.

17. Ibid.

18. Father David McElroy, "Chaplains for the Mexican War—1846," *Woodstock Letters*, vol. 15.

19. Letter of Marcy to Lt. Col. Thomas Hunt, May 29, 1846, National Archives.

20. Letter of Marcy to Taylor, May 29, 1846, National Archives.

Chapter 12: The Road to Monterrey

1. Father McElroy, *Woodstock Letters*, vol. 15.

2. Letter of U. S. Grant to his wife, May 11, 1846.

3. A sobriquet Santa Anna created for himself.

4. John Riley to the president of Mexico, British Public Records, Foreign Office, 203, 93: 367.

5. Justin Smith, *The War With Mexico*, vol. 1, 494, footnote 11.

6. *Diario del Gobierno*, September 8, 1846; National Archives, RG 59, September 12 and October 8, 1846.

7. Ramon Alcarez, *The Other Side*, 68.

8. Luther Giddings, *Sketches of the Campaign in Northern Mexico by an Officer of the First Regiment of Ohio Volunteers* (New York: George P. Putnam & Co., 1853), 83–84.

9. William B. Campbell, *Mexico War Letters*, 140–141.

10. Samuel Chamberlain, *My Confession*, 114.

11. George B. McClellan to his sister, May 13, 1846, Library of Congress.

12. Samuel Chamberlain, *My Confession*, 122.

13. Alexander Konze to the *Wisconsin Banner*, November 2, 1846.

14. Albert Lombard, *The High Private*, 22.

15. John Sedgwick, *Correspondence*, vol. 1, 37.

16. *New York Express*, August 29, 1846.

17. Kerby Miller, *The San Patricios* (documentary).

18. John Claiborne, *Correspondence of Major General John Quitman*, vol. 1, 235.

19. "Desertion Appeal of John Riley," Kendall Collection.

20. "Serious Military Insubordination near Matamoros," *The New York Herald*, September 15, 1846; "Riot at Burita," *The New York Herald*, September 16, 1846; George Potter, *To the Golden Door*, 475.

21. *The New York Herald*, September 16, 1846.

22. *Niles National Register*, August 22, 1846.

23. George Meade, *The Life and Letters of*, vol. 1, 161–162.

24. Philip Barbour, *The Journal of*, 46.

25. George Meade, *The Life and Letters of*, 161–162.

26. Zachary Taylor, *Letters*, 8.

27. *Niles National Register*, August 22, 1846, and November 6, 1847.

28. George Ballentine, *Autobiography of an English Soldier*, 34.

29. Ibid., 35.

30. General Ampudia's "Desertion Appeal," Yale University, September 15, 1846.

Chapter 13: "The Dastard's Cheek Blanched"

1. William S. Henry, *Campaign Sketches*, 221.

2. Taylor to the Adjutant General, Executive Document 60, 83.

3. John R. Kenly, *Memoirs of a Maryland Volunteer; War with Mexico in the Years 1846–7–8* (Philadelphia: J. B. Lippincott & Co., 1873), 119.

4. Luther Giddings, *Sketches*, 168–169.

5. Samuel French, *Two Wars*, 62.

6. Taylor to Adjutant General, Executive Document 60, 83.

7. Justin Smith, *The War With Mexico*, vol. 1, 251, 566.

8. William B. Campbell, *Mexican War Letters*, 144.

9. Luther Giddings, *Sketches*, 144.

10. John B. Robertson, *Reminiscences of the "Bloody First,"* 146.

11. George Meade, *The Life and Letters of*, vol. 1, 151.

12. George Deas, *Reminiscences*, 315.

13. William S. Henry, *Campaign Sketches*, 218.

14. Grant, *Memoirs*, 73.

15. George Deas, *Reminiscences,* 315; David Nevin, *The Mexican War* (Alexandria, VA: Time-Life Books, 1978), 78.

16. George Deas, *Reminiscences,* 223–224.

Chapter 14: "The Irish Volunteers"

1. *Diario del Gobierno,* December 2, 1846.

2. Samuel Chamberlain, *My Confession,* 124.

3. *New Orleans Daily Picayune,* September 9, 1847.

4. Zachary Taylor to the Advocate General, Executive Document 60, September 20, 1846.

5. Ibid.

6. J. Jacob Oswandel, *Notes of the Mexican War, 1846–47–48* (Philadelphia: n.p., 1885), 229–230.

7. Luther Giddings, *Sketches,* 276.

8. Taylor to Secretary of War Marcy, October 5, 1846, RG 59.

9. Letter of William Worth to his daughter, October 1846, Library of Congress.

10. *Diario del Gobierno,* October 2, 1846; *Niles National Register,* October 16, 1847.

11. *Niles National Register,* June 19, 1847.

12. Ibid.

13. "Mexicans to Catholic Irishmen," handbill, April 1847, Yale.

14. Ibid.

15. *Niles National Register,* October 16, 1847.

16. William S. Henry, *Campaign Sketches,* 240.

17. Zachary Taylor, "A Proclamation," Executive Document 60, October 1846, 287.

18. *Protestant Magazine,* Summer 1846.

19. George Ballentine, *Autobiography of an English Soldier,* 286.

20. Luther Giddings, *Sketches,* 275–277.

21. Ibid.

22. George Ballentine, *Autobiography of an English Soldier,* 332.

23. Ibid., 131.

24. Ibid.

25. Ibid., 333.

26. Samuel Chamberlain, *My Confession,* 192–193.

27. *Niles National Register,* October 9, 1847.

28. RG 153, EE 531, Case 17, William Keech.

29. Ibid.

30. RG 153, EE 531, Case 19, Heinrich Ockter.

31. RG 153, EE 525, Case 18, Lachlin McLachlin.

32. RG 153, EE 531, Case 6, Patrick Dalton.

33. George Ballentine, *Autobiography,* 14.

34. RG 153, EE 531, Case 6, Patrick Dalton.

35. John Riley to Charles O'Malley, RG 94, October 27, 1847.

36. *The London Times,* May 5, 1850.

37. George Potter, *To the Golden Door,* 47.

Chapter 15: "In High Disgrace the Holy Banner of St. Patrick"

1. Winfield Scott to Zachary Taylor, Executive Document 60, November 25, 1846, 373–374.

2. Charles Winslow Elliott, *Winfield Scott, the Soldier and the Man* (New York: MacMillan Company, 1937), 448.

3. Luther Giddings, *Sketches,* 279.

4. Taylor to Scott, Executive Document 60, January 15, 1847, 863.

5. Scott to Taylor, Executive Document 60, January 26, 1847, 864.

6. Zachary Taylor, *Letters Of,* 273–278.

7. Ibid.

8. *Niles National Register* (translation), March 13, 1847.

9. U.S. Senate Executive Document 1, 29th U.S. Congress, 2nd Session, 153–154.

10. John E. Weems, *To Conquer a Peace: The War Between the United States and Mexico* (Garden City: Doubleday & Company, 1974), 285.

11. Manuel Balbontin, *La invasion,* 60.

12. John A. Scott, *Encarnacion Prisoners, Comprising an Account of the March of Kentucky Cavalry from Louisville to the Rio Grande* (Louisville: Prentice & Weissinger, 1848), 43–45.

13. Ramon Alcarez, *The Other Side,* 114.

14. Ramon Alcarez, *The Other Side,* 118; John E. Weems, *To Conquer a Peace,* 288.

15. Executive Document 60, 98.

16. Ibid.

Chapter 16: "Take That Damned Battery!"

1. Blanche McEniry, Catholics in the War with Mexico (quoting Colonel Albert C. Ramsey), 51.

2. Samuel Chamberlain, *My Confession,* 118.

3. Zachary Taylor, Executive Document 1, 134.

4. Cadmus Wilcox, *History of the Mexican War,* 223.

5. Samuel Chamberlain, *My Confession,* 124.

6. Ibid., 124–126.

7. Fairfax Downey, *Sound of the Guns,* 103.

8. Ibid.

9. Lew Wallace, *Lew Wallace: An Autobiography,* 2 vols. (New York: Harper and Brothers, 1906), vol. 1, 174.

10. Ramon Alcarez, *The Other Side,* 141.

11. *Diario del Gobierno,* March 22, 1847.

12. James H. Carleton, *The Battle of Buena Vista* (New York: Harper and Brothers, 1848), 103.

13. Samuel Chamberlain, *My Confession,* 124; Taylor, Executive Document 60, 302–304.

Chapter 17: "Well, Pat, My Good Fellow"

1. Mejia's report after Buena Vista, *Diario del Gobierno,* April 7, 1847; *Diario del Gobierno,* August 18, 1847; Manuel Balbontin, *La invasion,* 91.

2. Jose Fernando Ramirez, *Mexico During the War with the United States* (Columbia: University of Missouri Press, 1970), 127.

3. George Ballentine, *Autobiography of an English Soldier*, 14.

4. Ibid.

5. George B. McClellan, McClellan Papers, letter to his sister, May 13, 1846.

6. George Ballentine, *Autobiography of an English Soldier*, 43–44.

7. George T. M. Davis, *Autobiography*, 131.

8. Vera Cruz Court-Martials, General Orders and Special Orders, 1847–48, Headquarters of the Army, April 1847.

9. George Ballentine, *Autobiography of an English Soldier*, 131.

10. George A. McCall, *Letters from the Frontiers* (Philadelphia: J. B. Lippincott and Company, 1868), 334.

11. Frederick Zeh, *An Immigrant Soldier in the Mexican War* (College Station: Texas A & M University Press, 1995), 4, 7, 55.

12. John F. Meginness, "A Collection of Incidents Connected with the Life of a Soldier (from His Enlistment) in Mexico, During a Part of the Campaign of 1847, from Vera Cruz to Puebla, Mexico, October 17, 1847," University of Texas, Special Collections, 279, 283, 287.

13. George Ballentine, *Autobiography of an English Soldier*, 285.

14. Winfield Scott, "Proclamation," Executive Document 60, April 11, 1847, 937.

15. George T . M. Davis, *Autobiography*, 138.

16. *The Flag of Freedom* reprinted this much-told "anecdote" on November 13, 1847.

17. Henry M. Judah, *Diary*, Library of Congress, April 1847 entry; Lloyd Lewis, *Captain Sam Grant*, 206.

18. George T. M. Davis, *Autobiography*, 228.

19. Ibid.

Chapter 18: "The Butcher's Bill"

1. U. S. Grant, *Memoirs*, 87; Lloyd Lewis, *Captain Sam Grant*, 207.

2. George Ballentine, *Autobiography of an English Soldier*, 174–185.

3. George Potter, *To the Golden Door*, 481.

4. George Ballentine, *Autobiography of an English Soldier*, 187–188.

5. Ramon Alcarez, *The Other Side*, 209.

6. George Ballentine, *Autobiography of an English Soldier*, 192.

7. Justin Smith, *The War with Mexico*, vol. 2, 54.

8. George Ballentine, *Autobiography of an English Soldier*, 192.

Chapter 19: "Come Over to Us"

1. National Archives Record Group 153, EE 531, Case 25, John Bartley, and Case 29, John Bowers.

2. Ibid.; RG 153, EE 531: Case 14, James McDowell; Case 24, Hezekiah Akles; RG 153, EE 525: Case 43, Abraham Fitzpatrick.

3. Letter to Ewan Mackintosh, British consul general, Mexico City, June 23, 1847, British Public Records, Foreign Office 203, 93: 105–106.

4. William Preston, *Journal in Mexico . . . November 1, 1847, to May 25, 1848* (Paris: privately printed, no date), 36–38.

5. W. C. S. Smith, *A Journey to California in 1849* (Bancroft Library, University of California, n.p.), 6.

6. George Ballentine, *Autobiography of an English Soldier*, 323–324.

7. William Preston, *Journal in Mexico*, 6.

8. Santa Anna's April 1847 Handbill, Yale University Library.

9. "Mexicans to Catholic Irishmen," supplement to Santa Anna's April 1847 handbill, Yale University Library.

10. George Ballentine, *Autobiography of an English Soldier*, 235.

11. J. Jacob Oswandel, *Notes of the Mexican War*, 229–230.

12. John R. Kenly, *Memoirs*, 381–382.

13. George Ballentine, *Autobiography of an English Soldier*, 332.

14. Thomas D. Tennery, *The Mexican War Diary Of* (Norman: University of Oklahoma Press, 1970), 88.

15. Winfield Scott, *The Memoirs of Lieutenant-General Scott, LLD*, 2 vols. (New York: Sheldon & Company, 1864), 466, note.

16. G. P. Stokes, "War With Mexico!" 43.

17. RG 153, EE 525, Case 16, Auguste Morstadt.

18. Winfield Scott, "A Proclamation," April 11, 1847.

19. Winfield Scott, "To the Mexican Nation," Executive Document 60, May 11, 1847, 971.

20. "Bucking and Gagging" (song).

21. George Ballentine, *Autobiography of an English Soldier*, 286.

22. U. S. Grant, *Memoirs*, 84.

23. John Riley to Charles O'Malley, RG 94, October 27, 1847.

24. Order of Santa Anna, printed in *Diario del Gobierno*, May 5, 8, and 10, and July 2 and 13, 1847.

25. *Diario del Gobierno*, August 18, 1847; *New Orleans Picayune*, September 28, 1847.

26. *Diario del Gobierno*, July 21, 1847.

27. Thomas E. Cotner, *The Military and Political Career of Jose Joaquin Herrera, 1792–1854* (Austin: University of Texas Press, 1949), 181.

28. John Riley to the president of Mexico, British Public Records, Foreign Office, 203, 93: 367.

29. "Desertion Appeal" of John Riley, August 1847.

30. Ibid.

Chapter Twenty: "A Bloody Field It Was"

1. Justin Smith, *The War with Mexico*, vol. 2, 101.

2. Ibid.

3. Winfield Scott, *Memoirs*, vol. 2, 481–482.

4. John S. D. Eisenhower, *So Far From God* (New York: Random House, 1989), 311.

5. Richard S. Ewell, *The Making of a Soldier: Letters of General R.S. Ewell*, ed. by Captain Percy G. Hamlin (Richmond: Whitlet & Sheppardson, 1935), 72.

6. Manuel Rincon's battle report for Churubusco, *Diario del Gobierno*, August 31, 1847.

7. Ephraim K. Smith, *To Mexico with Scott: Letters of Ephraim Kirby Smith to His Wife* (Cambridge: Harvard University Press, 1917), 201.

8. Ashbel Woodward, *Life of General Nathaniel Lyon* (Hartford: Connecticut Historical Society, 1862), 117.

9. Nathan C. Brooks, *A Complete History of the Mexican War: Its Causes, Conduct, and Consequences; Comprising an Account of the Various Military and Naval Operations, from Its Commencement to the Treaty of Peace* (Philadelphia: Grigg, Elliot & Co.), 85.

10. Fairfax Downey, *The Sound of the Guns*, 112; Justin Smith, *The War with Mexico*, vol. 2, 115.

11. Nathan C. Brooks, *Complete History*, 378–379 (reprinted letter from the *New York Courier*).

12. Ashbel Woodward, *Life of General Nathaniel Lyon*, 117.

13. J. Jacob Oswandel, *Notes of the Mexican War*, 472; General Worth's report on Churubusco, Executive Document 8, 319.

14. J. Jacob Oswandel, *Notes of the Mexican War*, 472.

15. George Ballentine, *Autobiography of an English Soldier*, 286.

16. George T. M. Davis, *Autobiography*, 203.

17. George Kendall, *War Between the United States and Mexico*, 725.

18. George T .M. Davis, *Autobiography*, 203.

19. George Kendall, *War Between the United States and Mexico*, 725.

20. George T. M. Davis, *Autobiography*, 203.

21. Othon de Groote, *El Correo Nacional*, October 11, 1848.

22. Ramon Alcarez, *The Other Side*, 299.

23. Worth's report on Churubusco (see note 15).

24. Ibid.

25. George Ballentine, *Autobiography of an English Soldier*, 286.

26. Fairfax Downey, *Sound of the Guns*, 113.

27. George Kendall, *War Between the United States and Mexico*, 718–719.

28. George T. M. Davis, *Autobiography*, 204.

29. Ibid., 205.

30. Ibid.

31. Ibid., 224.

Chapter 21: "Gloomy Curtains of Despair"

1. General Order 263, Mexican War, 1845–48, National Archives, August 22, 1847.

2. Sister Blanche McEniry, "Catholics in the War with Mexico," quotes Edward D. Mansfield, who wrote the passage in 1848, 54.

3. General Order 259, Mexican War, 1845–48, National Archives.

4. National Archives, Record Group 153, EE 525, Case 1, Friedrich Fogal.

5. *A Manual for Courts-Martial* (Washington D.C., U.S. Government Printing Office, 1920), 29; Michael Hogan, *The Irish Soldiers of Mexico* (Guadalajara: Fondo Editorial Universitario, 1997), 165.

6. Captain William C. DeHart, *Observations on Military Law, and the Constitution and Practice of Courts-Martial with a Summary of the Law of Evidence as Applicable to Military Trials* (New York: Wiley and Putnam, 1846), 168–169.

7. RG 153, EE 525 and 531, all cases brought against the captured San Patricios.

8. RG 153, EE 525, Case 18, Lachlin McLachlin.

9. RG 153, EE 525, Case 43, Sergeant Abraham Fitzpatrick.

10. General Order 283, September 11, 1847.

11. RG 153, EE 525, Case 16, Auguste Morstadt.

12. RG 153, EE 531, Case 13, Dennis Conahan; RG 153, EE 531, Case 3, Thomas Riley.

13. RG 153, EE 531, Case 19, Henry Ockter.

14. RG 153, EE 531, Case 20, Edward McHeran.

15. RG 153, EE 531, Case 6, Patrick Dalton.

16. Michael Hogan, *The Irish Soldiers of Mexico,* 170–171.

17. James Reilly, "An Artilleryman's Story," *Journal of the Military Service Institution* 33 (1903), 443.

18. William Chapman, "Mexican War Letters, 1845–48," West Point, United States Military Academy Library, August 28, 1847.

19. RG 153, EE 531, Case 27, John Riley.

Chapter 22: "Intense Dissatisfaction"

1. George T. M. Davis, *Autobiography,* 224.

2. Captain William C. DeHart, *Practice of Courts-Martial,* 168–169.

3. *New Orleans Daily Picayune,* September 9, 1847.

4. *American Star,* November 11, 1847.

5. *Daily Picayune,* September 9, 1847.

6. "Appeal for John Riley's Freedom," RG 94, Miscellaneous Papers, Box 7.

7. General Order 283, National Archives, Mexican War, September 11, 1847.

8. General Order 281, National Archives, Mexican War, September 8, 1847.

9. George T. M. Davis, *Autobiography,* 228–229.

10. General Order 281, National Archives, Mexican War, September 8, 1847.

11. George T. M. Davis, *Autobiography,* 225.

12. General Order 281, National Archives, Mexican War, September 8, 1847.

Chapter 23: "This Revolting Scene"

1. George T. M. Davis, *Autobiography,* 227.

2. *American Star,* September 20, 1847.

3. Ibid.

4. George T. M. Davis, *Autobiography,* 227.

5. Daniel M. Frost, "The Memoirs of Daniel M. Frost," edited by Dana O. Jensen, *Missouri Historical Society Bulletin* 26, number 3 (1970), 222.

6. *American Star,* September 20, 1847.

7. George T. M. Davis, *Autobiography,* 228.

8. Amasa G. Clark, *Reminiscences of a Centenarian, as Told by Amasa Gleason Clark, Veteran of the Mexican War, to Cora Tope Clark* (Bandera, TX: n.p., 1930), 14.

9. George T. M. Davis, *Autobiography,* 227.

Chapter 24: "A Fearful Dance of Death"

1. Ramon Alcarez, *The Other Side,* 359–360.

2. "General Harney," *Journal of the U.S. Cavalry Association* (March 1890), 1–8; Lloyd Lewis, *Captain Sam Grant,* 247.

3. Samuel Chamberlain, *My Confession,* 227; RG 94, National Archives, Harney's report on the executions, File 45.

4. Samuel Chamberlain, *My Confession,* 227; L. U. Reavis, *The Life and Military Service of General William Selby Harney* (St. Louis: Bryan, Brand, and Company, 1878), 8–12.

5. L. U. Reavis, *The Life of General Harney,* 10; Samuel Chamberlain, *My Confession,* 226.

6. L. U. Reavis, *The Life of General Harney,* 8–12.

7. L. U. Reavis, *The Life of General Harney,* 8–12; Samuel Chamberlain, *My Confession,* 227.

8. "General Harney," *Journal of the U.S. Cavalry Association,* 1–8.

9. *American Star,* September 20, 1847; James Reilly, "An Artilleryman's Story," 443–444; "General Harney," *Journal of the U.S. Cavalry Association,* 1–8.

10. James Reilly, "An Artilleryman's Story," 443.

11. Samuel Chamberlain, *My Confession,* 227.

12. Justin Smith, *The War with Mexico,* vol. 2, 153–154.

13. Ibid.

14. Lloyd Lewis, *Captain Sam Grant,* 247–248.

15. Ramon Alcarez, *The Other Side,* 359.

16. Samuel Chamberlain, *My Confession,* 227–228.

17. Lloyd Lewis, *Captain Sam Grant,* 248; Samuel Chamberlain, *My Confession,* 228.

18. James Reilly, "An Artilleryman's Story," 444.

19. Lloyd Lewis, *Captain Sam Grant,* 248.

20. James Reilly, "An Artilleryman's Story," 444.

21. Samuel Chamberlain, *My Confession,* 228; Lewis, p. 248.

22. William Austine, Letter to His Cousin, University of North Carolina, William Austine Collection, November 1, 1847.

Chapter 25: A War of Words

1. G. P. Stokes, "War with Mexico!" *Command Magazine* 40 (November 1996), 51.

2. *El Monitor Republicano,* September 28, 1847.

3. *The American Star,* October 2, 1847.

4. *The North American,* December 7, 1847.

5. Ibid., December 24, 1847.

6. Ibid.

7. Jose Fernando Ramirez, *Mexico During the War,* 160.

8. Guillermo Prieto, *Memorias de mis tiempos,* 173–174.

9. *Diario del Gobierno,* special supplement, September 10, 1847; *Niles National Register,* October 16, 1847.

10. *The North American,* January 7, 1848.

11. Raphael Semmes, *Service Afloat and Ashore During the Mexican War* (Cincinnati: William H. Moore & Co., 1851), 428.

12. *New York True Sun,* January 7, 1848.

13. Edward Mansfield, *The Mexican War: A History of Its Origin and a Detailed Account of the Victories Which Terminated in the Surrender of the Capital* (New York: A. S. Barnes, 1849), 280.

14. *The North American,* January 6, 1848.

15. *Niles National Register,* October 9, 1847.

16. *Cleveland Plain Dealer,* June 17, 1854.

17. *The 1856 Know-Nothing Almanac,* 14.

18. *The Boston Pilot,* September 14, 1847.

19. George Ballentine, *Autobiography,* 285–286, 332.

20. John Riley to Charles O'Malley, RG 94, October 27, 1847.

21. Charles O'Malley to Winfield Scott, RG 94, February 5, 1848.

22. National Archives, RG 153, EE 619, "Proceedings of General Court Martial, Lt. J. N. Whistler."

23. John Riley to British consul, January 7, 1848, British Public Records, Foreign Office, 204, 99.

24. Percy Doyle to John Riley, January 15, 1848, British Public Records, Foreign Office, 204, 99: 12.

25. *The American Star,* September 23, 1847; George T. M. Davis, *Autobiography,* 260–261.

26. General Order 296, National Archives, September 22, 1847.

27. Hunter Miller, ed., "Treaty of Guadalupe Hidalgo, Article IV," *Treaties and Other International Acts of the United States of America, 1776–1863,* vol. 5 (Washington, D.C.: Government Printing Office, 1937).

28. *El Siglo Diez y Nueve* (Mexico City), June 1, 1848; Robert R. Miller, *Shamrock and Sword,* 128.

29. General Order 116, RG 94, National Archives, June 1, 1848.

Chapter 26: "Back from the Lips of Fame"

1. John A. Perry, *Thrilling Adventures of a New Englander; Travels, Scenes, and Sufferings in Cuba, Mexico & California* (Boston: Redding & Co., 1853), 22.

2. *El Siglo Diez y Nueve,* June 6, 1848.

3. Ibid., June 11, 1848.

4. Carlos Franco to Mariano Riva Palacio, June 11, 1848, Riva Palacio Papers.

5. *El Siglo Diez y Nueve,* July 24, 1848.

6. *El Monitor Republicano,* July 28, 1848.

7. John Riley to Ewan Mackintosh, August 20, 1848, British Public Records, Foreign Office, 203, 93: 365.

8. John Riley to the president of Mexico, British Public Records, Foreign Office, 203, 93: 367.

9. Transfer notice of John Riley to Puebla, Mexico, *Archivo de Defensa Nacional,* January/February 1849.

10. John Riley to Ewan Mackintosh, Puebla, August 6, 1849.

11. John Riley to the British minister, British Public Records, Foreign Office, 204, 102: 313.

12. *Periodico Oficial,* August 14, 1850.

13. Letter of John Riley to Charles O'Malley, RG 94, October 27, 1847.

14. Emily Lawless, "With the Wild Geese" (poem).

15. *Griffith's Primary Valuation and Tithe Applotment Books, 1848–1864* (Dublin: National Archives, 1864), 85; Robert R. Miller, *Shamrock and Sword,* 176; Roman Catholic Church Records, Clifden, Galway, 1838–1900 (Galway: Galway Family History Society West).

16. Mark Day, "The Passion of the San Patricios," *Irish American Magazine* (May–June 1993), 44.

Epilogue

1. Bruce Catton, *The Civil War* (New York: Bonanza Books, 1982), 381.

2. Term used in Abraham Lincoln's antiwar speech, May 1846.

3. Ella Lonn, Quoted journal entry of army surgeon Thomas Ellis, *Foreigners in the Union Army and Navy* (New York: Greenwood Press, 1951), 646.

4. "Thomas Sherman," *Dictionary of American Biography,* vol. 9 (New York: Charles Scribner's Sons, 1928), 92.

5. Letter of Winfield Scott to William Robinson, July 2, 1850.

6. Letter of Albert Richardson to the Adjutant General, National Archives, RG 94, April 24, 1886.

7. Letter of War Department to Albert Richardson, National Archives, RG 94, May 24, 1886.

8. Letter of Daniel Maloney to the Adjutant General, National Archives, RG 94, March 1, 1896.

9. Memorandum from Adjutant General H. P. McCain to Congressman Frank L. Greene, National Archives, RG 94, May 20, 1915.

10. Ibid.

11. John Riley to Charles O'Malley, RG 94, October 27, 1847.

Bibliography

Primary Sources

Official Records and Archives

Great Britain Public Record Office

Foreign Office, 50. Diplomatic Correspondence, Mexico
Foreign Office, 203. Embassy and Consular Archives, Mexico
Foreign Office, 204. Embassy and Consular Archives, Mexico
War Office, 12. Army Muster Books and Pay Lists
War Office, 25. Army Deserters
War Office, 97. Army Service Records

Irish Archives

Galway Family History Society West. *Roman Catholic Church Records, Clifden, 1838–1900*. Galway.
National Archives. *Nineteenth-Century Census Returns*. Dublin.
———. *Griffith's Primary Valuation and Tithe Applotment Books, 1848–64*. Dublin.
National Library of Ireland, Dublin. *Roman Catholic Register, 19th Century*.
Registrar General. *Indexes of Births, Marriages, and Deaths, Pre-1922*. Dublin.

United States Government Documents

Records of the 29th and 30th Congressional Sessions

United States National Archives

Department of State, RG 59. Dispatches from U.S. Consuls in Mexico
Department of War, RG 94. Adjutant General's Office
Correspondence, File No. 27932
General Orders, Headquarters, Mexico, 1847–48

Miscellaneous Papers Relating to the Mexican War, Box No. 7
Registers of Enlistments in the U.S. Army, 1840–48
Department of War, RG 153. Judge Advocate General's Office
Proceedings of General Court-Martial at Tacubaya and San Angel, Mexico, 1847

University of California, Berkeley, The Bancroft Library

Archivo Historico Militar de Mexico, 1848–55, MSS
DeWitt Clinton Loudon MSS Diary, 1846–47
Thomas Carr Nugent MSS

University of Texas, Austin, Latin American Collection:

Riva Palacio Papers
Valentin Gomez Farias Papers

Periodicals

American Eagle (Vera Cruz)
American Review
American Star (Mexico City)
The Anglo Saxon
The Baltimore Sun
Brownson's Quarterly Review
Christian Examiner
Diario del Gobierno de la República mexicana (Mexico City)
Daily Picayune (New Orleans)
El Correo Nacional (Mexico City)
Flag of Freedom (Puebla)
The Freeman's Journal (Philadelphia)
Illinois State Register

The Liberator
The London Times
New England Magazine
The New York Herald
The New York Observer
The New York Journal of Commerce
The New York True Sun
The New York Times
Niles National Register (Baltimore)
The North American (Mexico City)
Periódico Oficial
The Pilot (Boston)
Protestant Banner
The Washington Union

Books and Journals

Alcarez, Ramon. *The Other Side; or Notes for the History of the War Between Mexico and the United States.* Translated and edited by Albert C. Ramsey. New York: John Wiley, 1850.

Anderson, Robert. *An Artillery Officer in the Mexican War, 1846–7: Letters of Robert Anderson, Captain 3rd Artillery, U.S.A.* New York: G. P. Putnam's Sons, 1911.

Austine, William. *Mexican War Letters of William Austine.* University of North Carolina, Chapel Hill: William Austine Collection.

Balbontin, Manuel. *La invasion americana, 1846 a 1847.* Mexico: Gonzalo A. Esterva, 1883.

Ballentine, George. *Autobiography of an English Soldier in the United States Army, Comprising Observations and Adventures in the States and Mexico.* New York: Stringer & Townsend, 1853.

Barbour, Philip N., and Martha I. Barbour. *Journals of the Late Brevet Major Philip Norbourne Barbour, Captain in the 3rd Regiment, United States Infantry, and His Wife, Martha Isabella Hopkins Barbour.* Edited by Rhoda van Bibber Tanner Doubleday. New York: G. P. Putnam's Sons, 1936.

Benham, Henry W. *Recollections of Mexico and the Battle of Buena Vista, February 22–23, 1847.* Boston: n.p., 1871.

Bowen, Isaac. Bowen Collection. Carlisle, PA: U.S. Military History Research Collection.

Calderon de la Barca, Frances. *Life in Mexico.* New York: Dutton (reprint), 1843.

Carleton, James H. *The Battle of Buena Vista with the Operations of the Army of Occupation for One Month.* New York: Harper and Brothers, 1848.

Carpenter, William W. *Travels and Adventures in Mexico.* New York: Harper and Brothers, 1851.

Chamberlain, Samuel E. *My Confession.* New York: Harper and Brothers, 1856.

Chapman, William. "Mexican War Letters, 1845–47." West Point: U.S. Military Academy Library.

Claiborne, John F. H. *Life and Correspondence of John A. Quitman, Major-General, U.S.A., and Governor of the State of Mississippi,* 2 vols. New York: Harper and Brothers, 1860.

Clark, Amasa G. *Reminiscences of a Centenarian, as Told by Amasa Gleason Clark, Veteran of the Mexican War, to Cora Tope Clark.* Edited by J. Marvin Hunter, Sr., Bandera, Tex.: n.p., 1930.

Clarke, Asa B. *Travels in Mexico and California.* Boston: Wright & Hasty's, 1852.

Coit, Daniel Wadsworth. *Digging for Gold Without a Shovel: The Letters from Mexico City to San Francisco, 1848–1851.* Edited by George P. Hammond. Denver: Old West, 1967.

Collins, Francis. "Journal of Francis Collins, An Artillery Officer in the Mexican War." Edited by Maria Clinton Collins. *Quarterly Publications of the Historical and Philosophical Society of Ohio* 10 (April–July 1915): 37–109.

Complete History of the Late Mexican War, Containing an Authentic Account of All the Battles Fought in That Republic ... by an Eyewitness. New York: F. J. Dow, 1850.

Dana, N. J. T. *Monterrey Is Ours! The Mexican War Letters of Lieutenant Dana, 1845–47.* Edited by Robert H. Ferrell. Lexington: University Press of Kentucky, 1990.

Davis, George T. M. *Autobiography of the Late Col. Geo. T. M. Davis, Captain and Aide-de-Camp Scott's Army of Invasion (Mexico).* New York: Jenkins & McCowan, 1891.

Deas, George. "Reminiscences of the Campaign on the Rio Grande." *Historical Magazine* 7 (January–May 1870): 19–22; 99–103; 236–38; 311–16.

DeHart, Captain William C. *Observations on Military Law, and the Constitution and Practice of Courts-Martial with a Summary of the Law of Evidence as Applicable to Military Trials.* New York: Wiley and Putnam, 1846.

Domenech, Abbe. *Missionary Adventures in Texas and Mexico.* London: Longman, Brown, Green, Longmans, and Roberts, 1858.

Donnavan, Corydon. *Adventures in Mexico Experienced During a Captivity of Seven Months.* Boston: George R. Holbrook, 1848.

Ewell, Richard Stoddert. *The Making of a Soldier: Letters of General R. S. Ewell* (ed. by Captain Percy G. Hamlin). Richmond: Whitlet & Sheppardson, 1935.

Ferris, A. C. "To California in 1849 Through Mexico," *Century* 42 (1891): 666–79.

French, Samuel Gibbs. *Two Wars, An Autobiography.* Nashville: The Confederate Veteran Press, 1901.

Frost, Daniel M. "The Memoirs of Daniel M. Frost." Edited by Dana O. Jensen. *Missouri Historical Society Bulletin* 26, no. 3 (1970): 200–26.

Frost, John. *The Mexican War and Its Warriors.* Philadelphia: H. Mansfield, 1848.

Giddings, Luther. *Sketches of the Campaign in Northern Mexico by an Officer of the First Regiment of Ohio Volunteers.* New York: George P. Putnam, 1853.

Grant, Ulysses S. *Personal Memoirs of U. S. Grant.* 2 vols. New York: C. L. Webster, 1885–86.

Hamilton, Charles. "Memoirs of the Mexican War." *Wisconsin Magazine of History* 14 (September 1930): 63–92.

Harney, William S. *Official Correspondence of Brig. Gen. W. S. Harney, U.S. Army, and First Lt. General, Late U.S. Army, with the U.S. War Department, and Subsequent Personal Correspondence.* Washington, D.C.: n.p., 1861.

Hartman, George W. *A Private's Own Journal: Giving an Account of the Battles in Mexico, under General Scott.* Greencastle, Pa.: E. Robinson, 1849.

Henry, William S. *Campaign Sketches of the War with Mexico.* New York: Harper and Brothers, 1847.

Hitchcock, Ethan A. *Fifty Years in Camp and Field: Diary of Major General Ethan Allen Hitchcock, U.S.A.* Edited by W. A. Croffut. New York: G. P. Putnam's Sons, 1909.

Jarvis, Nathan S. "An Army Surgeon's Mexican War Notes." *Journal of the Military Service Institution of the United States,* 40 (1907): 435–52; 41 (1907) 90–105.

Kendall, George W. *The War Between the United States and Mexico: Drawings by Carl Nebel.* New York: D. Appleton, 1851.

Kenly, John R. *Memoirs of a Maryland Volunteer: War with Mexico in the Years 1846–7–8.* Philadelphia: J. B. Lippincott, 1873.

"Letters of General Antonio Lopez de Santa Anna Relating to the War Between the United States and Mexico, 1846–1848." Edited by Justin H. Smith, *Annual Report of the American Historical Assoc. for the Year 1917.* Washington, D.C.: Government Printing Office.

Lombard, Albert. *The High Private, With a Full and Exciting History of the New York Volunteers.* New York: n.p., 1848.

McCall, George A. *Letters from the Frontiers.* Edited by John K. Mahon. Philadelphia: J. B. Lippincott, 1868.

McClellan, George B. *The Mexican War Diary of George B. McClellan.* Edited by William Starr Myers. Princeton: Princeton University Press, 1917.

McElroy, John. "Chaplains for the Mexican War, 1846," *The Woodstock Letters* 15 (1886): 198–202; 16 (1887): 33–39.

McSherry, Richard. *El Puchero: or, A Mixed Dish from Mexico.* Philadelphia: Lippincott, Grambo, 1850.

Macomb, Alexander. *The Practice of Courts Martial.* New York: Samuel Coleman, 1840.

Maury, Dabney. *Recollections of a Virginian in the Mexican, Indian, and Civil Wars.* New York: Charles Scribner's Sons, 1894.

Meade, George Gordon. *The Life and Letters of George Gordon Meade,* 2 vols. New York: Scribner's, 1913.

Meginness, John F. "A Collection of Incidents Connected with the Life of a Soldier (from His Enlistment) in Mexico, During a Part of the Campaign of 1847, from Vera Cruz to Puebla, Mexico, October 17, 1847." University of Texas, Arlington: Special Collections.

O'Brien, John P. J. *A Treatise on American Military Laws, and the Practice of Courts Martial, with Suggestions for Their Improvement.* Philadelphia: Lea & Blanchard, 1846.

Oswandel, J. Jacob. *Notes of the Mexican War, 1846–47–48.* Philadelphia: n.p., 1885.

Perry, John A. *Thrilling Adventures of a New Englander: Travels, Scenes and Sufferings in Cuba, Mexico & California.* Boston: Redding, 1853.

Preston, William. *Journal in Mexico, Nov. 1, 1847, to May 25, 1848.* Paris: Privately printed, n.d.

Prieto, Guillermo. *Memorias de mis tiempos, 1828 a 1853.* 2 vols. Mexico: Editorial Patria, 1948.

Ramirez, Jose Fernando. *Mexico During the War with the United States.* Edited by Walter V. Scholes. Translated by Eliott B. Sherr. Columbia, Mo.: University of Missouri Press, 1970.

Reilly, James. "An Artilleryman's Story," *Journal of the Military Service Institution* 33 (1903): 438–46.

Robertson, John B. *Reminiscences of a Campaign in Mexico by a Member of the "Bloody First."* Nashville: J. York, 1849.

Santa Anna, Antonio Lopez de. *The Eagle: The Autobiography of Santa Anna.* Edited by Ann Fears Crawford. Austin: Pemberton Press, 1967.

Scott, John A. *Encarnacion Prisoners, Comprising an Account of the March of the Kentucky Cavalry from Louisville to the Rio Grande.* Louisville: Prentice & Weissinger, 1848.

Scott, Winfield. *The Memoirs of Lieutenant-General Winfield Scott, LLD.,* 2 vols. New York: Sheldon, 1864.

Sedgwick, John. *Correspondence of John Sedgwick, Major General,* 2 vols. New York: Stoeckle, 1902–03.

Semmes, Raphael. *Service Afloat and Ashore During the Mexican War.* Cincinnati: William H. Moore, 1851.

Smith, Ephraim Kirby. Smith, Kirby, Webster, Black Family Papers. Carlisle, Pa.: U.S. Military History Research Collection.

Smith, Gustavus W. *Company A, Corps of Engineers, in the Mexican War.* Willetts Point, NY: Battalion Press, 1896.

Smith, W. C. S. *A Journey to California in 1849.* Berkeley: University of California, Bancroft Collection, n.p.

Taylor, Zachary. *Letters of Zachary Taylor from the Battle-Fields of the Mexican War.* Rochester, NY: William K. Bixby, 1908.

Tennery, Thomas D. *The Mexican War Diary of Thomas D. Tennery.* Norman: University of Oklahoma Press, 1970.

Thorpe, Thomas Bangs. *Our Army on the Rio Grande.* Philadelphia: Cary and Hart, 1846.

"To My Friends and Countrymen in the Army of the United States of America" (signed by John Riley). Austin: University of Texas, George W. Kendall Collection, August 1847.

Wallace, Lew. *Lew Wallace: An Autobiography,* 2 vols. New York: Harper and Brothers, 1906.

Wise, Henry Alexander. *Los Gringos: Or, an Inside View of Mexico and California.* New York: Baker and Scribner, 1849.

Zeh, Frederick. *An Immigrant Soldier in the Mexican War.* Translated and edited by William J. Orr, Jr., and edited by Robert R. Miller. College Station: Texas A & M University Press, 1995.

Secondary Sources

Alcaraz, Ramon, et al. (eds.). *Apuntes para la historia de la guerra entre Mexico y los Estados Unidos.* Mexico: M. Pyno, 1848.

———. *The Other Side: Or, Notes for the History of the War Between Mexico and the United States.* Translated by Albert C. Ramsey. New York: J. Wiley, 1850.

Baker, B. Kimball. "The Saint Patricks Fought for their Skins and Mexico." *Smithsonian* 8 (1978): 94–101.

Bancroft, Hubert H. *History of California.* Vol. 5, 1846–48. (Vol. 22 of *Works.*) San Francisco: The History Co., 1886.

Bauer, K. Jack. *The Mexican War, 1846–48.* New York: Macmillan, 1974.

———. *Zachary Taylor: Soldier, Planter, Statesman of the Southwest.* Baton Rouge: Louisiana State University Press, 1985.

Beals, Carleton. *Brass-Knuckle Crusade.* New York: Hastings House, 1960.

Berge, Dennis E., ed. and trans. *Considerations on the Political and Social Situations of the Mexican Republic: 1847.* Southwestern Studies, Monograph 45. El Paso: Texas Western Press, 1975.

Bill, Alfred H. *Rehearsal for Conflict: The War with Mexico, 1846–1848.* New York: Alfred A. Knopf, 1947.

Billington, Ray A. *The Protestant Crusade, 1800–1860.* New York: Rinehart, 1938.

"The Know-Nothing Uproar." *American Heritage* 4 (1954): 58–61, 94–97.

Bowman, Allen. *The Morale of the American Revolutionary Army.* Washington, D.C.: American Council on Public Affairs, 1943.

Brack, Gene M. *Mexico Views Manifest Destiny, 1821–1846: An Essay on the Origins of the Mexican War.* Albuquerque: University of New Mexico Press, 1975.

Brooks, Nathan C. *A Complete History of the Mexican War: Its Causes, Conduct, and Consequences; Comprising an Account of the Various Military and Naval Operations, from its Commencement to the Treaty of Peace.* Philadelphia: Grigg, Elliot, 1849.

Callcott, Wilfrid H. *Church and State of Mexico, 1822–1857.* Durham: Duke University Press, 1926.

———. *Santa Anna: The Story of an Enigma Who Once Was Mexico.* Norman: University of Oklahoma Press, 1936.

Carreno, Alberto M. *Jefes del ejercito mexicano en 1847: Biografias de generales de division y de brigada y de coroneles del ejercito mexicano por fines del ano 1847.* Mexico: Secretaria de Fomento, 1914.

Castillo Negrete, Emilio del. *Invasion de los Norte-Americanos en Mexico.* 4 vols. Mexico: n.p., 1890–91.

Catton, Bruce. *The Civil War.* New York: Bonanza Books, 1982.

Considine, Robert B. *It's the Irish.* New York: Doubleday, 1961.

Costigan, Giovanni. *A History of Modern Ireland, With a Sketch of Earlier Times.* New York: Pegasus, 1969.

Cotner, Thomas E. *The Military and Political Career of Jose Joaquin Herrera, 1792–1854.* Austin: University of Texas Press, 1949.

Cox, Patricia. *Batallon de San Patricio.* Mexico: Editorial Stylo, 1954.

Diccionario Porrua de historia, biografia y geografia de Mexico. 3 vols. S.v. Mexico: Editorial Porrua, 1986. "O'Reilly, Juan: San Patricio (Battallon de)."

Day, Mark R. "The Passion of the San Patricios." *Irish American Magazine* (May–June 1993), 44–48.

Dolph, Edward A. *"Sound off!" Soldier Songs from the Revolution to World War II.* New York: Farrar & Reinhart, 1942.

Downey, Fairfax. *Texas and the War with Mexico.* New York: American Heritage, 1961.

———. "Tragic Story of the San Patricio Battalion," *American Heritage* 6 (1955): 20–23.

———. *Sound of the Guns: The Story of American Artillery from the Ancient and Honorable Company to the Atom Cannon and Guided Missile.* New York: David McKay, 1955.

Dupuy, R. Ernest. *Where They Have Trod: The West Point Tradition in American Life.* New York: Frederick A. Stokes, 1940.

Eisenhower, John S. D. *So Far from God: The U.S. War with Mexico, 1846–48.* New York: Random House, 1989.

Elliott, Charles W. *Winfield Scott, The Soldier and the Man.* New York: Macmillan, 1937.

Enciclopedia de Mexico. 1978 ed. S.v. *"Guerra de E.U. a Mexico."*

Enciclopedia Britannica. 1954 ed. S.v. "Malplaquet."

Exley, Thomas M., ed. *A Compendium of the Pay of the Army from 1785 to 1888.* Washington, D.C.: Government Printing Office, 1888.

Federman, Stan. "Battalion of the Damned." *Army* (July 1979): 41–46.

Fernandez del Castillo, Francisco. *Apuntes para la historia de San Angel y sus alrededores.* Mexico: Museo Nacional de Arqueologia, Historis y Etnologia, 1913.

Fernandez Tomas, Jorge, et al. *Ahi vienen los del norte: La invasion norte-americana de 1847. (Mexico: Historia de un pueblo,* no. 8.) Mexico: Secretaria de Educacion Publica y Editorial Nueva Imagen, 1980.

Finerty, John F. *John F. Finerty Reports Porfirian Mexico,* 1879. Ed. Wilbert H. Timmons. El Paso: Texas Western Press, 1974.

Finke, Detmar H. "The Organization and Uniforms of the San Patricio Units of the Mexican Army, 1846–1848." *Military Collector and Historian* 9 (1957): 36–38.

"First Catholic Chaplains in U.S. Army and Navy," *The Woodstock Letters* 70 (1941) 466–67.

Flannery, John B. *The Irish Texans.* San Antonio: University of Texas, Institute of Texan Cultures, 1980.

Frost, John. *Life of Major General Zachary Taylor: With Notices of the War in New Mexico, California, and South Mexico; and Biographical Sketches of Officers Who Have Distinguished Themselves in War with Mexico.* New York: D. Appleton, 1847.

———. *Pictorial History of Mexico and the Mexican War.* Philadelphia: Thorne, Cowperthwait, 1849.

Gallagher, Thomas. *Paddy's Lament: Ireland 1846–47.* New York: Harcourt Brace Jovanovich, 1982.

Ganoe, William A. *The History of the United States Army.* New York: D. Appleton, 1942.

Griffin, William D. *The Book of Irish Americans.* New York: Times Books, 1990.

Grove, Frank W. *Medals of Mexico,* vol. 2, 1821–1971. San Antonio: Almanzar's Coins, 1972.

Harney, William S. "General Harney" (obituary), *Journal of the United States Cavalry Association* 3 (1890): 1–8.

Hasbrouck, Alfred. *Foreign Legionaries in the Liberation of Spanish South America.* New York: Columbia University Press, 1928.

Haynes, Martin A. *Gen. Scott's Guide in Mexico: A Biographical Sketch of Col. Noah F. Smith.* Lake Village, N.H.: Lake Village Times, 1887.

Heitman, Francis B., ed. *Historical Register and Dictionary of the United States Army from its Organization, September 29, 1789, to March 2, 1903.* 2 vols. Washington, D.C.: Government Printing Office, 1903.

Henry, Robert S. *The Story of the Mexican War.* Indianapolis: Bobbs Merrill, 1950.

Hicken, Victor. *The American Fighting Man.* New York: Macmillan, 1969.

Hogan, Michael. *The Irish Soldiers of Mexico.* Guadalajara, Mexico: Fondo Editorial Universitario, 1997.

Honeywell, Roy J. *Chaplains of the United States Army.* Washington, D.C.: Department of the Army, Office of Chief of Chaplins, 1958.

Hopkins, G. T. "The San Patricio Battalion in the Mexican War," *U.S. Cavalry Journal* 24 (1913): 279–84.

Ignatiev, Noel. *How the Irish Became White.* New York: Routledge, 1995.

Israel, Fred L., ed. *The State of the Union Messages of the Presidents, 1790–1966.* 3 vols. New York: Chelsea House, 1967.

Jenkins, John S. *History of the War Between the United States and Mexico.* Philadelphia: J. E. Potter, 1848.

Johannsen, Robert W. *To the Halls of Montezuma: The Mexican War in the American Imagination.* New York: Oxford University Press, 1985.

Johnson, Allen, and Dumas Malone, eds. "Winfield Scott" and "Zachary Taylor." *Dictionary of American Biography.* New York: Charles Scribner's Sons, 1928–44.

Jones, Oakah L., Jr. *Santa Anna.* New York: Twayne, 1968.

Katcher, Philip R. *The Mexican-American War, 1846–1848.* London: Osprey, 1976.

Knobel, Dale T. *Paddy and the Republic: Ethnicity and Nationality in Antebellum America.* Middletown, Conn.: Wesleyan University, 1986.

Koller, Larry. *The Fireside Book of Guns.* New York: Simon & Schuster, 1959.

Krueger, Carl. *Saint Patrick's Battalion.* New York: Dutton, 1960.

Kurtz, Wilbur G., Jr. "The First Regiment of Georgia Volunteers in the Mexican War." *Georgia Historical Quarterly* 27 (December 1943): 314–17.

Ladd, Horatio O. *History of the War with Mexico.* New York: Dodd, Mead, 1883.

Lavender, David. *Climax at Buena Vista: The American Campaign in Northeast Mexico, 1846–47.* Philadelphia: J.B. Lippincott, 1966.

Lewis, Lloyd. *Captain Sam Grant.* Boston: Little, Brown, 1950.

Liddell Hart, B. H. ed. *The Letters of Private Wheeler, 1809–1848.* London: Michale Joseph, 1951.

Livingston-Little, D. E. "Mutiny During the Mexican War: An Incident on the Rio Grande." *Journal of the West* 9 (July 1970): 340–45.

Lonn, Ella. *Foreigners in the Union Army and Navy.* New York: Greenwood Press, 1951.

McCaffrey, James M. *Army of Manifest Destiny: The American Soldier in the Mexican War, 1846–48.* New York: New York University Press, 1992.

McCampbell, Coleman. *Saga of a Frontier Seaport.* Dallas: South-West Press, 1934.

McCornack, Richard B. "The San Patricio Deserters in the Mexican War," *The Americas* 8 (1951): 131–42.

McDonald, Archie P., ed. *The Mexican War: Crisis for American Democracy.* Lexington, Mass.: D. C. Heath, 1969.

McEniry, Sister Blanche M. *American Catholics in the War with Mexico.* Washington, D.C.: Catholic University of America, 1937.

Mahoney, Tom. "50 Hanged and 11 Branded: The Story of the San Patricio Battalion," *Southwest Review* 32 (1947): 373–77.

Mansfield, Edward D. *The Mexican War: A History of its Origin and a Detailed Account of the Victories Which Terminated in the Surrender of the Capital.* New York: A. S, Barnes, 1849.

May, Robert E. "Invisible Men: Blacks and the U.S. Army in the Mexican War," *The Historian* 49 (August 1987): 463–77.

Mayer, Brantz. *Mexico As It Was and As It Is.* Philadelphia: G. B. Zieber, 1847.

Meehan, Thomas F. "Catholics in the War with Mexico." *U.S. Catholic Historical Record* 12 (1918): 39–65.

Merk, Frederick. *The Monroe Doctrine and American Expansionism, 1843–1849.* New York: Alfred A. Knopf, 1966.

Miller, Hunter, ed. "Treaty of Guadalupe Hidalgo," vol. 5. *Treaties and Other International Acts of the United States of America, 1776–1863.* Washington, D.C.: Government Printing Office, 1937.

Miller, Kerby A. *Emigrants and Exiles: Ireland and the Irish Exodus to North America.* New York: Oxford University Press, 1988.

Miller, Robert R. *Mexico: A History.* Norman: University of Oklahoma Press, 1985.

———. *Shamrock and Sword.* Norman: University of Oklahoma Press, 1989.

Millett, Allan R., and Peter Maslowskie. *For the Common Defense: A Military History of the United States of America.* New York: Free Press, 1984.

Muller, John. *A Treatise of Artillery.* Reprint. Ottawa: Museum Restoration Service, 1965.

Neve, Carlos D. *Historia grafica del ejercito mexicano.* Cuernavaca: Manuel Quesada Brandi, 1967.

Nevin, David. *The Mexican War.* Alexandria, Va.: Time-Life Books, 1978.

Nichols, Edward J. *Zach Taylor's Little Army.* Garden City: Doubleday, 1963.

Patron, James. *Life of Andrew Jackson.* 3 vols. Boston: Ticknor & Fields, 1866.

Pena, Jose Enrique de la. *With Santa Anna in Texas: A Personal Narrative of the Revolution.* Translated and edited by Carmen Perry, College Station: Texas A & M University Press, 1975.

Pioneer Society of the State of Michigan. *Collections of the Pioneer Society of the State of Michigan* 6 (1884): 349; 18 (1892): 694.

Pletcher, David M. *The Diplomacy of Annexation: Texas, Oregon and the Mexican War.* Columbia: University of Missouri Press, 1973.

Potter, George W. *To the Golden Door: The Story of the Irish in Ireland and America.* Boston: Little, Brown, 1960.

Power, Wally. "The Enigma of the Patricios," *An Cosantoir* (Irish Ministry of Defense) 21 (1971): 7–12.

———. "Facets of the Mexican War." *The Recorder* (American Irish Historical Society) 36 (1975): 135–43.

Randall, James G. *Lincoln the President.* Vol. 1. New York: Dodd, Meade, 1945.

Reavis, L. U. *The Life and Military Service of General William Selby Harney.* St. Louis: Bryan, Brand, 1878.

Reeves, Jesse S. *American Diplomacy Under Tyler and Polk.* Baltimore: Johns Hopkins University Press, 1907.

Richards, Leonard L. *The Life and Times of Congressman John Quincy Adams.* New York: Oxford University Press, 1986.

Richardson, James D., ed. *A Compilation of the Messages and Papers of the Presidents, 1789–1897.* Vol. 4. Washington, D.C.: Government Printing Office, 1897.

Richardson, Rupert N. *Texas: The Lone Star State.* Englewood Cliffs: Prentice-Hall, 1958.

Ripley, Roswell S. *The War with Mexico.* 2 vols. New York: Harper and Brothers, 1849.

Riva Palacio, Vicente, ed. *Mexico a traves de los siglos.* 5 vols. Mexico: Ballesca y Cia., 1887–89.

Rives, George L. *The United States and Mexico, 1821–1848.* 2 vols. New York: Charles Scribner's Sons, 1913.

Roa Barcena, José M. *Recuerdos de la invasion norte americana (1846–1848).* 3 vols. Mexico: Editorial Porrua, 1947.

Rubio Mane, Jorge I. "El Excmo. Sr. Dr. D. Martin Tritschler y Cordova, primer arzobispo de Yucatan," *Asbide, revista de cultura mexicana* 5: 9 (1941): 587–90.

The San Patricios. Documentary by Mark R. Day. Vista, Calif.: San Patricio Productions, 1996.

Sears, Louis M. *John Slidell.* Durham: Duke University Press, 1925.

Sellers, Charles. *James K. Polk, Constitutionalist, 1843–1846.* Princeton: Princeton University Press, 1960.

Singletary, Otis A. *The Mexican War.* Chicago: University of Chicago Press, 1960.

Smith, Arthur D. *Old Fuss and Feathers: The Life and Exploits of Lt.-General Winfield Scott.* New York: Greystone Press, 1937.

Smith, George Winston, and Charles Judah, eds. *Chronicles of the Gringos: The U.S. Army in the Mexican War, 1846–1848; Accounts of Eyewitnesses & Combatants.* Albuquerque: University of New Mexico Press, 1968.

Smith, Justin H. *The War with Mexico.* 2 vols. New York: Macmillan, 1919.

Spaulding, Oliver L. *The United States Army in War and Peace.* New York: G. P. Putnam's Sons, 1937.

Spell, Lota M. "The Anglo-Saxon Press in Mexico, 1846–1848," *American Historical Review* 38 (1932): 20–31.

Stenberg, Richard R. "The Failure of Polk's Mexican War Intrigue of 1845," *Pacific Historical Review* 6 (1935): 35–68.

Stevens, Peter F. "The Three Faces of John Riley." *The Boston Irish Reporter* (June 1998): 19.

———. "The Tragic Saga of the St. Patrick's Battalion." *The Boston Irish Reporter* (March and April 1996): 18–19; 16-17.

———. "The Proving Ground." *American History Illustrated 3* (February–March 1988): 38–44.

Stinson, Byron. "They Went Over to the Enemy," *American History Illustrated* 3 (1968): 30–36.

Stokes, G. P. "War with Mexico." *Command Magazine* 40 (November 1996): 34–51.

Sweeny, William M. "The Irish Soldiers in the War with Mexico." *American Irish Historical Society* 26 (1927): 255–59.

Swinson, Arthur, ed. *A Register of the Regiments and Corps of the British Army.* London: The Archive Press, n.d.

Upton, Emory. *The Military Policy of the United States.* Washington, D.C.: Government Printing Office, 1914.

Vasquez, Josefina Zoraida, and Lorenzo Meyer. *The United States and Mexico.* Chicago: University of Chicago Press, 1985.

Wallace, Edward S. "The Battalion of Saint Patrick in the Mexican War," *Military Affairs* 14 (1950): 84–91.

Warren, Harris G. *The Sword Was Their Passport: A History of American Filibustering in the Mexican Revolution.* Reprint, Port Washington, N.Y.: Kennikat Press, 1972.

Webb, Henry W. "The Story of Jefferson Barracks." *New Mexico Historical Review* 21 (1946): 185–208.

Weems, John E. *To Conquer a Peace: The War Between the United States and Mexico.* Garden City: Doubleday, 1974.

Weigley, Russell F. *History of the United States Army.* New York: Macmillan, 1967.

Wilcox, Cadmus M. *History of the Mexican War.* Edited by Mary Rachel Wilcox. Washington, D.C.: Church News Publishing, 1892.

Willson, Beckles. *John Slidell.* New York: Minto, Balch, 1932.

Winders, Richard Bruce. *Mr. Polk's Army: The American Military Experience in the Mexican War.* College Station: Texas A & M University Press, 1997.

Woodward, Ashbel. *Life of General Nathaniel Lyon.* Hartford, Conn.: Connecticut Historical Society, 1862.

Wynn, Dennis J. *The San Patricio Soldiers: Mexico's Foreign Legion.* Southwestern Studies, monograph 74. El Paso: Texas Western Press, 1984.

———. "The *San Patricios* and the United States-Mexican War of 1846–1848." Ph.D. diss., Loyola University of Chicago, 1982.

Zamacois, Niceto de. *Historia de las relacions entre Mexico y los Estados Unidos de America, 1800–1858.* 2 vols. Mexico: Editorial Porrua, 1965.

Index

About the Author

Peter F. Stevens is an award-winning author, historian, and journalist. His many articles on overlooked but significant aspects of American and Irish-American history are familiar to readers of *American History, American Heritage, Military History,* and many other publications. *The New York Times* has syndicated many of his historical features to newspapers nationwide. He is a feature columnist for *The Boston Irish Reporter* and was an on-screen commentator and consultant for the prize-winning documentary *The San Patricios.* Stevens's other books are *The Mayflower Murderer and Other Forgotten Firsts in American History* (William Morrow, Quill), *Notorious and Notable New Englanders* (Down East), and *Links Lore: Dramatic Moments and Forgotten Milestones from Golf's History* (Brassey's). He lives in Quincy, Massachusetts.